15°⁰/
~

# Behavior Modification Techniques for the Special Educator

Edited by
Stanley A. Winters
Eunice Cox

Queens College

**MSS Information Corporation**
655 Madison Avenue, New York, N.Y. 10021

This is a custom-made book of readings prepared for the courses taught by the editors, as well as for related courses and for college and university libraries. For information about our program, please write to:

MSS INFORMATION CORPORATION
655 Madison Avenue
New York, New York 10021

MSS wishes to express its appreciation to the authors of the articles in this collection for their cooperation in making their work available in this format.

**Library of Congress Cataloging in Publication Data**

Winters, Stanley A        comp.
   Behavior modification techniques for the special educator.

   Includes bibliographical references.
   1. Motivation in education--Addresses, essays, lectures. 2. Behaviorism (Psychology)--Addresses, essays, lectures. 3. Handicapped children--Education--Addresses, essays, lectures. I. Cox, Eunice, joint comp. II. Title.
LB1065.W55       370.15'4       72-86203
ISBN 0-8422-5000-X
ISBN 0-8422-0206-4 (pbk.)

# CONTENTS

# Behavior Modification:  An Introduction

The techniques used in shaping human behavior are not a new force in the field of human education.

Rewards and punishment for a person's actions have been used as long as people have existed.  A parent's glee at a baby's smile tends to reinforce the smile production; while a slap on the hand stops the spilling of baby food.  Almost any continued reaction of the parent will shape the child's adaptive functioning.

In essence behavior modification is the "application of the results of learning theory and experimental psychology to the problem of altering maladaptive behavior" (Ullman and Krasner 1965, p.2)

Laboratory work in this field started with Pavlov in the early part of this century and has been publicized and popularized by B.F. Skinner. Skinner is a behavioral psychologist who is interested in predicting peoples behavior.  He has assumed that a person's deviant as well as adaptive behavior is learned, therefore new learning or unlearning can alter in appropriate behavior.  Skinner's operant conditioning is well researched and demonstrates the efficacy of this approach to behavior modification.

It is not the purpose of this paper to go into great detail about the rational of "conditioning" per se, but, several points must be discussed.

The classroom teacher must be aware that to predict or engineer the child's response to a situation she must be aware of the essential element - reinforcement.  It is necessary to find the right reinforcement in order to strengthen the child's response.

The teacher must be aware of the child's level of development, his goals and the importance of the reinforcement in the organism's heirarchy.

A pat on the head may be meaningful to one student, a gold star may motivate another. Candy can lead one child to complete his assignment while another one is more pleased by a "well done" on the paper.

The child who has met failure because of emotional problems, less than normal intelligence or neurological impairment may be harder to motivate than a bright individual from a family that rewards learning. For some exceptional students, adult approved peer recognition, and disapproval or withholding of praise may serve to create problems rather than encourge new learning techniques.

A number of studies have suggested that tangible, immediate rewards serve as primary motivators. Later, the joy of learning and social approval become intrinsically important. We find then that the student will learn because he has a more adequate self-concept and better view of himself as a person.

One of the basic rules to be kept in mind is that behavior must be reinforced immediately. At the beginning, an M & M candy given at the completion of an assignment means more to the child than a box of candy at the end of the day.

It is the shaping of adaptive behavior by reinforcement at regular intervals that ultimately leads to a competent, secure learner.

Behavior modification techniques have been used in the amelioration of phobias, the curing of stammering and stuttering, with retarded, brain damaged, neurotic and psychotic individuals, in regular classrooms, special classes and individual tutoring, in public schools, State institutions, mental health clinics and by all of us at one time or another.

This collection of essays and research articles covers many of the areas mentioned. It should give the special educator confidence in using behavior modification in what circumstance he finds himself.

<u>References</u>

Eysenck, H.J. Ed. Experiments in Behavior Therapy, N.Y. MacMillan, 1964.

Forness, S.R. and MacMillan, D.L. "The Origins of Behavior Modification
With Exceptional Children." <u>Exceptional</u> <u>Children</u> 1970 Vol. 37 No.2
93-100.

Hilgard, E.R. , <u>Theories</u> <u>of</u> <u>Learning</u> New York Appleton, Centry Crofts,
1956.

Skinner, B.F. <u>Science</u> <u>and</u> <u>Human</u> <u>Behavior</u>, New York, MacMillan 1953.

Ullman, L. and Krasner, L. Ed. <u>Case</u> <u>Studies</u> <u>in</u> <u>Behavior</u> <u>Modification</u>;
New York, Hold Rinehart & Winston.

Stanley A. Winters, Ed.D.
Coordinator Special Education Program
Queens College, CUNY

The Flexible Box:

A Look at the Structured Classroom

In these days of the "open classroom" and student freedom", we are likely to forget that some children work best within a clearly defined classroom framework.

The framework for these students is the structured classroom. It is the establishment of a well organized, consistent method of experience and behavior.

The teacher can work within her competencies as an instructor but provide therapeutic learnings for the student, without being a psychotherapist. It allows the student to grow by discovering that behavior has consequences, and that he must learn to take responsibility for his actions. In this environment, behavior modification techniques play an important role in shaping behavior.

## The Physical Setting

The classroom should be bright and cheery but not overstimulating. Games, books and other material should be in closed cabinets or covered bookshelves. Burlap pinned to the outside of the shelves will serve the purpose. The student should have only those things absolutely necessary in front of him. When he is finished, they should be put away.

In decorating the room, care should be given to the choices of color for both the walls and carpeting. The colors may be light but should not be intense. Beige, light blue, pale yellow or green serve well to bring color into the room without overly stimulating the student.

## Structuring the Teaching

When a class is started, it is necessary to establish roles which limit activity and reduce the stimulus of the moving child. Youngsters
ORIGINAL MANUSCRIPT.

should not walk around the room, sharpen pencils or get material without permission. Even group participation should be reduced until the children know the rules and what is expected of them.

The curricula material for each child must be based on his ability. It is best to start on an academic level where he is sure to meet success without struggling.

Instant feedback is necessary as well. Correct each assignment as quickly as possible and allow the child to know how he is doing. Stress the positive not the negative. For example "You were able to get five right today. Tomorrow perhaps you'll get six correct." Not"well,only 50% correct, that is not passing."

If the teacher has planned correctly, then the student should be able to complete all his assignments. Insist that this be done before moving on to the next step. Remember it is not the teacher versus the child but "you have a job to do. When it is done, then you can go out for gym or play a game." Do not forget an assignment. The student must learn to take responsibility for his work. If he does not, then the teacher is rewarding maladaptive behavior not successful performance. Keep in mind as well, that we are talking about consequences not punishment.

No work. Then no gym, games, art, music, free play or participation in other pleasant activities.

Lecturing does not help. Children learn very quickly to turn off adults who talk too much. Let him know the rewards and consequences, praise good performance, give enough time and expect successful results.

Many times when a structured program is put into effect, children will test the limits. Expect that this will happen. Be calm, speak softly but stick to your rules. It is much easier to establish control from initial chaos than from chaos which has become set as usual behavior.

Some Reminders

1. Don't preach. It never works in a classroom.

2. Expect that missed work, because of absences be completed in class or at home. This will help to establish a work "set."

3. Know your students assets and disabilities. Build on what he can do-not what he has failed at.

4. Plan for each child individually even though he may be having many group experiences.

5. Set the limits in both time and manner of doing work and stick to them.

6. It gets rough sometimes - so praise and encourage but insist that the work be done.

7. Teachers are human beings, therefore, you may have tough days. Losing your temper, complaints, and punishment assignments don't work. Remember that self discipline and organization lead to success not threats and fear.

8. Behavior modification techniques can help to shape behavior. Use them.

The concept of the structured classroom is not a new one however, many educators have shied away from the term. Children with behavior and learning disorders thrive in this environment. When used constantly by a confident instructor significant results have occurred.

References:

Cruickshank, W.M., Bentzen,F.A. Ratzeberg R.H and Tannhauser <u>A Teaching</u>
    Method for Brain. Injured and Hyperactive Children, Syracuse, New York.
    Syracuse University Press 1961.

Haring, N.G. and Phillips E.L. <u>Educating the Emotionally Disturbed Child</u>.
    New York, McGraw-Hill Book Co. 1962.

Kephart N.C. <u>The Slow Learner in the Classroom</u>, Columbus, Ohio. Charles E.
    Merill 1960.

Mowrer, O.H. <u>Learning Theory and Behavior</u>, New York John Wiley and Sons, 1960.

Phillips, E.L. Wiener D.N. and Haring N.G., <u>Discipline Achievement and
    Mental Health</u>. Englewood Cliffs, New Jersey; Prentice Hall Inc. 1960.

Strauss, A.A. and Kephart, N.C. <u>Psychopathology and Education of the
    Education of the Brain Injured Child</u>; New York, Grune and Stratton 1955.

Stanley A. Winters, Ed.D.
Coordinator Special Education Program
Queens College, CUNY

12

# A PLAN FOR USING BEHAVIOR MODIFICATION TECHNIQUES WITH SEVERELY MENTALLY RETARDED CHILDREN AND YOUTH

by Eunice W. Cox

Radical changes within the past decade in legal, philosophic and treatment concepts are bringing into the public schools numbers of children and youth who are identified as severely mentally retarded (SMR). That is to say, these are members of a select population previously routinely denied admittance to public schools on the basis of their lack of potential for profiting from the school program. This lack of potential was typically determined through the results of individual intelligence tests administered by a qualified psychologist. The psychologist, in this role, follows in a train of clinical examination and decision-making set in motion more than fifty years ago when Binet was commissioned by authorities of the Parisian school system to devise a means for separating those unable to profit from the program of the public schools.

Sweeping innovations in transportation, media and other technological creations have served to introduce enormous possibilities for change within the traditional concepts of the school curriculum. However, changes of any real consequence in the programs of the schools is inextricably linked with social change as Sarason has so ably demonstrated (The Culture of the School and the Problem of Change; Allyn and Bacon,1971). Many of us find it extremely difficult to modify our concepts of our social institutions, perhaps, particularly, our schools, partially because of our strong desire and need to pass on to our children the cultural heritage basically unchanged. Since our culture has traditionally defined the curriculum of our schools in the narrouw terms of "readin', 'ritin' 'n 'rithmetic", the severely retarded individual was excluded by definition.
ORIGINAL MANUSCRIPT.

The impact of the repeated surges of change forces are breaching this narrow wall of concern and, at last, all of the children of all of the people are beginning to receive services in the public schools, however halting and imperfect these may be at this early stage.

Because of "tunnel vision" training programs, or in whatever metaphor one chooses to describe the fact, public school teachers have found it difficult to initiate and carry through educational programs for these "special" children and youth. Indeed, institutions staffed, equipped and charged with the care of these members of society, have not produced uniformly humanistically-oriented programs leading to useful and productiove lives for these wards.

One can assume this lack of developmental programming to be rooted in a philosophy of "deficit fixation". In other words, if one assumes incompetence as well as disability and lack of sensitivity and awareness as well as lack of motivation, it then becomes imperative to arrange for continuing care of these wards on a day-to-day basis. This philosophy of fixing upon the deficits makes it ethically and morally mandatory that no "unreasonable" demands be placed upon these diabled wards. So this philosophy of deficit fixation neatly reduces to the status of prized livestock  the members of this segment of our society. To pursue this metaphor a bit further, in times of deprivation and scarcity, the livestock may be neglected due to inadequate ability to supply the necessary services. Indeed, the prized livestock may even be thrown back upon their own foraging resources for sheer survival. Those without such resources suffer.

Children and adults, deprived of developmental opportunities, disallowed the freedom to develop a measure of independence, denied the concept of responsibility, with little or no sense of personal worth

and human dignity, can be retained in a lifelong status of extreme dependence, mentally and physically. This fact has been demonstrated
amply. But it is now also becoming clear that these disabled and disallowed citizens have an unplumbed depth of _positive_ potential. Perhaps, we need now to develop a philosophy of"_positive_ fixation" to
supersede the philosophy of deficit fixation. "I am what I think I am"
is a much more powerful mind-set than "I can't do it" or "I'm afraid to
try". Opportunities for developing and implementing such a positive
philosophy are becoming much more available in our public schools as
the climate of acceptance is becoming more benign.

How does the classroom teacher and/or aide, imbued with goodwill
and determination, set about establishing a developmental program that
will, to some degree, meet the needs of the SMR student? The positive
approach inherent in the belief that behavior is modifiable--even in
the severely mentally retarded--gives a useful conceptual framework
within which to approach the planning for such a group. A quick overview of certain notions will give us a mutually understood starting
point. The basic assumptions of behavior modification are at least as
old as as parenthood. When a mother patiently spoons food into an infant's mouth, guides the baby's fingers to grasp the spoon and leads
the hand to the dish for a spoonful, then guides the baby's hand to its
mouth, the mother obviously has assumed the infant will, in this manner,
learn to feed itself. The attention the mother pays to the child as
the task is carried out is a most unselfconscious form of reinforcement. The infant's reward in terms of hunger satisfaction is added
reinforcement obviously aiding in the maintaining of this explicit behavior of feeding oneself.

In this most ordinary example is the kernel of all behavior modification theory.  True, this theory has become so highly differentiated and detailed through the efforts of enormously curious and creative thinker that the above claim is dangeroulsy over-simplified.  However, to be generally useful, the theoretical must be made understandable at the level of the practitioner.  Our homely example does not intend to do violence to the thinkers who formulated the abstract theories; but, rather, to give a "handle" to the basic approach that may serve to make its usefulness accessible to the toiler in the vineyard.

If we elaborate a bit further upon the example of the mother and infant, we might suppose the infant shows no interest in learning the spoon-feeding technique.  After several weeks or months, the mother may become concerned that her method of teaching spoon-feeding is not producing desired results.  Obviously, other measures are indicated.  Since we are suuming that all behavior is modifiable, we expect this mother to vary her present approach.  If she understands the elements of behavior modification theory, she will know that at least three options are open to her:

(1) Extinction--involves the removal of those contingent stimulus events which are maintaining the non-learning behavior.

(2) Aversive stimuli--introduction of aversive components such as physical punishment or deprivation of desirable conse- quences (response cost).

(3) A strategy of reinforcing concurrent appropriate behavior patterns to compete with and replace the inappropriate be- havior.

Actually, the mother in our example may find herself using some combination of two or all of these together though she may never stop to analyze her actions in this framework.  This is the crucial dif- ference between the mother "doing what comes naturally' and the skilled

competent teacher. For the teacher, the skills of choosing the objective, analyzing the requirements of the task, structuring the environment accordingly, and engaging the student's cooperation in achieving
the objective constitute prerequisites to the fine art of teaching the
SMR child. Because the teacher deals with many children over a period
of time in an ordered manner, she has opportunity for developing expertise through a combination of study and practice. A skilled teacher,
confronted with the above situation might proceed in the following five-
step pattern to attempt to deal with the self-feeding problem in our
example.

(1) Clinical level observations, painstakingly recorded over a
reasonable period of time. In this example, two or three days may suf-
fice though a much longer period may be necessary. The value to the
teacher of recording the observations lies in the opportunity for studying and restudying the record to determine in what specific area and at
what developmental level the teacher will establish the initial learning objective. For example, does the child's failure to learn the desired self-feeding behavior appear to be primarily a motor problem (inability of the muscles to coordinate and carry through the grasping,
lifting and lowering of the spoon)? Or does it appear to be a perceptual problem (inability of the child to develop adequate visual and
auditory skills for accurately assessing areas necessary to achieving
the desired behavior that are not accessible to the sense of touch?
Does the child appear to have a memory deficit (he appears unable to
retain motorically and/or perceptually the information necessary to establish the habit pattern of self-feeding)? Or could it be that the
child's major problem is cognitive (he is unable to conceptualize the
paramaters of the proposed task in its entirety so that he is unable to
store the concept of the task as a whole and complete piece of behavior)?

17

Or, finally, is the child responding to language (able to understand the meaning of basic nouns and verbs such as "spoon", "hold", "food", "eat" and such) which can be helpful in aiding development of conceptualization of the proposed task?

In addition to recorded observations, both informal and standized testing can provide helpful information where these can be appropriately employed that can aid the teacher in determining the specific task area for concentration and in changing and supplementing the task assignment as progress allows.

(2) Study the learning behavior of the child. In teaching language, for example, it may be useful to attempt to ascertain whether the child's major problem appears to be in the area of reception or expression or the processing and association of stimuli. In this connection, too, the more accessible avenues for securing the child's interest and cooperation will be determined.

(3) Attempt to explore all possible factors that may be contributing to the non-learning. Direct cause-and-effect relationships may be difficult to establish and, with some tasks, not directly relevant to effective planning. Even so, it is helpful to be aware of all the possible contributing factors to the learning problem. These may be of emotional, environmental and/or psychological origins. Careful study of the record of observations may give indications of clusters of factors or characteristics that constitute an identifiable syndrome that can lead to pertinent analysis and more precise structuring of the teaching environment.

(4) Collate and interpret relevant data and formulate a plan for modifying the behavior. This plan should sum up all the information gleaned from the observation records and from any other source; and

should indicate the explicit structure to be employed in modifying the behavior. This step will be discussed in more detail immediately after the following paragraph.

(5) The plan for modifying the behavior is put into effect. Two major points must be keptin mind at this juncture. First, the plan for behavior modification must be developed by the person who will initiate and carry it through; and the plan should be adhered to zealously and consistently over a considerable length of time. Failure can be the result of naivete and/or impatience for too early signs of success. Second, the observation record should be maintained, on a day-to-day basis, as rigorously as during the preplanning stage. This record, carefully studied and analyzed at frequent intervals, will give the teacher a continuing diagnostic check on the child as he changes through the learning process; and will provide a basis for continuing evaluation of additional knowledge of the child acquired through the teaching process. In other words, at each task level in the achievement of the skill of self-feeding, for example, the pace and the content of the next level can only be determined for that individual on the basis of thorough knowledge of the preceding progress.

To return to the discussion for developing the plan for modifying the child's behavior: We can now assume that the objective, the piece of behavior which is to be modified, has been appropriately determined through observation. The plan for modifying this behavior can now be developed. The teacher will consider the three options from behavior modification theory mentioned earlier in this discussion, namely extinction, aversive stimuli and reinforcement of appropriate behavior patterns to compete with and replace the inappropriate behavior. In developing the plan, the person responsible for managing the behavior modification attempt will consider each of these three options with particular regard for the individual child. From the study of the records of observation and any other pertinent information, the stimulus events which are maintaining the non-learning behavior can be removed. For example, if the problem has been found to be largely that the child cannot control the large muscle groups necessary to lifting and lowering the spoon, the logical place to begin is with exercises planned to strengthen and train these muscles, thus effectively removing this block. If the child is reacting unfavorably to environmental stimuli, this can be ascertained and modified. The point is, the teacher will become sensitive to the child's view of the task in order to aid the child by removing whatever obstacles are discernible.

The use of aversive stimuli (physical punishment and/or deprivation) is a highly controversial component or behavior modification theory which many people feel is never justifiably used with the SMR child. An interesting and useful review of the literature dealing with this subject may be found in a recent text(Gardner, <u>Behavior</u> <u>Modification</u> <u>in</u> <u>Mental</u> <u>Retardation</u>, Aldine-Atherton, 1971). Two classes of punishment procedures with the mentally retarded are reported in the literature. These include the presentation of punishment stimuli immediately following a response to be eliminated; the second class includes those procedures for removal of certain stimulus conditions following the response to be eliminated. In simpler language, the child may be punished in his own person immediately upon the appearance of the undesired behavior. A shout, a slap, a shaking, an electic shock are some examples of this first class of punishments. The second class of punishments result typically in the child being removed from the setting to a less desirable surrounding--in short, the isolation technique. In addition to this physical removal, the child may lose certain tangible positive reinforcers available to him. For example, the child might be sent to bed without his supper.

The use of aversive stimuli is not without its proponents. However, it is highly suspect and not in general use because of its inhumane connotations.

The third option is, undoubtedly, the one most teachers would feel most comfortable with and would prefer. However, it is highly likely that this more abstract approach may not yield immediate results with some SMR children. This is not intended as a denigrating statement. It is intended, rather, to alert the manager of behavior to the aforementioned possibility of the need for time and patience in practicing behavior modification planning. This option presumes the teacher will be alert to each and every appearance of an appropriate piece of the desired behavior pattern and that immediate positive reinforcement will be forthcoming. This reinforcement will need to be planned carefully in terms of the child's values. What does the child see as a positive reward? Certainly, M&Ms will work with some SMR children some of the time. But even candy loses its charms for some children very quickly as a reinforcement option. Based on the observation record, the teacher may be able to glean a clue to a reinforcement technique which will work with a particular child.

When one is teaching a concrete behavior such as spoon-feeding, evaluation of the progress is fairly open to assessment. This step in the planning procedure is an integral component, however. It is imperative that the planner and manager of the behavior develop an attitude of constant evaluation and assessment of the child's progress. The fact of progress in itself can be a reinforcement to the SMR child who gains in his sense of personal self-worth and confidence as he develops skills.

In summary, the watchwords of the implementation of behavior modification techniques with the SMR child are observe, study, plan, initiate, evaluate and modify. The SMR individual can be productively viewed from a philosophical vantage of "positive fixation"; and, helped to develop skills employing a conceptual paradigm based on behavior modification theory.

<u>REFERENCES</u>

Baer, D.M., Perterson, R.F., and Sherman, J.A. "The Development of
  Imitation by Reinforceing Behavioral Similarity to a Model".
  <u>Journal</u> <u>of</u> <u>Experimental</u> <u>Analysis</u> <u>of</u> <u>Behavior</u>, 1967, 10, 405-416.

Bry, P.M. "The Role of Reinforcement in Imitation by Retardates." Unpublished doctoral dissertation, University of Missouri, 1969.

Crosson, J.E., "A Technique for Programming Sheltered Workshop Environments For Training Severely Retarded Workers." <u>American</u>
  <u>Journal</u> <u>of</u> <u>Mental</u> <u>Deficiency</u>, 1969, 73, 814-818.

Gardner, William I., <u>Behavior</u> <u>Modification</u> <u>in</u> <u>Mental</u> <u>Retardation</u>,
  Aldine-Atherton, Chicago, 1971

Sarason, S.B., <u>The</u> <u>Culture</u> <u>of</u> <u>the</u> <u>School</u> <u>and</u> <u>the</u> <u>Problem</u> <u>of</u> <u>Change</u>.
  Allyn and Bacon, 1971

Sheron, Arvilla A., "Social Exchange and Operant Conditioning with
  Applications to the Mentally Retarded." <u>Education</u> <u>and</u> <u>Training</u>
  of the Mentally Retarded; V4, N2, p65-70, April, 1969.

Sloane, H.N. Jr. and MacAulay, B.D. ed., <u>Operant</u> <u>Procedures</u> <u>and</u>
  <u>Remedial</u> <u>Speech</u> <u>and</u> <u>Language</u> <u>Training</u>, Houghton-Mifflin, 1968.

# TEACHING THE PROFOUNDLY RETARDED SELF-HELP ACTIVITIES BY BEHAVIOR SHAPING TECHNIQUES [1]

GERARD J. BENSBERG, PH.D.

*Southern Regional Education Board, Atlanta, Georgia*

AND

CECIL N. COLWELL, B.S. AND ROBERT H. CASSEL, PH.D.

*Pinecrest State School*

THE widely held notion that the profoundly mentally retarded are necessarily untidy and otherwise helpless is being questioned. At issue is not the matter of adding enough personnel so that the retardate can be "scheduled" for the toilet, thus curtailing the number of toilet accidents. Rather, the concern is to find a method to teach these individuals so that they will engage in basic self-help activities on their own. Ellis (1963) has presented a theoretical analysis of how toilet training might be accomplished and Dayan (1964) has reported some success with the method. Ferster and DeMyer (1961) found operant conditioning successful in changing the behavior of previously inaccessible autistic children. The present paper reports a pilot study using a combination of operant and classical conditioning and association,

here called "behavior shaping," to improve the self-help behavior of six severely retarded children.

Perhaps the biggest problem in trying to establish desired behavior in many of the severely retarded is that they are not amenable to verbal direction. Since operant conditioning has been very successful with non-language organisms, it was felt that this procedure would be an excellent one to bring about the initial modification of behavior in the retardate. It was hypothesized that once the retardate was responding to the conditioning, verbal instructions could be added and, in time, the retardate would associate particular verbal symbols to specific acts so that ultimately he would become amenable to certain verbal directions.

It was also believed that regular cottage personnel could learn and practice the method and that highly trained professional personnel would not be necessary except at the outset of the project.

[1] This study was partially supported by the National Institute of Mental Health as part of the SREB Attendant Training Project and the Louisiana Department of Hospitals.

AMERICAN JOURNAL OF MENTAL DEFICIENCY, 1965, Vol. 69, pp.674-679.

## Subjects

Seven boys, all from the same cottage, were chosen as Ss. They were recommended by attendant personnel to be the lowest level boys on the cottage. The chronological age (CA), MA (from the Kuhlmann Test of Mental Maturity) and SA (from the Vineland Social Maturity Scale) characteristics of the Ss appear in Table I.

The self-help level of all these Ss at the start of the experiment can be described in general as follows. None would sit on the toilet unattended long enough to evacuate and, of course, all were untidy. None made any attempt at dressing or undressing (at the proper time) and one continually ripped his clothing to shreds if not restrained. None made any effort toward washing or drying themselves, three resisted having their teeth cleaned and two resisted being bathed. Five ate with their fingers, one had to be fed and one used a spoon in a messy manner. None of the Ss used words to communicate. Four Ss were frequently disturbed. Five either did not mingle with the other residents at all or else created antagonisms quickly. Only one S was in any way amenable to verbal direction and this was only occasionally.

## Procedure

The first step in the project was to have one staff member trained in oper-

ant conditioning. One man was sent to the Animal Behavior Enterprises, Inc.,[2] of Hot Springs, Arkansas, to spend one week learning how to apply the principles of operant conditioning. Upon his return to Pinecrest, he taught these principles to six cottage attendants.

The conditioning procedure was as follows. Working with one S at a time in formal 15 to 30 minute sessions twice daily, the attendant would give some simple verbal directions to S and at the same time use gestures. Successive approximations of the desired behavior were immediately rewarded. The original rewards were pieces of cereal, broken cookies, and candy, all carried in a bag hung from the shoulder. Each time the edible reward was given a social reward was also given, e.g., "good boy." At first a "bridging signal" was given between the time of the occurrence of the desired behavior and the presentation of the reward, but this seemed superfluous and was eliminated. As the Ss learned to work for the reward, the ratio of reinforcement was increased so that larger and more complex units of behavior had to obtain for the reward to be given.

The first four Ss as listed in Table I were placed in a special unit with two attendants for each of the day shifts. The remaining three Ss stayed on the original cottage as a kind of control group. After four months of training, Ss E.T. and R.M. of the original control group were placed on the special training unit with the original four Ss. After five months on the training unit the edible rewards for the original four Ss were discontinued

TABLE I

CA, MA, and SA Characteristics for the Ss

| S | CA | MA | SA |
|---|----|----|----|
| C.G. | 8.4 | ... | 1.4 |
| C.I. | 15.5 | 0.8 | 1.3 |
| S.M. | 8.3 | 1.0 | ... |
| R.S. | 8.0 | 1.2 | 1.4 |
| E.T. | 14.7 | 1.0 | ... |
| R.M. | 7.7 | 1.2 | 1.1 |
| J.S. | 8.1 | 1.0 | 1.5 |

[2] Consultation was provided at Pinecrest by Mr. and Mrs. Keller Breland of the Animal Behavior Enterprises during the initial phases of the project.

TABLE II

RAW SCORES OF MODIFIED VSMS OF ALL Ss FOR FIRST SEVEN MONTHS OF THE PROJECT

| Month | Experimental Subjects | | | | Control Subjects | | |
|---|---|---|---|---|---|---|---|
| | R.S. | S.M. | C.I. | C.G. | J.S. | R.M. | E.T. |
| November | 31 | 25 | 31.5 | 24 | 32 | 29 | 24.5 |
| December | 46 | 51 | 45 | 46.5 | 36 | 30.5 | 26.5 |
| January | 52.5 | 57 | 42 | 55 | 36.5 | 33 | 31 |
| February | 66.5 | 63 | 49.5 | 59.0 | 36.5 | 33 | 33 |
| March | 62.5 | 70 | 52 | 58.5 | 34.5 | 38 | 33.5 |
| April | 59[a] | 70[a] | 57[a] | 58.5[a] | 40 | 48[b] | 54[b] |
| May | 65.5 | 73 | 56 | 56.5 | 38.5 | 61 | 59 |
| June | 65 | 72 | 57 | 56 | 39 | 60.5 | 63 |

[a] — S has been off food rewards one month.
[b] — S has been on Training Unit receiving conditioning for one month.

and only social rewards were used. Seven months after the start of the project all Ss were returned to their original cottage, a move determined by administrative expediency irrelevant to the project.

RESULTS AND DISCUSSION

Two measures were used in this study. One was periodic movies taken of the behavior of the Ss. The other was an empirical modification of the Vineland Social Maturity Scale consisting of 97 items.[3] These items were formulated for the specific facility and project and not necessarily for general usage. Even so, five items were subsequently discovered to be inapplicable. The Self Direction category of the VSMS was not represented as its items are at too high a development level. The basic modification had to do with breaking down items on the VSMS into stages. For instance, eating behavior is measured by five items, each of which represents a higher functioning level than the preceding one, viz.: 52. Makes some attempt to eat when fed; 53. Tries to eat but messy when fed; 54. Eats with fingers; 55. Eats with spoon, messy at least; 56. Eats

[3] Copies of this scale may be obtained from Pinecrest State School.

with spoon, neatly. The items are scored in sequence so that if S passes item 55, he also gets credit for items 54, 53, and 52. Although "No opportunity" and "No information" items were indicated on the score sheet, they received no credit. Ratings were taken each month.

In Table II are presented the scores of each S on the modified VSMS. The first score, i.e., November, was taken before the start of the project. The mean of the four experimental Ss was 27.9 and for the three control Ss 28.5. The most notable thing to be seen in the table is that in all cases the biggest gain in scores occurred during the first month of training. It seems clear that considerable behavior change obtained from first training to the last. For three of the four original Ss apparently the asymptote was reached in four months of training. It is also notable in the case of the four original Ss, dropping the food rewards at the end of the fourth month of training did not result in the appreciable drop in score. After three months of training, the mean for the experimental group was 59.5 and 34.2 for the control group.

At the end of the experiment the self help level of the six Ss exposed to conditioning was generally as follows. Two Ss have only occasional daytime toilet accidents, three take complete care of themselves at the toilet except for wiping, and two take complete care of themselves. Three completely dress themselves including buttoning but not tying and three dress and undress themselves but do not button or tie. Three $S$s dry their hands acceptably; all attempt to wash their hands and faces; and all now acquiesce to a bath and to having their teeth cleaned. All eat with a spoon and five do so neatly. All of the $S$s were more responsive to verbal directions. However, only one $S$ had begun to use single words such as "Hi" and "Bye." Three play with other residents for short periods of time, two for long periods of time, and one does not interact with the others. All are amenable to simple verbal instruction.

It is interesting that the so called social rewards actually motivated behavior. Verbal compliments and even pats on the head or back are used at times by all attendants, but it would appear that frequently they are given so long after the act that they are meant to praise is completed, it is difficult for the $S$ to associate the two. Nevertheless, these $S$s did condition to social rewards.

Certain pitfalls have to be avoided if the procedures are to be successful. The $S$ must be physically well: if he feels badly he will not cooperate and if he has an enteric disease, for instance, he cannot be toilet trained. The attention of the $S$ must be focused on the desired task or conditioning will obtain to some other task. At the outset, the behavior desired must be very simple and uncomplicated but gradually the complexity of the task can be increased. For instance, one $S$ was taught to ride a tricycle: first he was rewarded to sit on it, then to put each foot on the pedal, then to press on the pedal.

Once the cycle began to move, it was self reinforcing. Some ingenuity must be exercised in selecting tasks. Buttoning is best taught if the $S$ has first learned to unbutton, because unbuttoning is easier and less complicated.

Each $S$ has an individual tolerance level for what he will do to get a reward. The essence of the conditioning is to stretch this tolerance level but not to exceed it. It was surprising how long some $S$s would work, say, in trying to put on a sock, for a small reward. When the tolerance level is exceeded, frustration and anger result and learning is hampered. Related to this is the length of the training session which varies according to the $S$s.

The final problem is that the reward must be meaningful to $S$. One $S$ for instance would not perform for candy as the others would but did perform for small pieces of a particular breakfast cereal. One $S$ seemed uninterested in the reward itself but was motivated by the fact that he was getting something.

In the early stages of training, the sight of the food reward meant a great deal and it was necessary to show it to the child in order to get him to perform. In the later stages of training, particularly in the case of the dressing drills, getting to go outside for play was a very strong reward.

Initially, the training tasks were simple and uncomplicated. The $S$s were taught such things as sitting in a particular place, picking up a ball, throwing a ball, etc. Early in training, it was necessary for the attendant to stand close to the child and to keep verbal directions to a minimum and to rely heavily upon gestures. As training proceeded, the attendant could direct the child from some distance and the time interval between performing the task

27

and the reward could be made longer. While Ss were learning to follow the instructions of the attendants, much undesirable behavior, such as kicking, biting and temper tantrums, were being ignored. In a very short time these behaviors began to disappear and more socially mature behavior demonstrated.

Once the Ss were responding to verbal directions and were eager to perform for the attendant, the teaching of dressing skills was begun. The tasks were divided into stages and the simplest stage was taught first. Initially, rewards were given at the completion of each stage. In the latter stages of training, more and more was expected from S before he was rewarded. Several Ss were able to complete a series of tasks with only one command. For example, "Johnny, take off your shirt, put it in your drawer and bring me the broom."

Although difficult or new skills were developed in special training sessions, rewards were used throughout each day to reinforce desirable behavior. However, both in the training sessions and other daily activities, social praise was used more frequently and food rewards less frequently as the project proceeded.

Although there would appear to be no question that the self help behavior of these Ss has improved, this study still leaves many problems unanswered. Can it really be said that this change in behavior is the result of the behavior shaping procedures alone or is it in part, at least, related to the greatly increased amount of personal attention the Ss were afforded? A future project will be necessary in which the behavior shaping procedures are compared with a similar amount of increased attention alone.

Another question concerns possible extinction. The Ss have been returned to their original cottage and without the stimulus of the more individualized attention their self help behavior may extinguish. Although it would appear from the data that the zenith of self help behavior for these Ss has been reached, this is not necessarily so. Actually when the present level of behavior was reached, it was decided not to teach higher level activities. Whether it is possible to go further with these Ss cannot be predicted at this time.

An unanticipated dividend from this project concerns the attendants. Those employees who actually had contact with the Ss were tremendously heartened by the project. Their job changed from drab, custodial care to one of active participation in helping the Ss. It has also been found that more than a few attendants throughout the institution who heard about the project and its results were inspired to the extent of increasing their own efforts to train similar residents on their units.

Certain conclusions seem warranted from the findings of this study. First, the self help behavior of the Ss has been improved. Even though it cannot be said at this point specifically which procedures brought about the change, there would seem to be merit in recommending the general procedure for use in other institutions. Second, this was brought about by regular cottage personnel who had only brief instruction in behavior shaping. Third, for the self care program instituted, about four months of training the Ss is sufficient. Finally, this project did serve to inspire many attendants, who had nothing directly to do with it, to give better service to the residents in their charge.

## REFERENCES

Dayan, M. Toilet training retarded children in a state residential institution. *Ment. Retard.*, 1964, 2, 116–117.

Ellis, N. R. Toilet training the severely defective patient: an S-R reinforcement analysis. *Amer. J. ment. Defic.*, 1963, 68, 98–103.

Ferster, C. B., & DeMyer, Marian K. The development of performance in autistic children in an automatically controlled environment. *J. chronic Dis.*, 1961, 13, 312–345.

# Token Reinforcement for Learning

*by J. S. Birnbrauer*
*and Julia Lawler*

When Fred was admitted to Rainier School (in Buckley, Washington), he was described as an aggressive, destructive, extremely hyperactive child whose behavior was uncontrollable and violent. His Vineland Social Maturity Scale scores were: social age, two years and five months; social quotient, 38. (His age was six years and four months.) Psychological testing was not possible, and a recent attempt has been equally unsuccessful.

His attendants described Fred as "one of the most disturbed boys on our hall" and reported such behavior as "screaming and pounding on the table at mealtimes," tearing bedding, eating his clothing, and biting and kicking other children.

After 2½ years at Rainier, this child was still a severe behavior prob-

This article is based upon a paper read by the senior author at the Western Psychological Association convention in Portland, Oregon, April, 1964.

lem and was showing no signs of improvement, which, of course, is not unusual. However, we know that Fred will behave quite differently, for he has—during the 60 to 90 minutes that he spent daily in one classroom.

In class, Fred learned to sit quietly for about 60 minutes at a table with six other children, waiting his turn for individual instruction. He learned to hang up, put on, and zip his coat upon request, to respond to several other verbal requests, such as "sit down," "please close (open) the door," and "don't touch," and to identify parts of the body. By the end of the year he was beginning to discriminate pictures and colors, and rarely attacked another child or was self-destructive.

Fred was one of 54 children who attended the two Rainier School classrooms which were conducted according to operant learning, or reinforcement, principles (Bijou & Baer,

MENTAL RETARDATION, 1964, Vol. 2, pp. 275-279.

1961; Skinner, 1953) and in which token reinforcement systems were utilized. The children ranged from those like Fred, who was classified as profoundly retarded and ordinarily would not have been in a school program, to mildly retarded, educable 14-year-olds who had not progressed in academic subjects but did not necessarily present behavior problems.

We shall focus upon the classes for severely retarded children because they have been conducted by a teacher working alone with groups of from six to 13 pupils each. She has demonstrated that operant learning principles are practical and apparently quite effective. The procedures in the other classroom have been described elsewhere (Birnbrauer, Bijou, Wolf & Kidder, in press) and are quite similar.

In addition to describing the establishment of a token reinforcer system in some detail, we shall summarize the advantages of a token reinforcer over edibles, trinkets and other incentives, and outline our plan for "weaning" the pupils from the tokens. While Fred's greatly improved behavior in class is an important first step, it would be highly desirable to teach him to delay tangible reinforcement and respond more to instructions and other social cues.

## Operant Principles Applied to Severely Retarded Pupils

The teacher's aim was to carefully program the consequences of each child's behavior—to positively reinforce approximations to desirable social and studying behavior, to extinguish inappropriate and incorrect behavior, and to punish dangerous behavior.

To accomplish the first aim, she immediately proffered a tangible reinforcer when, and only when, a pupil complied with a verbal request or was exhibiting appropriate classroom behavior, e.g., sitting quietly, trying to hang up his coat. The reinforcers used were small chocolate-covered candies sold under the trade-mark M&M's. Later, a poker chip was also used.

Extinguishing incorrect behavior consisted of completely ignoring and perhaps turning away when a child behaved inappropriately, e.g., failed to comply with a request or responded incorrectly to a flash card. In other words, the teacher immediately attended to and tangibly reinforced correct behavior.

That behavior which could not be ignored because it endangered other children or the teacher was handled more directly. For example, whenever Fred started to attack another child, the teacher pinned his arms to his side until he relaxed. This procedure required only a few seconds, but was applied many times. Then, the teacher returned to the child whom she was instructing at the time. Another child who kicked other children and the teacher was restrained in a similar way until, after many bruises, the teacher observed that this child only kicked children who did not strike back. Thereafter, she defended herself and encouraged the other children to do likewise. In a short time, the boy no longer presented this problem.

To some teachers these procedures may not sound different from what they do. Indeed, many do conduct their classes with essentially these methods. However, the immediacy and consistency with which an *effective* reinforcer is used are important, if not necessary, elements. Token reinforcers permit a teacher to incorporate immediacy of reinforcement into her routine (if she has large pockets) and are effective even though she has pupils whose likes and dislikes vary.

At the beginning of the school term, the teacher used M&M's exclusively, dispensing them one at a time as a child exhibited approximations to the desired terminal behavior.

At the same time, she smiled, expressed approval verbally and, perhaps, patted the pupil. Within a month, most of the children were beginning to receive an occasional poker chip contingent upon correct behavior. When the child had "saved" two or three chips, the teacher exchanged the chips one-for-one with M&M's.

After the children had experienced trading, they ceased expressing disapproval when a poker chip was given. Then, the teacher gave more poker chips and fewer M&M's until finally the child was earning nothing but poker chips during class. At the end of the period, he exchanged his poker chips for an item from an array of choices (candy bars, balloons, whistles, and other edibles and trinkets).

The pupils were moved from M&M's to poker chips at individually determined paces. Still later, the teacher introduced a bonus chip for completely correct work and began to require some of the pupils to save their chips until the next day. That some of the children were still receiving M&M's had no effect upon others who had learned the value of the chips.

---

## about the authors . . .

*Jay S. Birnbrauer*, Ph.D., is an assistant professor of psychology at the University of Washington. Since 1962 he has been engaged in the applications of programmed instruction and operant procedures with retardates in the classroom. He is also engaged in laboratory investigations of discrimination learning of retardates at the Rainier School in Buckley, Washington, locale of the experiments reported here.
*Julia Lawler*, B.Ed., is a teacher at the Rainier School and has participated in classroom research on severe behavior problems in the trainable retarded.

The projects which the authors described in this article are supported by the White River School District and Mental Health Project Grant MH-01366 and Research Grant MH-2232.

At the end of the school year, with four exceptions the 37 pupils hung up their coats upon entering the classroom, took their seats quietly, and waited for their assignments with only an occasional reminder. Eleven children had advanced to the point of working alone and persistently on programmed multiple-choice prereading assignments which required from 10 to 30 minutes to complete. Of these 37, 14 had never attended school before, three had been dropped from school or would have been dropped for incorrigibility, and four are still considered "severe behavior problems." All had IQs of 40 or less.

The fact that many of these children have not changed in other situations is significant. It shows that the procedures used in this classroom are effective and that retarded children respond to their environments as do other humans. It is safe to say that these children are not treated in a systematic fashion in other situations.

Although we have not demonstrated experimentally that the token system, and not other factors, e.g., this particular teacher's "personality," was responsible for these changes, we can offer the following bits of circumstantial evidence:

(1) This teacher did not enjoy this kind of success during the preceding year with similar and, in some cases, the same children.

(2) In the classroom for educable pupils, each of the several teachers is effective and attended to as long as he dispenses tokens (check marks in a booklet which, when filled, is exchanged for an item of the student's choice).

(3) Fred, for example, displayed aggressive and destructive behavior in class on those days when the teacher tested his responses to only her approval, i.e., she tried *not* giving him tokens.

(4) Several studies have been published recently which show that these principles may be applied effectively and safely (e.g., Ayllon & Haughton,

1962, Ayllon & Michael, 1959, with chronic schizophrenics; Wolf, 1964, Wolf, Risley, & Mees, 1964, with an autistic child; Allen et al., 1964, Harris et al., 1964, with nursery school children).

Ullmann and Krasner (in press) have compiled many other examples of the applications of operant procedures to clinical and educational problems. However, our reason for writing at this time is to encourage the testing of these principles by others. Certainly, motivating retarded children is a significant problem and, for many, special procedures, such as token reinforcement, appear necessary.

## Why Token Reinforcement?

Children vary in what is reinforcing to them. This is true not only among children but also within a child at different times. Long, Hammack, May & Campbell (1958) observed that after several sessions, the performances of many children in their laboratory declined. After the reinforcer was changed, the children resumed their earlier "better" behavior. The token is the same for all children, but it derives its effectiveness from the "back-up" reinforcers which are available for exchange. Tokens will be generally effective to the extent that the exchange items are varied and sufficiently valuable (Sidman, 1962).

Tokens are quite economical. In the educable classroom (Birnbrauer et al., in press), literally thousands of immediate reinforcers were given, at an estimated maximum cost of $7 per child for the academic year.

Tokens do not interfere with ongoing activities. That is, there is nothing to unwrap, consume or investigate, and nothing with which to make a mess. Some tokens, however, may present their own problems; for example, poker chips in a tin pie plate make noise and the pupils sometimes engage in noise-making.

For one year, in the educable classroom, the tokens were tiny colored stars which the pupils pasted in booklets. These were difficult to recover from the floor and pasting them into the booklets often was quite time-consuming. For these reasons, check marks which the teachers inserted in the pupils' savings booklets were substituted. Staats, Finley, Minke, Wolf & Brooks (1964) have used still another variation in their research and discuss the advantages and problems of token reinforcement at length.

Tokens are intermediate between immediate and delayed tangible reinforcement. The tokens have power only in the future. In the classes for the severely retarded this delay has been extended from a few seconds to over an hour. Some of the educable children study for many days for only check marks and presumably the knowledge that they are approaching a goal.

## From Tokens to Other Reinforcers

While Fred is now spending the bulk of his class time more productively than previously with no reinforcers other than the chips (the teacher's praise and smiling apparently are not yet effective), he is not a socialized individual. He will not work, study, or play for relatively long periods with no tangible reinforcers (tokens, edibles, trinkets) in evidence.

We propose to approach this end in the same way that M&M's were replaced by poker chips. In the educable classroom, for example, the teachers first dispensed marks one at a time as the child made correct responses. Then the teacher absented himself and dispensed the marks when the lesson, which may have taken from five to 30 minutes, was completed. The next step was to delay the tokens until after several lessons were completed. At the end of the year, three of the 17 pupils were accomplishing a great deal of work in about 60 to 90 minutes before receiving any tokens. We do not anticipate difficulty in transferring this control to scores (grades) and praise with weekly and even less frequent exchange.

# References

Allen, K. E., Hart, B., Buell, J., Harris, F. & Wolf, M. M. Effects of Social Reinforcement on Isolate Behavior of a Nursery School Child. *Child Development,* 1964, *35,* 511-518.

Ayllon, T. & Haughton, E. Control of the Behavior of Schizophrenic Patients by Food. *Journal of the Experimental Analysis of Behavior,* 1962, *5,* 343-352.

Ayllon, T. & Michael, J. The Psychiatric Nurse as. a Behavioral Engineer. *Journal of the Experimental Analysis of Behavior,* 1959, *2,* 323-334.

Bijou, S. W. & Baer, D. M. *Child Development,* Volume I. New York: Appleton-Century-Crofts, 1961.

Birnbrauer, J. S., Bijou, S. W., Wolf, M. M. & Kidder, J. D. Programmed Instruction in the Classroom. In *Case Studies in Behavior Modification,* Ullmann L. & Krasner, L. (Eds.). New York: Holt, Rinehart & Winston, in press.

Harris, F., Johnston, M., Kelley, C. S. & Wolf, M. M. Effects of Positive Social Reinforcement on Regressed Crawling of a Nursery School Child. *Journal of Educational Psychology,* 1964, *55,* 35-41.

Long, E. R., Hammack, J. T., May, F. & Campbell, B. J. Intermittent Reinforcement of Operant Behavior in Children. *Journal of the Experimental Analysis of Behavior,* 1958, *1,* 315-339.

Sidman, M. Operant Techniques. In *Experimental Foundations of Clinical Psychology,* A. J. Bachrach (Ed.). New York: Basic Books, 1962.

Skinner, B. F. *Science and Human Behavior.* New York: Macmillan, 1953.

Staats, A. W., Finley, J. P., Minke, K. A., Wolf, M. & Brooks, L. O. A Reinforcer System and Experimental Procedure for the Laboratory Study of Reading Acquisition. *Child Development,* 1964, *35,* 209-231.

Ullmann, L. & Krasner, L. (Eds.). *Case Studies in Behavior Modification.* New York: Holt, Rinehart, & Winston, in press.

Wolf, M. M. Application of Operant Conditioning Procedures to the Behavior Problems of an Autistic Child —a Follow-up and Extension. Paper read at Western Psychological Assn. Convention, Portland, Ore., April, 1964.

Wolf, M. M., Risley, T. R. & Mees, H. L. Application of Operant Conditioning Procedures to the Behaviour Problems of an Autistic Child. *Behaviour Research and Therapy,* 1964, *1,* 305-312.

# The Use of Behavior Modification

## Techniques In An Urban Classroom

### Patricia Sachs

Class: The class was a Junior Guidance Halfway Class in the New York City Public School System. The population consisted of difficult, disruptive children, uncontainable in normal classes, as well as children with massive anxiety and depression patterns for whom there were no alternative classroom resources. The class was composed of 8 boys, aged seven to twelve and classified as socially maladjusted and/or emotionally disturbed.

Teachers: There were two female teachers, each of whom had taught in the regular classroom before working in the field of Special Education. Both teachers were graduates of Queens College and had received Master's Degree in Special Education.

Initial Reaction in Class Placement: All eight boys were extremely hostile, angry, and acting out. There were constant violent temper tantrums, furniture overturned, chairs thrown, and generally disruptive behavior. One child would become upset, and immediately, like a chain reaction, there were several children terribly upset. One boy would suddenly curse and scream, then overturn his desk. The boy sitting next to him would jump up immediately, ready to fight.

## A Typical Day In The Classroom

The teachers would arrive early, put sentence work on the blackboard one board having the sentences to be copied in manuscript, one board having the same work in cursive writing. (This work was done each day, one day the children would have to punctuate, the next day capitalize.)

The children were accompanied to the classroom by one teacher, who would go down and greet them. Some of the boys would line up at once,
ORIGINAL MANUSCRIPT

35

but two were continuing a fight which had begun on the bus that morning. Mrs. H. would have to calm them down and get them to the classroom, where the problem could be discussed. As the boys walked in Mrs. S. would greet them. Mrs. H. would walk to the board and give merits to the boys who had come up properly. She also gave merits to the two boys who had had the fight, saying: "I am giving you a merit for calming down and getting back on line. I'm glad you were able to do the right thing when you were told."

The boys went to the closet and hung their coats on the pegs with their names. They then sat down at their desks (the desks and chairs also had names on them). Each of six boys began to put on headings and to copy the work on the blackboard. Two boys, unable to copy from the board, began to work on a prepared sheet on their desks. As each boy began to work one teacher put a merit next to his name on the board.

While the boys were working quietly in their seats both teachers were circulating. One teacher would stop a boy, saying quietly, "Let's stop this for a while and read." She would sit down and read with the child individually, from a Library book the child had chosen. She would stay there for about ten minutes. When she felt the time was up she would put words or exercises the child needed in his notebook for homework. Before going on to another child she would go to the board and put up another merit saying, "I"m very proud of the way you stopped your work and read with me." She then went to the next child.

Each teacher would be working in the same pattern, only changing for a particular child's need. Before the boys had finished the morning work on the board Mrs. H. would take out the Homework Check Book and go to each boy individually, checking his assignment. If it was complete he received a check in the book and a merit on the board. If not it was recorded and he was given another day to catch up. (If the child completed all his homework for the month his name appeared on the school Honor Roll). By this time some of the boys finished the board work, and as the teacher checked his sentences he would then proceed to his workbook. For the two boys who could not work in such a book Mrs. S. sat down and gave work in their own notebooks, with those children listening. Some boys finished their work quickly and were ready for another task. However, the grouping was such that the entire class had to be ready for the next activity. Therefore those children were given specific housekeeping jobs. One boy was sent for a basin of water to wash off the lunch table, another to water plants, another child to straighten out the paper closet.

When all the boys were finishing up Mrs. H. gave the others quick jobs to do such as passing the basket. When all boys were in their seats and ready the class would take turns reading the sentences on the board aloud. The youngsters unable to read aloud were given jobs they could do for the group - "Can you tell us what today's date is? Come up and mark it on the calendar ."

After each child had been given an opportunity to read aloud, Mrs. S. would go to the Merit Chart on the board. She would start with each boy's name saying, "Anthony, you did very well this morning. You earned one merit for boardwork, one merit for reading, one merit for workbook, one merit for a job, and one merit for reading out loud." As she said this she marked the merits next to the child's name. (ex. Anthony *****). She might have said, "One half a merit for you job -- it could be done more neatly next time."

The next activity was a brief drill in calisthenics, ending with Simple Simon. The children were then given snack (milk, and cookies

37

provided by the teachers). As each child finished his snack he was permitted to use the bathroom. During snack the boys were allowed to discuss what they saw on television, or some current events. Some boys brought in newspaper pictures for the bulletin board. Each day the board was brought up to date: calendar, attendance, absentees, important notices.

The boys then were settled down in their seats for Math, each boy earning a merit as he got his book out and started working. There were two boards of work for two separate groups. Several others were given individual seat work with concrete materials. Mrs. H. went up to the board and gave merits to each boy who was working. Ray suddenly overturned his desk and began cursing and screaming. He kept screaming obscene words at the teacher and kicking his desk into the wall. Hubert jumped out of his seat and hit Ray. Mrs. H. quickly went to the board and gave merits to the boys sitting quietly. While Mrs. S. put Hubert in his seat, saying, "I know Ray upset you, but you must not use your fists." Mrs. S. continued to hold Hubert, calming him down while Mrs. H restrained Ray, and tried to get him to the "Angry Corner" where a screen had been placed. She was unsuccessful and Mrs. S. had to leave Hubert and help Mrs. H. drag Ray from the classroom. Mrs. S. stayed outside with Ray while Mrs. H. gave each boy who remained in his seat three merits for "being strong," and she gave Hubert one merit, saying, "I'm glad you were able to stop fighting when Mrs. S. went to you." The boys went on with their Math.

Mrs. H. quietly brought Ray back into the room to a table where they prepared an art activity for the class. As each boy completed his Math and had it checked he went to the back table where he began to work on a collage. When the boys were completing the collage others began

38

to clean up. Then Mrs. S. went to the board and gave each boy a merit as he returned to his seat. Then, again, she went down the list of names saying, "Anthony, one merit for completing your Math, and one for Art, one for cleaning up, and one for neatness." Then she would go on to each boy. When she came to Ray she made no mention of his outburst, merely saying, "One merit for Art, and one for cleaning up."

Then Mrs. H. called out three names for going to the kitchen and getting lunch. The other boys were given jobs such as putting the plates and napkins out, the salt and peper, the bag for the garbage pail. The other boys came in and all were told to sit down. The boys were given merits for their jobs. They were then called, one at a time, to bring their chairs to the lunchtable. (Each day the order of names called was rotated.)

The teachers would serve the boys as they passed their plates. When everyone had been served, and all the boys had napkins in their laps, they began to eat. The teachers ate the same lunch, along with the boys. As they finished the main course plates were passed and put in the garbage. Then dessert was served, the table cleared. During dessert the record player was put on. Jobs were given: washing the table cloth, emptying pots, bringing trays and pots back to the kitchen.

The boys were called to their seats and given merits for polite behavior at lunch and jobs. They then had to copy homework from the board, receiving a merit as they began, and one when they finished. As each boy finished he went to the back closet and picked a game. (In the back closet were many games such as Bingo, Lotto, Checkers, Chess, blocks, pegs, small cars, Junior Scrabble, and many more.)

By this time in the afternoon the children were more active and needed to move around. They were allowed to play other games such as

Ring-Toss and Nok-Hockey. After about twenty minutes the boys were
called to their seats and given merits for coming back, putting the
games away, and playing fairly.

When each boy was in his seat and ready, Mrs. H. would go to the
Merit Chart, going down the list of names, saying, "Anthony, you had a
very good day today--you earned thirty one merits--that is equivalent
to a star and six merits over." She would write this down in her Record Book, put a star on the Star Chart, next to Anthony's name, and then
go on to the next boy. (Since twenty-five merits equalled a star, and
at least thirty merits were possibly earned in a day, each boy could
possibly earn a star a day. When any boy had a star he got a candy bar.
When he earned ten stars he could pick from the Prize Box.)

The boys then got their coats, put up chairs and lined up. They
were escorted to the bus by the teachers. The boys who had earned candy bars were given them as they got on the bus.

## Conclusion

The boys in this class came in with little or no control over their
behavior, and no study habits. With the consistent use of behavior
techniques the boys learned to work, to control their behavior, and to
be proud of their accomplishments.

The techniques used began more simply than the merit system which
evolved. Initially the teachers used "M and M"s for immediate rewarding of acceptable behavior. Gradually they were able to change the
immediate rewards from candy to merits. The candy was still necessary
at the end of the day but the boys were able to wait for the oral gratification. Hopefully in time a system would evolve which could eliminate the candy altogether. In the future the children would be motivated by intrinsic reward.

Patricia Sachs is a Learning Disability Teacher Consultant at the North Hudson Jointure Commission for Special Education, Guttenberg, New Jersey.

## The Rationale For The Use Of Operant Conditioning Regarding The Transfer Of Training Of Therapeutic Techniques

Classroom teachers of physically handicapped children are an integral part of the habilitation team. Part of their educational sequence should incluse the area known as theraputic techniques. The problem of training teachers in physical therapy techniques can be viewed from either of two points of view (14,):

1. This is a problem in learning: teachers must master clinical techniques.

2. This is a problem in transfer of training: clinical procedures must be carred out in the classroom.

Neither of these points of view is likely to be productive by itself. What is, a clinical procedure observed in a demonstration or carried out by the learner in a clinic may not be equivalent to such a procedure carried out in a classroom. Resolution of the problem may require a third point of view, one which incorporates both learning and transfer.

The classical controversy between the identicala elements of transfer theory )Poffenberger) and the transfer of learned principles (Judd) is now largely resolved. Identical elements or components (Skinner) in the stimulus array must be present for a reliable transfer effect. In sofar.as principles are taught by the use of examples, there is oppor- for the elements in the learning situation to appear also in the performance situation. Thus, $S^d \xrightarrow{R} R^s$ represents the learning situation. When a response, R, occurs in the presence of a discriminative stimulus, $S^d$, the resulting operants, $R^s$, will tend thereater to be elicited in the presence of the stimulus. The letter definitions are:

$S^d$- The physically handicapped child in a given condition e.g. braces.

R - A therapeutic technique applied to the child
ORIGINAL MANUSCRIPT

$R^S$ - The operant (therapeutic technique) thereafter elicited in the presence of a handicapped child in that condition.

Let us first consider the physically handicapped child ($S^d$). The same children or class of children who furnish the stimuli in the physical therapy department must be present in the classroom. The transfer of training or stimulus induction (Skinner) is from physically handicapped children in the department of physical therapy to the same or similar physically handicapped children in the classroom.

Now, let us consider the therapeutic techniques applied to the child (R). A lecture-demonstration course involves explanation and demonstration with the transfer dependent upon the ingenuity of the student. The student is a passive participant in the lecture-demonstration course. While he may become familiar with the problems and the solutions, he does not physically particiapte in carrying through the evolved conclusions.

The educational methodology utilized should involve the participants in the following paradigm:

Presentation of problem →Problem solution→Reinforcement
Each student may then learn therapeutic techniques by carrying out speific courses of action. When the teacher actually locks the braces of a cerebral palsied child at the knees, the therapeutic technique represents a response. This response will emerge as an operabt controlled by a discriminative stimulus, the child, with braces, sitting down. The reinforcer, here, is the recognition of a satisfactory state of affairs brought about by the teacher's own behavior.

## RELEVANT RESEARCH

Transfer of training refers to the carryover of behavior from one performance situation to another, while transfer effect refers to the amount of this transfer reflected in the execution of the second performance. "The transfer effect may be positive or negative, beneficial or detrimental" (16:735). Transfer, then, consists of the difference in performance between that occurring in a learning situation and that occurring in another situation. Thus, a problem involving transfer requires analysis both of the conditions in the original learning situation and conditions in the new situation which may affect performance of the task learned. In some studies of transfer, the second situation may be a new learning task. In that case, the transfer effect refers to the influence of the original learning on the learning of the second task (16:734-735, 12:520).

With reference to the training of orthopedic teachers, the transfer task consists of the inspection of therapeutic equipment used by physically handicapped children in a classroom and facilitation of locomotion in that locale. While such behaviors are usually learned in in the physical therapy clinic, they must be carried out in the classroom.

Transfer effect in the performance situation may well be confounded by variables in that situation which were not present during the original learning. The usual analysis of a learning situation is appropriate in the present study of teacher training--stimulus variables, response variables, and reinforcing conditions can be isolated.

A. Stimulus Variables

Melton (10:337), distinguishes between the nominal and effective stimulus. A nominal stimulus is the obvious or apparent occasion for a response, e.g., a physically handicapped child with crutches and braces; the effective stimulus, on the other hand, may include the total learning environment or, possibly, some small part of it. Problem solving requires proficiency in making an appropriate response to both

aspects of the stimulus. Therefore, traces resulting from sensitiza-
tion to prior stimuli as well as those from immediate environmental
stimuli will determine the response (11:158).

With sub-human species, it has been found that a period of famil-
iarization with the learning environment facilitates subsequent learning of mazes and involves less exploratory behavior (16:640, 671, 13:
78). Thus, while novel stimuli tend to elicit responses which compete
with the learning of a task, after a few trials the original distract-
ors become background stimuli and may even help maintain the performance
(16:87). In the original learning, the learner observes or samples aspects of his environment and, as learning progresses, relies less frequently upon environmental information (2:260). Habituation to the
learning environment, then, involves a learning process in which responses are made to the constant features of that environment (5:78).
These constant stimuli become a ground on which are displayed those
stimuli to be learned, i.e., the child, his movements and his equipment.

In this study, the stimulus array in the learning situation was
closely similar to that of the performance situation. The array consisted of the handicapped children wearing braces and using crutches,
classroom desks, blackboards a teacher's desk positioned appropriately
with reference to the children's desks, and other general arrangements
of the learning space.

The stimulus variables included:

1. <u>Crutches and braces</u>: Insofar as the student discovered the
   relevant parts of the equipment, such a display constituted
   a part of the stimulus array to which he responded in a classroom for orthopedically handicapped children.

2. <u>The handicapped child using braces and crutches</u>. This constituted one kind of discriminative stimulus. Recognition of defects in the equipment served as another kind of discrimination
   stimulus.

3.  The classroom environment.  This constituted the constant
    features of the stimulus array.

Psychologists now commonly distinguish between instrumental and
classical conditioning.  The major difference is that, in instrumental
conditioning, the occurrence of reward or punishment upon the learner's
behavior, whereas in classical conditioning it is not (4:2).  Holland
and Skinner distinguish between them by restricting classical conditioning to learned changes in the internal economy of the body and by restricting instrumental conditioning to the operation of the skeletal
system (5:36-45).

Response behavior includes verbal and manipulative behavior.  Ma-
ipulative behavior.  Manipulative behavior is defined in terms of skills
and is concerned with transferable specifics, for example, the use of
braces and crutches.  Verbal behavior is involved with the nontrans-
ferable specifics, for example, the names of the various types of braces
and crutches (6:212).

Goss (3:250), asserts that the earliest behaviorists, e.g., Max
Meyer and John Watson, assumed an intervening environment in the form
of mediating verbal responses.  Verbal mediators are used in explanatory
accounts of learning:  verbal labels may serve as cues to arouse an appropriate response in the presence of a stimulus(15:231).

With reference to training, when a trainee has acquired a concept,
he is then able to acquire also a verbal label for that concept; the
label serves as a cue for his overt behavior (3:249).  Such verbal behavior becomes part of the response repertoire when the learner first
manipulates the braces and crutches and then discusses that action.  In
this study, verbal non-transferable behavior was not the goal of learning; rather it served a mediating function by producing cues for man-

ipulative transferable behavior.

1. <u>Verbal behavior</u>. This was exemplified by the name parts of the braces and crutches as well as by verbal description of the possible types of locomotion.

2. <u>Manipulative transferable behavior</u>. This behavior, instrument-ally learned, was exemplified by the adjustments of the braces and crutches as well as skills involving the provision of an opportunity for the child to ambulate optimally.

## C. REINFORCEMENT

The law of effect implies that a rewarded response increases in its likelihood of recurrence. Instrumental learning follows the law of ef-fect since reinforcers, such as food and water for a deprived animal and escape from punishment, reinforce the behavior which precedes their presentation (13:145-146, 7:40).

The definition of a reinforcer in a learning situation is highly controversial. Woodworth and Schlosberg (16:799), state that, when an individual succeeds in an endeavor, the success is its own reward. Hence, the awareness of success by the learner is the reinforcer. Koehler (8:122-125), when investigating nonoutcome problems (blank trials), re-quired a forced choice. He asserts that when the wrong choice is made, the learner realizes the alternate is correct, hence, such knowledge is reinforcing. The common element is the awareness of the learner. It is possible that, in the former interpretation, an individual could succeed in an endeavor and not be aware of the success. In this case, there would be no reinforcement.

Logically, then, the reinforcer requires awareness of the learner that a satisfactory state of affairs exists. Recognition of a satis-factory state on the part of the learner may be viewed as a reduction in uncertainty with a resultant tension decrease.

An immediate awareness of success implies an immediate reinforce-ment. Landsman and Turkewitz (9:66) found that immediate reinforcement

47

allows an individual to learn faster than does a delay of six seconds before presentation of the reinforcer. Many researchers (1:592, 7:23) support the hypothesis that the longer the delay in reinforcement, the greater the number of competing responses which may intervene and the poorer the resulting performance. Therefore, any condition which makes for an immediate awareness of success on the part of the learner should facilitate learning.

The present study utilized a reduction of stimuli, in effect, a forced choice discrimination task, and a reduction or responses, thus allowing reinforcement to occur at the moment of choice. By responding to a physically handicapped with braces and crutches in a learning situation closely resembling the performance or transfer situation, the learner is likely also to react appropriately in the transfer situation, the classroom.

This study was an attempt to train teachers in physical therapy techniques by the use of a programmed demonstration with maximum student involvement. Two groups received such training, each in one of two kinds of skill, at alternate times. Transfer to the classroom was evaluated.

### SUMMARY

Transfer effect may be confounded by variables in the performance situation which were not present in the learning situation. When considering the stimulus situation, background elements must be included. These constant features of the learning environment can influence both the original learning and the amount of transfer.

Habituation to the learning environment involves a learning process in which responses are made to the constant features of that environment. These constant stimuli become a ground on which are displayed those stimulit to be learned,i.e,. the child, his equipment and his method of environment.

In any learning situation the teacher must consider both discriminative stimuli, i.e., those which occasion particular responses, and responses variables. These include the manipulative transferable specifics and the verbal responses which may cue them. Once the manipulative skills are learned, verbal discussion can serve as cues to maintain the transferable behavior.

Awareness of the learner that a satisfactory state of affairs exists may be used as a reinforcer. Immediate reinforcement may be viewed as the reduction of uncertainty and the learner is at ease. Transfer of observing behavior and manipulative skills in the presence of appropriate discriminative stimuli in the classroom constitutes the goal with regards to skill learning in the educational process.

REFERENCES

1.  Champion, R. A. and D.A. McBride, ACTIVITY DURING DELAY REINFORCE-
    MENT IN HUMAN LEARNING. J. Exp. Psychol., 63 (6) 589-592.

2.  Fitts, Paul. "Perceptual Motor Learning" in CATEGORIES OF HUMAN
    LEARNING edited by Aurthur Melton. Academic Press, New York,
    1964. 244-283

3.  Goss, A.R. Verbal Mediating Responses and Concept Responses.
    PSYCHOL. REV. 1961, 68. 248-274.

4.  Grant, David A. "Classical and Operant Conditioning" in CATEGORIES
    OF HUMAN LEARNING edited by Arthur Melton. Academic Press,
    New York. 1964.

5.  Holland, James and B.F. Skinner. THE ANALYSIS OF BEHAVIOR. McGraw-
    HILL BOOK Co. New York 1961.

6.  Jones, H.E. and Batalla, M. Transfer in Children Maze Learning. J.
    EDUC. PSYCHOL. 1944, 35, 474-483. Cited by George Thompson,
    CHILD PSYCHOLOGY, Houghton-Mifflin Co., Boston, 1962.

7.  Kimble, Gregory, "Categories of Learning and the Problem of Def-
    inition" in CATEGORIES OF HUMAN LEARNING edited by Arthur
    Melton. Academic Press, New York. 1964.

8.  Koehler, J. Jr. Role of Instruction in Two Choice Verbal Condition-
    ing With Contingent Partial Reinforcement. J. EXP. PSYCHOLOGY.
    1961. 62, 122, 125.

9.  Landsman, Howard and Maring Turkewitz. Delay of Knowledge of Re-
    sults and Performance on A Cognitive Task. PSYCHOLOGY REP.
    1962. 1 (1) 66.

10. Melton, Arthur. CATEGORIES OF HUMAN LEARNING. Academic Press,
    New York. 1964.

11. Morrisett, Lloyd and Carl Hovland. TRANSFER OF LEARNING. Book
    edited by Robert Grose and Robert Birney, D. Van Nostrand Co.,
    New York. 1963.

12. Øsgood, Charles, METHODS AND THEORY IN EXPERIMENTAL PSYCHOLOGY.
    Oxford University Press, New York. 1953

13. Skinner, B.F. CUMULATIVE RECORD. Appleton-Century Crofts, New
    York. 1959

14. Swack, Myron J., Training Special Education Teachers in Physical
    Therapy Techniques By Means of Programmed Demonstrations.
    EXCEPTIONAL CHILDREN, April, 1967.

15. Underwood, Benton. The Representativeness of Rote Verbal Learning
    in CATEGORIES OF HUMAN LEARNING, edited by Arthur Melton.
    Academic Press, New York. 1964. 48-77.

16.  Woodworth, Robert and Harold Schlosberg. EXPERIMENTAL PSYCHOLOGY.
     Henry Holt and Company, New York. 1964.

Myron Swack, Ph.D*
Ellsworth Abare, M.A.**

*Professor & Chairman, Department of Special Education, William
  Paterson College of New Jersey, Wayne, New Jersey
**Assistant Profesor of Special Education, William Paterson College
  of New Jersey, Wayne, New Jersey

K. DANIEL O'LEARY
KENNETH F. KAUFMAN
RUTH E. KASS
RONALD S. DRABMAN

# The Effects of Loud and Soft Reprimands on the Behavior of Disruptive Students

A NUMBER of studies demonstrate that teacher attention in the form of praise can reduce disruptive classroom behavior (Becker, Madsen, Arnold, & Thomas, 1967; Hall, Lund, & Jackson, 1968; Madsen, Becker, & Thomas, 1968; Walker & Buckley, 1968). In these studies, praising appropriate behavior was usually concomitant with ignoring disruptive behavior. In addition, shaping appropriate behavior or reinforcing successive approximations to some desired terminal behavior was stressed. Despite the generally positive results obtained when a teacher used these procedures, a closer examination of the studies reveals that (a) they were not always effective (Hall et al., 1968), (b) the teacher did not actually ignore all disruptive behavior (Madsen et al., 1968), and (c) in one class of disruptive children, praising appropriate behavior and igoring disruptive behavior resulted in classroom pandemonium (O'Leary, Becker, Evans, & Saudargas, 1969).

One might argue that where praising appropriate behavior and ignoring disruptive behavior prove ineffectual, the teacher is not appropriately shaping the children's behavior. Although such an argument is theoretically rational, it is of little solace to a teacher who unsuccessfully attempts to reinforce approximations to desired terminal behaviors. Furthermore, the supposition that the teacher is not appropriately shaping ignores the power of peers to rein-

K. DANIEL O'LEARY *is Associate Professor of Psychology, State University of New York, Stony Brook, and* KENNETH F. KAUFMAN, RUTH E. KASS, *and* RONALD S. DRABMAN *are Graduate Students in Psychology, State University of New York, Stony Brook. The research reported herein was performed in part pursuant to Biomedical Sciences Support Grant No. 31-8200-C, US Public Health Service, 1967-69.*

EXCEPTIONAL CHILDREN, 1970, Vol. 37, No. 2, pp. 145-155.

force disruptive behavior. Disregard of disruptive behavior is based on two premises —that it will extinguish if it is not reinforced and that praising appropriate behavior which is incompatible with disruptive behavior will reduce the frequency of the latter. However, even when a teacher ignores disruptive behavior, other children may reinforce it by giggling and smiling. These peer reactions may occur only occasionally, but they may make the disruptive behavior highly resistant to extinction. Thus, the teacher may ask what she can do when praise and ignoring are not effective. The present studies were designed to assess one alternative to ignoring disruptive behavior: reprimanding the child in a soft manner so that other children in the classroom could not hear the reprimand.

The effectiveness of punishment in suppressing behavior of animals has been amply documented (Solomon, 1964). Similarly, the effectiveness of punishment with children in experimental settings has been repeatedly demonstrated (Parke & Walters, 1967). However, experimental manipulations of punishment or reprimands with disruptive children have not often been investigated in applied settings. One attempt to manipulate teacher reprimands was made by O'Leary and Becker (1968) who varied aspects of teacher attention and found that soft reprimands were effective in reducing disruptive behavior of a class of first-grade children during a rest period. Since soft reprimands seemed to have no adverse side effects in the study and since ignoring disruptive behavior is not always effective, further analyses of the effects of soft reprimands seemed promising.

Soft reprimands offer several interesting advantages over loud ones. First of all, a soft reprimand does not single out the child so that his disruptive behavior is made noticeable to others. Second, a soft reprimand is presumably different from the reprimands that disruptive children ordinarily receive at home or in school, and, consequently, it should minimize the possibility of triggering conditioned emotional reactions to reprimands. Third, teachers consider soft reprimands a viable alternative to the usual methods of dealing with disruptive behavior. Two experiments are presented here which assessed the effects of soft reprimands.

### Experiment I

Two children in a second-grade class were selected for observation because of their high rates of disruptive behavior. During a baseline condition, the frequency of disruptive behaviors and teacher reprimands was assessed. Almost all reprimands were loud, i.e., many children in the class could hear them. During the second phase of the study, the teacher was asked to voice her reprimands so that they would be audible only to the child to whom they were directed. The third phase of the study constituted a return to the teacher's former loud reprimand. Finally, during the fourth condition, the teacher was requested to again use soft reprimands.

*Subjects.* Child D was described as nervous and restless. He bit his nails, drummed his fingers on his desk, and stuttered. He was often out of his seat talking and bothering other children. D avoided any challenging work. He was quick to argue and was known to get into trouble in the neighborhood.

Child S was described as uncooperative and silly. He paid little attention to his work, and he would often giggle and say things out loud. His teacher said that he enjoyed having other children laugh at him and that he acted in this manner to gain attention.

*Observation.* Before base period data were collected, college undergraduates were trained over a 3-week period to observe in the classroom. During this time, the observers obtained reliabilities of child observations exceeding 70 percent agreement. There were two undergraduate observers. One observed daily, and the other observed less frequently, serving as a reliability checker. The observers were instructed to neither talk nor make any differential responses in order to minimize their effect on the children's behavior.

Each child was observed for 20 minutes

a day during the arithmetic lesson. Observations were made on a 20-second observe, 10-second record basis: The observer would watch the child for 20 seconds and then record in 10 seconds the disruptive behaviors which had occurred during that 20-second period. The disruptive behaviors were categorized according to nine classes modified from the O'Leary and Becker study (1967). The nine classes of disruptive behavior and their associated general definitions are:

1. *Out-of-chair:* Movement of the child from his chair when not permitted or requested by teacher. No part of the child's body is to be touching the chair.

2. *Modified out-of-chair:* Movement of the child from his chair with some part of the body still touching the chair (exclude sitting on feet).

3. *Touching others' property:* Child comes into contact with another's property without permission to do so. Includes grabbing, rearranging, destroying the property of another, and touching the desk of another.

4. *Vocalization:* Any unpermitted audible behavior emanating from the mouth.

5. *Playing:* Child uses his hands to play with his own or community property so that such behavior is incompatible with learning.

6. *Orienting:* The turning or orienting response is not rated unless the child is seated and the turn must be more than 90 degrees, using the desk as a reference point.

7. *Noise:* Child creating any audible noise other than vocalization without permission.

8. *Aggression:* Child makes movement toward another person to come into contact with him (exclude brushing against another).

9. *Time off task:* Child does not do assigned work for entire 20-second interval. For example, child does not write or read when so assigned.

The dependent measure, mean frequency of disruptive behavior, was calculated by dividing the total number of disruptive behaviors by the number of intervals observed. A mean frequency measure was obtained rather than frequency of disruptive behavior per day since the length of observations varied due to unavoidable circumstances such as assemblies. Nonetheless, only three of the 27 observations for child D lasted less than 20 minutes and only four of the 28 observations for child S were less than 20 minutes. Observations of less than 10 minutes were not included.

*Reliability.* The reliabilities of child observations were calculated according to the following procedure. A perfect agreement was scored if both observers recorded the same disruptive behavior within a 20-second interval. The reliabilities were then calculated by dividing the number of perfect agreements by the number of different disruptive behaviors observed providing a measure of percent agreement. There were three reliability checks during the base period (Loud I) and one during the first soft period for child D. There were two reliability checks during the base period and one reliability check during the first soft period for child S. The four reliability checks for child D yielded the following results: 81, 72, 64, and 92 percent agreement; the three for child S resulted in: 88, 93, and 84 percent agreement.

The reliability of the observations of the teacher's loud and soft reprimands to the target children was also checked. On two different days these observations were taken simultaneously with the observation of the target children. One reliability check was made during the base period and one check was made during the first soft period. A perfect agreement was scored if both observers agreed that the reprimand was loud or soft and if both observers scored the reprimand in the same 20-second interval. The consequent reliabilities were 100 percent and 75 percent during the base period and first soft period respectively.

## Procedures

*Base Period (Loud I).* During the base period the teacher was asked to handle the children as she normally would. Since few, if any, soft reprimands occurred during the base period, this period was considered a loud reprimand phase.

*Soft Reprimands I.* During this phase the following instructions were given to the teacher:

1. Make reprimands soft all day, i.e., speak so that only the child being reprimanded can hear you.

2. Approximately one-half hour before the observers come into your room, concentrate on using soft reprimands so that the observers' entrance does not signal a change in teacher behavior.

3. While the observers are in the room, use only soft reprimands with the target children.

4. Do not increase the frequency of reprimands. Reprimand as frequently as you have always done and vary only the intensity.

5. Use soft reprimands with all the children, not just the target children.

*Loud Reprimands II.* During this phase the teacher was asked to return to loud reprimands, and the five instructions above for the soft period were repeated with a substitution of loud reprimands for soft ones.

*Soft Reprimands II.* During this final period, the teacher was asked to return to the soft reprimand procedures.

## Results

*Child D.* Child D displayed a marked reaction to soft reprimands. The mean frequency of disruptive behavior during the four conditions was: Loud I, 1.1; Soft I, 0.8; Loud II, 1.3; Soft II, 0.9. A reversal of effects was evident. When the loud reprimands were reinstated disruptive behavior increased while disruptive behavior declined during the second soft period (Figure 1). In addition, in order to more closely examine the effects of the two types of reprimands, there was an assessment of the frequency of disruptive behaviors in the two 20-second intervals after a reprimand, when another reprimand had not occurred in one of the two intervals. The results revealed that the average number of disruptive behaviors in these two intervals during the four conditions was: Loud I, 2.8; Soft I, 1.2; Loud II, 2.6; and Soft II, 1.6.

*Child S.* Child S also displayed a marked reaction to soft reprimands. The mean frequency of his disruptive behavior during the four conditions was: Loud I, 1.4; Soft I, 0.6; Loud II, 1.1; Soft II, 0.5. Again a reversal of effects was evident when the loud reprimands were reinstated. The average number of disruptive behaviors in the two 20-second intervals just after a reprimand was made was as follows during the four conditions: Loud I, 2.0; Soft I, 1.5; Loud II, 2.1; Soft II, 0.9.

*Teacher.* Although teacher A was asked to hold constant the incidence of her reprimands across conditions, the mean frequency of her reprimands to child D during the four conditions was: Loud I, 7; Soft I, 5; Loud II, 12; Soft II, 6. Similarly, she also had difficulty in holding constant her reprimands to child S across conditions as the following data show: Loud I, 6; Soft I, 4; Loud II, 8; Soft II, 3. Thus, there is some possibility that the increase in disruptive behavior during the second loud phase was a consequence of increased attention to the behavior per se, rather than a consequence of the kind of attention given, whether loud or soft. As the disruptive behavior increased, teacher A felt it impossible to use the same number of reprimands that she had used during the soft period.

Because the frequency of loud reprimands was greater than the frequency of soft reprimands, one could not conclude from Experiment I that the loudness or softness of the reprimands was the key factor in reducing disruptive behavior. It was clear, however, that if a teacher used

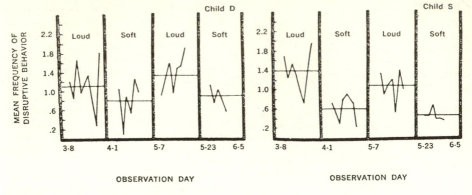

**FIGURE 1.** Disruptive behavior of children D and S in Class A.

soft reprimands, she could use fewer reprimands and obtain better behavior than if she used loud reprimands.

### Experiment II

Experiment II was conducted to assess the effects of loud and soft reprimands with the frequency held constant and to test whether all the children's disruptive behavior decreased when the teacher used soft reprimands. Experiment II is divided into three parts. Part I followed the same ABAB paradigm described in Experiment I (Loud, Soft, Loud, Soft), but Parts II and III involved variations which will be described later.

### Part I

*Subjects.* Class B, Grade 2: Child Z was a large boy who said that he wanted to be a bully when he grew up. He was the only child in the class who deliberately hurt other children. He constantly called out answers without raising his hand and his work habits were poor. Child V was extremely talkative. He loved to be with other children and he was always bursting with something to say. He was also mischievous, but never intentionally hurt anyone. His work habits were poor and his papers were never completed.

Class C, Grade 3: Child E was an extremely nervous child. When she

directed all her energy to her studies she could perform well. However, she was very undependable and rarely did her work. She was in and out of her seat and talked endlessly. Child W was a disruptive child whose reaction to most situations was to punch, kick, throw things, and to shove others out of his way. He did little work and devoted his time to such activities as chewing his pencils and punching holes in his papers.

*Observation.* The observational procedures described earlier in Experiment I were identical to those used in Experiment II. Each target child was observed during a structured academic lesson for 20 minutes each day on a 20-second observe, 10-second record basis. The nine classes of disruptive behavior were the same as those in Experiment I with some definitial extensions and a slight change in the definition of aggression. The dependent measure was calculated in the same manner as described in Experiment I.

To minimize the possibility of distance as the key factor in reprimanding the children, the target children in both classes were moved near the front of the room so that the teacher could administer soft reprimands without walking a great distance. This seating arrangement made it easier for the teacher to reprimand the target children either loudly or softly and decreased

56

the possibility of the teacher's serving as a cue for appropriate behavior by her walking to the child.

The occurrence of loud and soft reprimands was recorded throughout the study by a teacher-observer. As mentioned previously, the teachers were asked to hold the frequency of reprimands constant both to the target children and to the class throughout the study. The teacher was also asked to hold other behaviors as constant as possible so that behaviors such as praise, "eyeing down" a child, and reprimands to the class as a whole would not confound the results. A graduate student observed almost daily and gave the teachers feedback to ensure adherence to these requirements.

In addition to observations on target children, daily observations of disruptive behavior were taken on all the other children by a sampling procedure for one hour each day. Each nontarget child was observed consecutively for 2 minutes. The observer watched the children in a predetermined order each day, looking for the disruptive behaviors that had been observed in the target children.

*Reliability.* The reliabilities of child observations for both the target children and the class samples were calculated according to the procedures discussed in Experiment I. There were three reliability checks during the base period for both target children and the class sample. The average reliability for the target children was 84 percent and for the class sample was 79 percent. Nine additional reliability checks of the observations averaged 79 percent for the target children and 82 percent for the class sample.

The reliability of the observations during the base period of loud and soft reprimands used by Teacher B was 79 percent and 80 percent respectively. The reliability of the observation of loud and soft reprimands used by Teacher C was 82 percent and 72 percent respectively.

*Results.* Because there were definite decreasing trends of disruptive behavior during both soft conditions for three of

the four target children, the average of the mean levels of disruptive behavior during the last five days of each condition for the target children are reported in Table 1. There were changes in children's behavior associated with changes in teacher behavior (see Figure 2). There was a decrease in the children's disruptive behavior in the soft reprimand phase and then an increase in the disruptive behavior of three of the four children during the reinstatement of loud reprimands. Finally, the second soft period was marked by a decrease in disruptive behavior. Although the disruptive behavior of child V did not increase during the reinstitution of loud reprimands, a reduction of disruptive behavior was associated with each introduction of soft reprimands—particularly during the second soft phase. Consequently, soft reprimands seemed to influence the reduction of disruptive behavior of each of the four children. A mean reduction of 0.4 and 0.7 disruptive behaviors was associated with each introduction of soft reprimands for these children.

In order to demonstrate that the reduction of disruptive behavior was not a function of changes in frequency of reprimands, the frequencies of loud and soft reprimands are provided in Table 2. Although there was some slight reduction of reprimands for individual children during the soft reprimand phases, the teachers were able to hold the frequency of reprimands relatively constant across days and conditions, despite an obvious change in the children's behavior. The mean total reprimands, loud and soft, during the four conditions were as follows: Loud I, 5.7; Soft I, 4.6; Loud II, 5.3; Soft II, 3.7. Also

### TABLE 1

**The Average of the Mean Levels of Disruptive Behavior During the Last Five Days of Each Condition for the Target Children**

| | Condition | | | |
|---|---|---|---|---|
| Subjects | Loud I ($\overline{X} = 1.3$) | Soft I ($\overline{X} = 0.9$) | Loud II ($\overline{X} = 1.2$) | Soft II ($\overline{X} = 0.5$) |
| Child Z | 1.0 | 0.9 | 1.3 | 0.8 |
| Child V | 1.7 | 1.4 | 1.3 | 0.6 |
| Child E | 0.9 | 0.6 | 1.1 | 0.4 |
| Child W | 1.6 | 0.8 | 0.9 | 0.3 |

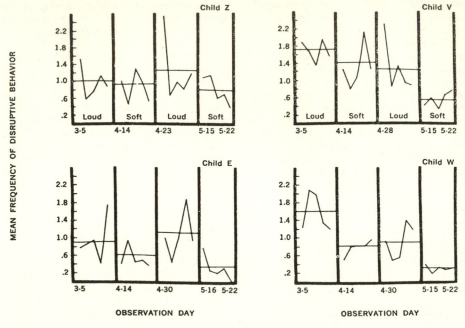

FIGURE 2. Disruptive behavior of children Z and V in Class B and children E and W in Class C.

of particular significance was the constancy of praise comments across conditions. There was an average of less than one

## TABLE 2

**Average Frequency of Loud and Soft Reprimands Per Day**

| Condition | Type of Reprimand to Child Z | | Condition | Type of Reprimand to Child V | |
|---|---|---|---|---|---|
| | Loud | Soft | | Loud | Soft |
| Loud I | 3.8 | 2.0 | Loud | 6.8 | 2.2 |
| Soft I | 0.6 | 2.6 | Soft | 0.5 | 6.7 |
| Loud II | 3.0 | 1.7 | Loud | 3.5 | 1.0 |
| Soft II | 0.1 | 2.6 | Soft | 0.1 | 3.6 |

| Condition | Reprimand to Child E | | Condition | Reprimand to Child W | |
|---|---|---|---|---|---|
| | Loud | Soft | | Loud | Soft |
| Loud I | 3.5 | 0.6 | Loud | 3.5 | 0.7 |
| Soft I | 0.4 | 5.0 | Soft | 0.4 | 2.3 |
| Loud II | 5.7 | 0.9 | Loud | 5.3 | 0.3 |
| Soft II | 0.2 | 3.4 | Soft | 0.1 | 4.6 |

praise comment per day given to each child in each of the four conditions. It can be inferred from these data that soft reprimands can be influential in modifying classroom behavior of particularly disruptive children.

The data from the class samples taken during the last five days of each condition did not show that soft reprimands reduced disruptive behavior for the whole class. Because of the variability within conditions and the lack of any clear relationship between type of reprimands and level of disruptive behavior, those data are not presented here. However, the changes in the behavior of the target children are evident when one considers that the mean frequency of disruptive behavior for the class sample B was .9 throughout the experiment and .8 during the second soft condition. The mean frequency of disruptive behavior for the class sample C was .6 throughout the experiment and .5 during the second soft condition. Thus one should note that the disruptive behavior of the four target children during the second soft period was less than the level of disruptive behavior for the class.

## Part II

Two target children and a class sample were observed in the class of a third-grade teacher. A baseline (Loud I) of disruptive behavior was obtained in this class during a structured academic lesson using the procedures described in Experiment I. In the second phase of the study (Soft I) the teacher was asked to use soft reprimands, just as the other teachers had done. Because of the infrequency of her reprimands in the second phase, the teacher was asked to double her use of soft reprimands in phase three (Soft II-Double). During phase four (Loud II), she was asked to maintain her more frequent use of reprimands but to make them loud. Both child and teacher observations were made in accord with the procedures described in Part I of Experiment II.

*Subjects.* Child B was reported to be a happy extrovert who was a compulsive talker. Child R was described by his teacher as a clown with a very short attention span.

*Reliability.* The reliability of child observations was obtained for the target children on seven occasions, and the reliability of the class sample on five occasions. The resultant average reliabilities were 87 percent and 87 percent, respectively.

The reliability of the observations of teacher behavior was checked on two occasions during the base period and once during the first soft period. The average reliability of the observations of loud and soft reprimands was 82 percent and 72 percent, respectively.

*Results.* Child B's disruptive behavior declined from 1.6 during the last five days of baseline (loud reprimands) to 1.3 during the last five days of soft reprimands. In contrast, child R's disruptive behavior increased from 1.5 in the last five days of baseline to 1.9 during the last five days of soft reprimands (see Figure 3). With the instructions to increase the use of soft reprimands during phase three (Soft II-Double), child B's disruptive behavior showed a slight drop to 1.1 while child R's increased slightly to 2.0. The return to loud reprimands was associated with an increase to 1.8 for child B and almost no change for child R.

The increase in child R's disruptive behavior from the loud to the first soft condition cannot be attributed to the soft reprimands. In fact, the change appeared to be due to a decrease in both loud and soft reprimands. Even with the instructions

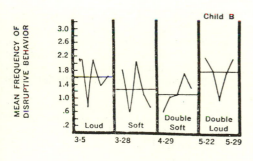
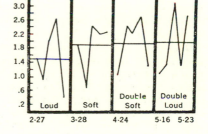

FIGURE 3. Disruptive behavior of children B and R in Class D.

59

to double the use of soft reprimands, the teacher observations reported in Table 3 indicate that the frequency of total reprimands during the double soft phase was less than during baseline. However, since child R's disruptive behavior did not increase with the return to loud reprimands, the experimental control over R's behavior was minimal or nonexistent. On the other hand, child B's disruptive behavior appeared to lessen with the use of soft reprimands.

**TABLE 3**

**Average Frequency of Loud and Soft Reprimands Per Day**

| Condition | Type of Reprimand to Child B | | Condition | Type of Reprimand to Child R | |
|---|---|---|---|---|---|
| | Loud | Soft | | Loud | Soft |
| Loud I | 2.0 | 0.4 | Loud | 1.5 | 0.2 |
| Soft I | 0.5 | 1.0 | Soft | 0.2 | 0.0 |
| Soft II | | | Double | | |
| (Double) | 1.8 | 1.1 | soft | 0.0 | 0.8 |
| Loud II | 3.1 | 2.3 | Loud | 2.5 | 0.0 |

| Condition | Reprimand to Child D | | Condition | Reprimand to Child J | |
|---|---|---|---|---|---|
| | Loud | Soft | | Loud | Soft |
| Loud | 4.5 | 1.3 | Loud | 1.3 | 0.2 |
| Soft | 0.2 | 3.2 | Soft | 0.0 | 2.2 |

Again, the data from the class sample did not show that soft reprimands reduced disruptive behavior for the whole class. Those data will not be presented here in detail. The mean frequency of disruptive behavior for the class sample throughout the experiment was .62.

*Discussion.* The failure to decrease child R's disruptive behavior by soft reprimands may have been due to his very deficient academic repertoire. He was so far behind his classmates that group instruction was almost meaningless for him. It is also possible that the teacher felt frustrated because of increases in child R's disruptive behavior when she used soft reprimands; teacher D found them particularly difficult to use. She stated, "It was difficult for me to give soft reprimands as I feared they were a sign of weakness. The walking

and whispering necessary to administer soft reprimands to the disruptive child were especially strenuous for me. As the day wore on, I found that my patience became exhausted and my natural tendency to shout like a general took over." Also of particular note was an observer's comment that when verbal reprimands were administered, whether in a loud or soft phase, they were rarely if ever soft in intensity. In summary, teacher D's data showed that soft reprimands did reduce disruptive behavior in one child. Because of lack of evidence for any consistent use of soft reprimands to the second child, nothing can be said conclusively about its use with him.

*Part III*

In a third-grade class of a fourth teacher, two target children and a class sample were observed during a structured academic activity. A baseline of disruptive behavior was obtained in the class with procedures identical to those of Experiment I. In the second phase of the study, the teacher was asked to use soft reprimands, just as the other teachers had done. Because of some unexpected results following this second phase, the general nature of the study was then changed and those results will not be presented here. Both child and teacher observations were made according to the procedures described in Part I of Experiment II.

*Subjects.* Child D was a very intelligent boy (135 IQ) who scored in the seventh-grade range on the reading part of the Metropolitan Achievement Test but he was only slightly above grade level in mathematics. His relations with his peers were very antagonistic.

Child J was occasionally considered disruptive by his teacher. However, he did not perform assigned tasks and would often pretend to be working while he actually was not.

*Reliability.* The reliability of child observations was obtained for the target children on 15 occasions, and the reliability of the class sample was obtained on

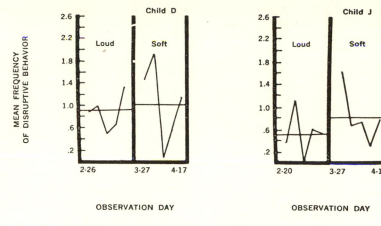

FIGURE 4. Disruptive behavior of children D and J in Class E.

three occasions. The resultant average reliabilities were 88 percent for the observations of the target children and 91 percent for the observations of the class sample.

The reliability of the observations of teacher behavior was checked on two occasions during the base period and once during the soft period. The average reliability of the observations of loud and soft reprimands on these three occasions was 78 percent and 79 percent respectively.

*Results.* Child D's disruptive behavior increased from .9 during the last five days of baseline (loud reprimands) to 1.0 during the last five days of soft reprimands. Child J's disruptive behavior increased from .4 to .8 from baseline to the soft reprimand period (see Figure 4). There was no change in the class sample from baseline to the soft reprimand period. The mean frequency of disruptive behavior for the class sample during the loud and soft phase was .6 and .5 respectively.

As can be seen in Table 3, teacher E's behavior with child D and child J did appear to have been influenced by the experimental instructions.

*Discussion.* The reasons that soft reprimands failed to decrease disruptive behav-

ior in this class are not clear. Several factors may have been important. First of all, teacher E was always very skeptical about the possibility that soft reprimands could influence disruptive behavior whereas the other teachers were willing to acknowledge the probability of their influence. Second, it is possible that the children learned to control the teacher's behavior since a soft reprimand had to be made while the teacher was close to the child. That is, a child might realize that he could draw the teacher to his side each time he misbehaved during the soft reprimand period. In addition, this teacher tolerated more disruptive behavior than the other teachers, and her class was much less structured. Probably most important, she wished to investigate the effectiveness of various types of instructional programs rather than soft reprimands.

### Conclusions

These two experiments demonstrated that when teachers used soft reprimands, they were effective in modifying behavior in seven of nine disruptive children. Because of a failure to document the proper use of soft reprimands by one teacher (D) to one child, it is impossible to assess the effec-

61

tiveness on that child. Of particular significance was the finding that soft reprimands seemed to be associated with an increase in disruptive behavior of one—and possibly two—target children in one teacher's class although the soft reprimands did not influence the level of disruptive behavior for the class as a whole. The results of Experiments I and II lead to the conclusion that with particularly disruptive children a teacher can generally use fewer soft reprimands than loud ones and obtain less disruptive behavior than when loud reprimands are used.

The authors wish to make clear that they do not recommend soft reprimands as an alternative to praise. An ideal combination would probably be frequent praise, some soft reprimands, and very occasional loud reprimands. Furthermore, it is always necessary to realize that classroom management procedures such as praise and types of reprimanding are no substitute for a good academic program. In the class where soft reprimands were ineffective for both target children, a type of individualized instruction was later introduced, and the disruptive behavior of both the target children and the class sample declined.

Because soft reprimands are delivered by a teacher when she is close to a child it is possible that a soft reprimand differs from a loud one in other dimensions than audibility to many children. Although observations of teachers in this study did not reveal that teachers made their soft reprimands in a less harsh, firm, or intense manner than their loud reprimands, it might be possible for a teacher to utilize soft reprimands in such a manner. If the latter were true, soft reprimands might require less teacher effort than loud reprimands. Ultimately soft reprimands might prove more reinforcing for the teacher both because of the relatively small expenditure of effort and the generally positive and sometimes dramatic changes in the children's behavior. The inherent nature of the soft reprimand makes its use impossible at all times, particularly when a teacher has to remain at the blackboard or with a small group in one part of the room. As one teacher mentioned, "I had to do more moving around, but there appeared to be less restlessness in the class."

In sum, it is the authors' opinion that soft reprimands can be a useful method of dealing with disruptive children in a classroom. Combined with praise, soft reprimands might be very helpful in reducing disruptive behavior. In contrast, it appears that loud reprimands lead one into a vicious cycle of more and more reprimands resulting in even more disruptive behavior.

### References

Becker, W. C., Madsen, C. H., Jr., Arnold, C., & Thomas, D. R. The contingent use of teacher attention and praise in reducing classroom behavior problems. *Journal of Special Education*, 1967, 1, 287-307.

Hall, R. V., Lund, D., & Jackson, D. Effects of teacher attention on study behavior. *Journal of Applied Behavior Analysis*, 1968, 1, 1-12.

Madsen, C. H., Becker, W. C. & Thomas, D. R. Rules, praise, and ignoring: Elements of elementary classroom control. *Journal of Applied Behavior Analysis*, 1968, 1, 139-150.

O'Leary, K. D., & Becker, W. C. Behavior modification of an adjustment class: A token reinforcement program. *Exceptional Children*, 1967, 33, 637-642.

O'Leary, K. D., & Becker, W. C. The effects of a teacher's reprimands on children's behavior. *Journal of School Psychology*, 1968, 7, 8-11.

O'Leary, K. D., Becker, W. C., Evans, M. B., & Saudargas, R. A. A token reinforcement program in a public school: A replication and systematic analysis. *Journal of Applied Behavior Analysis*, 1969, 2, 3-13.

Parke, R. D., & Walters, R. H. Some factors influencing the efficacy of punishment training for inducing response inhibition. *Monographs of the Society for Research in Child Development*, 1967, 32, (1, Serial No. 109).

Solomon, R. L. Punishment. *American Psychologist*, 1964, 19, 239-253.

Walker, H. M., & Buckley, N. K. The use of positive reinforcement in conditioning attending behavior. *Journal of Applied Behavior Analysis*, 1968, 1, 245-250.

MONTROSE M. WOLF
EDWARD L. HANLEY
LOUISE A. KING
JOSEPH LACHOWICZ
DAVID K. GILES

# The Timer-Game: A Variable Interval Contingency for the Management of Out-of-Seat Behavior

ALTHOUGH the ability to maintain an orderly classroom does not necessarily result in the achievement of academic goals, orderliness is often considered to be a prerequisite for effective teaching. Thus,

MONTROSE M. WOLF *is Associate Professor of Human Development and Research Associate, Department of Human Development and Bureau of Child Research, University of Kansas, Lawrence;* EDWARD L. HANLEY *is Assistant Professor of Education, University of Vermont, Burlington;* LOUISE A. KING *is Teacher, Wichita Public Schools, Wichita, Kansas;* JOSEPH LACHOWITZ *is Director of Research and* DAVID K. GILES *is Director, Southwest Indian Youth Center, Tucson, Arizona. The research reported herein was performed in part pursuant to Grant No. HD03144, National Institute of Child Health and Human Development.*

it is not surprising that the management classroom behavior has become a focus of applied behavioral research (Wolf, Giles, & Hall, 1968; Barrish, Saunders, & Wolf, 1969; Madsen, Becker, & Thomas, 1968; Hall, Lund, & Jackson, 1968; Thomas, Becker, & Armstrong, 1968; O'Leary, Becker, Evans, & Saudargas, 1969; Osborne, 1969).

Wolf, Giles, and Hall (1968) described an experimental remedial classroom for low achieving sixth-grade children in which academic behavior was supported by a token reinforcement system. One classroom problem was a moderately high rate of out-of-seat behavior, a common problem characterized by apparently aimless wandering, extended stays in the lavatory, prolonged pencil sharpening, and more visiting than is considered desirable. A technique was introduced for managing the out-of-seat behavior. It involved the occa-

EXCEPTIONAL CHILDREN, 1970, Vol. 37, No. 2, pp. 113-118.

sional ringing of a kitchen timer that was set by the teacher to ring after intervals of varying durations, averaging about 20 minutes. Every student who was in his seat when the timer rang avoided the loss of tokens. While it seemed that the timer game was effective in reducing out of seat behavior, no objective data was presented. The present study describes an empirical evaluation of the effects of the timer game.

## Experiment I

### Method

*Subjects and setting.* A group of 16 low-achieving children from a low-income, urban elementary school attended a remedial class every day after school. Fourteen of the children were fourth-graders and two were third-graders. The children met each afternoon for 3 hours. They were instructed to complete homework and remedial assignments. Tokens (points), which were given for correct answers, were supported by backup reinforcers such as snacks, candy, clothes, and field trips. The physical setting, token reinforcement contingencies, remedial education program, and materials have been described in detail elsewhere (Wolf et al., 1968).

*Response definition.* The out-of-seat behavior of the students was recorded by an observer. The one-hour session was divided into 30-second intervals. During each 30-second interval the observer would look at each student in a predetermined order and count the number who met the criterion for being out of their seats. The response definition required that "the seat portion of the child's body not be in contact with any part of the seat of the child's chair."

The out-of-seat behavior was independently measured by a second observer during two sessions. The number of instances of agreement about the presence or absence of the response in each 30-second interval for each student was calculated. The two sessions yielded agreements of 93 and 94 percent between the two observers.

*Experimental conditions.* There were three conditions. Baseline rate of the out-of seat behavior was first obtained for each child for seven sessions. The timer-game was then introduced. On the average of once every 20 minutes the timer rang. (The range of intervals between rings was zero to 40 minutes.) Every student who was in his seat when the timer rang earned 5 points. Five points was a very small proportion of the average student's accumulation of approximately 400 points per day. The timer-game was continued for six sessions. The baseline condition was then reinstated for seven sessions.

### Results

As Figure 1 shows, the timer-game was effective in reducing the out-of-seat behavior. Each dot corresponds to the number of intervals a particular student was out of his seat. The heavy line indicates the average amount of out-of-seat behavior for the entire class each day under each condition. On the average, 17 intervals containing out-of-seat behavior per child were recorded per session during baseline. The introduction of the timer game reduced the average to about 2 intervals per child. A return to the baseline condition resulted in an increase in the number of the out-of-seat responses to an average of 17 intervals per child.

## Experiment II

### Method

*Subject and setting.* One of the students (Sue) in Experiment I whose behavior was not greatly modified by the timer-game was the subject of this study. The classroom procedures and token reinforcement system were the same as in Experiment I. Out-of-seat behavior was recorded by an observer for 1½ hours each day using the same response definition as in Experiment I.

*Individual points condition.* Sue's out-of-seat behavior was observed under the baseline condition and two slightly different

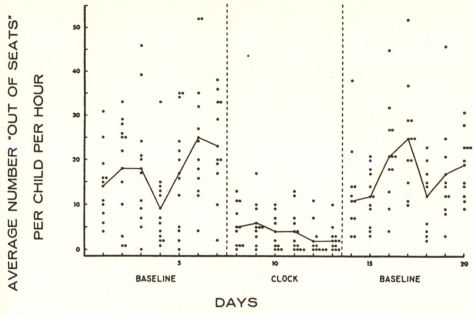

FIGURE 1. Experiment I. The heavy line represents the average number of 30-second intervals containing out-of-seat responses during a daily one-hour observation period. The individual dots represent the number of intervals containing out-of-seat responses for each of the children.

contingency conditions involving the timer-game. Under the first contingency condition Sue was told that she would have an opportunity to earn extra points by playing the timer-game. A 9 x 3 inch piece of construction paper was attached to the wall. The numbers 10, 20, 30, 40, and 50 were drawn on the paper with a marking pen. Sue was told that she would be given 50 points at the beginning of each session but that she would lose 10 of these points each time she was out of her seat when the timer rang. In such instances, the teacher would cross off the highest number on the paper, indicating the number of Sue's points that remained. The timer was set to ring after varying intervals but on an average of every 10 minutes.

*Peer points condition.* In the second contingency condition Sue and the other students were told that the rules of the game would be changed slightly so that more children could play. The new rule was that Sue would still be able to earn points for herself, but that she would also earn points for the four students who sat closest to her. At the end of the session the points remaining from the original 50 would be divided equally among Sue and her four peers. For example, if 40 points remained, Sue and the others would earn 8 points each.

*Results*

Figure 2 shows that the individual points condition resulted in an immediate decrease in the amount of out-of-seat behavior that occurred during the no points condition. However, the peer points condition resulted in even greater suppression although Sue earned only one-fifth as many points as she did under the individual points condition.

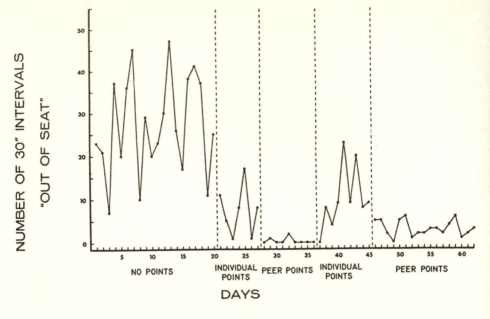

FIGURE 2. Experiment II. The number of intervals containing out-of-seat responses made by Sue throughout several experimental conditions.

*Discussion*

The timer-game was an effective technique for decreasing the out-of-seat behavior of the students in the remedial classroom. It was also practical since it did not require continuous monitoring by the teacher. The teacher needed to observe only the out-of-seat behavior that occurred when the timer rang. The purpose of the variable interval contingency rather than a fixed interval contingency was to reduce the likelihood that the students would discriminate the time when the bell was about to ring. The bell was just as likely to ring after having just rung as to ring only after a very long interval.

The peer points condition resulted in more control over Sue's out-of-seat behavior than the individual points condition. Exactly what the peers contributed to the effect must await further analysis. Our impression was that they provided a number of consequences and other functions for

Sue. For example, if she stood up, she was immediately reminded to sit down. If she broke her pencil, which she often did, one of the four peers would volunteer to sharpen it for her. If she went to the lavatory, she was reminded to hurry. However, the extent of their attending behavior was not determined.

The results of the peer points condition correspond to the results of a peer contingency in a classroom setting described by Patterson (1965) where he modified the hyperactive behavior of a second-grade child. Patterson arranged for the child to earn M & M's at the rate of one every 10 seconds when he was attending appropriately. The M & M's were then shared with all the members of the class. Patterson reports that while it was difficult to evaluate the roles of both the M & M's and the peers, his opinion was that the peers had some influence in reducing the hyperactive behavior. Since in Experiment II of this study the role of points for the indi-

66

vidual student was analyzed independently of the effects of points for the peers, it was clear that the peers did make a contribution beyond the points themselves. The question of how the peers made their contribution remains for further analysis. Other researchers (Graubard, 1969; Sloane, 1969) have reported success in adapting the timer-game to a variety of classroom situations.

It is likely that Sue's reaction to the peer condition may not be common to all students. There may very well be students for whom the peer attention generated by the peer points condition would serve to strengthen the out-of-seat behavior rather than reduce it. But the experimental conditions imposed here seemed to insure at least some degree of success in modifying out-of-seat behavior with the timer-game.

### References

Barrish, H. H., Saunders, M., & Wolf, M. M. Good behavior game: Effects of individual contingencies for group consequences on disruptive behavior in a classroom. *Journal of Applied Behavior Analysis*, 1969, 2, 119-124.

Graubard, P. Yeshiva University, New York City. Personal communication, 1969.

Hall, V. R., Lund, D., & Jackson, D. Effects of teacher attention on study behavior. *Journal of Applied Behavior Analysis*, 1968, 1, 1-12.

Madsen, C. H., Becker, W. C., & Thomas, D. R. Rules, praise, and ignoring: Elements of elementary classroom control. *Journal of Applied Behavior Analysis*, 1968, 1, 139-150.

O'Leary, K. D., Becker, W. C., Evans, M. B., & Saudargas, R. A. A token reinforcement program in a public school: A replication and systematic analysis. *Journal of Applied Behavior Analysis*, 1969, 2, 3-14.

Osborne, J. G. Free-time as a reinforcer in the management of classroom behavior. *Journal of Applied Behavior Analysis*, 1969, 2, 113-118.

Patterson, G. R., An application of conditioning techniques to the control of a hyperactive child. In L. P. Ullmann and L. Krasner (Eds.), *Case Studies in Behavior Modification.* New York: Holt, Rinehart & Winston, 1965. Pp. 370-375.

Sloane, H. University of Utah, Salt Lake City. Personal communication, 1969.

Thomas, D. R., Becker, W. C., & Armstrong, M. Production and elimination of disruptive classroom behavior by systematically varying teacher's behavior. *Journal of Applied Behavior Analysis*, 1968, 1, 35-45.

Wolf, M. M., Giles, D., & Hall, R. V. Experiments with token reinforcement in a remedial classroom. *Behavior Research and Therapy*, 1968, 6, 51-64.

# BEHAVIOR MODIFICATION AND THE BRAT SYNDROME [1]

MARTHA E. BERNAL, JOHN S. DURYEE,[2] HAROLD L. PRUETT,[3] AND

BEVERLEE J. BURNS [4]

*Neuropsychiatric Institute, UCLA Center for Health Sciences*

The purpose of this paper is to describe a behavior modification program designed for one "brat." A brat will be defined as a child who often engages in tantrums, assaultiveness, threats, etc., which are highly aversive and serve to render others helpless in controlling him. Collectively, such behaviors will be called "the brat syndrome" for purposes of convenience. Surveys of the relative frequency of presenting complaints at child guidance clinics indicate that brats, as defined above, are among the most frequent consumers of mental health services for children (Anderson & Dean, 1956; Wolff, 1961).

Within recent years, a number of papers (Boardman, 1962; Hawkins, Peterson, Schweid, & Bijou, 1966; Russo, 1964; Williams, 1959) have described the use of learning principles in the treatment of children who qualify as brats. These papers have emphasized the reprogramming of the child's

social environment by providing advice or training to the parent regarding techniques for reducing the child's aversive behaviors and strengthening more acceptable ones. Underlying the emphasis on training parents as therapists is the assumption that brat behaviors are learned, and are maintained by the child's parents (Wahler, Winkel, Peterson, & Morrison, 1965).

Two major findings have resulted from previous brat research: (*a*) simple learning principles are extremely useful in modifying this type of behavior, and (*b*) parents of children who are brats are capable of changing their behavior in such a way as to take over control functions with their children. These are encouraging findings that should have broad applicability in mental health settings. However, the success of any program for modification of brat behaviors ultimately depends upon the knowledge and sophistication of the professional who designs or engineers the program. There are large variations among brats and their interpersonal environments, and these differences require tailoring of programs to the idiosyncratic features of each child-parent combination. The behavioral engineer is confronted with the task of selecting learning principles, reinforcers, parent training techniques, and therapeutic strategies as he deals with each new child. Successful performance of these tasks requires that he learn both from his own experience as well as from the experience of others. The present paper is intended as an additional source of

[1] Portions of this paper were presented at the Society for Research in Child Development Meetings in 1967. Appreciation is expressed to Henry H. Work, Acting Chairman, Department of Psychiatry, UCLA, for his encouragement of this work. The authors are grateful to a number of people who assisted in data reduction and preparation of this manuscript: Janis Kimmelman, Jeffrey Kirschner, Judy Kollar, Merle Mishel, Albert Pinedo, and Sandra Sugent. Barbara A. Henker made valuable suggestions for design of the treatment program and Peter Gruenberg generously provided use of the television studio.

[2] Now at Columbia University.

[3] Now at the University of California at Los Angeles.

[4] Now at the University of Southern California.

JOURNAL OF CONSULTING AND CLINICAL PSYCHOLOGY, 1968, Vol 32, No. 4, pp. 447-455.

information from which the professional may draw ideas and guidelines for designing parent training programs. The program designed for one classical brat was similar to that used by Wahler et al. (1965) and in addition television was used to provide behavioral feedback to the mother.

## SUBJECT AND HISTORY

Jeff, age 8½ years, was referred to an outpatient psychiatric clinic because he had frequent temper tantrums and physically attacked his mother, teachers, and peers. "I have a right to do anything I want to do," as he put it, was his attitude toward life. Parental disciplinary attempts had included spanking and restriction of privileges, to no avail. An only child, he regulated family activities; for example, he dictated when his mother could sit in the living room.

Jeff was enrolled in a private school for emotionally disturbed children. In school, he was highly demanding of the teacher's attention and alternately bullied and tattled on the other children, depending upon their physical size and strength. While socially he was an ogre, academically he achieved at the fourth-grade level, and intellectually his IQ test scores ranged from 106 on the WISC Performance Scale to 143 on the Peabody Picture Vocabulary Test. Psychiatric and psychological diagnostic opinions ranged from adjustment reaction of childhood to schizophrenia.

Jeff had many other presenting problems. He wet his bed almost every night, suffered from skin allergies, and was susceptible to frequent respiratory illnesses including pneumonia, bronchitis, and chronic asthma. He sounded as if he had memorized his lines and was delivering them in a loud, stilted, and exaggerated manner. Frequent non sequiturs and odd phrases punctuated his verbal behavior. For example, he said, "you are distracting my image" in the context of being ignored. Other peculiar actions included a relatively high rate of rocking, drawing television channel symbols, and moving his head back and forth repetitively. His bizarreness, intellectual display of a vast vocabulary and fund of general information, and his incapacity to make or keep friends were probably

sufficient reasons for the neighborhood children's shunning him. He had neither playmates at home nor allies among his schoolmates.

Jeff was a sickly child from the time he had his first asthma attack at 16 months of age. Various respiratory illnesses followed in step with recurring asthmatic episodes, and the parents began to give in to his demands for fear of precipitating or aggravating his illnesses. When he was 3 years old they enrolled him in a nursery school where he engaged in frequent rocking and temper outbursts and was a social isolate. Advice from the nursery school teacher relating to management of Jeff's biting and hitting his mother consisted of substituting a rubber or plastic object for him to bite or a hitting bag so as to help him vent his anger. When he reached the age of 6 years, he was placed in a small private class but was withdrawn within 5 months because the faculty were not equipped to help him. Consultation with a school psychiatrist resulted in the public school system's refusal to admit him into a regular classroom. At age 7 years he was enrolled in the private school where he was attending at the time of the referral. In the school, individual psychotherapy was provided by a psychologist for about 3 months; the parents reported no improvement.

Questions regarding brain dysfunction as an explanation of Jeff's behavior disorder had been raised because he had suffered three grand mal convulsions associated with high temperatures at ages 4, 5, and 7 years. However, an electroencephalographic recording done just 3 months prior to the beginning of the present study was within normal limits, and neither neurologist nor psychologist reported evidence of major organic dysfunction.

From the time Jeff was a baby the parents had increasing marital difficulties and each had been in intensive psychotherapy for 3 years. At the time of referral, the father was living away from home except for weekends when he slept on the living room couch in the mother's apartment. Since the strain between the parents was very evident, the first step taken prior to any therapeutic commitment was to ask the parents to tell Jeff that they were separated and to request that the father live totally separate from Jeff and his mother, maintaining visits with Jeff without the mother's presence. This request was carried out 2 months prior to the first intervention.

## PART 1: JEFF AND MOTHER

The study was divided into two parts. Part 1 includes Weeks 0–13, constituting a period of time during which only Jeff and his mother were seen, and Part 2 includes Weeks 14–25, when another neighborhood child, Albert, was included in the treatment program with Jeff and his mother. Reasons for inclusion of Albert are given at the end of Part 1.

### Procedure

*Initial interview.* An initial interview was held with the parents to obtain specification of the presenting complaints. The parents agreed to permit audiotaped observations in the home and videotaped observations at the clinic. They were asked to tell Jeff that these recordings would be made in order that he and his parents might learn how to get along with each other. The mother was requested to begin keeping daily notes of conflicts with Jeff: what happened, what the child and mother did and said, and how the conflict ended. Since the father was about to move to another city temporarily, only the mother was included in treatment.

*Treatment plan.* During observation, it was noted that the mother had a high rate of indiscriminate response; she attended and verbally responded to him constantly in a meek, soft monotone, even when correcting him. Much of her behavior seemed to be in the class of escape and avoidance reactions, that is, she tried to pacify Jeff at all costs. For instance, if she refused to give him a snack, he would respond, "If you don't I'll scream," or "I'll hit you," or "I'll have an asthma attack," whereupon the mother would give in. If she did not, the boy would carry out his threat. Jeff's control of his mother was so complete that she generally exerted no control functions. No expressions of warm emotional response between Jeff and his mother were noted in any of these pretreatment observations. When asked how she felt about Jeff, the mother stated that she did not like him, and was terrified of him.

The first step in training was to teach the mother to reduce her verbal output and to selectively ignore all of Jeff's abusive behaviors, from sulking to direct physical assault. This plan was intended to help her make decisions about her own behavior as she and Jeff interacted, and to extinguish his abuse.

Step 2 was to establish certain maternal behaviors as conditioned negative reinforcers by associating them with physical punishment. The behaviors or cues consisted of ignoring abuse and if ignoring did not stop it, the mother was to express anger and order him to stop. Finally, if he did not stop, she was to spank him. Hopefully, these cues, ignoring, frowning, angry tone of voice, the word "don't" etc., if clearly presented and consistently paired with punishment when the boy did not obey, would take on properties of conditioned negative reinforcers. The conditioned negative reinforcers would assume control functions when produced contingent upon the child's "bad" behavior or when removed contingent upon "good" behavior.

Several important considerations were involved in the design of instructions to the mother. She reported that, in moments of extreme frustration, she had severely spanked him. These spankings, however, were not consistently associated with cues which might serve as discriminative stimuli for the boy, as an aid in determining when his behavior would earn punishment. It was hoped that by instructing the mother on the use of punishment such severe spankings would be avoided. A second consideration was that the mother had seldom carried out her threats of punishment. The training would have to stress the reduction of threats so that when the mother said she was going to punish, punishment would follow. Unless such consistency was maintained by the mother, it seemed likely that the angry cues would fail to acquire stimulus functions.

The third step was to have the mother identify acceptable behaviors as they occurred, positively reinforce them by responding warmly and praising him, and specify to Jeff which of his behaviors were acceptable. When during positive reinforcement training, the mother responded both to his acceptable behavior and to his peculiar or "silly" talk, it became necessary to try to help her discriminate these two behavior classes, so that she would not maintain the peculiar verbalizations.

*Treatment.* The treatment steps were divided into five lessons, called interventions; the series of interventions was defined as treatment. Treatment of Jeff's other deviant behaviors was postponed pending establishment of maternal control.

The first videotaped session, made before any interventions occurred, was called Pretreatment. During filming of the Pretreatment and all subsequent sessions, Jeff and his mother interacted freely, and Jeff sometimes had a game to play. The mother was given specific instructions during intervention sessions. One uninstructed Posttreatment videotaped session was held approximately 11 weeks after Pretreatment.

The format of the interventions was as follows: The mother and one of the experimenters met without Jeff for 30 minutes and instructions were reviewed with her. Excerpts from the most recent videotape were played to demonstrate points at which the new operants were to be used and to identify discrepancies between her performance and any previous instructions. She and Jeff were then videotaped for approximately 15 minutes and a brief tone was played over the intercom system to cue her reinforcement of Jeff's abusive behaviors. Following the interaction, the mother was warmly praised for adequate performance. The mother's questions regarding problems arising at home were

TABLE 1

TSS OF MOTHER'S PERFORMANCE OF INSTRUCTIONS

| Session and instruction | Jeff abuses | Mother ignores abuse | Percentage abuse ignored | Percentage of session mother ignores | Number commands Jeff obeys | Percentage of session mother affectionate |
|---|---|---|---|---|---|---|
| Pretreatment | | | | | | |
| No instruction | 9 | 1 | 11 | 3 | 0 of 4 | 0 |
| Intervention 1 | | | | | | |
| Ignore abuse | 13 | 13 | 100 | 73 | — | 0 |
| Intervention 2 | | | | | | |
| Spank if he hits you | 13 | 11 | 85 | 72 | — | 0 |
| Intervention 3 | | | | | | |
| Differentiate positive and negative response | 13 | 13 | 100 | 43 | 1 of 2 | 7 |
| Posttreatment | | | | | | |
| No instruction | 2 | 2 | 100 | 7 | 2 of 2 | 20 |

always answered by indicating that she would receive assistance only with problems occurring under observation at the clinic.

## Results

*Videotaped interaction data.* The primary method of data reduction for the interaction sessions was the time sampling technique (Arrington, 1939; Koch, 1948). Behavior categories of interest were delineated and each interaction session was divided into 30-second samples. Each first occurrence of the specified behaviors within each sample was given a time sampling score (*TSS*) of 1; additional occurrences within a sample were unscored. Thus, a maximum *TSS* of 30, representing 15 minutes of interaction time, was possible for any single session.

The scored categories were: (*a*) Jeff abuses (Jeff refuses to obey requests or commands, uses foul language, threatens, screams, bites, hits, throws objects, kicks, makes loud noises), (*b*) Jeff obeys, (*c*) mother ignores Jeff's abuse (mother does not visually attend or speak contingent upon Jeff's abuse), (*d*) mother ignores Jeff regardless of his behavior, (*e*) mother commands or requests, (*f*) mother is affectionate (mother smiles, praises, encourages, or caresses Jeff), (*g*) mother spanks Jeff.

Initially, two observers trained in scoring by going through the Pretreatment and Intervention 1 tapes three times and stopping every 30 seconds to discuss the scoring of the behavioral events; they made no scores at this time. Then they independently scored the two tapes and all other tapes except Intervention 5, viewing them once for scoring of Jeff's behaviors and again for scoring of the mother's behaviors. Proportion of agreement between observers was determined by dividing the number of agreements (both occurrence and nonoccurrence of behavior) by 30. Agreement on Jeff's behaviors ranged from .86 to 1.00 with a mean of .94. Agreement for the mother's behaviors ranged from .80 to 1.00 with a mean of .95. *TSS* data for all sessions except Interventions 4 and 5 are shown in Table 1. The general nature of instructions to the mother is written under the designated session.

During the Pretreatment session, before the mother received any instructions, she ignored only one scored occurrence or 11% of Jeff's abuse, and Jeff obeyed no commands. When instructed to ignore his abuse during Intervention 1, the mother succeeded in ignoring 100% of the scored occurrences of Jeff's abuse. She gave no commands during either Intervention 1 or 2. The instructions for Intervention 2 were designed to help her control Jeff's physical attacks on her. During this intervention, he bit her hand once and she carried out her instructions. There were no other occurrences of physical attacks during Intervention 2, but she continued to ignore 85% of his abuse. It was noted that during Interventions 1 and 2 she was very successful in ignoring Jeff most of the time, whether he was being abusive or not (73% and 72% for Interventions 1 and 2, respectively). When instructed to react warmly to Jeff's acceptable behavior during Intervention 3, the mother was affectionate for the first time, but her score was only 7% for the session. Her ignoring of Jeff's abuse remained consistent (100%), and there was a drop in ignoring of Jeff during the session (43%). Results for Intervention 4 when she was asked to discriminate Jeff's acceptable verbalization from his "silly" talk will not be presented because they could not be clearly evaluated.

Intervention 5 started off with the mother immediately commanding Jeff to sit in a chair next to her. He refused, and the mother proceeded to practice her instructions. Data for the struggle that followed were obtained by using an event recorder to note covariations among the mother's actions and the time that Jeff spent sitting in the designated chair. In order to maintain chronological continuity, Intervention 5 data shown in Figure 1 will be discussed, then the reader will be referred back to Table 1. In Figure 1, the mother's commands to sit are shown as a cumulative curve, and the hatchmarks indicate when she spanked Jeff. Time throughout the 24.5 minute session is divided into consecutive 30-second intervals along the abcissa. The shaded area corresponds to the number of seconds within each interval that Jeff was seated. Four spankings were administered, and then he sat for most of the rest of the session. When he asked to get up, or actually left the chair, the mother's commands were successful in inducing him to obey. During the session, the mother's verbal and facial expressions were angry, and the boy's appreciation of her anger was expressed in his question, "Are you angry?" which he asked just after the third spanking. While he sat in the chair, he continued to swear, scream, and threaten.

The Posttreatment session followed Intervention 5; the data are shown in the last row of Table 1. The mother successfully ignored both occurrences of Jeff's abuse, but ignored him very seldom during the session (7%) while scoring higher (20%) for affectionate behavior than in previous sessions. Jeff obeyed both commands given him. Following Posttreatment it was judged no further instruction was necessary unless the mother requested it, and treatment was terminated with the understanding that she would call should there be further difficulties.

Five weeks after Intervention 5, the mother called to report that she could not manage Jeff when a normal 9½ year-old neighborhood boy, Albert, was in their home. Albert had entered Jeff's life earlier in treatment, and while there had been reports of Jeff's rudeness

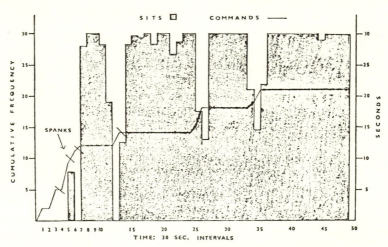

Fig. 1. Intervention 5: Establishment of control.

TABLE 2

| Session | Abuses mother | Abuses Albert | Soft voice | Breaks rules | Plays amicably |
|---|---|---|---|---|---|
| Pretreatment 1 | 26 | 11 | 2 | 7 | 0 |
| Pretreatment 2 | 1 | 2 | 0 | 7 | 7 |
| Posttreatment 1 | 1 | 0 | 27 | 1 | 27 |
| Posttreatment 2 | 0 | 0 | 30 | 0 | 28 |

to Albert, those incidents were relatively mild. Coincident with the telephone call, the mother wrote in her notes that Jeff was extremely antagonistic toward Albert, and wondered if she showed "too much friendship" toward Albert in Jeff's presence. An appointment was set up for the following week.

## PART 2. JEFF, ALBERT, AND MOTHER

### Procedure

In Jeff's presence, the mother asked Albert to join Jeff in his television program so that they might learn how to get along better. Albert probably saw the request as a service he was asked to perform in order to be of help to Jeff.

Jeff, Albert, and the mother were first videotaped on two consecutive weeks; the boys played a game and the mother was asked to proceed as if they were at home. Following the two videotapings, the tapes were studied in order to determine how to help the mother control Jeff as well as facilitate amicable play with Albert. Three major events seemed outstanding in the interactions: The mother was not carrying out her instructions, that is, she failed to ignore his abuse and her angry cues were not delivered with conviction, and she asked Albert to deal with Jeff rather than intervening herself, for example, she urged Albert to hit Jeff back when Jeff hit him. In addition, when Jeff continued his tantrumous behavior, the mother turned to Albert and invited him to talk and interact with her. The mother was then seen for two 1½ hour sessions; these were called Interventions 6 and 7.

*Intervention 6.* A lecture on basic operant principles was given the mother, with examples drawn from incidents between Jeff and herself. Instructions previously given the mother were properly labeled and reviewed.

*Intervention 7.* The two videotapes were reviewed, and the mother was encouraged to stop the tape and praised whenever she could formulate reasonable alternatives to her behavior. Direct intervention with Jeff was emphasized and attention was focused on the effects of her favoritism toward Albert.

On the following 2 weeks, the boys and the mother were again videotaped. She was asked to use the information imparted during Interventions 6 and 7. At no time during the four interaction sessions involving Albert was the mother cued by the tone.

### Results

*Videotaped interaction data.* Data for the four sessions were reduced as in Part 1. The first of the four videotapes was first viewed twice by the observers and discussed in order to arrive at a consensus on the definition of the new behavior categories. Interobserver agreement ranged from 82% to 100% with means of 92%, 94%, 95%, and 99% for Sessions 1–4, respectively.

The following categories were scored: (*a*) Jeff abuses mother or Albert (defined as in Part 1), (*b*) Jeff speaks in a soft voice (Jeff's speech is clearly characterized as "nice," and tone of voice is at normal conversational level), (*c*) Jeff breaks rules (Jeff refuses to play by the rules of the game or the conditions specified by Albert or mother), (*d*) amicable play (Jeff and Albert play a game in a friendly manner, with no incident of conflict between the two).

Time sampling data are displayed in Table 2; the two interactions before Interventions 6 and 7 are designated Pretreatments 1 and 2, and Posttreatment sessions 1 and 2 occurred following instruction of the mother. Comparison of Pretreatment and Posttreatment sessions shows improvement in all categories.

*Mother's notes and other observations.* The mother's notes of conflicts between herself and Jeff at home were divided into weeks, beginning on a Wednesday, when interventions were scheduled. Two research assistants who had no knowledge of interventions performed independently scored two event classes: *general abuse*, which included profanity, refusal to obey, sulking, rudeness, demands, whining, and threats, and *physical abuse*, which included hitting, biting, kicking, screaming, tantrums, and throwing things. The mother described incidents occurring at different times of the day, and within each incident the exact number of occurrences of abuse could not be determined, therefore, only first occurrences of behavior for each incident were scored. Thus, the frequency scores are underestimations of abusive occurrences. Pearson product-moment correlations between scorers were .97 for general abuse and .98 for physical abuse. The frequencies for the two event classes per week were divided by the number of days during which the boy was with his mother (he spent some weekdays and weekends with his father) to obtain rate of daily occurrences per week. Figure 2 displays the rates of abuse over a period of 25 weeks. Interventions are noted under the abscissa. The figure shows that a sharp reduction in general abuse occurred beginning with the first intervention, and that at no time during subsequent weeks was the rate of general abuse comparable to the pretreatment weeks.

During Week 3, when the mother was instructed to begin ignoring the boy's abuse, an increase in physical abuse occurred. On Week 4, following Intervention 2 wherein the mother was instructed in control of the boy's physical attacks, a drop in this form of abuse occurred, and its rate in subsequent weeks was below the mean level of the first 3 weeks, reaching a zero level by the last 5 weeks.

Validation of problems with Jeff and Albert can be seen during Week 14 where the general abuse rate shows a sharp rise. Finally, Jeff was generally abusive only eight times during the last 5 weeks of the project; such an approximate rate might be considered comparable to that of the average child who from time to time becomes difficult, but is not unmanageable.

The mother's notes suggested that much of her control was acquired through establishment of cues denoting anger as conditioned negative reinforcers. In support of this conclusion is the tally of the number of spankings administered by the mother; she spanked him four times at the clinic during Intervention 5, and then reported only nine more spankings. The effectiveness of her anger was apparent by Week 10, when she reported:

I had occasion to speak harshly to Jeff, and now he asks "How do you feel?" If I say angry he is given an explanation if he asks why, but he knows. Together with ignoring him, showing him I'm really angry by voice is working quite well. He mumbles under his breath and occasionally there is a bad word, but he responds within a reasonable time. No swats necessary.

Improvement in the relationship was gradual; there was much "testing" of the mother's authority during and after treatment.

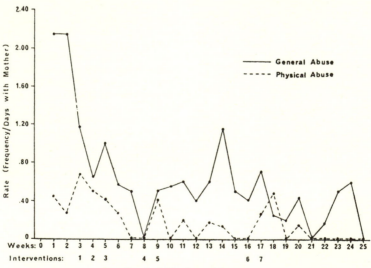

Fig. 2. Jeff's abuse at home.

Confronted with his tyrannical behavior, she had to practice her instructions as best she could, varying them to meet the situation. The following note from Week 14 demonstrates a typical exchange:

> On the freeway, I started to sing to myself. Jeff told me to stop, as he always has, and to turn off the radio. I realized I was being ordered by my child, so I told him, loudly, firmly, and without misunderstanding that I would sing anytime I felt like it. Instant tantrum. I ignored him and continued humming. He begged me to stop, and finally asked, "Why can't you stop when I tell you?" I said because I was the boss and if I felt like doing something, I would. No argument, he calmed down and asked for donuts at the drivein. I stopped and we got a different order from the last time. He questioned the selection, but didn't argue or pout. "Okay, mother, whatever you feel like," he said. I very nearly choked.

Her success in controlling him in spite of his tantrums and pleas, his positive response to her firmness, and praise from relatives and friends probably served to strengthen her new reactions to him. Each test with which Jeff confronted her could be regarded as a learning trial for both of them.

Change in the mother was very apparent and could best be typified as an increase in assertiveness and self-esteem in her relations with others and confidence in her role as mother. Her increased assertiveness may well have been initiated by the impact of watching herself on television with Jeff for the first time; her terse comment, "What a dishrag!" expressed its impact upon her.

Freed of her terror of the boy, she gradually grew to like him, and he in turn began to express affection. During Week 18 the following occurred after Jeff had gone to bed:

> He asked to talk to me. He asked if he could take piano lessons. I told him he had a bigger project first—learning to get along with others, including children—and in a few years perhaps he could take lessons. As I went out the door he said, "I love you." I replied the same and told him how pleased I was with him. After the door was closed I heard him say to himself, "She's swell! I feel great!"

In contrast to the positive changes in Jeff and his mother, there was no evident reduction of the other presenting complaints except for the enuresis problem. Just after Intervention 2, he stopped wetting himself, and only one further wetting incident occurred 15 weeks later. So far as could be determined without the aid of records, the other presenting complaints did not intensify.

## DISCUSSION

The treatment program designed for Jeff was successful in establishing maternal control over a period of 25 weeks. The design of the study did not provide for evaluation of the generalization of treatment effects to persons other than the mother.

A number of factors probably contributed to the effectiveness of the program. As Hawkins et al. (1966) have noted, a cooperative parent is critical for successful training. Jeff's mother's cooperation was evident in willingness to follow instructions, the voluminous notes she wrote, and a record of no appointments missed. Lang (1966) pointed up the desirability of providing some record of progress, or feedback, during training of social agents as reinforcers. Such feedback to Jeff's mother was provided by television replay, the tone cue, and friends and relatives. Two patient variables were probably important. Jeff was an only child, and lived alone with his mother. There was no one in the home regularly to interfere with her new role as the major disciplinary agent in his life. Additionally, Jeff's rate of problem behavior upon which the treatment focused was high both in the television studio and at home. Its high rate permitted a large number of occasions for modification. It is conceivable that some brats would behave very well in the clinic or television studio while being intolerable at home. In such a case, techniques such as those developed by Hawkins et al. (1966) for training the parent at home may be more useful than those described here. Finally, television provided a record of interactions that was immediately replayable. The recordings permitted very careful assessment of ongoing events and consequently facilitated tailoring of the program to the uniqueness of the relationship as it was originally and as it changed during treatment.

One unique feature of parent training programs deserves comment. It seems unnecessary to blame a mother for her childrearing mistakes without the offer of some alternative as to what she can do that is helpful. Training the parent to respond in new ways to her child emphasizes the parent's successes and minimizes dwelling upon previous mistakes or the parent's psychodynamic structure as explanations for problem behaviors. In the design of the present program, it was considered most useful and humane to phrase the instructions in terms of what she could do to help her child and to strongly emphasize correct performance. This plan was particularly pertinent during the initial stages of training, when she was struggling to deal with a child who terrified her. Later on, when she had difficulty in handling Jeff in Albert's presence, it was judged that she had experienced enough success to permit more extensive discussion of her errors, as, for example, when she was asking Albert to discipline Jeff. On occasion, she expressed her regrets regarding the manner in which she had raised Jeff. Typically, these comments received the response that what had happened before was in the past and that now she was dealing with him in a constructive manner.

## REFERENCES

ANDERSON, F. N., & DEAN, H. C. Some aspects of child guidance clinic intake policy and practices. *Public Health Monograph,* 1956, 42, 1–16.

ARRINGTON, R. E. Time-sampling studies of child behavior. *Psychological Monographs,* 1939, 51(2, Whole No. 228).

BOARDMAN, W. K. Rusty: A brief behavior disorder. *Journal of Consulting Psychology,* 1962, 26, 293–297.

HAWKINS, R. P., PETERSON, R. F., SCHWEID, E., & BIJOU, S. W. Behavior therapy in the home: Amelioration of problem parent-child relations with the parent in a therapeutic role. *Journal of Experimental Child Psychology,* 1966, 4, 99–107.

KOCH, H. M. Methods of studying the behavior and development of young children. In T. G. Andrews (Ed.), *Methods of psychology.* New York: Wiley, 1948.

LANG, P. F. The transfer of treatment. *Journal of Consulting Psychology,* 1966, 30, 375–378.

RUSSO, S. Adaptations in behavioural therapy with children. *Behaviour Research and Therapy,* 1964, 2, 43–47.

WAHLER, G., WINKEL, G. H., PETERSON, R. F., & MORRISON, D. C. Mothers as behavior therapists for their own children. *Behaviour Research and Therapy,* 1965, 3, 113–124.

WILLIAMS, C. D. The elimination of tantrum behavior by extinction procedures: Case report. *Journal of Abnormal and Social Psychology,* 1959, 59, 269.

WOLFF, S. Symptomatology and outcome of preschool children with behavior disorders attending a child guidance clinic. *Journal of Child Psychology and Psychiatry,* 1961, 2, 269–276.

# POSITIVE REINFORCERS FOR EXPERIMENTAL STUDIES WITH CHILDREN—CONSUMABLES AND MANIPULATABLES

Sidney W. Bijou* *and* Persis T. Sturges[1]

*University of Washington*

This paper is an analysis of the kinds and the ways that positive reinforcers may be used in experimental studies with children. For the purpose of this presentation they have been classified as follows: (a) consumables, (b) manipulatables, (c) visual and auditory stimuli, (d) social stimuli, and (e) tokens. The first two categories will be considered here; the other three, in a paper to follow.

The material is from three sources: (a) papers published before 1947 dealing specifically with motivation in children; (b) experiments, technical notes, and theoretical analyses published between 1947 and the present; and (c) studies conducted at the University of Washington since 1954.[2] In regard to the second category, no attempt was made to summarize all experiments using positive reinforcers. Instead, studies were selected which illustrate typical practices.

The present discussion is limited to the relationship between positive reinforcers and instrumental or operant behavior. Let us spell out what we mean by the two key terms. By *positive reinforcers* we refer to those classes of stimuli which upon presentation strengthen the behavior that they follow. It cannot be said that stimuli referred to as "rewards," "incentives," or "goal objects" in studies with children are necessarily positive reinforcers. They may be for some subjects, not for others. The only way to find out is by submitting each to an experimental test: observe the behavior prior to the introduction of the stimulus and note the changes in behavior after presentation contingent upon a response. If the frequency of response is increased, then the stimulus is a reinforcer for that organism in that situation (18, 34, 36). By *operant behavior* we refer to those classes of responses that have effects upon the surrounding environment (34) and "for which eliciting stimuli have not necessarily been determined" (36, p. 22). We are therefore concerned with studies dealing with acquisition of sensorimotor skills, learning discriminations, formulating concepts, learning ab-

---
* Institute of Child Development, University of Washington, Seattle.

[1] Some of this material was presented at the 1957 meeting of the W. P. A. at Eugene, Oregon, by the junior author.

[2] Research reported here was supported by the National Science Foundation (G-2141)

CHILD DEVELOPMENT, 1959, Vol. 30, pp. 151-170.

stractions, solving problems, or responding to schedules of reinforcement. All or most of these problems have been treated in the laboratory with some variation of multiple-choice and free operant techniques.

In discussing consumables and manipulatables, attention is given to some of the conditions influencing their effectiveness. These include the age of the child and such situational factors as the kind of experimental task, the instructions about the nature of the task and about disposition of the reinforcers, the method of presenting the reinforcers, and the behavior of the adult in the experimental room. Of course, historical conditions also play a part. To take them into account, however, would be to go beyond the limited objective of this analysis.

<h2 style="text-align:center">CONSUMABLES</h2>

Procedures in which consumables, edibles and drinkables, are contingent upon an instrumental act are discussed here. Those in which the consumables are delivered after completion of a series of responses linked with tangible conditioned reinforcers will be treated in a discussion of tokens in a paper to follow.

### Edibles

Edibles, of various kinds, frequently have been used as positive reinforcers in both multiple-choice and free operant experimental studies with children. These procedures will be discussed in the following order: (a) experimental studies with preschool children, (b) those with older children, and (c) those with deviant children.

*Preschool children.* Multiple-choice experiments are particularly suited for the use of edible reinforcers and may either give the child freedom to do as he pleases with the edibles or instruct him to save them until the experiment is over. A study by Hunter on transposition behavior (16) is an example of a multiple-choice procedure with preschool children in which $S^3$ may either eat or save what is received. The question at issue was whether behavior on a transfer task is determined by the absolute sizes or the relative differences in size of pairs of circles. Three experiments were performed with two distinctively different procedures. In the first and second, with raisins as reinforcers and Ss from 4-11 to 5-3 and 5-0 to 5-11 respectively, E described the task as a game and explained the rules:

> Each time, you have to look at both cards and see which is right for, if you pull out the drawer—look, there's a drawer here and another there— beneath the right card, you get a raisin. You like raisins? If you get a raisin you can keep it or eat it or do what you like with it. If you pull out the drawer under the wrong card, there will be no raisin there and you won't get any. Now let's pull out the drawer under this card. (Pull out drawer

---

3 In describing procedures the subject will be designated as S and age of subject will be expressed by two figures indicating years and months. Thus, the age of a 3½-year-old child will be noted as 3-6. The experimenter will be referred to as E.

beneath wrong card.) There's nothing there so that must be the wrong card. Now let's pull out the drawer under this card. (Pull out drawer beneath right card.) Oh, look, there's the raisin. Take it (16, pp. 117-118).

The first time the "right" drawer was opened $S$ took the raisin. The first time the "wrong" drawer was opened the experimenter, who was seated at the opposite end of the table, "held the other drawer from behind so that the subject could not open it, and informed the subject that he must open the 'right' drawer the first time, otherwise he could not get the raisin," (16, p. 117). From then on $E$ arranged the cards for the trials, "baited" the drawers, kept records, and held fast to the "right" drawer on errors to prevent spontaneous corrections.

In the third experiment, materials and instructions were tailored for $Ss$ between ages 1-2 and 2-8. $E$ sat on a low stool on the opposite side of a table from $S$ with a stack of blocks and a sack of currants on the floor by his side to be used as reinforcers. At the beginning of each trial a currant was placed under a block of appropriate size and pushed within reach of $S$. Correction was sometimes allowed and sometimes not, at the experimenter's discretion, "since a rigid scheme was not found optimal for learning" (p. 124). Furthermore, since some of the blocks were difficult for the $Ss$ to manipulate, $E$ now and then gave a little unobtrusive aid.

These procedures include a considerable amount of "flexible" adult-child interaction. Perhaps in working with 1- and 2-year-olds, a certain amount of guidance is necessary to help the child "in the situation"; however, it is difficult to evaluate the relative influence of the edibles and the social interactions, verbal and otherwise. It would facilitate analysis if variations followed a definite plan that could be unambiguously described (as for example, successive approximations with objective behavioral criteria).

Multiple-choice experiments may be arranged so that $S$ sees and even handles the edible reinforcers, but is instructed to save them until the end of the session. Let us describe two studies with this variation. In the first, by Alberts and Ehrenfreund (1), $Ss$ were required to discriminate white squares on a black background. One pair of squares at a time was presented to $Ss$ from 3-0 to 3-11 and 4-5 to 5-6, from the State College of Washington Laboratory Nursery School. The response was opening compartment doors. Correct choices resulted in finding a gumdrop. $S$ was brought into the room after a "warming-up" procedure with a toy dog, and was given instructions by $E$ who remained behind the apparatus panel where he arranged the problems and recorded responses. "When a trial was successful (i.e., $S$ opened the smaller door), $S$ took the gumdrop and placed it upon the napkin which had been spread on another small chair nearby, while $E$ closed the door and the curtains" (1, p. 33). Since some $Ss$ reacted emotionally to nonreinforcement, positive social stimulation followed an incorrect response. "$S$ was assured of another opportunity to find the candy. . . ."

In the second study, Brackbill and O'Hara (8) were interested in comparing the relative effectiveness of reward and punishment for discrimination learning. An M&M candy was given for a correct response and one was taken away for an error. The stimuli were three boxes differing in color and size. The task, for 43 boys with a mean age of 5-10, was to learn a simple position alternation sequence between the first and second boxes. At the beginning of the session S, who sat opposite E at a small table, was "staked" to a box of M&Ms, after which E said to the Ss in the reward-punishment group:

> Now, I have something very special for you to do, and if you can do it, you can have some more of the candy. I'm going to put one candy at a time under one of these boxes. And every time you pick up the box that has the candy under it, you can keep the candy. But, every time you pick up the WRONG box, you'll have to GIVE BACK one of your candies. (E pointed to S's pile.) Understand? Now! THERE IS A WAY TO FIND THE RIGHT BOX EVERY SINGLE TIME. SEE IF YOU CAN FIND THE WAY (8, p. 3).

The same instructions were read to the Ss of the reward-only group, except that nothing was mentioned about withdrawing an M&M after a wrong response. Following the first correct response, E said to all Ss: "Now every time you get a candy, pick it up and put it down there, and all the candy that you put there will be for you to keep." Following the first incorrect response for the reward-punishment group, E said: "That was the wrong box, so you'll have to give back one of your candies." At the end of the session E put the M&Ms in S's box into a sack and gave it to him.

In this, as well as in the Alberts and Ehrenfreund study, E played an active role in dealing with the reinforcers and S's reactions to various parts of the experiment. Because of such interaction it is difficult to determine the effectiveness of the candy relative to the social reinforcement that may have been involved. There is no objection to the use of social reinforcement. The only question is which set or sets are operating in the experiment. The challenge for future research is to carry out the procedures required under circumstances that are explicit regarding the reinforcements in operation.

The free operant technique is, of course, a natural for edible reinforcers, and in recent years an increasing number of such studies with children have appeared. A terse statement of the salient characteristics of the method is given by Ferster: "The use of the free operant is a method of wide generality; it refers to any apparatus that generates a response which takes a short time to occur and leaves the animal in the same place ready to respond again. The free operant is used in experiments when the main dependent variable is the frequency of occurrence of behavior" (12, p. 263). Three examples with preschool children will be considered here. Each has a bearing on some of the factors influencing the use of edibles as reinforcers. In the first, Warren and Brown (37) used hemispherical pellets of candy made of sugar, corn syrup, and gelatin ("Little Gems"), delivered by a vending-type machine modified for lever pressing. Ss, 2-0 to 5-0 in age, performed alone in the experimental room, decorated and arranged for preschool children. The preliminary part of the procedure was described as follows:

> For each experimental period one of us brings the child individually from his house to the psychological laboratory, enters the playroom with him, and if necessary plays with him for a few minutes. Then the subject is locked in the room with a toy, book, and lever. The toy and book generally occupy the child's interest when he is not at the lever. . . . If for any reason the subject becomes overexcited, the experimenter enters the playroom. If necessary, the experiment is stopped and continued the next day (37, p. 183).

Each S was seen once a day for 22 minutes, and each, serving as his own control, was observed under five conditions (operant conditions, extinction, spontaneous recovery, disinhibition and periodic reconditioning) over 15 experimental days. Strength of drive for "Little Gems" was measured by behavior. Ss who ate all the candy while in the playroom or shortly thereafter were rated as having strong drive; those who ate little or no candy or objected to receiving candy were judged as having weak drive, and those who behaved somewhat in between were classified as having medium drive. One of the findings was that "the strength of the child's appetite for candy reward used in this experiment determines the orderliness of conditioning, extinction, and periodic reconditioning" (37, p. 203).

The second investigation, by Siegel and Foshee (33), was concerned with the relationship between number of reinforcements and rate of extinction. Ss from ages 2-11 to 3-8 were also required to press a bar for cylindrical-shaped party mints, each weighing approximately .2 of a gram. One person stayed with the child throughout, "making for a uniform social environment." He attempted to keep his behavior neutral and constant. Observations, made two to three hours after breakfast, were initiated by inviting S to come and see a new game.

> If he indicated acceptance, he was led to a nearby experimental room and told that he could sit or stand before the apparatus. The E then pointed to a single pellet in the tray and asked, "What is it?" If S indicated recognition, he was told that he could eat it. If no recognition was apparent, E told the child that it was candy and that he was free to eat it. Next, E pointed to the lever and inquired, "What do you think would happen if you pushed this?" If S pressed the lever, ate the candy, and pressed again, E said nothing further. If S pressed the lever and then failed to eat the candy, E said, "You may have as much as you like." No further comment was offered (33, p. 13).

The third study, by Baer (3), resembled Warren and Brown's in that it aimed to explore operant processes, and Siegel and Foshee's in that an adult was in the experimental room. Ss, from 4-0 to 4-6, were attending the University of Chicago Nursery School. The task was to press down on a wooden door knob for M&M candies delivered in paper cups by a revolving dispenser modeled after a lazy-susan. After orienting S to the situation and to the task as a game, E waited until S responded to the first candy, and then suggested that he could eat it if he wished. (All $Ss$ ate them immediately.) The notation on the relationship between $E$'s behavior and the $S$'s performance during the period of nonreinforcement is of particular interest. "The extinction rate apparently was affected by a grossly defined social condition in which the experimenter injected his attention and approval into the extinction process" (3, p. 17).

In these three studies, it is apparent that in addition to candy *per se*, other factors were influential. First, there were differences in kinds of candy. It will be recalled that Warren and Brown found that differences in strength of appetite for candy influenced the orderliness of performance. Different kinds of candy assuredly have differential appeal and should also be expected to produce variations in performance. Second, the activities of the adult in the experiment unquestionably influenced performance. Baer's finding of the effect of attention and approval on extinction adds to the accumulating evidence. His findings are particularly significant since he did not make his attention and approval contingent upon a response although $S$ may have so interpreted it. Third, differences in instructions—statements to induce $S$ to participate and orient him to the experiment task—must have made for differences in performance. Although no studies have been cited here to demonstrate this, a large number of investigations on adult $Ss$ (especially those using "projective techniques") indicate that it is a safe assumption (32).

*Older children.* Let us now consider two studies with older children showing how instructions and social participation may be drastically reduced. The first is by Lasko (23), illustrating a simple but ingenious method of studying intermittent reinforcement. $Ss$, 11-year-old school children, were presented with an apparatus consisting of a box with 96 holes across the front panel. They were to start at one end and insert a stick into the holes. The stick ejected an individually-wrapped, penny Hershey bar. One group was reinforced after each response; the other group, after every other response. Little or no social action was necessary.

The second investigation, by Azrin and Lindsley, was concerned with cooperative behavior (2). $Ss$, ranging in age from 7 to 12 and drawn from two settlement houses in Boston, were brought to the experimental room, two at a time. They sat at long ends of a table 6 ft. in length and 3 ft. in width. Physical contact between the children was prevented by a wire screen mounted on the table. Each $S$ had a stylus which could be inserted in any of three holes in the table. $E$ gave the following instructions and then left the room.

> This is a game. You can play the game any way you want to or do anything else that you want to do. This is how the game works: Put both sticks (styli) into all three of the holes. (This sentence was repeated until both styli had been placed in the three available holes.) While you are in the room some of these (the experimenter, $E$, held out several jelly beans) will drop into this cup. You can eat them if you want to or you can take them home with you (2, p. 100).

The Ss had to discover that, if one of them inserted his stylus in one of the holes on his side of the table within 0.04 sec. after the other had inserted his stylus in a comparable hol: on his side, a red light flashed and a jelly bean tumbled down a chute into a tray accessible to both Ss. Azrin and Lindsley stated that instructions were kept brief so that the initial acquisition of cooperative behavior could be studied; the procedures could be used with subjects having difficulty in understanding instructions, such as the retarded or disturbed; and the effect of instructions on behavior would be minimized.

*Deviant children.* Let us now turn attention to the use of edibles with deviant children. As has been mentioned earlier, in a multiple-choice type of instrumentation there is a tendency to combine edibles with social factors. Here are two examples with deviant children. A study by House, Zeaman, Orlando, and Fischer (15) was concerned with discrimination learning and transfer in institutionalized imbeciles. Stimuli varying in form were presented two at a time by means of the Wisconsin General Apparatus Test. Correct responses were rewarded by an M&M candy in the hole beneath the stimulus object and the word "good" delivered by *E*. Incorrect responses were followed by a "No." For the most part, the correctional method was used and *S* could do as he pleased with the candy. *E* operated from behind a one-way screen. He arranged the stimuli for each presentation, pushed the tray to *S*'s side of the screen for a trial, and pulled it back after a response. The procedure relevant to reinforcers is as follows:

> On the subject's initial exposure to the experimental situation, two or three pretraining trials were given as demonstration with a minimum of verbal explanation. The subject was first asked if he liked candy and was given a small piece. If he responded positively to the candy (i.e., either ate or hoarded it), he was told that he was going to play a game for candy. For the first presentation of the stimulus tray, both food cups were left uncovered with candy placed in one of them. The experimenter asked, "Can you find the candy?" and pointed it out if the subject failed to see it. On the next trial, a grey wedge was placed over the food cup containing the candy, with the other cup left uncovered. Again *S* was asked to find the candy and aided by the experimenter if he failed to move the wedge. Another trial with the wedge was given at this point if the subject seemed slow. At this point, discrimination trials were begun (15, pp. 6-7).

In another multiple-choice study on the institutionalized retarded, Cantor and Hottel (11) were interested in the effect of amount of reinforcement on rate of learning. *E* explained and demonstrated a form discrimination task and arranged the problems by placing one peanut or four peanuts under the correct stimulus box. "When *S* made a correct choice, he was allowed to eat the food reward; when an incorrect choice was made, *S* was not allowed to lift the correct box, thus being deprived of the reward." Each of the authors served as *E* for half the Ss. The performance of the low and higher reward groups was not significantly different, but there was a significant interaction (at the 5 per cent level) of *rewards* by *experimenters*, indicating that the behavior of *E* had some control over the *S's* performance.

The next two examples on deviant children are of the free operant type. They suggest, at least with this type of method, that it is not essential to compound edibles with social reinforcers. The first one is part of a project on psychotic behavior by Lindsley (25). The experimental situation was a specially constructed cubicle in which *S*, working alone, was required to pull a plunger to obtain reinforcers delivered automatically. The reinforcers consisted of a mixture of candies including jelly-beans, corn candies, gumdrops, sour-balls, peanuts, chiclets, M&Ms, small Hershey bars, and Tootsie Rolls. Since the *Ss*, ranging in age from 7 to 14, would not stay in the room alone at first, they were oriented and given preliminary training in gradual stages similar to Warren and Brown's free operant technique. Of special interest here is the attempt to evaluate the effect of food deprivation on performance. The report states:

> In our usual experimental procedure the patients come to the experimental rooms an average of two hours after they have eaten. In order to obtain an exploratory determination of the effects of food deprivation on candy-reinforced behavior, three patients missed breakfast before the experimental session. These children showed no significant changes in the number of responses per hour as a result of this 20-hour food deprivation. These preliminary results suggest that short periods of food deprivation will not significantly increase the rate of responding for candy reinforcement (25, p. 5).

A second research program by House, Zeaman, Orlando, and Fischer (15) was on the developmentally retarded and was patterned after Lindsley's. Major interest was on the process of operant discrimination; hence, the apparatus was modified so that *S* faced a panel with two windows for presenting stimuli and a plunger for responding under each. Presentation of stimuli and delivery of reinforcers were controlled by electric devices. "The reinforcers are small, commercially available candies including: miniature marshmallows, candy corn, M&Ms, and chocolate chips (the kind that go into Toll-House cookies)" (15, p. 87).

## Drinkables

There is no reason why drinkables should not serve as effective reinforcers. Small amounts of juice or milk can be delivered in sealed sanitary cups, or squirted into a stationary cup or glass. Yet, only two investigations using some kind of drink have come to our attention. For example, under Notes and Discussion in the 1949 volume of the *American Journal of Psychology,* Fuller reports a provocative investigation of operant conditioning of arm movement in an 18-year-old "vegetative idiot" using a warm milk-sugar solution (13). Observations were conducted before breakfast so that *S* was without food for 15 hours prior to training. Although the attending physicians at the institution thought that the subject could not learn anything, the response of arm movement was conditioned in four experimental sessions. The milk was delivered directly to *S's* mouth. In addition to demonstrating the feasibility of drinkable reinforcers, the study suggests that we have yet to apply known learning principles to the training of the retarded in a thorough and systematic way.

*Summary*

Consumables, edibles and drinkables, have been discussed as reinforcers in experiments with children. Edibles were considered first. A large variety of edibles has been used effectively with children in both multiple-choice and free operant tasks. Procedures involving multiple-choice tasks may either give the child freedom to do as he pleases with the edibles, or instruct him to save them until the experiment is over. Three experiments on pre-school children were cited in illustrating the first practice, and two the second. It was pointed out that all involved the experimenter in the procedures, thereby making it difficult to evaluate the reinforcing function of the edibles as such. Procedures following free operant techniques almost have to allow the child to do as he pleases with the reinforcers. Procedures from three studies on preschool children were described, and it was noted that kind of candy, instructions to the child, and the behavior of the experimenter influenced the behavior of the child. Six additional studies were cited: one restricted operant and one free operant showing techniques with middle childhood children, two multiple-choice types on retarded children, one free operant on retarded subjects, and one free operant on emotionally disturbed youngsters.

Mixtures of edibles are most serviceable in studies requiring the child to come to the laboratory for many sessions. Mixtures of edibles and manipulatables will be discussed in the following section. Drinkables were treated only briefly. Although drinkables may serve as reinforcers only a few studies have used them. One was cited involving a grossly retarded subject.

Findings from this analysis and from experiences at this Laboratory have been brought together in the form of practical suggestions for the use of consumables as reinforcers:

1. Prior to initiating a study with consumables, it is suggested that parents, teachers, principals, and/or superintendents be briefed on the kind and amount of consumables each child will receive from participation in the investigation. In most situations the information will be gratefully received and cooperation will be enhanced. In some cases, parents may express reservation on the basis that sweets are detrimental to the child's teeth or health and interfere with his eating routines, and teachers may add that foods brought from laboratory tend to "mess up" the class room and school equipment. Under such circumstances it is obviously advisable to plan on alternate reinforcers such as toys, trinkets, hobby items, music, movies, or social interaction.

2. Select the type of consumable that is acceptable to parents, teachers, or other adults responsible for the children, as well as advantageous to the purpose of the study and to the ease of reporting and replicating. It is suggested that the reinforcers have low calories, be individually wrapped, or

have a hard consistency or at least a hard surface, so that they will not readily stick, melt, or crumble.[4] It is also recommended that consumables be small (about half the size of jelly beans) and uniform in size, and that they be easily identifiable and readily reproducible or obtainable. Mixtures of candies with tiny cookies, Trix cereal, nuts, and raisins are advocated for studies requiring long periods of observations or a series of observations extending over several months.

3. To reduce the influence of uncontrolled reinforcing stimuli, it is suggested that minimum instructions be used, that all instructions be given in a standardized manner, that reinforcers be presented by mechanical or electronic means—unless social reinforcers are also experimental variables —and that, if an adult must be present in the experimental situation, his behavior be evaluated experimentally or statistically.

4. To encourage investigations aimed at duplicating, elaborating, and extended findings, it is suggested that a complete and detailed account be given of the consumables used, the instructions employed, the method of dispensation, and the controls exercised over other social and physical stimuli.

Manipulatables

Manipulatables refer to toys, trinkets, and hobby items—objects which apparently derive their reinforcing properties from tactile, visual, and auditory stimulation. Some of the practices with manipulatables will be considered here, others in the section on tokens in the paper to follow.

## Toys

Toys—the five-and-ten-cent-store variety as well as the more expensive kinds—may serve as reinforcers in at least three ways: (a) presented for play for short periods during the experiment, (b) presented for play during the experiment and given to keep at the end, and (c) displayed during the experiment and given to keep at the end.

Limited periods of toy play as reinforcement are exemplified in a study on inferential behavior by Kendler and Kendler, and on concept learning by Roberts. In both, preschoolers were the Ss. The Kendler and Kendler experiment (19) used Ss from a private nursery school, ranging in age from 2-10 to 4-11. In the preliminary phase of the study S was required to pull a ribbon to obtain a small stuffed red ladybug, and a gold chain for a small stuffed gray chicken. "Although a string was clipped to both subgoals to prevent them from being pulled more than a few inches past the apparatus, there was sufficient play in it to allow S to handle the stuffed toy. After a few moments of handling, the ladybug was retracted by E" (19, p. 312). S was then asked to pull the ribbon again. This time it not only brought forth the ladybug but also a toy foreign sports car. The child

---

[4] The Kirkman Pharmacal Co., Seattle, Wash., is exploring possibilities of a standard experimental sugarless candy in attractive colors with fruit flavors.

"was permitted to play with the car about one minute. During this time he made it go around the room once and tooted the horn two or three times" (19, p. 312). *E* took an active role throughout.

In the Roberts' study (31) the *S*s were from 2-0 to 5-9 in age. Each was shown a two-story gray wooden house with a roof made of glass. The house had three different colored doors, and the upper part of the door had a ridge upon which an airplane (the same color as the correct door) was sitting and which could be triggered so that the airplane would fall off. *E*, who remained with the child, gave the following instructions: "This house has three doors; all of them open, but only one door makes the air-plane fall. You open one door and see if you can make an airplane fall" (31, p. 120). If *S* opened the correct door, he could play with the airplane while *E* completed his records of the response and prepared for the next trial. If he opened the wrong door, *E* said: "No, that door doesn't make an airplane fall. See, this is the one. This door makes an airplane fall." She then opened it, but the child could not play with the airplane since it and the house were removed at once. However, he could play with the other toys in the room until the next trial. As in the Kendler and Kendler study, *E* took an active role in the proceedings.

Giving youngsters toys to play with during the session and to keep afterwards was the practice followed by Stevenson (35) in a study on latent learning and by Lewis (24) on a problem dealing with "intermittent rein-forcement." In the first study *S*s, who were from a university housing project, ranged in age from 3-0 to 6-0. After preliminary training in open-ing locks, each was required to run down one side of a large V-shaped "maze" and open a box with a key. On the reinforced trials, *S* found a bird-, a flower-, or an animal-sticker. ". . . *E* asked him to bring the reward to the starting point and paste it on a large placard placed there. As the child pasted, the assistant replaced the lock, key and reward" (35, p. 18). As is apparent, *E* and his assistant were actively involved throughout.

Stevenson noted that the behavior of the older *S*s (ages 5 and 6) ap-peared to be directed toward obtaining the reinforcements and complying with E's requests, and their performance showed a consistency and directed-ness that was missing in many of the younger *S*s. The younger *S*s (ages 3 and 4) seemed to regard the reinforcement as but one of a number of inter-esting aspects of "the game" and showed considerably more manipulation of the irrelevant objects. A similar observation on differences in behavior of younger and older preschoolers in relation to trinkets will be discussed in the next section.

In the Lewis study (24) each *S* was given 20 plastic toys (cowboys, foot-ball players, and the like) at the beginning of the session and was told that it was possible to win many more but that it was possible to lose all of them, too. The youngest child in the group was 6-5, the oldest 7-5. Each subject was presented with four electrical switches and told that, if the correct one were pushed, a red light would flash and he would receive an additional toy; if the wrong one was pressed, a blue light would flash and a toy would be taken away. The lights were controlled by *E* in order to distribute the reinforcers in predetermined percentages. At the end of the session the subject was told that he could keep the toys remaining. As in the other three studies, *E* took an active part in giving instructions and in presenting and withdrawing the toys. Incidentally, it may be recalled that Brackbill and O'Hara used a similar procedure with M&M candy to study the relative effectiveness of reinforcement and punishment in discrimination learning (8). Was the Brackbill and O'Hara study concerned with intermittent reinforcement or was the Lewis study concerned with reinforcement and punishment? According to the definition of terms ordinarily used in an objective behavioral analysis (34, 36), Lewis must have been dealing with reinforcement and punishment—in a complicated situation.

In a study of transposition behavior with *S*s 2-6 to 5-10, Kuenne (22) used a variation of the above procedure. The child was given toys to handle and play with during the session and was given his choice of one of the toys to keep. Each *S* was seated in front of a panel with two hinged lids, behind each of which was a box. "In the event of a correct response, the box opened and a toy was found inside, while in the event of an incorrect response, the box was found to be locked" (22, p. 478). Colorful wood and cardboard toys of the five-and-dime variety were used and were collected in a cardboard box which the child held on his lap. At the conclusion of the experiment the box of toys was turned back to the *E* and the child was offered one selection from the cardboard toys to take home.

The third procedure with toys—presented contingent upon a response yet unavailable for possession or play until the end of a session—requires some kind of a dispensing apparatus and a clear plastic box to serve as a "showcase." With such an arrangement toys may be presented according to experimental plan, be seen during the experiment, and be given to keep at the end of the session. Studies following this procedure will be described in the section on trinkets.

### Trinkets

One of the earliest notes on the effectiveness of trinkets as reinforcers is in a review of child development for 1952 by Nowlis and Nowlis (26). Since then multicolor and multiform plastic and metal trinkets, or charms, as they are sometimes called, have served in studies with boys and girls from 2 to 12. In some, they have been delivered but were not available for handling until the end of the experiment; in others, they were immediately available.

An example of the "you-can-see-but-can't-touch" method with nursery school children was described by Bijou (4). The apparatus was a wooden box with two holes, one above the other. When a ball was dropped into the upper hole, it rolled through a series of tubes and came out the lower hole. (Since the child must wait 3.3 sec. for the ball to return to make the next response, the situation is a restricted rather than a free operant.) To the left of the bottom opening was a clear plastic box with a closed cover to receive trinkets. In preparing for the study, the *E*, a young woman, first made herself known to the children by watching them at play in the yard and in the school rooms. This phase ended when the children began to regard her as a member of the nursery school staff. The study got under way when the first child was selected to come and "play with some toys." The preliminary experimental procedure was as follows:

> On entering the laboratory, she suggests that the child sit at a table upon which are a plastic dog and a tin dog house. After a few introductory remarks, the experimenter puts the dog in the house and shows the child that tapping on the table will make the dog shoot out. She next demonstrates that the dog will also pop out if called by his name, "Sparky." The subject is then encouraged "to make the dog come out." Once the child takes charge of the toy, play is permitted until he has made the dog come out at least four times. A delay of 15 sec. or more between insertion and pop-out is the criterion for termination of warm-up activity (4, pp. 165-166).

The child was then invited to sit in front of the table with the apparatus. A plywood screen was removed and *E* followed this procedure:

> She shows a handful of trinkets and says: "You can get some of these to keep, to take home with you." She hands the child the ball and says: "When you put the ball in there (pointing to the upper opening) some of these toys will come down here (pointing to the covered plastic box). The ball will come out here again. You can put it back into the top hole as many times as you like. We will leave all the toys that come down in the box until we are finished, and are ready to go." The experimenter takes a seat six feet to the rear of the subject and offers no further suggestions or instructions. Comments and questions addressed to her are reacted to in a pleasant non-directive fashion, e.g., "You think the thing is broken." "You think no more will come out." When the experiment has been completed the receiving box is opened, the trinkets are given to the child, and the child is returned to his group (4, p. 166).

This procedure was used in two studies on intermittent reinforcement (5, 29) and one on the relationship between strength of response and number of reinforcements (30). A variation was employed by Kogan (21) in an analysis of presenting and withdrawing trinkets. *S*s ranging in age from 3-0 to 5-11 were drawn from a university housing unit. To reinforce a response, a trinket appeared in a plexiglas window suspended from a hook on a horizontal chain which moved the trinket into view. To remove a reinforcer, chain movement was reversed causing a trinket to disappear from sight. At the end of the session *S* was given the trinkets displayed in the window. It was hoped that this procedure would eliminate the need for an adult to present and withdraw reinforcers as in the Brackbill and O'Hara and the Lewis studies. The device was not entirely satisfactory, however, since considerable training was required before *S* learned that every time one moved out of sight it was his loss. Further investigations have produced other devices and procedures which accomplish this purpose in a more efficient manner.

An example of a free operant method in which trinkets were available following a response has also been described by Bijou (6). The apparatus was a box with a lever for responding and a tray for receiving trinkets. The initial part of the procedure followed the practice of having an adult become acquainted with the children in the nursery school and then inviting them in, one at a time, to the laboratory to play games and get some trinkets. The latter part of the procedure was as follows:

> On entering the laboratory, she closes the door, takes him to the middle of the room, and says, "You can play with the toys as long as you like." She disappears behind the cardboard screen, sits down, clips the ear-piece on her left ear (away from the side where the child would see it if he were to approach), and pretends to be reading or writing. During the experiment, if the youngster leaves the "toys" to peek around the screen, she looks at him pleasantly. If the child comes to talk about the trinkets, toys or anything else, she also reacts in a pleasant manner but says nothing. In response to direct questions she says, "You can play with the toys as long as you like." This is all she is permitted to say. All her other behavior toward the child is prescribed by E and communicated to her through the ear-piece (6, p. 247).

In one of the studies with this procedure interest was focused on determining the minimum number of trinkets necessary to obtain stable performance within a session and between sessions. The $Ss$, from the University of Washington Nursery School, ranged in age from 2-6 to 4-11. In each session seven trinkets were dispensed but 19 reinforcements in all were given. For some $Ss$, the remaining reinforcers were pieces of brightly colored paper; for others, they were simply the humming sound of the dispenser motor. Interval and ratio schedules were set up so that the first two reinforcements were trinkets and the interval between trinkets increased progressively. Thus trinkets were dispensed on the 1st, 2nd, 4th, 7th, 11th, 15th, and 19th reinforcement. As can be seen, the blocks of responses between trinkets were 0, 1, 2, 3, 3, 3. With both trinkets and hum, and trinkets and paper, a relatively steady rate was maintained by only one from the junior group (ages 2-6 to 3-3) and by five $Ss$ from the senior group (3-3 to 4-6), out of a total of 25. For the remaining 19 children, the sessions became shorter, response rates decreased, and there were frequent refusals to return. Actually this was a double schedule—the distribution of reinforcements on an interval or ratio schedule, and the distribution of trinkets among the reinforcements on an increasing ratio basis (7). As will be discussed in the next section, mixtures of edibles and trinkets have resulted in stable performance over a number of sessions.

Casual observations in this and in other studies using the free operant method indicate age differences in response to trinkets, comparable to those with stickers described by Stevenson (35). Performance of the $Ss$ in the older groups (ages 3-3 to 4-6) gave strong indication that they were "working for the trinkets," since they spent relatively little time with the other toys in the room. For the $Ss$ in the younger group (age 2-6 to 3-3) apparently the trinket was only another interesting aspect of the total situation, and they often spent as much time playing with the other toy in the situation as they did with the manipulandum.

Trinkets may, of course, be made immediately available in multiple-choice situations. Such a procedure was used by Calvin and his associates in a series of discrimination studies (9, 10, 27) on normal children and by Plenderleith on retarded children (28). In one of the Calvin studies (10) interest was centered on the effect of nondifferentiated reward and non-reinforcement on discriminative learning in 10 Ss 10-0 to 11-0. S was presented with two identical plain opaque red plastic cups, mouth down and 4 in. apart. Two 3 × 4½ in. white cardboard cards which served as cues were placed in horizontal positions, one in front of each cup. The procedure was described as follows:

> If S pointed to the cup with the reward (a small plastic toy of the kind given in gum-ball machines) under it, E picked it up and gave the reward to S; whereas if S pointed to the cup with nothing in it, E first picked up the chosen cup to show that it had not covered a reward and then immediately lowered the screen to terminate the trial without giving S a reward (10, pp. 439-440).

The Plenderleith study (28) was a test of Lewin's concept of rigidity as a personality trait of the retarded. Normal and retarded Ss ranging in mental age from 5-6 to 5-11 were observed in discrimination learning tasks involving pairs of pictures. The procedure of orienting the S to the situation, giving instructions, setting up the choices, dealing with behavior arising from nonreinforcement and other conditions, was as follows:

> The stimuli used in this study were a series of pairs of pictures. No two pictures were the same. The pictures were inserted into slots in a movable frame behind which was a concealed reward trough. The child was instructed to select one of the two pictures by pushing the card, and if the correct card was chosen the child found a reward (small charms purchased at novelty counters) in the trough behind it. If the wrong card was chosen, no reward was found. The noncorrection method was used throughout (28, p. 108).

In both multiple-choice studies description of procedures is too brief to permit comment on the influence of the instructions and of E's behavior in the situation.

### Mixture of Trinkets and Edibles

Trinkets and edibles may be used together to provide (a) variation in strengths of reinforcers and (b) variety among reinforcers to forestall satiation in experiments requiring many sessions. The procedure in a problem-solving study by Kendler, Kendler, Pliskoff, and D'Amato (20) is an example of the first type of usage. Interest was centered on the influence of reinforcement during training and during the test trials on inferential behavior. Some responses (pushing a lever inward) produced a raisin' as a weak reinforcer and a trinket or charm as a strong reinforcer. An example of the second usage of a mixture of trinkets and edibles is a methodological investigation conducted at this Laboratory in 1956. The question was whether a mixture would produce, over a number of sessions, stable response patterns which could serve as a baseline for evaluating other experimental variables. If it could be accomplished, the way would be opened to study systematically social, emotional, and symbolic conditions on individual subjects. The mixture was trinkets, dime-sized cookies, colored corn cereal (Trix), and M&M candy. Reinforcers were available on delivery according to one of four schedules—fixed ratio, variable ratio, fixed interval, and variable interval. The Ss, 18 in number, were from a private day-care center and ranged in age from 2-6 to 5-0. All were seen more than once; some as many as 10 times. There was a total of 81 sessions with intervals between sessions ranging from 2 to 17 days. In essence, it was found that the mixture strengthened lever-pressing behavior and maintained it at fairly constant rates in all but two children. One was a 4-year-old boy whose rate in the first session was abnormally slow compared to the other Ss. In subsequent sessions his rate gradually decreased, and finally he refused to return. His history and his behavior in the nursery school suggested severe emotional problems. The other exception was a 2½-year-old child—the youngest in the group. He refused to play with the trinkets or eat the edibles. Everything that came from the chute was pushed in the hole in the lever box. His rate of responding showed negligible change following reinforcement, and he spent more and more time playing with the other toys and pulling at the window shades. These two exceptions are further examples of the influence of age and historical factors on the effectiveness of experimentally manipulated reinforcers.

Two years later this procedure was used in a single-lever-type discrimination study with the following refinements: (a) the mixture was trinkets, dime-sized cookies, corn cereal (Sugar Corn Pops), and specially prepared sugarless candy in the proportions of 5 : 3 : 3 : 1; (b) each session was 20 minutes long; and (c) intervals between sessions were six days. Complicated discriminations were learned (two minutes of responding on a variable ratio of 25 or 50 on the occasion of an amber light and two minutes of no responding on a blue light) and some of the Ss were seen as many as 12 times, with maintenance of stable performance.

## Hobby Items

Hobby items should serve satisfactorily as reinforcers for middle childhood, preadolescent, and adolescent Ss. The items would, of course, have to be selected in accordance with the known hobbies of the Ss. One of two procedures could be followed—tailor the items to each S's hobbies or select a group of Ss with the same hobby and use a common set of reinforcers. Many possibilities for suitable material come to mind—stamps, small jewelry, items such as pop beads, pictures of baseball players, airplanes, boats, historical figures, and the like. Unfortunately, examples of research using hobby items cannot be given since none has as yet been reported in the literature.

*Summary*

The use of toys, trinkets, trinkets and edibles, and hobby items as reinforcers in experiments with children has been considered. Toys may be used in multiple-choice types of experiments to give a child a limited play period during the experiment or given as a gift during or at the end of an experiment. Studies have been described using these procedures or some combination of them. It was pointed out that some of the practices cited involved the active participation of the experimenter, making it difficult to separate the reinforcing property of the toy from the behavior of the experimenter. Trinkets, on the other hand, are usually given as gifts. Sometimes they are displayed following a response and given at the end of the experimental period, and sometimes they are immediately available following a response. The first procedure was illustrated by two studies on preschool children, one using a restricted operant, the other a free operant. The second procedure was exemplified by a free operant study on preschool children, and two multiple-choice situations, one on middle childhood children and one on the retarded. A combination of trinkets and edibles may be used to introduce variation in strength of reinforcers or to supply variety in experiments requiring a large number of sessions. One multiple-choice study on preschoolers was cited to illustrate the first, and two free operant investigations on preschoolers were cited to illustrate the second. Finally, it was pointed out that hobby items can serve as reinforcers for children above the preschool level. Procedures might involve tailoring the item to each subject's interest or preselecting subjects with a common interest and using a common set of hobby items.

The following suggestions for using manipulatables as reinforcers seem indicated:

1. In the suggestions for using consumables as reinforcers, it was recommended that prior to initiating a study, parents, teachers, principals and/or superintendents be told what, in general, the experiment is about and what kind of reinforcers would be involved. Naturally, the same practice is recommended when manipulatables are to be used. If it is planned to give manipulatables to the child to keep, it may be reassuring to show some samples. In the event of objections to children's receiving toys, trinkets, hobby items, and perhaps edibles as well, it is suggested that the experimental procedure be modified to use limited toy play in situations, as in the Kendler, Kendler, Pliskoff, and D'Amato study (20). If this type of reinforcement is not appropriate for the study, it is suggested that motion pictures, TV, music, or social reinforcers be tried. [See articles by Jeffrey (17) on music and by Gewirtz and Baer (14) on social reinforcers.]

2. In selecting manipulatables for a study, it will be advantageous to take several things into account. First, they ought to be appropriate for the particular group of subjects under study. That is, the material ought to

be chosen in the light of such factors as the age, sex, socioeconomic status, and living conditions (residential institution, day care centers, private school, etc.). Second, materials that may readily cause hurt or disturbances in the school or home should be avoided. These would include buttons that can easily be put into the mouth or nose, noise makers, wind-up toys, balls, and symbolic objects that may be contrary to parents' practices and teachings, e.g., certain types of religious symbols or items suggesting aggression. Third, for the convenience of interested investigators the materials used should be easily identifiable and obtainable. And fourth, it is recommended that mixtures of manipulatables or mixtures of manipulatables and edibles be considered in studies requiring many repeated measures.

3. It is suggested here again that reinforcers other than those experimentally introduced be maximally controlled by using minimum amount of instructions (to bring the child to the situation and to explain the task) and delivered in a consistent and standard fashion, and by presenting the manipulatables in such a way that social factors are eliminated, controlled, or evaluated.

4. To make clear the conditions under which the reported behavior was observed, it is suggested that complete and detailed information be given in the procedure section of the report of the study. That portion dealing with reinforcement should tell what type of manipulatable was received, and how it was received. If given during the session, what was the child allowed to do with it? If displayed during the session, how was it displayed and what were the instructions prior to the experiment? If delivered by $E$, what was $E$ allowed to do and say at the time of the delivery and between deliveries?

## REFERENCES

1. ALBERTS, E., & EHRENFREUND, D. Transposition of children as a function of age. *J. exp. Psychol.*, 1951, 41, 30-38.

2. AZRIN, N. H., & LINDSLEY, O. R. The reinforcement of cooperation between children. *J. abnorm. soc. Psychol.*, 1956, 52, 100-102.

3. BAER, D. M. A use of the free operant in the study of children's behavior. *Stud. Res. Psychol., Univer. Chicago*, 1957, 1, 5-18.

4. BIJOU, S. W. A systematic approach to an experimental analysis of young children. *Child Develpm.*, 1955, 26, 161-168.

5. BIJOU, S. W. Patterns of reinforcement and resistance to extinction in young children. *Child Develpm.*, 1957, 28, 47-54.

6. BIJOU, S. W. Methodology for an experimental analysis of child behavior. *Psychol. Rep.*, 1957, 3, 243-250.

7. BIJOU, S. W. Operant extinction after fixed interval schedules with young children. *J. exp. Anal. Behav.*, 1958, 1, 25-29.

8. Brackbill, Yvonne, & O'Hara, J. Discrimination learning in children as a function of reward and punishment. Paper read at Western Psychol. Ass., Eugene, Oregon, 1957.

9. Calvin, A. D., & Clifford, L. T. The relative efficiency of various types of stimulus-objects in discriminative learning by children. *Amer. J. Psychol.*, 1956, 69, 103-106.

10. Calvin, A. D., Perkins, M. J., & Hoffman, F. K. The effect of non-differentiated reward and non-reward on discrimination learning in children. *Child Develpm.*, 1956, 27, 439-446.

11. Cantor, G. N., & Hottel, J. V. Discrimination learning in mental defectives as a function of magnitude of food reward and intelligence level. *Amer. J. ment. Def.*, 1955, 60, 380-384.

12. Ferster, C. B. The use of the free operant in the analysis of behavior. *Psychol. Bull.*, 1953, 50, 263-274.

13. Fuller, P. R. Operant conditioning of a vegetative human organism. *Amer. J. Psychol.*, 1949, 62, 587-590.

14. Gewirtz, J. L., & Baer, D. M. The effect of brief social deprivation on behaviors for a social reinforcer. *J. abnorm. soc. Psychol.*, 1958, 56, 49-56.

15. House, Betty J., Zeaman, D., Orlando, R., & Fischer, W. Learning and transfer in mental defectives. Progress Report, No. 1, Oct., 1957.

16. Hunter, I. M. L. An experimental investigation of the absolute and relative theories of transpositional behavior in children. *Brit. J. Psychol.*, 1952, 43, 113-128.

17. Jeffrey, W. E. New techniques for motivating and reinforcing children. *Science*, 1955, 121, 371.

18. Keller, F. S., & Schoenfeld, W. N. *Principles of psychology.* New York: Appleton-Century-Crofts, 1950.

19. Kendler, H. H., & Kendler, Tracy S. Inferential behavior in preschool children. *J. exp. Psychol.*, 1956, 51, 311-314.

20. Kendler, H. H., Kendler, Tracy S., Pliskoff, S. S., & D'Amato, May F. Inferential behavior in children: 1. The influence of reinforcement and incentive motivation. *J. exp. Psychol.*, 1958, 55, 207-212.

21. Kogan, C. L. Withdrawal of a positive reinforcer and strength of behavior in children. Unpublished doctoral dissertation, Univer. of Washington, 1956.

22. Kuenne, Margaret R. Experimental investigation of the relation of language to transposition behavior in young children. *J. exp. Psychol.*, 1946, 36, 471-490.

23. LASKO, A. A. A theoretical study of partial reinforcement within the framework of Rotter's social learning theory of personality. Unpublished master's thesis, Ohio State Univer., 1950.

24. LEWIS, D. J. Partial reinforcement in a gambling situation. *J. exp. Psychol.*, 1952, 43, 447-450.

25. LINDSLEY, O. R. Status Report III, Report of the first half of the second year on the Study of Psychotic Behavior, Studies in Behavior Therapy, Metropolitan State Hospital, Waltham, Mass., 1954.

26. NOWLIS, V., & NOWLIS, HELEN H. Child psychology. *In Ann. Rev. Psychol.*, 1952, 3, 1-28.

27. PERKINS, M. J., BANKS, H. P., & CALVIN, A. D. The effect of delay on simultaneous and successive discrimination in children. *J. exp. Psychol.*, 1954, 48, 416-418.

28. PLENDERLEITH, MAVIS. Discrimination learning and discrimination reversal learning in normal and feebleminded children. *J. genet. Psychol.*, 1956, 88, 107-112.

29. PUMROY, D. K. The effects of intermittent reinforcement on resistance to extinction and emotional behavior in preschool children. Unpublished doctoral dissertation, Univer. of Washington, 1954.

30. PUMROY, SHIRLEY A. S. The effects of amount of reinforcement on extinction and emotional behavior with preschool children. Unpublished doctoral dissertation, Univer. of Washington, 1954.

31. ROBERTS, K. E. The ability of preschool children to solve problems in which a simple principle of relationship is kept constant. *J. genet. Psychol.*, 1932, 40, 118-135.

32. SARASON, S. B. *The clinical interaction.* New York: Harper, 1954.

33. SIEGEL, P. S., & FOSHEE, J. G. The law of primary reinforcement in children. *J. exp. Psychol.*, 1953, 45, 12-14.

34. SKINNER, B. F. *Science and human behavior.* New York: Macmillan, 1953.

35. STEVENSON, H. W. Latent learning in children. *J. exp. Psychol.*, 1954, 47, 17-21.

36. VERPLANCK, W. S. *A glossary of some terms used in the objective science of behavior.* Washington, D.C.: Amer. Psychol. Ass., 1957.

37. WARREN, A. B., & BROWN, R. H. Conditioned operant response phenomenon in children. *J. gen. Psychol.*, 1943, 38, 181-207.

# THE DEVELOPMENT OF SOCIALIZATION SKILLS
## IN AN ELECTIVELY MUTE CHILD

Phillip Blake and Thelma Moss

Neuropsychiatric Institute, University of California, Los Angeles

Effective treatment of the electively mute child has been demonstrated in recent years, using various operant conditioning procedures (Ferster and DeMyer, 1961; Wolf *et al.*, 1964; Metz, 1965; Hewett, 1965; Straughan *et al.*, 1965; Cook and Adams, 1966; Lovaas *et al.*, 1966; Blake *et al.*, 1966; Jenson and Womack, 1967). In addition, Williams (1959) and more recently Hart and her co-workers (1964) have evolved special techniques for the management of disruptive behavior such as temper tantrums and operant crying—both of which are often observed in these children. A neglected area in this research has been the development of techniques which would make possible a preliminary assessment of such children's verbal repertoires. The establishment of this kind of behavioral baseline has proved of value in defining those areas from which to proceed in the development of specific behavior patterns (Fineman, 1966).

This study first assessed both the verbal and non-verbal behavior potentials of the S, a little girl named Dolly; after which both types of skills were taught. Almost immediately it was realized that Dolly's disruptive behavior prevented the acquisition of any skills. As a result, procedures were devised which hopefully would extinguish both her operant crying and temper tantrums. The work proceeded in four somewhat overlapping stages: (1) the baseline assessment of those vocalizations Dolly already had in her repertoire; (2) the extinction of her disruptive behavior; (3) shaping of eye contact and teaching Dolly to follow instructions; and (4) teaching of non-verbal imitative behavior, and two discriminable verbal responses.

BEHAVIOR RESEARCH AND THERAPY, 1967, Vol. 5, pp. 349-356.

Dolly was an attractive, 4-yr-old, blond girl, who made only three or four sounds (similar to a baby's babbling) when first seen. She would not imitate non-verbal behavior, such as handclaps, nor would she imitate verbal sounds. She had no expressive meaningful language, nor did she make positive affectionate responses to her family or people with whom she was familiar. She was able to participate in play activities (although her interest was not maintained) but she did not play with other children. She had no eye contact, nor did she use objects appropriately. Often she displayed severe temper outbursts, occasionally banging her head; and she had automatisms of rocking, swaying, and staring at the back of her hand. Dolly's parents had sought help from psychiatrists, most of whom had noted in their reports that Dolly had developed an understanding of what was said to her; an understanding commensurate with her chronological age. But her expressive language deficit and bizarre motor behavior indicated a severe emotional disturbance. Neurological tests showed no impairment.

## METHOD

*Apparatus.* A special teaching booth, designed to shut out external stimuli, afforded Dolly maximum opportunity to focus her attention both on E, and the stimuli E wished to present. This booth is described in detail by Hewett (1965). Here, it is enough to say that the booth is divided into two sections by a shutter, which can be raised and lowered by E. The section reserved for the child contains a chair, facing the shutter—which, when raised, reveals the other section in which E sits, facing Dolly. Lighting was focussed on E's side of the booth, where all positive reinforcements were stored. Thus, when the shutter was lowered, Dolly was deprived of light, rewards, and the presence of E.

Usually at the start of a session, the shutter was already lowered, and Dolly found herself in darkness. A ball-drop device was used, to signal the start of a session. E would release the ball inside the box, which would roll down into a cup near Dolly, ringing a bell as it reached the cup. Dolly would then take the ball and place it in a hole at the top of the device; the ball would roll down the tube and ring the bell again. This second bell ringing was the cue for E to raise the shutter, and begin the session.

An Esterline-Angus 20-event cumulative recorder was used in all sessions, making possible a quantification of those behavioral events under investigation.

*Reinforcers.* The most effective of the reinforcements was food; in particular, frosted flakes. Almost as effective was the manipulation of light. The absence of light proved an excellent means of promoting behavior, since Dolly would work to avoid being left in darkness. During the baseline assessment period, another excellent reinforcer was the "color organ". This instrument, described by Fineman (1966), is able to translate sounds, uttered into a microphone, into an array of fusing colors on a screen, which is the face of the "organ". Intensities of the colors varied in proportion with the intensities of sounds emitted into the microphone; the overall effect of this instrument is not unlike that of a kaleidoscope.

## TREATMENT

*Stage* 1 (*The baseline assessment, Session A*). In this pre-treatment session, Dolly was brought into the booth—crying—and seated on the chair. All lights were on, and the shutter up. The E made sounds into the microphone, which caused the "color organ" to produce an array of colors. Then E stopped making the sounds. Gradually, Dolly noticed that when she stopped crying, the colors on the screen would go off. At first she deliberately made crying noises (presumably to keep the color lights playing), but these crying noises slowly shifted to babbling sounds ("s"; "ee"; "ah"; "sh"; and plosives were frequent). Finally these sounds became a definitely repeated "ee" sound. And then, "mama" was said six consecutive times.

At this point, 15 min of the 30-min session had passed, and the "color organ" was removed. The rest of the session was devoted to assessing the reinforcing properties of stimuli other than the "color organ." Dolly rejected all food which was offered (candy, drink, ice cream), but eventually accepted a tactual reinforcement—a beanbag—which she played with for a time. In addition, she became familiar with the ball-drop device. However, most of the session was punctuated with severe operant crying (see Fig. 1).

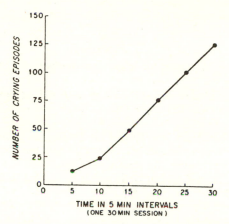

Fig. 1. Baseline assessment: Number of crying episodes (duration of 5 sec or more).

On the basis of this assessment, it was decided that Dolly's disruptive behavior—particularly her crying—was too powerful to attempt the development of verbal or non-verbal skills. Thus the next phase of work was chiefly devoted to the extinction of this inappropriate behavior.

It was arranged that Dolly be seen three times a week for half-hour sessions, on an out-patient basis.

*Stage 2 (Sessions 1 through 9).* For eight of these sessions, when Dolly first saw E, she immediately started to cry, and continued to cry all the way into the booth. (Her movements of propelling herself out of the chair in the booth were so forceful that she was finally kept in the chair by means of an automobile harness.) The shutter was down, and the lights out. When Dolly stopped crying—for a minimum 3 sec—the shutter was lifted, the lights went on, and E at the same time said, "Hi, Dolly!"—offering her a frosted flake, as he spoke. On the first two occasions, Dolly pushed the flake away and began to cry again. Immediately when she started to cry, the shutter was lowered. It was necessary to continue this method of extinguishing her crying for eight sessions. In the ninth session, as soon as Dolly began to cry E said, "Stop crying, Dolly." If she stopped within 3 sec after the command, the shutter was kept raised. If not, the shutter was dropped for 15 sec. In the tenth session, there was not a single episode of crying (see Fig. 2). Crying was minimal for the remaining thirty sessions—most of which could be stopped by E saying, "Stop crying, Dolly."

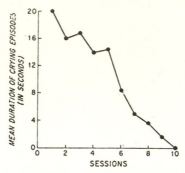

FIG. 2. Extinction of operant crying.

At times during these early sessions, attempts at imitative non-verbal behavior (hand clapping) were made, but with little success until the fifth session. Gradually, this response improved.

*Stage* 3 (*Sessions* 10 *through* 20). *Session* 10. During this half-hour, eye contact was shaped using the following technique. At the start, Dolly was in total darkness. Every 5 sec, E would open the shutter and put on the lights, saying at the same time: "Hi, Dolly—look at me!" Almost always, Dolly would be looking in E's direction—and she would be rewarded for doing so, by being given a spoonful of ice cream. If Dolly was looking elsewhere, the shutter would be dropped for 15 sec. Only a few trials were required for Dolly to look directly into E's eyes—at which time, she would receive the ice cream. After approximately seventy-five trials, 100 per cent performance of the eye contact response had been shaped, paired with the words "Look at me!" The remaining 10 min of the session were devoted to asking Dolly to "Give me the beanbag" or "Put the bag over here"—most of which requests she followed. There was no problem with eye contact after this session.

*Sessions* 11 *through* 20. During these sessions, about 80 per cent of all disruptive behavior had been eliminated, so that new behavior could be attempted more easily. The handclapping response was taught through the "fading" technique described by Kerr (1965). In the beginning, E would clap his hands, and proceed to put Dolly's hands through the motions of handclapping. It was not long before E had only to lift Dolly's hands in the air about a foot apart and let go; and Dolly would close them herself. Gradually E was able to shift the responsibility for executing the handclapping from himself to Dolly. Eventually E had only to say "Clap your hands!" Dolly would comply, and get a reward.

Starting with Session 11, a new non-verbal behavior was reinforced. This consisted of E saying, "Pull my ear, Dolly!"—at which time, E would take Dolly's hand and put it to his ear. Over the next nine sessions, simply pointing to his ear, or E turning his head toward Dolly, paired with the request "Pull my ear" was enough to evoke the response.

100

By Session 20, 90 per cent success was achieved by this request. (See Fig. 3 for the development of these responses. Please note that in Session 14 both handclapping and earpulling showed a sharp decline. This was probably due to the fact that Dolly was ill that day. As can be seen, on the following Session 15, there was a dramatic rise in response rate, when she had recovered.)

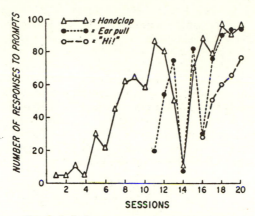

Fig. 3. Imitative responses over twenty sessions.

Starting with Session 12, verbal responses were attempted. This was begun with a free operant training procedure in which every discrete sound (with a 2 sec interval between sounds) was rewarded with a food reinforcer. Any sound which was not a cry or whimper was reinforced. Dolly's vocal output increased dramatically using this technique (see Fig. 4). In Session 15 it was decided to differentially reinforce one particular sound:

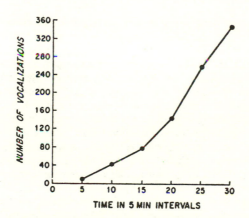

Fig. 4. Number of vocalizations (free operant) with reinforcements: Session 12.

"Hi!" All vocalizations which approximated this sound were rewarded. In the first 5 min, no such sound was produced. But after 20 min, over 100 approximations had been uttered. However, the quality of the sound was "Eye" rather than "Hi!" In Session 16, "Hi" was achieved by shaping the "H" sound—Dolly imitating E's blowing on her hand —then combining the two sounds. It was only when Dolly combined the sounds, saying "Hi" that she was rewarded with food. Next the "Hi" response was brought under stimulus control—that is, when E said "Hi", Dolly said "Hi"; in Session 16 with 30 per cent success. By Session 20, this response rate of success had increased to 76 per cent. The contingency had been learned (see Fig. 3). "Hi!" was later paired with a hand wave, which was greeted with a spontaneous hand wave from Dolly.

*Stage* 4 (*Sessions* 21 *through* 40). Starting with Session 21, differential reinforcement was begun for approximations of the word "eat"—all sounds containing an "ee" sound were immediately rewarded with food. This meant, temporarily, extinction of the "Hi!" sound. In the free operant condition, Dolly kept saying "Hi" rather than "ee"—and in fact, Session 22 was a regression: Dolly stopped all vocalizations in that session. But in Sessions 23, "ee" approximations began in the second 5-min interval, and with reinforcements the clarity of the "ee" sound improved. With this accomplished, discrimination between the two sounds could be established (see Fig. 5).

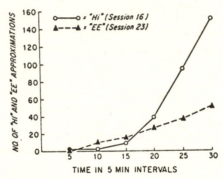

FIG. 5. Differential reinforcement of verbal response approximations.

In Session 32, E attempted to get the "ee" response under stimulus control; and over the next three sessions approximately 75 per cent success was achieved. In Sessions 36 through 39, recovery of the "Hi" sound, differentiated from the "ee" sound was accomplished. Session 40 was devoted to a resumé of the four learned responses.

Starting with Session 21, after the formal work in the booth, E had a "social session" with Dolly outside the booth, in which three types of games were played consistently. The first of these was the "tickle" game, in which E said, "Tickle me!!"—at the same time taking Dolly's hands and placing them on E's chest. E would giggle four or five times aloud; and then proceeded to tickle Dolly—who giggled spontaneously. Soon E was able to say, "Tickle me!" and Dolly would move her hands on E's chest; then wait to be tickled by E.

The second game was "Old McDonald." This consisted of E's humming the song— but only when Dolly took E's hands and made them clap together. E would hum the tune up to the part of the song where "Ee-eye-ee-eye-oh" was sung aloud. After a few trials, E took Dolly's hands, and clapped them for her as he hummed the song, and sang the refrain. Eventually, E was able to clap Dolly's hands, while she hummed the tune and sang "Ee-eye-ee-eye-oh." These sounds, however, were not made by Dolly until she had learned them in the booth. In the third game, E placed Dolly on his lap, facing him. Then he would take Dolly's finger and point to parts of E's face, labelling each in turn (eye, nose, mouth, etc.). Gradually Dolly began to point with her finger, herself, at E's eyes, wait until he said the word "eyes"; then go on to nose, and mouth, each time waiting for E to give the words. Finally Dolly herself said "ice", when pointing to E's eyes—an event which occurred spontaneously. Again, though, it should be noted that this response did not occur before Dolly had produced the "Hi" sounds in the booth.

These play periods between E and Dolly proved a useful adjunct to the formal periods in the booth; particularly in the development of social initiative which had previously been absent. It is important to stress the distinction between the "formal" sessions in the booth and the "social" sessions. In the latter, no primary reinforcers (such as food) were used: only social approval.

## DISCUSSION

### Eye contact

So far as the authors are aware, there has been no study in which light has been used to shape eye contact, in the manner here described. We believe that eye contact is an important factor in attention; and attention is considered an important factor in shaping behavior. Thus, in a sense, the shaping of *attention* was achieved by this technique.

### Verbal responses

The two sounds "Hi!" and "ee" were successfully shaped and maintained as discriminable responses within the subject's repertoire. The authors believe that some meaning was conveyed to Dolly with the sound "Hi!"; because she would respond with "Hi!" and a hand wave, when she was addressed by other people in the area, as well as by her mother who called for her at the end of the sessions. It had been hoped that the "ee" sound would begin to have meaning connected with the act of eating (evolving from the sound "ee" to "eat"·. This did not occur by Session 40—at which time, due to unfortunate circumstances, the sessions had to be discontinued.

Now, some 8 months later, circumstances have improved and Dolly is once more beginning her work with us. It is hoped that some maturational development has occurred in the interim which will facilitate the teaching of new and meaningful communicative and social skills. Already, Dolly has regained what she had previously learned—which signifies to us a breakthrough in her attainment of some minimal behavior necessary for an enriched life.

*Acknowledgements*—The authors wish to express their gratitude to Drs. FRANK HEWETT and NORMAN TIBER, and to Mr. FRANK LANGDON and Mr. KENNETH FINEMAN for their co-operation, and for the use of special equipment. In addition, we are grateful to the Division of Child Psychiatry of the Neuropsychiatric Institute, and the Psychological Research and Service Center at the University of Southern California for the facilities used in this study.

## REFERENCES

BLAKE P. R., TIBER N., KOGUS M. and MAHON M. (1966) The effects of single and multiple experimenter conditions on the acquisition and generalization of operantly conditioned verbal responses in autistic children. Unpublished paper.

Cook C. and Adams H. E. (1966) Modification of verbal behavior in speech deficient children. *Behav. Res. & Therapy* 4, 265–271.

Ferster C. B. (1964) Psychotherapy by machine communication in disorders of communication. *Res. Publs Ass. Res. nerv. ment. Dis.* 12, 317–333.

Ferster C. B. and DeMyer M. K. (1961) The development of performance in autistic children in an automatically controlled environment. *J. chron. Dis.* 13, 312–345.

Fineman K. (1966) Developing sounds and word approximations in a deaf mute through systematic visual stimulation. Unpublished paper.

Hart B. M., Buell J. S., Harris F. R. and Wolf M. M. (1964) Effects of social reinforcement on operant crying. *J. E. Child Psychol.* 1, 145–153.

Hewett F. M. (1965) Teaching speech in an autistic child through operant conditioning. *Am. J. Orthopsychiat.* 35, 927–936.

Jenson G. D. and Womack M. G. (1967) Operant conditioning techniques applied in the treatment of an autistic child. *Am. J. Orthopsychiat.* 1, 30–34.

Kerr N., Meyerson L. and Michael J. (1965) A procedure for shaping vocalizations in a mute child. In *Case Studies in Behavior Modification.* (Eds. Ullman L. P. and Krasner L), pp. 366–370. Holt, Rinehart and Winston, New York.

Lovaas O. I., Berberich J. P., Perloff B. F. and Schaeffer B. (1966) Acquisition of imitative speech in schizophrenic children. *Science* 151, 705–707.

Metz J. R. (1965) Conditioning generalized imitation in autistic children. *J. E. Child Psychol.* 4, 389–399.

Sidman M. (1961) *The Tactics of Scientific Research.* Basic Books, New York.

Straughan J. H., Potter W. K. and Hamilton S. M. (1965) The behavioral treatment of an elective mute. *J. Child Psychol. Psychiat.* 6, 125–130.

Williams C. D. (1959) The elimination of tantrum behavior by extinction procedures. *J. abnorm. soc. Psychol.* 59, 269.

Wolf M. M., Risley T. R. and Mees H. I. (1964) Application of operant conditioning procedures to the behavior problems of an autistic child. *Behav. Res. & Therapy* 1, 305–312.

# Psychotic Children and Behavior Modification

BY DON W. CHURCHILL, M.D.

*The author describes the techniques of an operant conditioning treatment program for psychotic children that has both curative and palliative objectives. He outlines several major implications of the work for the understanding of these children. Of particular interest was the surprisingly limited response capability of some of the children, even when motivation was high.*

THE PURPOSE OF this paper is twofold: first, it describes some specialized techniques currently in use for treating psychotic children; second, it deals with some implications for our understanding of these children, derived from the application of these techniques.

Fifteen children (11 boys and four girls) between the ages of three and seven were diagnosed by the Clinical Research Center as either autistic or early childhood schizophrenic, according to the DeMyer classification(8). They are all characterized by severe and irregular developmental lags manifest within the first two years of life.

They have little or no language for communication and are either socially withdrawn or relate to others in very irregular ways. Their self-care skills are minimal. Their adaptation to their environment, including such things as play with toys or appropriate use of other objects, is almost nonexistent except where it may be characterized by perseverative or obsessive preoccupation with one object or class of objects, often in bizarre or idiosyncratic ways. They are noted for inconsistency of response and the difficulty with which they are controlled. As one father, near the end of his rope, put it: "There is not much that I can count on Teddy to do. And even worse, there is nothing—absolutely nothing—I can count on for sure that Teddy will *not* do."

The treatment techniques described here are limited almost exclusively to the application of principles derived from operant conditioning. However, our concern has been somewhat different from that which has traditionally occupied operant conditioners. While experimentalists have concentrated on the environmental contingencies that strengthen or weaken a given response, we have been especially preoccupied with the conditions under which new responses are acquired in the first place and with in-depth sampling of the kinds of responses that can be shaped at all—hence, a kind of limit testing.

This is a condensed version of a paper read at the 124th annual meeting of the American Psychiatric Association, Boston, Mass., May 13-17, 1968.

Dr. Churchill is associate professor, department of psychiatry, Indiana University Medical Center, and assistant director, Clinical Research Center for Early Childhood Schizophrenia, LaRue D. Carter Memorial Hospital, 1315 W. Tenth St., Indianapolis, Ind. 46202.

This work is being supported in part by Public Health Service grant MH-05154 from the National Institute of Mental Health and in part by Carter Memorial Hospital, State of Indiana.

AMERICAN JOURNAL OF PSYCHIATRY, 1969, Vol. 125 NO. 11, pp. 1585-1590.

In using this approach we have assumed the attitude that any new therapy, to be preserved, must meet at least one criterion or—we hope—two. First, it must yield results at least as good as traditional methods. Second, it should increase our knowledge of the persons we are treating and the disorders we are studying. A new treatment, so long as it does not fail the first criterion, can claim its rightful place if it can demonstrate superiority on the second criterion alone.

Operant conditioning was first utilized in the study and treatment of autistic children by Ferster and DeMyer(1), using an automated enivronment. This work has been continued by Hingtgen and others(3, 4). In the last several years a number of other workers have also reported in detail the basic technique and demonstrable results of modifying behavior of psychotic children through operant conditioning(2, 5, 6, 7). Like others, we have moved away from the automated environment and are using so-called hand-shaping techniques, which are well described in the literature. Essentially what we are trying to do is to establish a basic repertoire of very simple but, for these children, new behaviors. Upon this basic repertoire we try to build increasingly complex chains of behavior and to induce these behaviors under increasingly more "natural" environmental conditions.

## Objectives of Treatment Program

Our experience in trying to help psychotic children has been one of minor victories and major defeats. We thus conceive of second-order as well as first-order objectives—in a sense hedging our bet. First, we still aspire to cure each child, assuming that each has the potential to proceed to normal and independent development if he can be helped over certain hurdles. At present we tend to view cure for these children less in terms of helping them make affective contact with the world or in resolving fundamental emotional or interpersonal conflicts, and more in terms of helping them overcome specific learning disabilities that interfere with their acquisition of a variety of precision skills.

As a second-order objective we try to ensure that, if we cannot cure, all is not lost. If the child cannot be helped in any very important sense at least we ought to make him as easy as possible to live with; this should minimize the morbidity within the family that harbors him. For this second portion of our program we begin by delineating very specific target behaviors, judged by the parents and by our staff as being: a) most desirable and b) least desirable. We rank each in hierarchical fashion according to its importance along several parameters, e.g., how it appears to foster or interfere with the child's development; how pleasant or unpleasant it makes the child to live with, and so forth. To a large degree the subsequent success in strengthening desirable behaviors and reducing, modifying, or eliminating undesirable behaviors hinges on the specificity or narrowness with which we define the target behaviors, e.g., throwing food at the table, screaming when approached, and so forth. We then note carefully the events antecedent and consequent to these behaviors and make a very specific prescription as to what the new consequences of each behavior shall be. It is then possible to determine whether the behavioral prescription has had the predicted effect.

## Specific Techniques

The particular method we have used with ten children begins with isolating the child in a small, bare room. (The five others were treated with some form of operant conditioning but were not treated with isolation.) He stays there 24 hours a day, seven days a week, usually for three weeks. During this period he has no contact with anybody except two or three adults who are working with him in shifts totaling approximately six hours throughout the day. The room has a potty chair and at night there is a mattress on the floor. Otherwise there is nothing except the materials used in individual sessions with the child.

By careful attention to the child's physical condition, weight, intake, and output we can safely arrange that all food and drink is obtained, bite by bite and sip by sip, at appropriate times from those adults who are

106

working with him. These primary reinforcers are paired with affectionate words, gestures, and physical contact, as described by Lovaas(5), in an attempt to establish such conventional social responses as conditioned reinforcers of desirable behavior. We have not found it necessary to use any dramatic punishment in order to train children in this way. However, the fact that we make the children sit facing us and do not let them escape by running away, ritualizing, turning their heads, or having a tantrum—and if necessary we use physical restraint—may readily be construed as a form of aversive stimulus.

The new behaviors that are shaped have also been described in detail elsewhere(3). To begin with, we emphasize training in three general areas: general body imitation, use of objects, and imitative vocalization. Body imitation consists of such simple things as touching the nose, clapping hands, and putting hands up over the head after the adult has done these things. It is usually necessary at first to actually put the child through the motion, and then the prompt can be gradually faded out until the child responds upon seeing the adult do it. Eventually quite intricate adult models are imitated. When the child can imitate new models on first presentation he is considered to have established an imitative set.

In the use of objects a similar stepwise procedure is used; it is possible in a relatively short time to shape such behaviors as cutting on a line with scissors, building with blocks, loading and shooting a dart gun at targets, and writing on the blackboard. The latter skill begins with copying horizontal and vertical lines, then circles and crosses, and eventually letters.

In shaping imitative vocal responses it may be necessary at first to simply reinforce any spontaneous vocalization, then to differentially reinforce open- or closed-mouth sounds, and finally to shape sounds in imitation of the adult. While it may be necessary at first to position the child's mouth or to use sounds that have clear visual components on the adult's face, it is eventually possible for the child to imitate virtually any sound simply upon auditory cue alone.

The amount of progress made during the initial three weeks of relative isolation varies from child to child. But by the end of this time, regardless of progress in the selected tasks the children invariably appear to be attentive, cooperative, and highly motivated to perform. The child then resumes living on the ward, where training sessions are continued under more natural circumstances. His parents are brought in—first to observe, next to participate under supervision, and finally to work with the child at home on weekends with a prescribed program and reporting procedure.

When the child is ready, either before or after leaving isolation, his very rudimentary skills (particularly those having direct relevance to communication) are expanded as follows: Letters are built into printed words which are then attached to objects, and phonemes are built into vocalized words which are also attached to objects. We work to get associations across as many different modalities as possible, i.e., visual-vocal, visual-visual, auditory-visual, auditory-vocal, etc., and also to achieve as much generalization as possible. It is in this particular area that we become aware of the relative ease or difficulty with which the child can acquire new behavior.

Outside of these individual precision skill training sessions we employ operant techniques to develop self-care skills, game play, independent work, and social interaction.

## Results and Discussion

### Second-Order Objectives

To take the second-order objectives first (i.e., the palliative effort), two things may be said concerning our results. It is almost always possible to effect some specific change in certain isolated behaviors of psychotic children which, while they may seem insignificant in terms of the over-all clinical problem, nevertheless may be viewed as of substantial benefit to the family and may facilitate the child's finding a more comfortable and accepted place within the family. The children can be taught to dress and feed themselves and usually to take care of their own toileting. At the table they can not only learn not to throw food but can even attain a level of decorum that is acceptable in public places. Thus a family may be permitted to eat in restaurants again, something that they may not have done in years.

Families find that it is neither necessary nor desirable to be tyrannized by all of the child's idiosyncracies. The children can be taught to perform simple and useful acts such as helping with the dishes, emptying trash, and helping set the table. These are things which can be measured in terms of newly acquired behavior and the reduction or elimination of undesirable behavior.

More difficult to measure but of great importance is an apparent change in parental attitude toward a psychotic child handled in this way. Finding that they have both the ability and the right to control certain aspects of the child's behavior, finding that their own range of pleasures is extended with a better controlled child, and having a carefully defined training program in which they themselves participate and can see the child making small but definite steps—all these things tend to counteract the familiar vicious cycle of parental hostility, rejection, and guilt and help to provide a new and unexpected acceptance for the child at home.

## First-Order Objectives

As for the first-order objectives, efforts to train psychotic children in precision skills have led to several unexpected observations that have interesting implications for our concepts of psychotic children.

The child, after passing through the initial negativism and uncooperativeness, the tantrums and rituals, and after he has become hungry enough and appears to know that food is given contingent upon his responses, enters into a phase in which he is very highly motivated. His attention is riveted on the adult; the interfering behaviors drop away completely. Response latencies are extremely short and, indeed, if the adult is not quick enough the child tries to prompt him to present the next cue.

By now the child has been trained to give several different responses upon presentation of an adult model for that response— say, clapping hands and holding hands high over the head. If presented randomly with simply these two models to "imitate," the child may never achieve more than a chance number of successes. That is, with every indication of the highest possible motivation the child may attentively watch the adult clap hands and then put his own hands over his head! He then looks for his reward and displays evidence of great frustration that it is not forthcoming. Similar examples could be presented in great number but the point is this: There is a situation of extremely high motivation and of astonishingly poor performance—astonishing, that is, in terms of our previous expectations.

While judgments about what a child *cannot* do versus what he *will not* do have logical and heuristic shortcomings, such judgments are nevertheless implicit in much of our thinking about and planning for psychotic children. Within this context the described procedures distinguish rather sharply between what these children cannot do and what they will not do. Our experience suggests that these children are often given credit for many response capabilities that they simply do not have and that it is erroneous to argue that the bizarre, negativistic, and idiosyncratic behaviors represent some willful holding back of hidden potential.

It appears more likely that these children do not perform appropriately because they cannot, or because the environmental variables, unless very specially arranged, are insufficient to support their performance.

We have a second set of observations concerning the behaviors that are usually taken to represent the quintessence of such children's "craziness." Sometime during or after the initial three-week period, when a child has had enough experience working with an adult at designated tasks and at being regularly reinforced for successful performance of very low-level tasks, he begins to appear less and less psychotic. He is no longer withdrawn, the rituals are gone, and he can no longer be described as negativistic. The child is attentive to the task. One even imagines that he is enjoying it a bit, and there may be some spontaneous display of affection or of other interest in the adult. At this point the child is working at tasks previously mastered and is doing well.

If the level of difficulty is raised or changed in some way so that the child begins failing, a number of interesting things ensue. The rituals return, the child's attention wanders, and he begins to act in a teasing or negativistic way. Response latencies become very long, and indeed it might be said that the child has withdrawn altogether from "reality." It is almost as if the signs of psychosis can be turned on and off during the hour simply by varying the success/failure ratio. One wonders to what degree the bizarre and autistic features manifested by psychotic children are really secondary phenomena—the results of unrelieved frustration and inevitable failure in an incomprehensible world.

A third set of observations comes from our experience that while it seems possible to take any psychotic child and within a relatively short time teach him a variety of low-level skills, when it comes to building these skills into more complex behaviors we regularly encounter what appears to be a hard and fast block to further learning. This occurs at different places in different children, but some of our failures may be especially illuminating. We encounter what we call a cross-modal defect.

What we see is this: We are working with a child on a blackboard, writing letters. We print either *A*, or *O*, or *E*. The child by now readily prints these letters after us—in fact, he will copy intricate designs in detail. Also confining ourselves to three long vowels we say *ā*, or *ō*, or *ē* and the child repeats each sound after us. He can also repeat any other sounds that we make for him. In short, he is a very good imitator of sounds that he hears and a very good copier of lines that he sees.

What we try to do next is to get him to write *A* on the blackboard after we do and then to spontaneously say *ā* when he sees that. Now he may say *ā* but he may just as likely say *ō* or *ē*. On the other side we say to him, *ā*, and point to the blackboard. He may then write *A* but he is just as likely to write *O* or *E*. This chance performance continues after thousands and thousands of trials, even though the child's motivation may be very dramatic. He can write what he sees. He can say what he hears. But he cannot say what he sees, and he cannot write what he

hears. When this is observed, neither persistence nor ingenuity has produced association of information across these two sensory modalities.

Finally, this intrusive and coercive approach, which focuses on the acquisition of selected behaviors and the learning of certain precision skills, preempts our concern for making affective contact or establishing a relationship with the child. Yet in our experience these things do occur, although no special effort has been made initially to develop a positive attachment and much of the early adult-child interaction might be considered detrimental to it. But the child does not become more mechanical or robot-like; he generally becomes more affectionate and attached to the adults working with him.

Indeed, it is common for visitors, including those who are well acquainted with autistic children, to remark that the children do not seem autistic. Perhaps these attachments to adults develop simply as a function of a certain duration of forced interaction. However, it is also possible that some minimum behavioral repertoire must be learned before a relationship with an adult is possible.

## Summary

A program applying operant conditioning techniques to the treatment of psychotic children has been described. The problem is seen in terms of modifying specific behaviors and teaching certain precision skills. Four implications of these studies are considered: 1) the surprisingly limited response capability, even when motivation is high; 2) the traditional behavioral signs of psychosis as a function of success/failure ratio in a given milieu; 3) the appearance of specific learning defects, most notably a "cross-modal defect," which may put an absolute ceiling on ability to respond to certain stimulus combinations; and 4) the appearance of positive attachments to adults, possibly dependent on some minimum learned behavioral repertoire.

### REFERENCES

1. Ferster, C. B., and DeMyer, M.: The Development of Performances in Autistic Children in an Automatically Controlled Environment,

J. Chron. Dis. 13:312-345, 1961.

2. Hewett, F. M.: Teaching Speech to an Autistic Child Through Operant Conditioning, Amer. J. Orthopsychiat. 35:927-936, 1965.

3. Hingtgen, J. N., Coulter, S. K., and Churchill, D. W.: Intensive Reinforcement of Imitative Behavior in Mute Autistic Children, Arch. Gen. Psychiat. 17:36-43, 1967.

4. Hingtgen, J. N., Sanders, B. J., and DeMyer, M. K.: "Shaping Cooperative Responses in Early Childhood Schizophrenics," in Ullman, L., and Krasner, L., eds.: Case Studies in Behavior Modification. New York: Holt, Rinehart & Winston, 1965.

5. Lovaas, O. I., Berberich, J. P., Perloff, B. F., and Schaeffer, B.: Acquisition of Imitative Speech by Schizophrenic Children, Science 151:705-707, 1966.

6. Metz, J. R.: Conditioning Generalized Imitation in Autistic Children, J. Exp. Child Psychol. 2:389-399, 1965.

7. Risley, T., and Wolf, M.: Establishing Functional Speech in Echolalic Children, Behav. Res. Ther. 5:73-88, 1967.

8. White, P. T., DeMyer, W., and DeMyer, M. K.: EEG Abnormalities in Early Childhood Schizophrenia: A Double-Blind Study of Psychiatrically Disturbed and Normal Children During Promazine Sedation, Amer. J. Psychiat. 120:950-958, 1964.

# COMPLIANCE AND RESISTANCE IN THE CONDITIONING OF AUTISTIC CHILDREN: AN EXPLORATORY STUDY

PHILIP A. COWAN

University of California, Berkeley

B. A. HODDINOTT and BARBARA ANNE WRIGHT

Thistletown Hospital

*Twelve autistic children between 4 and 9 years of age were asked to choose red objects and square objects from a stimulus array. Ten Ss made correct choices significantly less often than chance, that is, they avoided emitting correct responses.*

*Ss were given 60 conditioning trials in which choices of either red or square objects were reinforced. Those who attained either concept subsequently performed perfectly when asked to produce both red and square concepts; the other Ss continued giving fewer-than-chance correct responses. Thus, conditioning trials elicited in some Ss an increased tendency to comply with the experimenter's instructions. The results suggest that more attention should be paid to the distinction between responses that autistic children are unable to make and responses that they are unwilling to make.*

Two primary symptoms of early infantile autism are "extreme self isolation" and "obsessive insistence on sameness" (Kanner, 1957). These symptoms imply, in part, that the autistic child fails to respond to environmental stimuli usually considered reinforcing and that he modifies his response patterns very slowly when conditions of reinforcement are changed. Failure to respond and resistance to change have usually been interpreted in four ways: (1) lack of capacity—usually some underlying biological malfunction is posited in order to explain inadequate performance (see Bender, 1956);

The data were collected while the senior author was employed at Thistletown Hospital, Rexdale, Ontario, and some of the results were presented at the 1963 annual meeting of the Canadian Psychological Association. Cowan's address: Department of Psychology, University of California, Berkeley 94720.

CHILD DEVELOPMENT, 1965, Vol. 36, pp. 913-923.

111

(2) lack of experience—a change in patterns of stimuli and reinforcement is necessary and sufficient for the development of acceptable levels of behavior (see Ferster, 1961); (3) lack of general motivation or drive, that is, indifference or apathy; (4) resistance or negativism—motivation *not* to do what is requested. At times autistic children may be able to respond appropriately, may be aware of the requirements of the stimulus situation, but may stubbornly resist complying with the instructions given by E, therapist, or parent (Ekstein, Bryant, & Friedman, 1958).

In the operant conditioning experiments by Ferster and DeMyer (1961; 1962) several children whom they described as autistic slowly learned to make a number of discriminative responses to sophisticated elaborations of operant conditioning apparatus. There have been other successful attempts to condition an autistic child (Davison, 1964; Wolf, Risley, & Mees, 1964) and to condition a schizophrenic child who has autistic symptoms (Lovaas, Freitag, Gold, & Kassorla, 1965). These studies show that various combinations of social and primary reinforcement can elicit and maintain prosocial behavior. This fact does not rule out the possibility that autistic children are biologically deficient, because malfunctioning organisms may still be able to learn. In addition, it is not possible to determine in these experiments whether nonperforming subjects lacked reinforced training with the stimuli, whether they lacked drive, or whether they were being negativistic. The results, then, show that autistic children can learn, but they learn slowly. It has not been possible to decide whether their slow learning results from a deficit in capacity, experience, motivation, or from resistance to the demands of the situation.

This question, of course, cannot be entirely resolved by one experiment. The present two-part study represents only a preliminary approach. As no objective evidence has confirmed or disconfirmed the repeated clinical description of autistic children as negativistic, Part I focuses on the problem of identifying children who are unwilling rather than unable to emit correct responses.

A method is used that yields an objective criterion for differentiation between those children who cannot and those children who *will* not demonstrate that they can use simple color and form concepts in response to E's requests. In Part II of this study, operant conditioning is explored as one method of overcoming the resistance of those children who will not comply.


PART I

*Method*

*Subjects.*—Thistletown Hospital is a residential treatment, teaching, and research center for emotionally disturbed children. Two years prior to the present study, one small ward containing 12 beds was set aside for observation of schizophrenic and autistic children. They lived in the ward for periods of 3 months. Of the 42 children seen in this way, 12 were selected for further hospitalization in connection with a two-year experimental-treatment project. Every effort was made to see that these children formed a homogeneous group conforming to Kanner's description (1957) of early infantile autism.

All the children came from intact families (either natural or adoptive). The educational and occupational level of the parents was much higher than that typically seen in the hospital, but the parents were not all at the high level that Rimland (1964) suggests is usual in the families of autistic children. At the time of the experiment, the children, ranging in age from 4-6 to 9-3, had been living in the hospital for 7 months. Their disturbed behavior had been evident before the age of 2 but was not linked with known organic damage. They spent little time voluntarily engaged in interpersonal contact. They engaged in many repetitive movements and failed to react adaptively to much, but not all, stimulation; this was especially true when the stimulation was of a social nature. All the children had severe speech and communication difficulties. At the time of this study three had no speech at all, seven used isolated words, and only two spoke in sentences. The language of these latter two children was bizarre, and the level of language development was markedly retarded.

From the observations of the ward staff there was much clinical evidence that none of the children was mentally defective, but the psychometric evidence was equivocal. On the Leiter International Performance Scale (Leiter, 1948), the only intelligence test that could be given in its entirety to these Ss, five obtained IQ's above 90, four obtained IQ's between 35 and 71, and three Ss could not respond consistently enough for an IQ to be measured.

In general, few predictable verbal or nonverbal responses were elicited by verbal or gestural requests or commands. The staff was never certain whether the children could not understand the request or whether they were stubbornly refusing to comply.

*Apparatus and procedure.*—All Ss were tested individually in a classroom just off the ward. It was a quiet room, relatively free of distracting visual displays. The tester (B.A.W.) was an interne who had previously spent a short time on the ward over a period of 4 weeks. There was no indication that any of the children had formed either a positive or negative relationship with her.

In the simple discrimination or concept-formation task used in the present experiment, each child selected objects of the color or shape verbally requested by E. S then dropped the objects into a box. Before beginning the experiment proper, it was necessary to establish the topographical features of the desired response. Seven skeins of colored wool were chosen from the Gelb-Goldstein Color Sorting Test (Goldstein & Scheerer, 1941). The skeins were placed in a random array in front of S, who was seated at a table

113

opposite *E*. Experimenter demonstrated the procedure three times; she dropped a gray skein into the box and gave herself a piece of popcorn, saying, "I put one here and I get popcorn." Popcorn was chosen as a reinforcer simply because many of the children appeared to like it. It may not, of course, have been reinforcing for all the children.

After the third demonstration, the gray skein was withheld, and *S* was instructed, "Now *you* put one in the box." When *S* complied, he received a piece of popcorn, and *E* said, "Johnny gets popcorn." The responses were often difficult to elicit. Sometimes *S* had to be chased, caught, put back in the chair, and given the instructions again. After *S*'s first response, the demonstration skein was replaced in the array, and the skein that *S* had placed in the box was withheld, out of sight, for one trial. The withholding procedure, repeated on each trial, prevented *Ss* from perseverative responding with the same skein. Popcorn was given for 10 placements of a skein in the box regardless of *S*'s choice of color. It was found that there was no tendency for any child to choose skeins of any particular hue.

On the following day the 12 tiles of the Weigl-Goldstein-Scheerer Color Form Sorting Test (Goldstein & Scheerer, 1941) were placed on a table in front of *S* in random order. This "test" consists of small tiles in three different shapes—circles, squares, and triangles. Each shape is duplicated in each of four colors—red, blue, yellow, and green. Experimenter pointed to the array of tiles and asked *S* to "put a square one in the box." Regardless of the correctness of *S*'s response he was given popcorn. The tile that he had placed in the box was then withheld by *E*, leaving *S* 11 tiles in a different random array from which to choose on the next trial. Again, *S* was asked to "put a square one in the box." This procedure, including the withholding for one trial of the last tile placed in the box, was repeated for 25 trials and constituted the pretest for the use of the concept square (the "Square Pretest"). In order to keep *S* interested in the task, every response was rewarded regardless of its correctness. The same procedure was repeated for an additional 25 trials, except that this time *S* was asked to "put a red one in the box" (the "Red Pretest"). Thus, *S* was given two sets of 25 trials in order to assess his ability to respond to *E*'s instructions with appropriate choices of color or form.

The multiple-choice procedure employed in Part I makes possible the gathering of evidence concerning negativism. In the Square Pretest, *Ss* choose among 12 tiles that include four squares. Subjects can make approximately eight correct choices in 25 trials even if they are guessing. In the Red Pretest, 3 of the 12 tiles are correct; *Ss* who are guessing can make approximately 6 correct choices out of 25 by chance. The "chance" figures are approximate because of rounding. They are also approximate because, after the first trial, the last tile chosen is withheld. *S* continues to choose among 11 tiles. If the withheld tile is classified as a correct response, 2 of the remaining 11 tiles (18 per cent) are red. If the last response is incorrect, 3 of the remaining 11 tiles (27 per cent) are red. Given Ss' propensity to respond incorrectly consistently, 25 per cent is actually a slightly conservative underestimate of the proportion of responses likely to be correct by chance.

Children who choose red and square objects on demand significantly more often than chance demonstrate functional use of color and form concepts. Children who respond at chance levels probably do not understand the concept, or they are indifferent; however, a negativistic child who emits a correct response at sporadic intervals may also appear to exhibit a random pattern of responding.

There is one additional outcome directly relevant to the diagnosis of negativism. It is possible for the child to choose the correct color or form significantly *less* often than chance. Significantly few correct responses can occur in two ways:

1. The child can make wrong responses *systematically* with respect to color or form dimensions (e.g., always choosing green instead of red objects). Systematic errors may reflect negativistic resistance, or color blindness, or misinformation concerning the connection between a particular verbal sign (red) and its referent. However ambiguous these alternatives may be, it is obvious that a child making systematic errors is able to discriminate between color (or brightness) and form attributes. A child who responds with 25 circles when asked 25 times to produce a square has failed the task, but he can obviously discriminate between circles and squares.

2. The child may make significantly few correct responses and have errors that are unsystematic. If 3 of 12 objects are red, the child should choose red 25 per cent of the time even if he were blindfolded. If he *never* chooses a red object and he also does not choose any other color systematically, he must know what "red" means. The only possible way the child can choose colors and shapes "randomly" without *ever* making a correct choice is consistently to avoid complying with E's instructions.

Counterbalancing of requested colors or shapes and order of presentation of tasks would have been desirable, but the number of available Ss was too small. The decision was made to ask for red as the color concept and for square as the form concept. Pretests were presented in the same order for all Ss—first square, then red.

*Results and Discussion*

The data for both parts of the experiment are shown in Table 1. Two Ss, the only two in the sample who used language, obtained a perfect score of 25 in the Square Pretest. All other Ss made fewer than chance (8) correct responses; 1 S had 3 correct, 1 S had 1 correct, and 8 Ss made *no* correct responses in 25 trials. The two Ss with perfect scores in the Square Pretest also obtained perfect scores in the Red Pretest. The remaining 10 Ss made fewer than the 6 correct choices in the Red Pretest, which would be ex-

## TABLE 1

### NUMBER OF CORRECT PRETEST, CONDITIONING, AND POSTTEST CHOICES IN BLOCKS OF FIVE TRIALS: DATA FROM EACH SUBJECT FOR PARTS I AND II

| S | Age | Language | IQ | Square Pretest ($p = .33$) | Σ | Red Pretest ($p = .25$) | Σ | Conditioning | Σ | Square Posttest | Σ | Red Posttest | Σ |
|---|-----|----------|----|-----------------------------|---|--------------------------|---|--------------|---|-----------------|---|--------------|---|
| A | 7–1 | No | 133 | 0 1 1 0 1 | 3 | 2 3 0 0 0 | 5 | 5 0 1 4 5 5 5 5 5 5 5 5 | 50 | 5 5 5 5 5 | 25 | 5 5 5 5 5 | 25 |
| B | 9–1 | No | 58 | 0 0 0 0 0 | 0 | 0 1 0 0 0 | 1 | 1 1 0 2 0 1 3 2 4 5 | 30 | 5 5 5 5 5 | 25 | 5 5 5 5 5 | 25 |
| C | 5–9 | No | … | 0 0 0 0 0 | 0 | 1 1 0 1 0 | 3 | 0 2 0 1 1 1 0 3 0 1 | 9 | 1 0 0 0 1 | 2 | 3 0 0 0 0 | 3 |
| D | 5–9 | No | … | 0 0 0 0 0 | 0 | 0 0 0 0 0 | 0 | 0 0 0 1 0 0 0 1 2 0 | 5 | 0 0 1 0 0 | 1 | 1 1 0 1 0 | 3 |
| E | 6–7 | No | 35 | 0 0 0 0 0 | 0 | 0 0 1 0 0 | 1 | 0 0 0 0 2 0 1 0 0 1 | 5 | 0 0 0 1 0 | 1 | 1 1 0 0 0 | 2 |
| | | | | | | | | _Conditioning Red_ | | | | | |
| F | 4–6 | No | 145 | 0 0 0 0 0 | 0 | 4 0 0 0 0 | 4 | 4 5 5 5 5 4 5 5 5 5 5 5 | 58 | 5 5 5 5 5 | 25 | 5 5 5 5 5 | 25 |
| G | 5–2 | No | 93 | 0 0 1 0 0 | 1 | 1 1 0 0 0 | 1 | 1 1 1 5 5 5 5 5 5 5 5 5 | 48 | 5 5 5 5 5 | 25 | 5 5 5 5 5 | 25 |
| H | 6–7 | No | 71 | 0 0 0 0 0 | 0 | 1 0 0 1 0 | 2 | 0 1 0 1 0 0 0 0 0 1 1 0 | 4 | 1 1 0 1 0 | 3 | 0 0 0 1 0 | 1 |
| I | 5–11 | No | … | 0 0 0 0 0 | 0 | 0 1 0 1 0 | 2 | 4 1 1 0 0 1 2 0 3 0 0 1 | 13 | 0 1 0 1 0 | 2 | 0 1 0 1 0 | 2 |
| J | 5–10 | No | 54 | 0 0 0 0 0 | 0 | 0 1 0 0 0 | 1 | 0 0 0 0 1 0 0 0 0 0 0 0 | 1 | 0 0 0 0 0 | 0 | 0 0 0 0 0 | 0 |
| K | 9–3 | Yes | 117 | 5 5 5 5 5 | 25 | 5 5 5 5 5 | 25 | . . . . | . . | . . . . | . . | . . . . | . . |
| L | 8–6 | Yes | 122 | 5 5 5 5 5 | 25 | 5 5 5 5 5 | 25 | . . . . | . . | . . . . | . . | . . . . | . . |

pected on the basis of random guessing. One S had 5 correct, 1 S had 4 correct, 1 had 3 correct, and 7 Ss had 2 or fewer correct in 25 trials. Group data showed a decline in number of correct choices in each succeeding block of 5 trials. In the last 15 trials 10 Ss were responding at a level significantly below chance in both the Red Pretest and the Square Pretest.

There was one ambiguity in the meaning of an incorrect response. At times, four Ss refused to select just one tile from the array; they threw a handful into the box instead. The four Ss gave a mean of 20 out of 25 "handful" responses in the Square Pretest and a mean of 16 handful responses in the Red Pretest. Their remaining single-object responses were correct less often than chance. It appears that these four Ss may have been resisting the demands of the situation so much that they were not even willing to produce a topographically correct response. This interpretation is supported by some data from Part II. During the conditioning trials when *only* correct responses were rewarded, three of the four Ss stopped giving handful responses, and the other S reduced his proportion of handful responses from 80 per cent to 38 per cent. However, the four Ss still made fewer-than-chance correct choices.

None of the Ss made systematic errors; the wrong answers were randomly chosen (e.g., yellow and blue tiles were chosen in random order when red was asked for). This rules out the possibility that the children merely assumed that red or square referred to another color or shape. There is no basis for thinking that the children tried to comply but, for some reason, could not do so. They picked a large number of single tiles without choosing the particular one requested. When asked for red they did choose squares, that is, they did not avoid a particular shape *unless this shape had been requested by* E. No hypotheses concerning loose thought associations or other perceptual or conceptual distortions of color and form can possibly explain the low number of correct choices given by most children. This is especially true when the wrong answers follow no discernible pattern. The children *knew* the correct responses; they were able to emit them but did not do so on demand. This is negativism by definition. Negativism, rather than indifference, lack of capacity, or lack of experience, is the only possible way of accounting for the failure of the 10 Ss to give correct responses.

In one sense this part of the experiment served only to demonstrate empirically what is clinically "obvious" and accepted—that autistic children tend to be negativistic. But all previous estimates of negativism in the literature confound judgments concerning negativism with judgments concerning ability. For example, staff ratings of high negativism are usually based on the fact that the child could recently perform some act but does not do so in the present. While this may represent negativism, it is also compatible with the possibility that the physical-organic state of the organism may change from day to day. The child may not be *able* to do today what he did yesterday with ease. The present multiple-choice method allows O, given certain outcomes, to label negativism at a given point in time where the state of the organism is relatively unchanging.

This part of the experiment had initially been planned as an attempt to teach, by operant conditioning, concepts that were not in the repertoires of some of the autistic children. In Part I it was shown that all the autistic children were perfectly capable of making color and form discriminations. Therefore, the conditioning trials described below were instituted to encourage concept utilization or emission rather than concept attainment. The central question was if the negativism could be overcome when the incentive conditions were changed.

## Method

*Subjects.*—On the third day of the experiment the 10 Ss from Part I who gave significantly few correct responses were divided randomly into two groups of equal size.

*Apparatus and procedure.*—The Weigl-Goldstein-Scheerer tiles used in the pretests were placed before each individual S. Subjects in Group R were rewarded only for responding correctly to the instruction to "put a red one in the box." The one difference between the pretest and the conditioning procedure was that *only* correct choices were rewarded with popcorn in the conditioning trials. Sixty trials were given individually to each of the five Ss. If these Ss did not give five consecutive correct responses during these trials, they were given another 60 trials.

Exactly the same procedure was followed for five Group S Ss who were asked to "put a square one in the box." In the conditioning trials Ss were trained in only one concept—red or square. Two days after the conditioning trials, both Square and Red Posttests were administered to all Ss using the procedures for the pretests described in Part I.

## Results and Discussion

By the end of 60 conditioning trials, two of the five Ss in Group R and two of the five Ss in Group S had given correct responses for at least the last 10 consecutive trials (see Table 1). None of the other six Ss, three in Group R and three in Group S, gave more than one correct response in the last 10 trials. These six Ss failed to improve with an additional 60 conditioning trials and virtually always gave fewer-than-chance correct responses in each block of 10 trials. Again, it is evident that all the Ss understood the concepts but that only some Ss complied with requests for specific color or form choices, even when rewards were given *only* for correct responses.

The results from the Red and Square Posttests shed some light upon the way in which conditioning affected Ss' responses. The 2 Ss in Group R who performed correctly in the last 10 "red" conditioning trials now performed perfectly in the 25-trial Red Posttest, but they also performed perfectly in the Square Posttest for which no conditioning trials had been given. The 2 Ss in Group S, who performed perfectly in the last 10 "square" conditioning trials now performed perfectly both in the 25-trial Square Posttest and in the Red Posttest. The other 6 Ss still made fewer correct choices in both posttests than would have been expected had they been guessing. The inference can again be made that these Ss were resisting E's instructions. The particular reinforcement offered in the present experiment was sufficient to overcome the negativistic behavior of 4 of 10 Ss. The other 6 Ss, it has been demonstrated, were still negativistic children who could discriminate, but would not. The question of whether other or larger rewards would have been more effective in motivating compliance was not explored in the present study.

Differential reinforcement of correct and incorrect responses in this experiment does not affect responses to a particular class of stimuli (red or square). It seems to affect the willingness of some Ss to comply with instructions which they understood before the experiment began. The effects of primary reinforcement in this study cannot be assessed fully unless additional control groups are added in order to separate the effects of social reinforcement and primary reinforcement (e.g., a control group given contact with E, but no conditioning between test and retest). This lack of control groups does not affect the interpretation of the prevalence of negativism found in some children in both stages of this study.

The six children who complied with instructions initially or after conditioning (the compliers) showed similarities to and differences from the six children who rarely made correct choices (the resisters). There was no difference in their understanding of the color and form concepts demanded in the present experiment. Also, the groups did not differ in age. The two best (compliant) performers were the children with the highest level of language development, but there was no evidence of gradation in language ability which would separate the six resisters from the remaining four compliers.

We have additional data which suggest that the difference between the compliers and the resisters is not a finding isolated from other aspects of these children's behavior. For example, the groups differ dramatically in IQ scores. Five of the six compliers had an IQ greater than 90 as measured by the Leiter International Performance Scale (Leiter, 1948). Three of the six resisters had an IQ below 75, and three did not respond consistently enough for an IQ to be measured. It will be noted that the three resisters who did respond were making some of the color and form discriminations necessary to produce correct answers on the Leiter IQ test.

It would be circular to explain the better performance of the compliers on the basis of higher intelligence. It would also be circular to explain the low IQ performance of the resisters in terms of negativism; however, the children *were* negativistic on the Weigl-Goldstein-Scheerer tests, and it may be reasonable to investigate further the general hypothesis that inadequate IQ-test performance of many autistic children may be attributable to motivational factors. The results of Part II of this study suggest that contingent reward may help to raise the scores of some autistic children. Further approaches in this direction might ultimately help to clarify the differential diagnosis between mental deficiency and autism, on the assumption that operant conditioning would not substantially raise the score of a "truly defective child." This approach still leaves unanswered the problems of diagnosing those autistic children who do not respond to contingent reward.

Results obtained from two additional unpublished studies conducted with these children indicate that the compliers show other pervasive differences from the resisters. The first study was undertaken 2 weeks after the present one. Subjects were given blue and yellow circles and triangles from the Weigl-Goldstein-Scheerer Color Form Sorting Test. Each of the 12 children was asked to "give me a dax" and to "give me a mib" for 25 trials, that is, the requests were stated with nonsense syllables. All six compliers spontaneously chose a concept—either form or color—and made at least 15 consecutive systematic responses. The six resisters all responded randomly with respect to color or form.

The second study, conducted by H. Day, involved an attempt to condition cooperative behavior; it took place 7 months after the present one. In a pretest, seven random pairs of compliers and seven pairs of resisters were placed consecutively in a room where the floor was marked off in 2-foot squares. On the average, in a 5-minute period the compliers spent four times as much time together in the same square as did the resisters. Because of high variability this difference was only significant at the 10 per cent level. With such a small number of pairs, after a 6-month period, we believe that these results indicate a relatively stable difference between compliant and resistant autistic children.

### Conclusions

We do not know what variables determined compliance or resistance in the multiple-choice perceptual motor task. It is possible that more patience or more careful choosing of primary reinforcement would have induced more resistant children to comply. It is possible that resistance is a general trait present in all phases of the autistic child's behavior, with some children being more resistant to environmental demands than others. These possibilities are being examined in a new study.

We do know that in this experiment some autistic children were aware of environmental demands but stubbornly resisted compliance. This has been a frequent clinical observation (Szurek, 1956), but objective evidence has not been available. We also know that some children seem to give up this negativism fairly easily when their negativistic responses are no longer rewarded.

The children who complied initially and those who relinquished negativism easily showed a number of differences from the resisters. They had higher IQ's, they organized color and form concepts more spontaneously, and they spent more time with each other in an experimental room. These differences are not necessarily explained by the concept of negativism alone. However, the multiple-choice method of measuring resistance and the application of conditioning procedures (which may measure the strength of resistance) seem to identify behavior which is part of a large network of relationships among variables. If the conclusions of this experiment stand the test of further replication and generalization, this resistance phenomenon, the method of measuring it, and an operant conditioning method of dealing with it may have important implications both for psychometric testing and for treatment of autistic children.

## REFERENCES

Bender, L. Schizophrenia in childhood: its recognition, description and treatment. *Amer. J. Orthopsychiat.*, 1956, **26**, 499–506.

Davison, G. C. A social learning therapy programme with an autistic child. *Behav. Res. Ther.*, 1964, **2**, 149–159.

Ekstein, R., Bryant, K., & Friedman, S. Childhood schizophrenia and allied conditions. In L. Bellak (Ed.), *Schizophrenia*. New York: Logos Pr., 1958.

Ferster, C. B. Positive reinforcement and behavior deficits of autistic children. *Child Developm.*, 1961, **32**, 437–456.

Ferster, C. B., & DeMyer, M. The development of performances in autistic children in an automatically controlled environment. *J. chron. Dis.*, 1961, **13**, 312–345.

Ferster, C. B., & DeMyer, M. A method for the experimental analysis of the behavior of autistic children. *Amer. J. Orthopsychiat.*, 1962, **32**, 89–98.

Goldstein, K., & Scheerer, M. Abstract and concrete behavior: an experimental study with special tests. *Psychol. Monogr.*, 1941, **53**, No. 2 (Whole No. 239).

Kanner, L. *Child psychiatry.* (3rd ed.) Springfield, Ill. Charles C Thomas, 1957.

Leiter, R. C. *The Leiter international performance scale.* Chicago: C. H. Stoelting, 1948.

Lovaas, O. I., Freitag, G., Gold, V. J., & Kassorla, I. C. Experimental studies in childhood schizophrenia: analysis of self destructive behavior. *J. exp. child Psychol.*, 1965, **2**, 67–84.

Rimland, B. *Infantile autism: the syndrome and its implications for a neural theory of behavior.* New York: Appleton-Century-Crofts, 1964.

Szurek, S. A. Psychiatric episodes and psychiatric maldevelopment. *Amer. J. Orthopsychiat.*, 1956, **26**, 519–543.

Wolf, M., Risley, T., & Mees, H. Application of operant conditioning procedures to the behavior problems of an autistic child. *Behav. Res. Ther.*, 1964, **1**, 305–312.

# BEHAVIOR MODIFICATION AND THE PSYCHOSES OF CHILDHOOD:

## A REVIEW [1]

ROBERT LEFF [2]

*University of Pennsylvania*

Over the course of the last 15 years, various types of behavior modification, that is, modification procedures which are directed primarily at the behavioral symptoms of a psychological disorder, have been effectively used in a wide variety of applications. Grossberg (1964) reviewed the large body of literature that has rapidly accumulated in this general field. More recently, an increasing number of investigators have been devoting their attention to experimental inquiries into the efficacy of behavior modification with the most severe of the childhood disorders—the childhood psychoses, including early infantile autism. Virtually all of the methods employed in this work to date are direct derivatives of the operant-learning procedures which have been established in the comparative laboratories.

The primary behavior disorders of childhood which characterize the subjects of the research discussed in this review have been

[1] This review is based upon a paper submitted to the faculty of the Graduate School of the University of Pennsylvania in partial fulfillment of requirements for the PhD degree. The author expresses his gratitude to Justin Aronfreed, James Geer, Harvey Winston, and Julius Wishner for their helpful critical comments. This work was done during the author's tenure as a United States Public Health Service Predoctoral Fellow and was supported by National Institute of Mental Health Grant No. 5 TI MH-8209.

[2] Now at Children's Treatment Center, 3418 Harper Road, Madison, Wisconsin 53704.

labeled variously childhood schizophrenia, early infantile autism, and symbiotic autism. According to Bender (1953), childhood schizophrenia is a disorder of the entire organization and maturation of behavior processes. Manifest in such primary disturbances of function is a "global instability and poor integration of the control and direction of behavior at all levels [p. 415]." Also typical of these cases are pan-anxiety and secondary disturbances in the basic perception of the self as an object in the psychological world, including perturbations in body image, identity, and orientation to the objects and forces of the external world. On the more specific level of symptomatology, the schizophrenic child is often subject to somatic complaints, shows abnormal EEG activity, and indulges in bizarre regressive behavior, repetitive motor actions, and tantrums. Also noted are speech and thinking disturbances.

Early infantile autism is a diagnostic entity, first described by Kanner (1943) and eventually recognized by him and his co-worker (Eisenberg, 1957, p. 79) as "the earliest possible manifestation of childhood schizophrenia." The criteria that Kanner proposed for diagnosis of this "disturbance of affective contact" with other persons are: (*a*) definite early onset, before the age of 2; (*b*) demonstration of at least selected age-appropriate intellectual abilities; (*c*) early preference for extreme

PSYCHOLOGICAL BULLETIN, 1968, Vol. 69, No. 6, pp. 396–409

"self-isolation" or "aloneness"; and (d) obsessive insistence on the preservation of "sameness" in the environment. In addition, there are several subordinate, distinguishing features of this childhood disorder, reviewed by Rimland (1964), among which are (a) the low incidence of psychotic progenitors and the lack of clinically detectable hallucinations or delusions in autistic versus schizophrenic children, (b) the very frequent fetishlike preoccupation with mechanical objects, and (c) the extremely high and peculiar incidence of extraordinary spatial memory and musical ability.

Rimland (1964), on the basis of these and other factors enumerated in his book, maintains that autism deserves the status of a separate and unique diagnostic category. He deplores the practice of misnaming true autism "childhood schizophrenia," and the more frequent indiscriminate use of the autism diagnosis to include cases which do not meet Kanner's (1943) original criteria. To some extent, Kanner, himself, may have become responsible for the trend toward a diluted concept of autism when, in 1956, he isolated as the pathognomonic, primary symptoms of autism only the extreme self-isolation and the obsessive insistence on the preservation of sameness (Eisenberg & Kanner, 1956). Compounding the effects of Kanner's implied reduction of the stringency of criteria for autism is the observation that there apparently is a great deal of overlap in symptomatology between the early autistic and childhood-schizophrenic syndromes. Finally, it appears possible that several of the studies reported here may have confused the diagnoses somewhat, while others have employed mixed samples of autistic and schizophrenic children. All the children dealt with here, however, are quite clearly severely disturbed (psychotic), and all seem to respond similarly, on the whole, to the treatments applied. Thus, at least within the present context, that is, that of the effects of behavior-modification techniques with the primary disorders of childhood, differential diagnosis will not be considered a crucial issue.

Instead, major emphasis will be given to the problem of the efficacy of the behavior-modification procedures discussed. Traditional psychodynamic methods of therapy, in all their diversity, have failed to demonstrate any reasonable degree of efficacy with psychotic children. In 1956, Eisenberg reported a follow-up study of 63 autistic children, and, in 1957, after a thoughtful review of the literature on childhood schizophrenia, he concluded that there was little or no reason to believe that any of the techniques employed to that date, including classical psychotherapy and electrical and chemical shock, had been shown to have beneficial effects on the patients treated. On the other hand, the rapidly growing body of literature reporting positive results of behavior-modification methods attests to the potential power of this "new" therapy. Many investigators have reported successful therapeutic manipulation of the behavior of hospitalized psychotic adults (e.g., Ayllon & Haughton, 1962; Ayllon & Michael, 1959; King, Armitage, & Tilton, 1960; Sherman, 1965). In addition, the deviant behavior patterns of normal, neurotic, and retarded children have been shown to be readily amenable to the control of various operant-training procedures (Baer, 1962; Bijou, 1957; Harris, Wolf, & Baer, 1964; Lazarus, Davison, & Polefka, 1965; Wolf, 1965).

No such application of the established principles of operant learning to the specific problems of the autistic or schizophrenic child appeared in the literature until 1961. The appearance in that year of two papers (Ferster, 1961; Ferster & DeMyer, 1961a) gave major impetus to subsequent research in this field. In these publications, Ferster presented his thesis that autism, like any other behavioral phenomenon, is best understood and treated within the framework of a social-learning theory. The autistic child is not seen as qualitatively different from the normal one; rather, he is distinguished from the normal organism only by the relative frequency of occurrence of all the performances in his repertoire. Thus, for example, the autistic child engages in a great deal less behavior which influences his social environment, and a great deal more behavior intended to influence only the physical environment than does the normal child.

Though Ferster regards lack of positive

reinforcement (especially parental attention) as the fundamental agent in the production of many autistic deficits, he also recognizes that a consistent program of active restriction of a child's behavior may produce the severely limited behavioral repertory that is characteristic of the autistic child. Illustrative of this type of etiology is Ferster's (1965a) recent description of a mother who appeared, on casual observation, to be continuously involved in normal interaction with her child. Closer observation, however, indicated that the mother's only true interactive behavior with her son was comprised of restrictions of the boy's attempted manipulations of his environment. Thus, Ferster (Ferster & DeMyer, 1961a) stated that:

all of the basic processes by which new performances are generated, strengthened, maintained, eliminated, punished, suppressed, or controlled by special aspects of the environment are relevant to an analysis of how a particular history could produce a weak, positively maintained repertoire [p. 344].

The next logical step in the consideration of an appropriate behavior-modification program, therefore, consists of an arrangement of reinforcement contingencies so as to establish conditioned and then generalized reinforcers, many of which are social in nature. Most investigators would agree that the primary goal of this modification, whether it be predominantly accomplished through the use of positive reinforcement or avoidance-learning techniques, is to render other human beings "meaningful in the sense of becoming rewarding to the child [Lovaas, Schaeffer, Benson, & Simmons, 1965, p. 108]."

The focus of this paper will be upon operant training, since it has been employed far more extensively with psychotic children than the desensitization or "deconditioning" techniques that are more closely associated with the principles of Pavlovian or classical conditioning. The term "operant training" refers to a diversity of procedures that have been derived directly from principles of behavior that were established in the basic operant-research laboratory. Both appetitive and aversive paradigms are used. In the former type of procedure, reinforcement contingencies are arranged in order to produce

new behavior (shaping) or to modify existing behavior via, for example, the method of successive approximations.

Aversion therapy is another class of treatments, one component of which is passive-avoidance training. This method incorporates the traditional concept of punishment, where noxious stimulation regularly follows undesired behavior. Positive-reinforcement withdrawal or deprivation will be subsumed under this category of passive-avoidance techniques, consistent with the view of withdrawal of positively reinforcing stimuli as one form of aversive contingency. Active-avoidance learning, on the other hand, involves situations in which the attenuation or elimination of aversive stimuli is made contingent upon desired, adaptive responses.

In the studies conducted thus far with psychotic children, positive reinforcement and/or avoidance techniques are the methods upon which the behavior modifiers have relied most heavily. Typically, modification goals have been relatively circumscribed and clearly specified. Since most of the work is recent, there has been little opportunity for adequate long-range follow-up reports. This precludes the possibility of fruitful analyses of extended therapeutic efficacy in terms of percentages of patients who met a long-term criterion of improvement. But such longitudinal outcome criteria would not be appropriate for many of the studies reviewed because they were not addressed to the issue of long-duration change. Furthermore, group-statistic criteria are not necessary for a rigorous demonstration of the potency of operant-training methods.

The operant approach leads, instead, to a research design in which evaluation of results is accomplished by means of successive experimentation with the same organism. The subject thus becomes his own control in a program that has carefully specified target behaviors and modification goals. Typically, the subject's "base-rate" behavior, recorded prior to the application of the modification procedure, is compared with behavior measures taken after the introduction of experimental manipulations. An evaluation of outcome may subsequently be achieved by temporary discontinuance of the modification procedure (i.e., return to base-rate conditions), followed by reinstatement of the procedure.[3] Systematic variation of behavior in accordance with the changing experimental conditions provides conclusive evidence of efficacy.

Since much of the work reviewed has been reported in preliminary and case studies, complete demonstrations of experimental control such as that outlined above were not often incorporated. The outcomes, then, of a good deal of this work must be evaluated with respect to the degree to which the results reflect dramatic changes in behavior that appear to be reasonably permanent and to contribute substantially to the adaptation of the children so treated. The studies are grouped according to the type of basic procedure used —positive reinforcement, active avoidance, or passive avoidance.

## OPERANT-TRAINING TECHNIQUES

### Positive Reinforcement

It should be recognized, of course, that the great majority of experiments reported in this review incorporate *some* positive-reinforcement contingencies in their procedures, but the studies grouped here are distinguished by their sole reliance upon positive reinforcement. Ferster and DeMyer (1961a) showed that the response patterns emitted by two schizophrenic children who were exposed to fixed-ratio (FR) and variable-interval (VI) schedules under nonverbal reinforcement approximated the characteristic functions obtained with animals and normal humans under such schedules. In addition, a conditioned, or "generalized" reinforcer (coin) was established. The children failed to learn on a multiple schedule (FR-VI) and had great difficulty in a relatively simple transfer-of-training task, where learned discriminative control could not be maintained upon introduction of a new, slightly different apparatus. Nevertheless, both subjects exhibited more experimentally controlled behavior and less tantrum activity with increasing exposure to the automatic environment.

[3] An alternative design recently presented by Browning (1967) also uses a self-control procedure, but avoids some of the practical drawbacks of the above-described method when it is applied in the setting of a residential treatment center.

In 1962, Ferster and DeMyer further demonstrated the practicability of controlling key-press behavior in two autistic children through nonverbal intermittent-reinforcement schedules. The children, who eventually performed discriminative acts quite well for intermittent food reward, nevertheless exhibited very restricted behavioral repertoires, in that their operant activity was largely uninfluenced by a wide variety of available stimuli which are reinforcers for normal children. Both these demonstration experiments were informative because they showed that conventional learning technology is adequate for the experimental analysis of this previously refractory disorder.

Metz (1965) obtained "generalized imitation" in two schizophrenic children using conditioned verbal and nonverbal reinforcers ("good" and tokens) in a gradual shaping procedure which began with the experimenter passively "putting the subject through" the action he was to imitate later and rewarding him with food and verbal praise ("good") after each passive demonstration. The experimenter's guidance was progressively withdrawn ("fading" technique) until eventually only an occasional verbal reinforcement was necessary to maintain imitative performances. The problems encountered in this program involved slow learning rates and strong tendencies toward "superstitious" responding, based on inadvertently administered rewards during training. In addition, occasional "regressive" behaviors occurred, that is, responses previously appropriate were emitted in subsequent situations where they were inappropriate. More than balancing the effects of these setbacks, however, were Metz' (1965) observations that: (a) many imitative responses "persisted and increased, in a context of reward for imitation, *without specifically being rewarded* [p. 397, italics added]"; (b) the frequency of inappropriate, ritualistic, and emotional behavior (tantrums) decreased as appropriate activity increased; and (c) these withdrawn, autistic children eventually "expressed joy or delight upon 'solving' a problem . . . sought the model out whenever he appeared on the ward . . . etc. [p. 398]."

Two comments are in order here: First,

this investigator enjoyed a greater degree of control over the motivational states of the subjects than is usually possible, since the subjects were deprived of their breakfast daily, and their lunch consisted solely of the reinforcements earned in the experiment. The second point, this one made by the author, limits the interpretation of the results somewhat since no control subjects or procedures were run, and, in light of the diverse extra-experimental experiences undergone daily by these institutionalized children, no strong inference can be made that the increased generalized imitative performance was the specific result of the operant-training procedures.

In an interesting experiment by DeMyer and Ferster (1962) that was conducted on the ward, rather than in a laboratory, new social behaviors were taught to eight schizophrenic children (aged 2–10) by the regular hospital staff of nurses and attendants, who had received explanatory lectures on the basics of operant learning. Each worker spent a great deal of time with the child according to regular hospital routine, but, in addition, each of these "experimenters" had the task of discovering those particular adult behaviors which were especially reinforcing to each of the children involved. Such reinforcers ranged from verbal praise and reassurance to holding the child, playing music, and dancing. When the worker to whom the child seemed most responsive was found, he began the shaping program that constituted the "therapy" of this study. The authors, in conjunction with each worker, decided what sort of behavior was to be shaped with each child, and the worker spent $\frac{1}{2}$ hour a day, three or four times a week, engaged in these activities.

This individually tailored program clearly represents a departure from the less personal and more formally organized tactics employed in other behavior-modification studies and comes closer to the love-oriented techniques of psychoanalytic therapies. Since most of the workers relied heavily on bodily contacts, such as holding and rocking the children, the therapy was more practicable with the younger children, and, indeed, the children under 6 showed the greatest positive effects. Results were reported in terms of individual improvements for each child, with the general conclusion that "there were classes of behavior which definitely seemed to improve as a result of this therapy and other, more general behavior changes, not directly attributable to the specific procedures employed [DeMyer & Ferster, 1962, p. 460]." The authors did not fail to mention the inherent difficulty of evaluating these results due to the subjects' numerous uncontrolled contacts with other institutional personnel during the course of the study. But it is noteworthy that untrained, nonprofessional workers probably did accomplish some important behavioral changes in the appropriate direction.

That the strategy of employing inexperienced nonprofessionals in operant-training programs for severely disturbed children can be successful has been further demonstrated in a study by Davison (1965). Here, four college undergraduates were given 1 month of classroom training in the basic concepts of social reinforcement and operant learning. The undergraduate "therapists," working in teams of two, then applied their newly learned techniques to modifying the behaviors of two autistic children. They returned daily reports to the author-supervisor, and he in turn made suggestions and changes during the course of the program. Working conditions in the day-care center at which this experiment was performed were far from ideal. The psychotic children were exposed to the student therapist for less than 15% of their waking hours for a total of only 4 weeks. Also, as a result of unanticipated situational problems with the children, the author was prevented from carrying out his postmeasure of behavioral change as originally planned. Since the pre- and postmeasurements were quite dissimilar, the only firm conclusion that was warranted was that "the therapists *probably* were able to control the child better after the treatment [Davison, 1965, p. 148]." (The more successful team achieved an average increase of about 40% in the number of commands obeyed.) Of course, the failure in experimental rigor involving measures and the limitations imposed by uncontrolled institutional settings limit interpretation of these results. But one highly significant implication of this work is that intelligent, highly motivated students may be trained in a very short time to execute a behavior-control program that requires the application of learning principles to the manipulation of psychotic behavior in children.

Perhaps most universally characteristic of children who are labeled schizophrenic is their withdrawal from interpersonal relationships. It has become a classically noted feature of childhood schizophrenia that very little physical contact occurs between afflicted children. Yet, Hingtgen, Sanders, and DeMyer (1965) observed that their six schizophrenic subjects did eventually engage in such behavior, despite the fact that reinforcement was never made directly contingent upon social contacts. The children were seen experimentally for one session per day, 5 days a week. They were first taught to press a lever to obtain coins on a fixed-ratio (FR) schedule of reinforcement. Then the six subjects were paired into three teams, the members being taught, through nonverbal shaping procedures, to emit cooperative responses, that is, they were eventually required to alternate their bar presses in order to obtain rewards, one subject's response allowing the other subject to obtain reinforcement. The results indicated that it was possible to shape these alternative cooperative responses in early childhood schizophrenics within an average of 23 sessions. (However, it must be noted that each of the subjects here had received several months of preexperimental operant training.) This cooperative behavior is clearly attributable to the training program employed.

However, as mentioned above, it was also noted that other, more general behavior changes occurred as the experiment progressed. The increase in physical contact activity between the children was one of the most striking of these changes. Children who typically behaved as if they were unaware of the presence of other humans were now seen to direct a good deal of their attention and their activity toward another child, within the confines of an experimental setting. As the experimenters have noted, their subjects were exposed, during the remainder of each experimental day, to play therapy, psychotherapy, occupational therapy, music therapy, and so forth. Yet it seems likely that the observed increase in forms of social interaction

which were not directly reinforced was also primarily due to the experimental manipulations, since the behavior referred to increased in the experimental room, but not on the ward.

If it is accepted that the experimental manipulations incidentally established certain situation-specific social interactions, then a critical evaluation of this result becomes necessary. Such an evaluation will be facilitated by a closer examination of the types of interpersonal behavior which occurred. While some of the contact actions involved one subject's guiding the hand of the other to the lever, there were other "cooperative" interactions of a less passive nature, in which one subject would slap or otherwise attack the other in order to rouse him to action. It is obvious that behavior such as this may be called "cooperative" only within the context of this experiment, that is, a subject who forces his teammate to act in order to render his own actions effective in securing reinforcement is not cooperating or "operating jointly with another" in the usual sense of that definition. Rather, he is coercing another solely in order to further his own ends—in this case, the acquisition of material rewards.

The above analysis is not meant to imply that the so-called cooperative behavior is of no potential value in an operant-learning approach to a therapeutic training program for psychotic children. Though the physical prompting of a teammate cannot be classified as true cooperative behavior, it does entail reality testing and the tacit recognition of other human beings as significant mediators of desired ends. Action taken with reference to the instrumental value of others is indicative of an adaptiveness that is characteristically absent in the autistic or schizophrenic behavioral repertoire. Thus, the elicitation here of such adaptiveness through the use of reinforcement-contingency techniques suggests that these operant-training methods may constitute a fruitful approach to the problems of the primary behavior disorders of childhood.

Indeed, a follow-up study by Hingtgen and Trost (1964) provides added support for this inference. In an attempt to induce more general behavioral changes, the authors made provision for the direct reinforcement of vocal and physical interactions between four young nonverbal schizophrenic children. After an average of 46 sessions, the two pairs of children (who had all had approximately 1 year of previous experience in operant-learning procedures) exhibited a low but stable rate of interactive behavior. This level of contact action was significantly greater than that measured in a series of preexperimental toy-play observations in which the subjects participated. Moreover, in line with the authors' expectations, physical contact and vocal behavior were observed to increase in the ward setting, as well as in the home.

Further evidence for the power of operant-training methods is provided by the work of Hewett (1964, 1965). This author has been able to engineer and maintain a consistently enforced training program with his hospitalized subject population. In the course of 1 year of daily individual training, a 13-year-old autistic boy who had not developed useful speech was taught a 55-word sight vocabulary (Hewett, 1964). This was accomplished by using gumdrop reinforcers for correct matching of visually presented words with corresponding pictures. Eventually, picture cues became unnecessary, and the child could select any word card on the verbal command of the teacher. Finally, the subject was taught the alphabet and was required to write out any requests that he wished to make of the hospital personnel.

In connection with the author's long-term goal—the socialization of this psychotic child—there were other behavior modifications which accompanied those described above. The author described the subject's growing interest in his education and his increasing conformity to his teacher's instructions, even under conditions of decreasing reinforcement. The child showed enjoyment of his work by emitting laughter and other vocalizations. He also frequently initiated new learning tasks by bringing the teacher pictures whose symbolic designation he was eager to master. Finally, the subject gave definite indications that the teacher had acquired secondary reinforcement value for him. The child began to look directly at the teacher's face, rather than only at his hand (the immediate reinforcement-delivery mechanism), and drew simple sketches which symbolized events of great importance in his life.

All of these changes, and especially the latter ones which represent the definite attempts of a previously intractable autistic child to communicate with his adult teacher, are behavior modifications which were not directly reinforced in this child's educational program. In the absence of even rudimentary control procedures, it would be unwarranted to attribute these changes solely to the operant-reinforcement program per se. The author, for instance, did not describe the extraexperimental daily activities engaged in by the subject. Nor did he characterize in any detail the nature of the teacher's behavior toward the child, that is, it cannot be ascertained from this report whether the relationship between the teacher and child was warm and solicitous or mechanically impersonal. These variables could conceivably play an important role in the behavior-modification program. Such deficiencies in descriptive information notwithstanding, it seems likely that the dramatic general improvements shown by this child were largely the outgrowth of the experimental manipulations. In strong support of this statement is the fact that the subject had remained virtually inaccessible to all previous socialization attempts during the first 13 years of his life. Only when reinforcement became reliably contingent, through human mediation, upon certain goal-directed behaviors did the child acquire rudimentary communication skills. And it would seem that in large measure the acquisition of these skills facilitated the further socialization of this autistic boy.

Several other papers which describe therapeutic programs for psychotic children are of direct relevance here. Though the practitioners involved are psychodynamically oriented, they have explicitly incorporated basic tenets of reinforcement theory in their therapies. Weiland and Rudnik (1961), for example, made an 8-year-old autistic boy's receipt of his favorite toy contingent upon his verbalization of the word "ball," thus widening the child's vocabulary until he was eventually singing songs. The authors stated:

In the ideal therapeutic program, the total environment of the child should be organized to allow all of his gratifications to be offered by some single person who could erect such barriers as to make it impossible for the child to achieve these gratifications by himself (autistically). . . . Gratification without asking for the assistance of his specific worker(s) would not be permitted, while withdrawal would be obstructed by the persistent efforts of the worker. The child would be offered certain activities or objects which were known to be of high desirability to him. These would be given, however, only if the youngster specifically asked the worker for them [p. 560].

Thus would these workers establish the secondary or generalized reinforcing power of other human beings for the schizophrenic child.

Dubnoff (1965), who successfully treated a child who had been diagnosed as "early infantile autistic" by Kanner, similarly mentioned that such a child in her therapeutic program "is expected to verbalize his demands before they are gratified. . . . Only appropriate behavior is gratified [p. 386]." This kind of therapy seems a long conceptual way from the all-accepting, permissive, and indiscriminately rewarding type of treatment advocated by some psychoanalysts (e.g., Bettelheim, 1952, 1965). However, despite this apparent gulf that seems to exist between behavior-modification approaches to therapy and the more traditional psychodynamic model, it seems probable that the most successful therapeutic strategy will evolve from a close collaboration between the two.

An example of such a collaboration is provided in two recent papers by Ferster (1965a, 1965b) who described a program in which he cooperated with the clinical director of a treatment center for autistic children. Ferster stated that in the course of their work together, he was continuously impressed by the underlying similarity of their two superficially disparate approaches. In describing his previous investigations of the phenomena of operant learning, Ferster (1965a) stated that his "customary approach to an experiment is essentially clinical." That is, procedures in his animal and human experiments "are carefully designed to meet the repertoire of each individual subject; there is a day-by-day interaction with the experiment in which each procedure derives from the results of

previous procedures [p. 14]." Conversely, emphasized Ferster, careful observation of the clinical director's therapeutic activity revealed that:

many of her procedures consisted of direct and forceful manipulation of the milieu directly contingent upon the child's behavior [1965b, p. 3]. She places limits on the child's behavior, gives or withholds food, attention and automobile rides and toys [1965a, p. 14].

It is in practices such as these that many therapists, either wittingly or unwittingly, often make effective use of the basic principles of operant learning. The evidence suggests that therapeutic potency is a direct function of the degree to which these principles are *systematically* applied.

*Positive Reinforcement and Passive-Avoidance Learning*

Lovaas, Freitag, Gold, and Kassorla (1965) performed a series of well-controlled experiments, the results of which supported many of the implications about children's psychotic behavior derived from the findings of earlier studies. In their first study, Lovaas and his co-workers increased the "appropriate music behavior" and simultaneously decreased the seriously self-destructive behavior of a 9-year-old schizophrenic girl. In acquisition periods, music was played and social reinforcements (smile and "good") were delivered only following appropriate behaviors, such as clapping in rhythm. Significantly, control or extinction periods were also run, during which music was again played, but no social rewards were forthcoming. Appropriate changes in the subject's behavior from acquisition to extinction periods revealed that the behaviors in question had come under experimental control.

A second study, this time using a bar-press response, confirmed the finding of the first study, that is, frequency of self-destructive behavior is a function of the presentation and withdrawal of reinforcement for other behaviors in the same situation. The third study reported in this article demonstrated the tremendous importance of the parental or adult "attention" variable. The authors showed that delivery of sympathetic comments ("I don't think you're bad") contingent upon the occurrence of self-destructive behavior *increased* the frequency and magnitude of such undesirable behavior over levels of performance obtained in base-line control sessions, which were interspersed among experimental sessions. Furthermore, a reduction in tantrum and destructive behaviors was observed in sessions in which the experimenter was nurturant and attentive to the subject *except* when the subject indulged in tantrum or destructive behavior, at which times he was ignored. Such results make it difficult to escape the authors' conclusion that the types of self-destructive acts they examined are best understood "as learned, operant, or instrumental behavior [Lovaas, Freitag, Gold, & Kassorla, 1965, p. 79]."

Wolf, Risley, and Mees (1964) described their rather dramatic therapeutic intervention into a case which had proven intractable to conventional therapies. They used shaping procedures with a food-deprived hospitalized schizophrenic boy of $3\frac{1}{2}$, who was characterized by severe self-destructive behavior and refusal to wear eyeglasses (which were necessary to save his sight) and to sleep at night. Using bits of food as reinforcement and isolation from all social contacts as punishment (analogous to time out from positive reinforcement), these therapists were highly successful in decreasing the child's tantrums and increasing his eyeglass wearing to an acceptable level. When the child began to throw the glasses, isolation, made contingent upon such throwing, effectively reduced this unwanted behavior. Subsequent eating-habit problems were similarly eliminated. The child (who had complex but noncommunicative verbal habits at the outset) was trained to imitatively name pictures and use pronouns correctly in social speech. Verbal stimuli such as "no" came to suppress undesirable nonverbal behavior, probably as a result of frequent pairing with the experience of being sent into isolation. Perhaps most impressive is the authors' account of the mother's report, 6 months after the child's return home: "Dicky continues to wear his glasses, does not have tantrums, has no sleeping problems, is becoming increasingly verbal, and is a new source of joy to the members of his family [Wolf et al., 1964, p. 312]."

Risley and Wolf (1964) used shaping procedures based on ice-cream-bite rewards and incorporated prompting and fading procedures in a program of therapy with a 6-year-old autistic child. They succeeded in enlarging the child's verbal repertoire from echolalic speech to appropriate picture naming and eventually to appropriate answers to questions such as, "What's your name?" and "Where are you going?" Unique in this study was the follow-up procedure conducted with the child's parents. The mother, who had observed several laboratory sessions, was instructed and supervised in the basic operant techniques so that she could continue the therapy at home. Though she manifested an early tendency to urge and prompt the child too frequently, she soon came to understand the necessity for strict adherence to a schedule of contingent rewards and in this manner was able to make remarkable progress with the boy. Praise became an effective reinforcer, though not quite as effective as food was in motivating learning. Tantrum screaming, formerly a serious problem, was reduced greatly by sending the child to his room whenever he engaged in such "atavistic" behavior. Chanting, repetitious verbalizations were converted, through gradual shaping and imitative learning, into meaningful sentences. The authors concluded on an optimistic note, stating that seven other sets of parents are effectively working with their disturbed children in this way.

A talkative (but uncommunicative) schizophrenic child who met criteria of (*a*) being in no individual therapy, (*b*) having no known physiological damage, (*c*) receiving no medication, and (*d*) accepting a candy when offered to her was chosen by Davison (1964) as the subject in an experiment which used previously inexperienced undergraduates as behavior modifiers. The students received training similar to that described in Davison (1965). They saw the psychotic child in the uncontrolled environment of a day-care center where they occupied only 8 of the child's 25 weekly institutional hours. According to the author, "the crux of this therapy was to utilize play situations for the differential reinforcement and extinction of various behaviors [p. 150]." The extinction referred to, as in other studies, was a sort of time-out procedure, in which the positively reinforcing therapists withdrew a certain distance from the subject if the subject misbehaved. The results of the short "therapy" indicated that both therapists had achieved a markedly greater degree of control over the subject than they had had at the outset in terms of the number of commands issued to the child that were obeyed.

But, in addition, and somewhat to the author's surprise, the child also obeyed an equally high percentage of the standard commands given by both a nonprofessional worker who spent a great deal of time with the child and a college student never before seen by the child. The author tentatively concluded that the child had become, as a result of the behavior therapy, more responsive to adults in general. Other positive features of the results were the incidental apparent desensitization of several phobic fears, and the fact that adults seemed to have acquired the status of generalized reinforcers to whom the child was attracted. Finally, the "extinction" procedures evidently eliminated at least two deviant behaviors—kicking and pouring sand on others. It is tempting to conclude that the behavior-modification program was responsible for all these changes, but there was obviously insufficient control of the child's activities to warrant any strong conclusions of this nature.

Ferster and DeMyer (1961b) described the salutary effects of prochlorperizine administered to an autistic child who was required to perform a matching-to-sample discrimination task. Correct matches enabled the child to get a wide variety of reinforcers; incorrect matches were followed by short time outs from positive reinforcement. Analysis of results indicated that matching to sample was significantly better under drug than under placebo conditions. However, since the authors' only statement about the effects of the drug was that it "increased the amount of his behavior," it is difficult to tell whether the improved matching performance was due specifically to the drug's psychological effects or whether it was merely a function of the child's hyperactivity. If it were the former, such a drug might prove to be an important educational aid in behavior-therapy programs for psychotic children.

## Positive Reinforcement and Active-Avoidance Learning

Hewett (1965) reported that he was able to teach a mute autistic child 32 words over a 6-month period using a paradigm that combined both reinforcement and active-avoidance procedures. The 4-year-old subject, sitting in a special teaching booth, was exposed to a variety of reinforcing stimuli when he responded correctly, but was subjected to isolation in the darkened booth if he failed to respond correctly on cue. In preliminary training, the child was required to perform a series of imitative acts, such as touching appropriate facial features. Subsequently, an undifferentiated vowel sound that was frequently uttered by the child was used as the basis for the verbal learning program. The method of shaping, using successive approximations and the fading technique that was previously described in connection with Metz' (1965) paper, was employed. Ward personnel and the child's parents observed many of these procedures and continued to require the newly learned words from the child, reinforcing him only at appropriate times. Though the subject's acquired speech did not approach normal language, Hewett (1965, p. 935) was justified in stating that the child "generalized an experimentally acquired vocabulary to the larger environment and uses it to verbally express his needs (e.g., 'I want toilet.')." The successful training given to this child is particularly impressive in view of the extremely poor prognosis that is typical for the psychotic child who fails to develop language by the age of 4 or 5.

The last study reviewed here was conducted by Lovaas, Shaeffer, Benson, and Simmons (1965). Schizophrenic twins were given escape-avoidance training in a room with an electrified-grid floor. The children were first physically guided, then more and more required to initiate the approach response when they heard the experimenter's command, "Come here!" At first they responded in order to escape painful shock, but they soon learned that a low-latency response (less than 5 seconds) would enable them to avoid shock.

In addition, the children were shocked whenever they began to emit tantrum behavior. These procedures resulted in a long-lasting response tendency to the "come here" command (9–10 months passed before extinction began to occur) and good suppression of the tantrums. Pairing the word "no" with shock gave it the status of a conditioned suppressor, demonstrated by its reduction of the frequency of a child's bar press for positive reinforcement.

In a second part of this study, the subjects received further shock-avoidance training with a portable subject-mounted shock apparatus. The children, who were required to hug and kiss the experimenter, showed increased affectionlike behavior as a result of training. Nurses who rated the subjects immediately after the avoidance sessions, but who were unaware of the purpose of the experiment, described the children as more dependent upon adults, more responsive and affection seeking, and more anxious and fearsome. They saw the children as less happy and content, but emitting less pathological behavior. It is well known that professional raters of such general classes of behavior as those preceding often have difficulty in agreeing upon what they observe. Relatedly, it was also explicitly pointed out by Harris et al. (1964) that teachers, nurses, and attendants who are direct participants in shaping procedures often produce completely fallacious estimates of behavior change resulting from such procedures (as checked against objective records). Admittedly the nurses in the present study were not involved in the therapy procedures nor, say the authors, did they know about them. Yet it would seem appropriate to use caution in accepting such nonprofessional, nonitemized behavior ratings.

The last experiment reported by Lovaas, Shaeffer, Benson, and Simmons (1965) in this article described children's learning to press a bar for candy and the sight of the experimenter's face. Accompanying this was shock-escape training in which the subjects had to go to the experimenter. Eventually, the subjects pressed the bar for the sight of the experimenter alone, without showing any generalized increase in activity resulting from the shock sessions. Here again, one has the nurses' informal observation of a perhaps generalized tendency resulting from this training. The children, who previously showed only immobility when hurt, now sought out other human beings when hurt in a variety of extraexperimental situations.

## DISCUSSION

The results of these studies indicate that behavior-modification techniques may be extremely useful tools in the education and rehabilitation of psychotic children. None of the investigators whose work was reviewed here would claim that they have cured their subjects. But many can justifiably state that they have equipped their subjects with several of the basic skills and habits necessary for the most rudimentary of adjustments to their social environment. Furthermore, behavior "therapists," guided by social-learning models which are more parsimonious than traditional psychodynamic theories, have been able to effectively control, and in several cases eliminate, much of the undesirable and maladaptive behavior of these children. Results such as these, achieved with types of patients that had formerly proven largely intractable to other therapeutic approaches, are sufficient to warrant further exploratory research in this area.

An examination of what appear to be the potential advantages of the behavior-modification methods described here is in order. One such advantage may be the speed with which these procedures work. Davison (1964), for example, working under the poorest of nonlaboratory conditions and seeing the subject for only a short time each day, achieved significant control over the child in 4 weeks. Exemplified also in Davison's (1964, 1965) work, as well as that of others (e.g., DeMyer & Ferster, 1962; Risley & Wolf, 1964), is the fact that such programs can apparently be executed by rapidly trained nonprofessional workers and continued in the home by parents. If this is generally the case, it might eventually be feasible for a small core of professional therapist-trainers to supervise simultaneously many therapeutic workers in behavior-modification programs with large numbers of clients.

An instructive outcome of this behavior-

In addition, the children were shocked whenever they began to emit tantrum behavior. These procedures resulted in a long-lasting response tendency to the "come here" command (9–10 months passed before extinction began to occur) and good suppression of the tantrums. Pairing the word "no" with shock gave it the status of a conditioned suppressor, demonstrated by its reduction of the frequency of a child's bar press for positive reinforcement.

In a second part of this study, the subjects received further shock-avoidance training with a portable subject-mounted shock apparatus. The children, who were required to hug and kiss the experimenter, showed increased affectionlike behavior as a result of training. Nurses who rated the subjects immediately after the avoidance sessions, but who were unaware of the purpose of the experiment, described the children as more dependent upon adults, more responsive and affection seeking, and more anxious and fearsome. They saw the children as less happy and content, but emitting less pathological behavior. It is well known that professional raters of such general classes of behavior as those preceding often have difficulty in agreeing upon what they observe. Relatedly, it was also explicitly pointed out by Harris et al. (1964) that teachers, nurses, and attendants who are direct participants in shaping procedures often produce completely fallacious estimates of behavior change resulting from such procedures (as checked against objective records). Admittedly the nurses in the present study were not involved in the therapy procedures nor, say the authors, did they know about them. Yet it would seem appropriate to use caution in accepting such nonprofessional, nonitemized behavior ratings.

The last experiment reported by Lovaas, Shaeffer, Benson, and Simmons (1965) in this article described children's learning to press a bar for candy and the sight of the experimenter's face. Accompanying this was shock-escape training in which the subjects had to go to the experimenter. Eventually, the subjects pressed the bar for the sight of the experimenter alone, without showing any generalized increase in activity resulting from the shock sessions. Here again, one has

the nurses' informal observation of a perhaps generalized tendency resulting from this training. The children, who previously showed only immobility when hurt, now sought out other human beings when hurt in a variety of extraexperimental situations.

## DISCUSSION

The results of these studies indicate that behavior-modification techniques may be extremely useful tools in the education and rehabilitation of psychotic children. None of the investigators whose work was reviewed here would claim that they have cured their subjects. But many can justifiably state that they have equipped their subjects with several of the basic skills and habits necessary for the most rudimentary of adjustments to their social environment. Furthermore, behavior "therapists," guided by social-learning models which are more parsimonious than traditional psychodynamic theories, have been able to effectively control, and in several cases eliminate, much of the undesirable and maladaptive behavior of these children. Results such as these, achieved with types of patients that had formerly proven largely intractable to other therapeutic approaches, are sufficient to warrant further exploratory research in this area.

An examination of what appear to be the potential advantages of the behavior-modification methods described here is in order. One such advantage may be the speed with which these procedures work. Davison (1964), for example, working under the poorest of nonlaboratory conditions and seeing the subject for only a short time each day, achieved significant control over the child in 4 weeks. Exemplified also in Davison's (1964, 1965) work, as well as that of others (e.g., DeMyer & Ferster, 1962; Risley & Wolf, 1964), is the fact that such programs can apparently be executed by rapidly trained nonprofessional workers and continued in the home by parents. If this is generally the case, it might eventually be feasible for a small core of professional therapist-trainers to supervise simultaneously many therapeutic workers in behavior-modification programs with large numbers of clients.

An instructive outcome of this behavior-modification research has been the demonstration that certain types of behavior, previously conceptualized by psychodynamic theories of psychopathology as complex reactions to internal states, are more realistically and profitably conceived as socially learned and maintained acts. An example of the rapidly achieved benefits of such reanalysis was the above-described virtual elimination of self-destructive tantrums without recourse to harsh, suppressive punishments. Such tantrum behavior was found to be maintained by adult attentiveness to it and was eliminated by withdrawing attention or merely by occupying the child with incompatible behavior (Davison, 1964; Lovaas, Freitag, Gold, & Kassorla, 1965).

The foregoing discussion of the potential assets of operant-learning therapeutic models is based on evidence from a variety of essentially clinical studies. It is obvious that further demonstration of the adequacy and efficacy of behavior modification with psychotic children is necessary. Future investigations must employ better controlled procedures and long-term follow-ups with larger subject populations in order to relate general as well as specific enduring results to the techniques used. Negative side effects of treatment procedures must be recognized and evaluated by competent observers. A major problem concerns the generality of therapeutic effects. Although several of the above studies reported "generalized," long-lasting results, most of the behavior changes accomplished have been relatively limited ones.

The restricted nature of the behavior changes reported in these studies is, of course, not surprising. When a program of behavior modification is planned, it is usually designed with a carefully specified goal or set of goals in mind. Certain undesirable behavior must be eliminated; adaptive skills and habits must be imparted. The aims of this sort of procedure contrast sharply with those of various orthodox therapies which direct their efforts at more molar goals, such as attitude change and the modification of personality traits. Yet, the authors of several of the studies reviewed here (Hewett, 1965; Lovaas, Schaeffer, Benson, & Simmons, 1965; Metz, 1965; Risley & Wolf, 1964; Wolf et al., 1964) reported that positive, generalized changes did accompany the more circumscribed changes resulting from their experimental manipulations. Phenomena like these raise important questions concerning their determinants, for it seems clear that the task of greatest ultimate significance will be the development of those procedures that have maximal catalytic effects in appropriate or adaptive directions.

Perhaps the simplest hypothetical explanation for the unique success of behavior-modification techniques specifies that much of psychotic (and especially autistic) deficit is due to the disturbed child's *inability to learn under ordinary circumstances*. Whether it is due to organic malfunction or parental influence, early failure to solve extremely simple problems would be expected to interfere with subsequent learning. Such interference would, in turn, be expected to increase exponentially, with successive failures producing progressively greater decrements in learning skills.

It follows, then, that the infant with such a developmental history would be for the most part helpless to organize or adapt to his environment and would therefore tend to withdraw from interaction with his surroundings. If this sort of etiological conception is accepted, then it may be hypothesized that behavior-modification methods achieve their striking effects simply because they order the environment sufficiently so that even the most severely impaired child can successfully manipulate it. Once the subject begins to experience manipulative successes, it is possible that a facilitation process may begin, whereby an eventual approximation to normal intellectual growth can occur.

Presumably spurring such growth would be the child's recognition of and orientation toward varied sources of reinforcement to which he was previously unresponsive. In their recent discussion of the role of behavior modification in producing generality of adaptive change, Baer and Wolf (1967) have conceptualized this therapeutic process as one in which initial modification of certain of the subject's key behaviors promotes his "entry into natural communities of reinforcement" that were hitherto ineffective in influencing his behavior. Thus, for example, after having received appropriate language or motor training from an adult, a socially isolated or immobile psychotic child might suddenly "discover" the reinforcement potential of his agemates or of activities that are available to him. It would be expected that behavior emitted with reference to such new communities of reinforcers would be instrumental in the consolidation of earlier changes and in the amplification and extension of therapeutic gains that were achieved in the laboratory.

It seems likely that the process by which widespread changes are accomplished must make use of motivational and learning or cognitive factors which are relatively novel in the experience of the psychotic child. That is, it is hypothesized that (a) the sensation of "mastery" resulting from successful control of the environment, and (b) the establishment of learning sets or "strategies" in such children interact in a manner that is crucial to the child's eventual general improvement. It would seem important, in this context, to avoid the use of the term "generalization" to describe nonspecific, adaptive change, since the phenomenon under discussion has little in common, structurally, with stimulus or response generalization. That is, the broader behavior and attitude changes that may result from behavior-modification procedures cannot properly be described in terms of their location on any true generalization gradient, except insofar as one refers to a continuum of "adaptiveness" or "improvement" to describe the nature of the change. Knowledge of the determinants of this process of nonspecific, adaptive change will obviously be invaluable in the construction of efficacious therapeutic methods.

A promising approach to the problem would seem to be one that emphasizes the establishment of learning and behavior strategies or, in operant terminology, complex response chains with general applicability, as opposed to an approach that emphasizes discrete response learning. Operationally, the teaching of such learning strategies may take the form of training in a small number of increasingly complex response chains. Alternatively, and perhaps more basically, such training may depend heavily upon the teacher's ability to modify the child's typical attentional behav-

ior, that is, it may be of central importance to first teach the child to orient toward a variety of potential reinforcement sources and "reinforceable" types of behavior that are appropriate and adaptive in character, but toward which he was generally indifferent prior to training.

The preceding discussion of the modification of behavior of childhood psychotics is, of course, highly speculative. But while the evidence to date is inconclusive, it certainly is strongly suggestive. The implication of these data is that effective new techniques of therapeutic behavior modification may be developed from the basic principles of operant-learning technology. If such techniques do prove to be statistically successful, it appears that they will have the additional virtues of simplicity and easy communicability. With these qualities, operant methodology could facilitate the realization of widely available, rapidly effective therapy for at least one area of psychopathology, that is, the psychoses of childhood.

## REFERENCES

AYLLON, T., & HAUGHTON, E. Control of the behavior of schizophrenic patients by food. *Journal of the Experimental Analysis of Behavior*, 1962, 5, 343–352.

AYLLON, T., & MICHAEL, J. The psychiatric nurse as a behavioral engineer. *Journal of the Experimental Analysis of Behavior*, 1959, 2, 323–334.

BAER, D. M. A technique of social reinforcement for the study of child behavior: Behavior avoiding reinforcement withdrawal. *Child Development*, 1962, 33, 847–858.

BAER, D. M., & WOLF, M. M. The entry into natural communities of reinforcement. Paper presented at the meeting of the American Psychological Association, Washington, D. C., September 1967.

BENDER, L., & HELME, W. H. A qualitative test of theory and diagnostic indicators of childhood schizophrenia. *AMA Archives of Neurology and Psychiatry*, 1953, 70, 413–427.

BETTELHEIM, B. Schizophrenic art: A case study. *Scientific American*, 1952, 186(4), 30–34.

BETTELHEIM, B. Early ego development in a mute, autistic child. Freud Lecture presented at the meeting of the Philadelphia Association for Psychoanalysis, University of Pennsylvania, May 1965.

BIJOU, S. W. Methodology for an experimental analysis of child behavior. *Psychological Reports*, 1957, 3, 243–250.

BROWNING, R. M. A same-subject design for simultaneous comparison of three reinforcement contingencies. *Behaviour Research and Therapy*, 1967, 5, 237–243.

DAVISON, G. C. A social learning therapy programme with an autistic child. *Behaviour Research and Therapy*, 1964, **2**, 149–159.

DAVISON, G. C. The training of undergraduates as social reinforcers for autistic children. In L. P. Ullman & L. Krasner (Eds.), *Case studies in behavior modification*. New York: Holt, Rinehart & Winston, 1965.

DEMYER, M. K., & FERSTER, C. B. Teaching new social behavior to schizophrenic children. *Journal of the American Academy of Child Psychiatry*, 1962, **1**, 443–461.

DUBNOFF, B. The habilitation and education of the autistic child in a therapeutic day school. *American Journal of Orthopsychiatry*, 1965, **35**, 385–386.

EISENBERG, L. The autistic child in adolescence. *American Journal of Psychiatry*, 1956, **112**, 607–612.

EISENBERG, L. The course of childhood schizophrenia. *AMA Archives of Neurology and Psychiatry*, 1957, **78**, 69–83.

EISENBERG, L., & KANNER, L. Early infantile autism, 1943–1955. *American Journal of Orthopsychiatry*, 1956, **26**, 556–566.

FERSTER, C. B. Positive reinforcement and behavioral deficits of autistic children. *Child Development*, 1961, **32**, 437–456.

FERSTER, C. B. An operant reinforcement analysis of infantile autism. Unpublished manuscript, Institute for Behavioral Research, Silver Spring, Maryland, 1965. (a)

FERSTER, C. B. Operant reinforcement in the natural milieu. Paper presented at the meeting of the Council for Exceptional Children, Portland, Oregon, April 1965. (b)

FERSTER, C. B., & DEMYER, M. K. The development of performances in autistic children in an automatically controlled environment. *Journal of Chronic Diseases*, 1961, **13**, 312–345. (a)

FERSTER, C. B., & DEMYER, M. K. Increased performances of an autistic child with prochlorperizine administration. *Journal of the Experimental Analysis of Behavior*, 1961, **4**, 84. (b)

FERSTER, C. B., & DEMYER, M. K. A method for the experimental analysis of the behavior of autistic children. *American Journal of Orthopsychiatry*, 1962, **32**, 89–98.

GROSSBERG, J. M. Behavior therapy: A review. *Psychological Bulletin*, 1964, **62**, 73–88.

HARRIS, F., WOLF, M. M., & BAER, D. M. Effects of adult social reinforcement on child behavior. *Young Children*, 1964, **20**, 8–17.

HEWETT, F. M. Teaching reading to autistic children through operant conditioning. *The Reading Teacher*, 1964, **17**, 613–618.

HEWETT, F. M. Teaching speech to autistic children through operant conditioning. *American Journal of Orthopsychiatry*, 1965, **35**, 927–936.

HINGTGEN, J. N., SANDERS, B., & DEMYER, M. K. Shaping cooperative responses in early childhood schizophrenics. In L. P. Ullman & L. Krasner (Eds.), *Case studies in behavior modification*. New York: Holt, Rinehart & Winston, 1965.

HINGTGEN, J. N., & TROST, F. C., JR. Shaping cooperative responses in early childhood schizophrenics: II. Reinforcement of mutual physical contact and vocal responses. Paper presented at the meeting of the American Psychological Association, Los Angeles, September 1964.

KANNER, L. Autistic disturbances of affective contact. *Nervous Child*, 1943, **2**, 217–250.

KING, G. F., ARMITAGE, S. G., TILTON, J. R. A therapeutic approach to schizophrenics of extreme pathology: An operant-interpersonal method. *Journal of Abnormal and Social Psychology*, 1960, **61**, 276–286.

LAZARUS, A. A., DAVISON, G. C., & POLEFKA, D. A. Classical and operant factors in the treatment of a school phobia. *Journal of Abnormal Psychology*, 1965, **70**, 225–229.

LOVAAS, O. I., FREITAG, G., GOLD, V., & KASSORLA, I. Experimental studies in childhood schizophrenia: Analysis of self-destructive behavior. *Journal of Experimental Child Psychology*, 1965, **2**, 67–84.

LOVAAS, O. I., SCHAEFFER, B., BENSON, R., & SIMMONS, J. Q. Experimental studies in childhood schizophrenia: Building social behaviors in autistic children by use of electric shock. *Journal of Experimental Research in Personality*, 1965, **1**, 99–109.

METZ, J. R. Conditioning generalized imitation in autistic children. *Journal of Experimental Child Psychology*, 1965, **2**, 389–399.

RIMLAND, B. *Infantile autism*. New York: Appleton-Century-Crofts, 1964.

RISLEY, T., & WOLF, M. Experimental manipulation of autistic behaviors and generalization into the home. Paper presented at the meeting of the American Psychological Association, Los Angeles, September 1964.

SHERMAN, J. A. Use of reinforcement and imitation to reinstate verbal behavior in mute psychotics. *Journal of Abnormal Psychology*, 1965, **70**, 155–164.

WEILAND, I. H., & RUDNIK, R. Considerations of the development and treatment of autistic childhood psychosis. *The Psychoanalytic Study of the Child*, 1961, **16**, 549–563.

WOLF, M. Reinforcement procedures and the modification of deviant child behavior. Paper presented at the meeting of the Council for Exceptional Children, Portland, Oregon, April 1965.

WOLF, M., RISLEY, T., & MEES, H. Application of operant conditioning procedures to the behaviour problems of an autistic child. *Behaviour Research and Therapy*, 1964, **1**, 305–312.

# POSITIVE REINFORCEMENT AND BEHAVIORAL DEFICITS OF AUTISTIC CHILDREN

## C. B. FERSTER

*Indiana University Medical Center*

Infantile autism, first described by Kanner (6), is a very severe psychotic disturbance occurring in children as young as 2 years. At least outwardly, this childhood schizophrenia is a model of adult schizophrenia. Speech and control by the social environment are limited or absent; tantrums and atavistic behaviors are frequent and of high intensity; and most activities are of a simple sort, such as smearing, lying about, rubbing a surface, playing with a finger, and so forth. Infantile autism is a relatively rare form of schizophrenia and is not important from an epidemiological point of view. The analysis of the autistic child may be of theoretical use, however, since his psychosis may be a prototype of the adult's; but the causal factors could not be so complicated, because of the briefer environmental history. In this paper, I should like to analyze how the basic variables determining the child's behavior might operate to produce the particular kinds of behavioral deficits seen in the autistic child. To analyze the autistic child's behavioral deficits, I shall proceed from the general principles of behavior, derived from a variety of species, which describe the kinds of factors that alter the frequency of any arbitrary act (3, 10). The general principles of behavior applied to the specific situations presumably present during the child's developmental period will lead to hypotheses as to specific factors in the autistic child's home life which could produce the severe changes in frequency as well as in the form of his behavior. As an example, consider the effect of intermittent reinforcement, many of the properties of which are comparatively well known from animal experiments. To find how intermit-

CHILD DEVELOPMENT, 1961, Vol. 32, pp. 437-456.

tent reinforcement of the autistic child's behavior might produce deficits, we would first determine, in the general case, what specific orders of magnitude and kinds of schedules produce weakened behavioral repertoires. The factors in the child's home life could be examined to determine estimates of what kind of circumstances could conceivably cause schedules of reinforcement capable of the required attenuation of the child's behavior. The analysis will emphasize the child's performance as it is changed by, and affected in, social and nonsocial environment. As in most problems of human behavior, the major datum is the frequency of occurrence of the child's behavior. Although the account of the autistic child's development and performance is not derived by manipulative experiments, it may still be useful to the extent that all of the terms of the analysis refer to potentially manipulable conditions in the child's environment and directly measurable aspects of his performance. Such an analysis is even more useful if the performances and their effects on the environment were described in the same general terms used in systematic accounts of behavior of experimental psychology.

Some of our knowledge of the autistic child's repertoire must necessarily come from anecdotal accounts of the child's performance through direct observation. Although such data are not so useful as data from controlled experiments, they can be relatively objective if these performances are directly observable and potentially manipulable. A limited amount of experimental knowledge of the dynamics of the autistic child's repertoire is available through a program of experiments in which the autistic child has developed a new repertoire under the control of an experimental environment (5). These experiments help reveal the range and dynamics of the autistic child's current and potential repertoires. In general, the autistic child's behavior will be analyzed by the functional consequences of the child's behavior rather than the specific form. The major attempt will be to determine what specific effects the autistic child's performance has on that environment and how the specific effects maintain the performance.

### SPECIFICATION OF THE AUTISTIC CHILD'S PERFORMANCE

We must first describe the current repertoire of the autistic child before we can describe possible environmental conditions that might produce gross behavioral deficits. A topographic description of the individual items of the autistic child's repertoire would not, in general, distinguish it from the repertoires of a large number of functioning and nonhospitalized children, except perhaps in the degree of loss of verbal behavior. The autistic child's behavior becomes unique only when the relative frequency of occurrence of all the performances in the child's repertoire is considered. In general, the usual diagnostic categories do not adequately characterize the children in the terms of a functional analysis of behavior. Hospitalization of a child usually depends upon whether the parent can keep the child in the home, rather than a functional description of the role of the parental environment in sustaining or weakening the child's performance.

*Range of Performances*

Although the autistic child may have a narrower range of performances than the normal child, the major difference between them is in the relative frequencies of the various kinds of performances. The autistic child does many things of a simple sort—riding a bicycle, climbing, walking, tugging on someone's sleeve, running, etc. Nevertheless, the autistic child spends large amounts of time sitting or standing quietly. Performances which have only simple and slight effects on the child's environment occur frequently and make up a large percentage of the entire repertoire, for example, chewing on a rubber balloon, rubbing a piece of gum back and forth on the floor, flipping a shoelace, or turning the left hand with the right. Almost all of the characteristic performances of the autistic child may be observed in nonhospitalized children, but the main difference lies in the relative importance of each of these performances in terms of the total repertoire. Conversely, isolated instances of quite "normal" performances may be seen in the autistic child. Again, the relative frequency of the performances defines the autistic child.

*Social Control over the Child's Performance*

The major performance deficits of the autistic child are in the degree of social control: The kinds of performances which have their major effects through the mediation of other individuals.

The main avenue of social control in a normal repertoire is usually through speech, a kind of performance that is unique because it produces the consequences maintaining it through the mediation of a second person (12). Autistic children almost always have an inadequately developed speech repertoire, varying from mutism to a repertoire of a few words. Even when large numbers of words are emitted, the speech is not normal in the sense that it is not maintained by its effect on a social environment. When normal speech is present, it usually is in the form of a *mand* (12). This is a simple verbal response which is maintained because of its direct reinforcement, e.g., "Candy!" "Let me out." The main variable is usually the level of deprivation of the speaker. It lacks the sensitive interchange between the speaker and listener characteristic of much human verbal behavior, as for example, the *tact* (*see* below). The reinforcement of the mand largely benefits only the speaker. In the case of the autistic child, it frequently affects the listener (parent), who escapes from the aversive stimulus by presenting a reinforcing stimulus relevant to the child's mand. At suppertime, the child stands at the door screaming loudly and kicking the door because the ward attendants in the past have taken the child to supper when this situation became aversive enough. Sometimes, the form of the mand is nonvocal, although still verbal, as when the mand involves tugging at a sleeve, pushing, or jostling. The dynamic conditions which could distort the form of a mand into forms most aversive to a listener will be described below. In contrast to the mand, the tact (12) is almost completely absent. This form of verbal behavior benefits the listener rather than the speaker and is not usually relevant to the current deprivations of the speaker. This is the form of verbal behavior by which the child describes his environment, as, for example, "This is a chair"; "The mailman is coming." This latter kind of verbal control is generally absent or weak, as with other kinds of verbal behavior except an occasional mand.

*Atavisms*

Tantrums, self-destructive behavior, and performances generally aversive to an adult audience are relatively frequent in the autistic child's repertoire. Most autistic mands depend on an aversive effect of the listener for their reinforcement. To the extent that social behavior is present at all, its major mode is through the production of stimuli or situations which are aversive enough so that the relevant audience will escape or avoid the aversive stimulus (often with a reinforcer). For example, on the occasion of candy in the immediate vicinity, the child screams, flails about on the floor, perhaps striking his head, until he is given some candy. There is evidence that much of the atavistic performance of the autistic child is operant, that is, controlled by its consequence in the social environment. The operant nature of the autistic child's atavisms is borne out by experiments where a child was locked in an experimental space daily for over a year. There was no social intervention, and the experimental session was usually prolonged if a tantrum was underway. Under these conditions, the frequency of tantrums and atavisms declined continuously in the experimental room until they all but disappeared. Severe tantrums and attempts at self-destruction still occurred when sudden changes in the conditions of the experiment produced a sudden change in the direction of nonreinforcement of the child's performances. Severe changes in the reinforcement contingencies of the experiment produced a much larger reaction in the autistic than in the normal child. Consequently, we learned to change experimental conditions very slowly, so that the frequency of reinforcement remained high at each stage of the experiment. Much of the atavistic behavior of the autistic child is maintained because of its effect on the listener.

*Reinforcing Stimuli*

The reinforcers maintaining the autistic child's performance are difficult to determine without explicit experimentation. Small changes in the physical environment as, for example, direct stimulation of the mouth, splashing water, smearing a sticky substance on the floor, breaking a toy, or repeated tactile sensations, appear to sustain the largest part of the autistic child's repertoire. Nevertheless, these may be weak reinforcing stimuli which appear to be strong, because the response produces its reinforcement continuously and because alternative modes of responding are also maintained by weak reinforcers. The durability and effectiveness of a reinforcer can usually be determined best by reinforcing the behavior intermittently or by providing a strong alternative which could interfere with the behavior in question. In the controlled experiments with autistic children, most of the consequences we supplied to sustain the children's performance, such as color wheels, moving pictures, music, and so forth, were very weak reinforcers compared with food or candy. Food generally appeared to be an effective reinforcer, and most of the performances associated with going to the dining room and eating are frequently intact. In contrast, the normal children could sustain very large amounts of behavior through the nonfood reinforcements. It is difficult to guess the potential effectiveness of new reinforcers, because the estimate depends upon some performance being maintained by that reinforcer.

In the everyday activities of the autistic children, little behavior was sustained by conditioned or delayed reinforcers. But, in a controlled experimental situation, such activities could be sustained by explicit training. For example, (a) The sound of the candy dispenser preceding the delivery of candy served as a conditioned reinforcer. The fine-grain effects of the schedules of reinforcement show this. The difference in performance produced by two different schedules of reinforcement could have occurred only if the effective reinforcer were the sound of the magazine rather than the delivery of a coin. The actual receipt of the coin or food is much too delayed to produce the differences in performances under the two schedules without the conditioned reinforcer coming instantly after a response. (b) With further training, the delivery of a coin (conditioned reinforcer) sustained the child's performances. The coin, in turn, could be used to operate the food or nonfood devices in the experimental room. (c) Still later, coins sustained the child's performance even though they had to be held for a period of time before they could be cashed in. The child worked until he accumulated five coins, then he deposited them in the reinforcing devices. (d) Even longer delays of reinforcement were arranged by sustaining behavior in the experimental room with a conditioned reinforcer as, for example, a towel or a life jacket which could be used later in the swimming pool or in water play after the experimental session terminated. The experimental development of these performances shows that, even though the usual autistic repertoire is generally deficient in performances sustained by conditioned reinforcement and with delay in reinforcement, the children are potentially capable of developing this kind of control.

Little of the autistic child's behavior is likely to be maintained by generalized reinforcement, that is, reinforcement which is effective in the absence of any specific deprivation. A smile or parental approval are examples. The coins delivered as reinforcements in the experimental room are potentially generalized reinforcers, since they make possible several performances under the control of many different deprivations. However, we do not know whether the coin has actually acquired the properties of a generalized reinforcer.

*Stimulus Control of Behavior*

It is very difficult to determine the stimulus and perceptual repertoire of autistic children. When a child responds to a complex situation, it is not usually clear what aspect of the situation is controlling the child's behavior. In most cases, it is difficult to determine to what extent these children can respond to speech discriminatively, since the situations are usually complex and many stimuli may provide the basis for the simple performances. Similarly with visual repertoires. Controlled experiments showed unequivocally that behavior can come under the control of simple stimuli when differential effects of the performances were correlated with the different stimuli. When a coin was deposited in a lighted coin slot, it operated the reinforcing device. Coins deposited in unlighted slots were wasted. The children soon stopped putting coins in the unlighted slots. The previously developed stimulus control broke down completely when these stimuli were placed in a more complicated context, however. A new vending machine was installed with eight columns, eight coin lights, and eight coin slots, so the child could choose a preferred kind of candy. The slight increase in complexity disrupted the control by the coin light, and it took several months and many experimental procedures before the stimulus control was reestablished. A better designed procedure, in view of the minimal perceptual repertoire of these children, would have been a gradual program by which variations in the specific dimensions of the coin slot and coin light were changed while the reinforcement contingency was held constant in respect to the essential property.

In summary, the repertoire of the autistic child is an impoverished one. Little is known about the perceptual repertoire, but the available evidence suggests that it is minimal. The absolute amount of activity is low, but this deficit is even more profound if the specific items of activity are evaluated in terms of whether they are maintained by significant effects on a social or even nonsocial environment. Most of the child's performances are of a simple sort, such as rubbing a spot of gum back and forth, softening and twisting a crayon, pacing, or flipping a shoelace. Those performances in the child's repertoire having social effects frequently do so because of their effects on the listener as aversive stimuli. Atavisms and tantrums are frequent.

### The Emergence of Performance Deficits During the Early Development of the Autistic Child

Having characterized the autistic child's repertoire, the next step is to determine the kinds of circumstances in the early life of these children which could bring about the behavioral deficits. The general plan is to state how the major behavioral processes and classes of variables can drastically reduce the frequency of occurrence of the various behaviors in the repertoire of any organism. Then, the parental environment will be examined to determine circumstances under which the actual contingencies applied by the parental environment to the child's behavior could weaken the child's performance similarly. The datum is the frequency of occurrence of all of the acts in the child's repertoire, and the independent variables are the consequences of these acts on the child's environment, particularly the parental environment. All of the terms in such a functional analysis are actually or potentially directly observable and manipulable. In general, the performances in the child's repertoire will be simultaneously a function of many factors, each contributing to changes in the frequency of the relevant performances. It is important, therefore, to consider relative changes in frequency rather than simple presence or absence of various performances. The datum is the frequency of occurrence of the behavior. In the same vein, singly identifiable factors may be interrelated and functioning simultaneously.

The major paradigm for describing the behavior of an organism is to specify the consequences of the act (reinforcement) which are responsible for its frequency. In this sense, the major cause of an instance of behavior is the immediate effect on the environment (reinforcement). The continued emission of the verbal response "Toast" depends on its effect on the parent in producing toast. Every known behavioral process influencing the frequency of a positively reinforced performance is relevant to the problem of defining conditions under which we may produce a behavioral deficit. Given the variables which maintain it, a performance may be weakened by their absence or by changing the order of magnitude. It is perhaps surprising to discover that large behavioral deficits are plausible without any major appeal to punishment or suppression of behavior by aversive stimuli.

## Intermittent Reinforcement and Extinction

Intermittent reinforcement and extinction are the major techniques for removing or weakening behavior in a repertoire. The most fundamental way to eliminate a kind of behavior from an organism's repertoire is to discontinue the effect the behavior has on the environment (extinction). A performance may also be weakened if its maintaining effect on the environment occurs intermittently (intermittent reinforcement).[1] Behaviors occurring because of their effects on the parent are especially likely to be weakened by intermittent reinforcement and extinction, because the parental

---

[1] The reader may suggest at this point an apparent contradiction with the fact that extinction after intermittent reinforcement is more prolonged than after continuous reinforcement. This aspect of intermittently reinforced behavior's durability is not a general proposition, however, and does not hold for behavior which is still being maintained. Behavior reinforced intermittently will, in general, be emitted less frequently and be more easily weakened by emotional factors, changes in deprivation, punishment, and physiological disturbances than continuously reinforced behavior.

reinforcements are a function of other variables and behavioral processes usually not directly under the control of the child. The reinforcement of the verbal response, "Give me the book," may go unreinforced because of many factors which determine the behavior of the listener. He may be preoccupied, listening to someone else, disinclined to reinforce, momentarily inattentive, etc. In contrast, the physical environment reinforces continuously and reliably. Reaching for a book is usually followed by the tactile stimulation from the book. Verbal behavior, particularly, depends entirely for its development and maintenance on reinforcements supplied by an audience (usually a parent). Because of the possibility of prolonged extinction and infrequent, intermittent reinforcement, speech and social behavior are the most vulnerable aspects of the child's repertoire. The young child is particularly vulnerable to the extinction and intermittent reinforcement occurring in social reinforcement because only the parental environment mediates nearly all of the major reinforcers relevant to his repertoire. Large parts of the child's repertoire are reinforced by first affecting a parent who in turn produces the reinforcer for the child. The 2-year-old child who asks for a cookie from a parent and gets no response usually has no alternative audience who will reinforce this vocal behavior. The result will either be the extinction of the child's verbal behavior or the reinforcement of nonvocal verbal forms when the child produces a cookie by a tantrum from which the parent escapes by giving the cookie.

### Factors in the Parental Repertoire Affecting the Frequency of Reinforcement of the Child's Performances

To find the conditions under which the child's repertoire will be weakened, therefore, we must look for conditions influencing the parents' behavior, which will alter the parental performances, in turn providing reinforcement of the child's performances. These might be:

1. The general disruption of the parental repertoire. Any severe disruption of the parental repertoire will severely affect the frequency with which the parent reinforces the behavior of the child. Consider, for example, the depressed parent whose general level of behavior is very low. One consequence of this low level of behaving will be a lessened frequency of reacting to the child. Therefore, many items in the child's repertoire will be less frequently reinforced in the depressed than the normal parent. The verbal responses, "May I have some bread" or "I want to go outside," might go unreinforced or be emitted many times without reinforcement. Various kinds of somatic disturbances, such as alcoholic "hangover," drug addiction, severe headache, somatic diseases, etc., could also produce large changes in the over-all reactivity of the parent to a child. To the extent that the child's performances occur because of their effect on the parent, the severely weakened parental repertoire may correspondingly weaken the child's behavior. If the parental extinction of the child's behavior is systematic and periodic, much of a child's behavior could be eliminated.

2. Prepotency of other performances. Whether or not a parent reinforces a child's performance also depends upon the alternative repertoire available to the parent. For example, the parent who is absorbed in various kinds of activities such as housecleaning, a home business, social activities and clubs, active telephoning, and so forth, may at various times allow many usually reinforced performances to go unreinforced. In general, the likelihood of omitting reinforcement would depend upon the strength of the prepotent repertoire. As an example of a prepotent repertoire, the housewife absorbed in a telephone conversation will not be inclined to answer a child or comply with a request. Housecleaning might be another repertoire controlling some parents' behavior so strongly that it is prepotent over behavior in respect to the child. In both cases, the essential result is the nonreinforcement of the child's behavior in competition with the prepotent parental repertoire. Mothers of autistic children often appear to have strong repertoires prepotent over the child. This may be at least a partial reason why mothers of autistic children are so often well-educated, verbal, and at least superficially adequate people.

3. A third factor producing intermittent reinforcement of the child's behavior is related to the first two factors listed above. If the parent finds other reinforcers outside of the home more rewarding than dealing with the child, the child becomes an occasion on which the significant elements of the parental repertoire cannot be reinforced. A parent changing diapers, or otherwise taking care of a child, cannot telephone a friend, be out socializing, be on a job, or doing whatever the autistic mother finds rewarding. The child acquires the properties of a conditioned aversive stimulus because it is an occasion which is incompatible with the parents' normal repertoire. This is of course the major method of aversive control in human behavior—the discontinuation of positive reinforcement. Another basis for establishing the child as a conditioned aversive stimulus to the parent is the emergence of atavisms and a large degree of aversive control of the parent by the child. To the extent that the parent is reinforced by escaping from the child because of his conditioned aversive properties, the frequency of the parental reinforcement of the child's behavior is further reduced.

The development of the atavistic behavior in the child by the parent is necessarily a very gradual program in which the beginning steps involve small magnitudes of behavior such as whining, whimpering, and crying. As the parent adapts to these or becomes indifferent to them because of the prepotence of other kinds of activity, then progressively larger orders of magnitude become reinforced. The large-magnitude tantrum may be approximated or "shaped" by gradual differential reinforcement. The parents of one autistic child, for example, at one period took turns all night standing in the child's room because one step out of the room would immediately produce a severe tantrum in the child. When the child functions as a conditioned aversive stimulus for the parent, the parent is less likely to reinforce the child's behavior positively. This lack of positive reinforcement, in turn, emphasizes the atavistic responses on the child's part as the major mode of affecting the parent.

The usual limiting factor in preventing excessive development of tantrums is the emergence of self-control on the part of the parent in escaping from the aversive control by the child rather than reinforcing it. Here, again, the repertoire of the parent is relevant. The development of self-control requires a highly developed repertoire which depends for its development on the ultimate aversive consequences of the child's control of the parent. The child's control becomes more aversive to the parent if it interrupts strong repertoires. Specifically, a parent engrossed in a conversation will find a child's interruption more aversive than a parent who is simply resting. If, in fact, there is no strong behavior in the parent, then the child's control is not likely to be aversive, and there is no basis for developing self-control.

All three of the above factors—over-all disturbances in the parental repertoire, prepotent activities, and escape from the child because of his aversiveness—reduce the amount of parental reinforcement of the child's performances. The over-all effect of the nonreinforcement on the repertoire of the child will depend upon the length of time and number of items of the child's repertoire that go unreinforced, as well as the existence of other possible social environments that can alternatively maintain the child's behavior (*see* below).

### Differential Reinforcement of Atavistic Forms of Behavior by the Parent

The schedule by which the parent reacts to the child is also relevant to the development of atavistic behavior. Initially, a tantrum may be an unconditioned consequence of parental control as, for example, sudden nonreinforcement or punishment. Eventually, however, the child's tantrums may come to be maintained by their effect on the parental environment, because they present an aversive situation that can be terminated if the parent supplies some reinforcer to the child. The reinforcer presented by the parent to escape from the aversive consequences of the tantrum also increases the subsequent frequency of atavistic responses.

The effect on the parent of the given form and intensity of tantrums will vary from time to time, depending on the conditions maintaining the parents' behavior. This variation in sensitivity of the parent to aversive control by the child results in a variable-ratio schedule of reinforcement of the child's tantrum by the parent—a schedule of reinforcement potentially capable of maximizing the disposition to engage in tantrums. This is the schedule of reinforcement that produces the high frequencies of performances as in gambling (10). The sensitivity of the parent to aversive control by the child will depend on the general condition of the parental repertoire as discussed above. The same factors in the parental repertoire that tend to produce nonreinforcement of the child's behavior—general disruption of the parent or other behaviors prepotent over the child—correspondingly produce reinforcement of large-order-of-magnitude tantrums. The parent whose total repertoire is severely enough disrupted to interfere with the normal reinforcement of the child's behavior will also react only to tantrums that are of large order of magnitude of aversiveness. A range of sensitivity of the parent to aversive control by the child produces ideal conditions for progressively increasing the intensity or frequency of tantrums. A high sensitivity to aversive control guarantees that some tantrums will be reinforced at least periodically. A low sensitivity differentially reinforces tantrums of large orders of magnitude. At one extreme, the parent may be hypersensitive to the child and, at other times, so depressed that only physical violence will produce a reaction. The schedule by which the parent's behavior terminates the tantrum is a second factor which will increase the range of reactivity of the parent. As more behavior is required of the parent to terminate the tantrum, the parent's inclination to do so will fall. When the parent is less inclined to reinforce a given intensity of tantrum, any variation in tantrum intensity is tantamount to differential reinforcement of extreme forms, if the parent now reacts to the larger-order-of-magnitude tantrum.

How much the parent differentially reinforces tantrums in the child depends, in part, upon the child's other positively reinforced repertoires. When, for example, a child's performance suddenly goes unreinforced, as when a parent may refuse a request, the likelihood and severity of a tantrum will in part depend on the parent's ability to "distract" the child. This, in turn, depends upon whether alternative modes of behavior are in fact available to the child. When conditions are present for the progressive reinforcement of more and more severe tantrums, the process is potentially non-self-limiting. Autocatalysis is likely to occur, particularly if the parent has little disposition to reinforce the general items in the child's repertoire for reasons other than terminating the aversive demands of the child.

## Nonsocial Reinforcers

Some of the child's behavior is maintained by his direct effect on the physical environment without the intervention of other individuals. In general, very small effects on the environment will sustain performances with which the parent usually has little reason to interfere. For example, the child plays with his own shoelace, moves his fingers in his own visual field, emits minimal nonverbal, vocal responses, and so forth. Larger effects on the physical environment as, for example, moving objects about the house, speaking to the parent, playing with toys, touching and handling usual household objects, are more likely to enter upon the parental repertoire and so may produce a response whose effect is to discontinue the behavior or interfere with its reinforcement. The punishment aspect of the parental interference with the child's activities will be dealt with separately below. The relative possibility of parental interference and nonreinforcement of the hierarchy of performances may account for the large part of the autistic child's repertoire, which consists of behaviors having small, limited effects on the physical environment. Occasionally, even behaviors that are maintained by the most simple effects on the environment are extinguished or punished when they occur in the presence of a parent. For example, the father of one autistic child reports that the child reached for a chandelier while he was holding him. The father instantly dropped the child, with a reaction of considerable disapproval because "You should pay attention to me when you're with me." Aside from the secondary effect on the child, the immediate result of the incident is the nonreinforcement of the child reaching for a common physical object.

The existence of "nonverbal" vocal behavior in some autistic children may be related to forms of vocal behavior with which the parent will or will not interfere. Vocal behavior maintained by its effect on a parent (verbal) is susceptible to weakening by parental extinction. A parent interferes less easily with vocal behavior maintained by its direct effect (nonverbal) comparable with making noise by rubbing a stick over a rough surface. Further, such nonverbal vocal responses can emerge readily at any stage of the child's life, unlike verbal behavior, because it does not depend on a generalized reinforcement.

*Failure to Develop Conditioned and Generalized Reinforcers*

The normal repertoire of the child consists almost entirely of sequences of behavior that are maintained, in a chain or sequence, by conditioned and generalized reinforcers (10). An example of a chain of responses would be the behavior of the child moving a chair across the room and using it to climb to a table top to reach a key which in turn opens a cupboard containing candy. This complicated sequence of behavior is linked together by critical stimuli which have the dual function of sustaining the behavior they follow (conditioned reinforcement) and setting the occasion for the subsequent response. The chair in the above example is an occasion on which climbing onto it will bring the child into a position where reaching for food on the table top will be reinforced by obtaining food. Once this behavior is established, the chair in position in front of the table may now be a reinforcer, and any of the child's behavior which results in moving the chair into position will be reinforced because of the subsequent role of the chair in the later chain of behaviors. A minimal amount of behavior is necessary before a chain of responses can develop. The development of the control by the various stimuli in the chain, both as discriminative stimuli setting the occasion for the reinforcement of behavior and as reinforcers, depends upon a high level of activity, so that the responses will occur and come under the control of the stimuli. This is even more true for the development of the generalized reinforcer. When the child has moved enough objects about the house and achieved a variety of effects on his environment relative to a range of deprivations and reinforcers, simply manipulating the physical environment may become a reinforcer without reference to a specific level of deprivation. This, of course, is the uniquely human reinforcer that makes possible much of verbal behavior, education in general, and self-control. Again, large amounts of behavior—many chains of behavior with many different kinds of conditioned reinforcers—are a necessary condition for the emergence of a generalized reinforcer. To the extent that the child's repertoire becomes weakened by intermittent reinforcement and extinction, as mentioned above, and punishment and aversive control (*see* below), the possibility of the development of generalized reinforcers, and hence more complex behavior, becomes less and less likely. Parental "attention" is probably one of the most important generalized reinforcers normally maintaining the child's behavior. Parental attention is an occasion upon which the child's performances may have an important effect on the parent. Inattention is an occasion on which the child's responses are likely to have little effect. Hence, the parents' performances in smiling, saying, "Right," "Good boy," or "Thank you," all come to function as conditioned reinforcers. Their emergence as generalized reinforcers again depends upon the existence of a large behavioral repertoire. A large number of chains of responses will produce important positive effects when the parent smiles or says, "Good boy." Lower frequencies of reinforcement follow for these same activities when the parent is frowning or says, "Bad boy."

Any large reduction in the child's over-all performance will interfere with the initial development of conditioned reinforcers or their continued effectiveness. The control by the environment over the child's behavior depends first upon the emission of the behavior. This follows from the manner in which the environment comes to control the child's performance: the successful execution of an act on one occasion, coupled with the unsuccessful act in its absence. Until a child climbs on chairs, as in the previous example, a chair has little chance of becoming a discriminative stimulus. Without the development of stimulus control, conditioned reinforcers cannot develop. The reinforcing effect of the chair in the above example depends upon its being the occasion on which further performances may be reinforced. In this way, a low general level of behavior may impede the enlargement of the child's repertoire because it does not allow stimulus control and in turn prevents reinforcement of new behavior. A limited development of simple conditioned reinforcers in turn prevents the development of a generalized reinforcer. Parental responses, such as smiling, "Good," or "Right," can have little effect on the child if there is not a history by which many different forms of the child's performance have produced various reinforcers on these occasions. Without parental generalized reinforcement, educational processes and positive parental control are all but impossible. This control is normally carried out by the use of praise and parental attention, coupled with mild forms of threats of discontinuing the reinforcers. Even after a generalized reinforcer has acquired its function, its continued effectiveness depends on the various stimuli continuing to stand in a significant relation to the child's performance. The actual form of the parents' generalized reinforcer is not nearly as important as the parents' subsequent reinforcement practices with the child. The reinforcing effects of the smile derive from the reinforcing practices associated with it. A smile usually functions as a generalized reinforcer in most people because a smiling person is more likely to reinforce. The correlation between smiling and reinforcement is by no means inevitable, however. Some individuals may be more disposed to punish than reinforce when smiling in some situations. In a similar vein, if the child has no behavior in his repertoire that will be more likely to be reinforced on the occasion of a parental smile, it matters little what the parent's reinforcing practices are when smiling as against when frowning.

## STIMULUS CONTROL

The specific occasions on which a child's performances have their characteristic effects on the environment will subsequently determine whether the child acts. In the absence of the characteristic circumstances under which the behavior is normally reinforced, the child will be less disposed to act in proportion to the degree of similarity with the original situation. Changing a stimulus to one which has not been correlated with reinforcement is another way of weakening a repertoire. New stimuli also elicit emotional responses and general autonomic effects that may interfere with established performances. Here, simply repeated exposure to the stimuli may produce adaptation to the stimuli and eliminate their emotional effects. Ordinarily, the infants' performances are under the control of a limited range of stimuli, usually one or two parents in a limited part of a specific home environment. The discriminative repertoire broadens as the child grows older and other individuals come to be occasions on which his performances have significant effects. The parental environment of the very young child narrows the control of the child's performance to a limited range of stimuli, largely because the parent mediates almost all of the important events affecting the child. A major factor which brings the child's behavior more narrowly under the control of the parent is the nonreinforcement of much of the child's behavior in the absence of the parent. The close control of the child's behavior by the parent weakens the child's repertoire in the absence of a parent much more when there has been explicit differential reinforcement than when there has been simply a limited reinforcing environment.

Sudden shifts in the child's environment may or may not produce major performance deficits. At one extreme, a sudden shift of the stimuli in the child's controlling environment will have little influence if the child already has been reinforced on the occasion of a wide range of circumstances and individuals. At another extreme, a repertoire can be eliminated almost completely if the child has had a history in which major kinds of performances have gone unreinforced except on the occasion of a single person in a specific environment. The sudden shifts in the situations and persons controlling the child's behavior may occur under a variety of circumstances, such as a sudden change in a constant companion, death of a parent, or a sudden shift in the physical environment. A sudden shift in the environment of one of the subjects reported in the previously mentioned experiment could conceivably have been the major factor in her autistic development. Many of the activities of the child's mother were prepotent over dealing with the child, and she solved the problem by hiring a teenage baby sitter as a constant companion and nursemaid. After a year, the baby sitter left, suddenly and abruptly, leaving the child with the mother. Within four months, the child began to behave less in general, lost speech, and showed increasing frequency of atavisms. The child's repertoire possibly was under such close control of the baby sitter that the very sudden change to the mother created an environment which in the past had been correlated with nonreinforcement. If the child's behavior were under very narrow control by the baby sitter, because of the nonreinforcement on all other occasions, a sudden shift, as in the loss of the baby sitter, could produce a dramatic deficit in the child's repertoire.

## Disruptive Effect of Sudden Stimulus Changes and the Amount, Durability, and Range of Behavior

A novel reinforcing environment will not sustain a child's performance unless the repertoire contains behavior of a sufficient range and durability. The new environment weakens the performance because it nearly always requires slightly different forms of behavior. For example, a new person entering a child's home is not so likely to respond successfully to the incompletely developed verbal behavior of a child as the parent. The possibility of the child's affecting the stranger will depend upon his having verbal responses different from those usually reinforced by the parent and, also, durable verbal behavior that will continue to be emitted under the intermittent reinforcement that is likely to occur. If the child's repertoire is durable and extensive enough so that the verbal response may be repeated several times and supplemented by auxiliary behavior, the child has a greater chance of affecting the new person or of being shaped by him. Similarly with other kinds of social behavior. The wider the range of behavior and the greater the disposition to emit it the more likely that the child's performance will be within the range of responses potentially reinforcible by the new environment.

For a stimulus to acquire control over behavior, the child must first emit behavior in the presence of the stimulus. Consider, for example, the performance of a child at a children's party at which there are lots of toys and games, such as bicycles, swings, and so forth. The likelihood of the child's behavior coming under the control of any of the other children as reinforcers is minimal if the new environment suppresses or makes the child's entire repertoire unavailable because it is a novel stimulus and is an occasion on which the child's behavior has never been reinforced. If the behavior of playing with a swing or riding a tricycle is sufficiently strong that it may be emitted even under the adverse conditions of the very strange party environment, then the simple emission of the previously developed behavior provides a situation under which other children at the party may potentially reinforce or otherwise affect the child's repertoire. Simply the acts of eating cake, candy, or ice cream, or picking up a toy put some of the child's behavior under the control of the new environment. Each new performance which can potentially occur at the party provides a basis for the child's reinforcing some behavior of other children at the party or of his coming under the control of the other children's reinforcers. On the other hand, a sudden exposure to a new environment with a weak and narrow repertoire may produce a severe behavioral deficit. In any case, the child will be much less disposed to go to the party if he had behaved unsuccessfully in the new environment. This lower disposition to attend and engage in the party would in turn make it less likely that the child will emit behavior that would be reinforced in the party environment.

### Adaptation

The emotional and elicited autonomic effects of novel environments may also interfere with a child's performances. Adaptation to new environments occurs with gradual exposure. A sudden exposure to a new environment will produce gross emotional and autonomic responses which will in turn interfere with, or even completely suppress, the emission of possible operant behavior potentially reinforcible by the new environment. The rate at which the child is exposed to the new environments will determine the magnitude of disturbance. Exposure to a new environment and adaptation of the emotional responses do not necessarily create the potential basis for responding, however. A repertoire that will make contact with the new environment is also necessary.

### Amount of Prior Nonreinforcement

The more closely controlled the child's performances are by specific stimuli, the more likely a sudden shift in the environment will produce a cessation of responding. For example, the child receiving minimal care from a parent probably will be less affected by a sudden shift in environment than a child closely affected and controlled by parental response. It is paradoxical that the parent who responds sensitively to the child's performance may be potentially weakening it more than the parent who exerts little control over the child. It is the alternate reinforcement and nonreinforcement that place the child's behavior narrowly under the control of very specific stimuli so that it is much more vulnerable to sudden changes. The range of stimuli in whose presence the child's behavior goes unreinforced will determine the narrowness of the stimulus control.

The continuous development of more and more complex forms of a child's behavior is normally achieved because the parents and community approximate the required performances. At each stage of the child's development, the community reinforces the child's current repertoire even though it is more disposed to react to small increments in the child's performance in the direction of the required complex performances. Should any of the above processes produce a deficit in performance or an arrest in the development of the child's performance, further development of a repertoire would depend upon the community's relaxing its requirements and reinforcing performances in an older child that it normally accepts only from a younger one. Ordinarily, the reinforcing practices of the community are based on the chronological age and physical development of the child.

Only between the ages of $1\frac{1}{2}$ to 4 years does the parent have sufficient control of the child to weaken his performance to the degree seen in infantile autism. This is a critical period in the child's development during which his behavior is especially susceptible to extinction, because the traditional social pattern in the usual family restricts the child's experience to one or two parents. Before the age of $1\frac{1}{2}$, the child has few performances with which the parent will interfere or that have important effects on the parent. Much of the infant's behavior is maintained by simple and direct effects on its environment. As the child approaches 2 years, the rapid development of a behavioral repertoire, particularly social and verbal behavior, makes possible extinction and other forms of weakening. The effectiveness of the parental environment in weakening the child's repertoire depends upon the availability of concurrent audiences for the child's behavior. In general, the 2-year-old child is limited to the home and comes into increasing contact with other environments as he grows older, perhaps reaching a maximum at school age. The presence of an older sibling might appear to preempt the possibility of a sufficient degree of isolation to account for an aversive behavioral deficit. A sibling could provide an alternative to the parent as a reinforcing environment. The behavioral or functional influence of a sibling would depend on the amount and nature of interaction between the children. For example, an older child might possibly completely avoid the younger one or tend to have the same patterns of reaction as the parent. In many cases, the older sibling has playmates outside the home to the complete exclusion of the younger child. The older sibling, in many circumstances, punishes as well as extinguishes the younger child for any attempted participation in his play. There are very few facts as to the exact nature of the interactions in most cases.

The parent as the sole maintainer of the child's behavior is perhaps even more likely when the child is raised in a rural or isolated community, and perhaps with one of the parents largely absent. The above analysis suggests that a survey of severely autistic children would, in general, show them to be first-born children; or, if other siblings were available, they would have provided little interaction with the child. It also suggests that the child would be raised in a house physically or socially isolated from other families or children such that there were no alternative social environments that could provide reinforcement for the child's behavior. When the child was exposed to both parents, it would be expected that both parents were consistent in their nonreinforcement of the child's performances.

## Aversive Control and Punishment

It has been possible to describe conditions which might produce major behavioral deficits without dealing with punishment or aversive control. A similar account might present a functional analysis of how performance deficits might occur as a result of aversive control. Many writers have already described some of these factors by extending general principles of aversive control to human behavior (7, 8, 11). For the purposes of the analysis presented in this paper, I should like to restrict the discussion of aversive control to its relation to positive reinforcement. Much of human aversive control is carried out by discontinuing or withdrawing reinforcement (3, 10). For example, a frown or criticism may function as an aversive stimulus because these are occasions on which reinforcements are less likely to occur. Even when corporal punishment is given, it is not clear as to whether the resulting effect on the child's behavior is due to a slap or to the lower inclination of a punishing parent to reinforce. Most parents who spank a child will be indisposed to act favorably toward the child for some period of time subsequently. As a result, one major by-product of frequent punishment may be a larger order of interference with the child's normal repertoire along the lines of the positive reinforcement deficits described above.

The obvious effectiveness of punishment in some kinds of human control appears to contradict experimental findings with animals which show punishment to have only a temporary effect on behavior (1, 2, 9). The role of positive reinforcement factors helps resolve the dilemma. The effectiveness of punishment depends on how strongly the punished behavior is maintained by positive reinforcement. The apparent effectiveness of punishment in the control of children may occur when weak repertoires are punished or when the punishment indirectly produces extinction. Most animal experiments using electric shock as an aversive stimulus have used strongly maintained positively reinforced operant behavior as the base-line performance to be punished. The aversive control might be more effective when the performances to be punished are less strongly maintained.

## Conclusion

As might be expected from the relatively low frequency of infantile autism, the combination of circumstances hypothesized above would occur only rarely. The above hypothesis provides a framework for investigating the circumstances surrounding the development of the autistic child. All of the variables that might weaken the behavior of a child are directly or potentially observable. The data required are the actual parental and child performances and their specific effects on each other, rather than global statements such as dependency, hostility, or socialization. Not all of the factors responsible for a child's performance may be present currently. Using retrospective accounts, however, makes it difficult to determine the actual correspondence between the verbal statements of the parent and their actual practices in raising the child. The alternatives are, first, an objective assessment of the child's repertoire in a wide enough range of environments so as to allow an assessment of the nature of the environmental control of the child's current behavior; and, second, actual home observations of the specific social consequences of the child's performances early in the development of the disease.

The same kind of functional analysis can be made for the performance of the adult psychotic although the specific deficits observed in autistic children and their manner of occurrence may not be relevant. In particular, the analysis of the adult's behavior would be more concerned with the factors which weaken behavior already in the repertoire rather than the development of new repertoires as with the analysis of the autistic child's behavior. Maintaining already-established behavior is more at issue in the adult than the initial development of a performance as in the case of the child (3).

REFERENCES

1. AZRIN, N. H. Punishment and recovery during fixed-ratio performance. *J. exp. anal. Behav.*, 1959, 2, 301-305.

2. ESTES, W. K. An experimental study of punishment. *Psychol. Monogr.*, 1944, 57, No. 3 (Whole No. 623).

3. FERSTER, C. B. Reinforcement and punishment in the control of human behavior by social agencies. *Psychiat. Res. Repts. 10*, 1958, 12, 101-118.

4. FERSTER, C. B., & DEMYER, M. K. A method for the experimental analysis of the behavior of autistic children. *Amer. J. Orthopsychiat.*, in press.

5. FERSTER, C. B., & DEMYER, M. K. The development of performances in autistic children in an automatically controlled environment. *J. chronic Dis.*, 1961, 13, 312-345.

6. KANNER, L. Early infantile autism. *J. Pediat.*, 1944, 25, 211-217.

7. MILLER, N. E., & DOLLARD, S. *Personality and psychotherapy.* McGraw-Hill, 1950.

8. ROTTER, JULIAN. *Social learning and clinical psychology.* Prentice-Hall, 1954.

9. SKINNER, B. F. *The behavior of organisms.* Appleton-Century-Crofts, 1938.
10. SKINNER, B. F. *Science and human behavior.* Macmillan, 1953.
11. SKINNER, B. F. Some contributions of an experimental analysis of behavior to psychology as a whole. *Amer. Psychologist,* 1953, 8, 69-78.
12. SKINNER, B. F. *Verbal behavior.* Appleton-Century-Crofts, 1957.

# BEHAVIOR THERAPY WITH CHILDREN[1]

## C. B. FERSTER
*Institute for Behavioral Research*

## JEANNE SIMONS
*Linwood Children's Center*

Even though there is no widespread use of behavior therapy in clinics there have been many demonstrations in clinic settings of how to apply a functional analysis of behavior. For example, Wolf, Risley, and Mees (1964) dramatically changed the behavior of an autistic child by carefully arranging large parts of the child's total hospital environment. They made the environment specifically reactive to those behaviors they wanted to develop, and nonreactive to those behaviors they intended to weaken. Lovaas (1965) has carried out experiments which were essentially therapeutic procedures. In these he carefully measured the child's behavior in relation to its functional environment; he actually synthesized speech and social behavior by a graded series of reinforcement procedures carefully adjusted to each child. Experiments with retarded children, such as those by Girardeau and Spradlin (1964) and Birnbrauer and Bijou (1965) show how elements of a normal repertoire, such as reading and writing or eating with utensils and putting on clothes, may be created and maintained with reinforcement procedures. Other examples are nursery school experiments by Bijou's group (Harris et al., 1964) at the University of Washington and the classroom demonstration experiment by Zimmerman and Zimmerman (1962), who weakened primitive behavior in the classroom by making the teacher's attention occur as a result of productive school work rather than annoying behavior.

Because it is difficult to control children verbally and because research in operant behavior has predominantly used food reinforcement, many of the clinical demonstrations with children (as well as psychotic adults) have also used food reinforcement. These food reinforcement

1 This research was carried out with a grant from the Aaron E. Norman Fund and the Office of Education, Grant No. 32-20-7515-5024, Division of Handicapped Children and Youth. The paper was delivered at the symposium on "An appraisal of operant techniques in the therapeutic modification of children's behavior" at the American Psychological Association, September, 1965.

PSYCHOLOGICAL RECORD, 1966, Vol. 16, pp. 65-71.

procedures are often valuable because they develop performances that may be maintained in other places by direct effects on the environment, natural to the behavior and unrelated to getting food. The general case is illustrated in a recent talk by Skinner, who spoke of a normal child who memorizes the multiplication tables in class but later behaves arithmetically elsewhere because material reinforcers take control of the same repertoire. We know little technically of the conditions under which this transfer from one reinforcer to another takes place, but we know that it does. Lovaas, for example, developed speech and soical behavior in autistic children with frosted cereal flakes as a reinforcer, but these same performances were maintained later, naturally, because the new performances made possible new experiments in the social environment.

To the extent that it is successful, much conventional therapy is behavior therapy. Some of the apparent difference between the activity of clinicians and behavior therapists comes from the frequent use of food as a reinforcer in behavior therapy. Whenever we have observed successful clinicians at work, we have seen them change verbal and nonverbal behavior and manipulate the environment, much as in behavior therapy. The potential contribution of behavior therapy comes when natural-science, laboratory principles are self-consciously applied to clinical problems. With such a natural-science approach to clinical problems, the objective and functional description of the environment makes it possible to describe what particular aspects of a complex interaction are having what particular effects on the patient. Hence new procedures can be developed, and old ones refined and their application intensified. With such a natural-science philosophy of human nature, the behavior of the therapist is constantly shaped differentially and reinforced by its effect on the patient.

Therapy with children gives many chances to reinforce behaviors by a natural effect on the environment, inherent in the performance itself, rather than food. Many of the performances and available reinforcers which are effective with children are easily applied without extensive control of the child's life, and the traditional treatment center offers many opportunities for many non-food aspects of the child's life. We speak of reinforcements as being natural when the other environments available to the child (such as the parental environment) would also reinforce the same behavior in the same way.

Our experiences at the Linwood Children's Center in Ellicott City, Maryland, provide opportunities to describe how the natural environment of a treatment center may be used to produce new behaviors. Jeanne Simons, the Director of Linwood, and Kathryn Schultz, Medical Director, are collaborating with Dr. John Cameron and myself in a project in which we are combining clinical procedures and a functional analysis of behavior. In many ways Miss Simons has manipulated the environment of the treatment center to change and develop children's behavior with a surprisingly large number of instances in which highly effective reinforcers were used which had no relation to eating or drinking.

Many reinforcers, special for each child, are discovered and applied on the spur of the moment. For example, one boy, Jackie, was reluctant to leave the room one day after Jeanne Simons had been swinging and tumbling with him. Instead of continuing to play with him or sending him away, she held him in front of a puzzle, put one piece in his hand and held his hand over the appropriate place until he dropped it. The puzzle was of the simplest form, so a slight nudge on his part jarred it into place. When he fit the puzzle into its exact place Miss Simons reacted instantly and enthusiastically. She led him to an open area where she roughhoused with him, but only for about a minute. They then went back to the puzzle, where this time he not only dropped it into the right place, but he nudged it into position without Miss Simons guiding his hand during the final maneuver. She approved immediately, as before, and played with him again for another minute. In each of perhaps ten such successive experiences (a total of about ten or fifteen minutes), she required a little more of the boy each time until finally he picked up a piece, put it into place, walked to where she had been taking him for play and lay on the floor with his hands up, wanting Miss Simons to play with him. We judged his puzzle activity was under close control of its reinforcer, the roughhousing with Miss Simons. On successive days the roughhousing activity was contingent on more sustained and complicated performance with the puzzles. Finally, Jackie assembled three or four different puzzles, some much more difficult than the first one, before being reinforced. The reinforcer was remarkably durable probably because some of its effect came from Jackie's relationship with Miss Simons and his other rewarding experiences in the room.

The puzzle itself is an example of a natural reinforcer. The difficulty of the puzzle specifies a schedule of intermittent reinforcement. Its physical design determines much of the behavior appropriate to completing it. In a very simple puzzle, almost any performance gets the piece in place and hence reinforcement is virtually continuous; but as the pieces become even slightly irregular, the child may need to make several attempts, only one of which will be reinforced. With more difficult puzzles, there are more possibilities of nonreinforced responses, and a graded series of puzzles is a convenient device for changing from continuous reinforcement to a difficult puzzle where some behavior may go unreinforced. Eventually the reinforcement again becomes continuous when the child achieves an effective repertoire. Laboratory experience shows that such a graded experience from continuous to intermittent reinforcement is the best way to develop a persistent, durable repertoire. The small amount of restraint imposed on Jackie when Miss Simons held her arms around him the first time he was in front of the puzzle reduced the frequency of many behaviors which might be prepotent over dropping the puzzle into place. The actual reinforcer maintaining the puzzle activity was Miss Simons' immediate verbal response, which in turn derived some of its effect from the roughhousing. Eventually Miss Simons shifted the control to the puzzle itself, which later came to be the only event preceding the roughhousing.

A second child frequently played with a set of cups which stacked inside each other. These cups were used to reinforce puzzle activities as with the boy I just described. Initially the puzzle was of the simplest sort and all that was required of the child was to push the piece into its hole. The first response was chosen as one that was surely in the child's repertoire, so that almost all behavior could be reinforced. Without this careful successive approximation, the reinforcer would probably not have been durable enough.

Jackie had to be protected from some staff members who were disposed to swing Jackie "free" because they were reinforced by seeing him enjoy himself; others were inclined to let the second child play with the cups until he tired of them.

Even though a child may be strongly inclined to play on the rocking horse or dress himself, he may still need an adult to help him, because he cannot climb on the horse or put on or take off his clothes. Such sequences of performances leading to rewarding activity are a chance to increase the child's repertoire. For example, a child who enjoyed rocking was lifted up one foot on one stirrup, her hands held, and the final step of swinging one leg over was left to the child. The first approximation was carefully chosen to be clearly within the child's potential behavior and successive approximations resulted in the child taking responsibility for more and more of the behavior needed to get onto the horse until, finally, she climbed on herself. Being on the horse was the reinforcer and the therapist arranged how much on the child's part was needed to get on the horse. Each increment in the child's performance got him onto the horse, and slightly more was required on the child's part and slightly less on the therapist's part on successive occasions.

One time, taking off Kathy's sweater, Miss Simons stopped with one hand in the sleeve and said, "Now you take your hand out of the arm." Kathy withdrew her hand. This contingency reinforced undressing because it actually "took the sweater off." On later days Kathy did more as Miss Simons withdrew her support and Kathy acquired performances further back along the chain of behaviors leading to the sweater coming off. We do not know in this case why getting the sweater off is reinforcing. Kathy might be too warm; following Jeanne Simons' instructions might be becoming a reinforcer; the sweater might be restrictive; or she might take it off because in her experience with Jeanne Simons, nothing else could happen until she complied. Given the sweater as a reinforcer, the procedure was functionally parallel to animal training procedures where the last member of the chain is brought under the control of a reinforcer and the antecedent members added one at a time. In the present case, the whole chain of performances is executed each time, but only the last performance occurs under the control of the natural reinforcer. The earlier members, while not in the child's repertoire, are suported by the therapist as she "helps the child onto the horse."

Regular meals were used indirectly as a reinforcer by requiring all of the children to have a poker chip, sometimes of a particular color, to enter the dining room. The immediate events, reinforcing the behavior with the tokens, are social and outside the dining room, even though food ultimately maintains the performance. A staff person at the entrance admits a child only if he has a token of the correct color. Someone else, 15 feet or so from the dining room, gives out the tokens. If a child comes to the door without a token, he is sent back for one, but the procedures are adjusted for new children so that the requirement is clearly within their capability. In practice no child misses lunch but is simply delayed until all of the children have entered the dining room and the child's behavior can be supplemented by a staff member. Almost without plan, the requirement advances in tiny increments until all of the children are under close control of the token and its related procedures. Occasionally a child shuffles back and forth between the two people because he does not take or give a token, but this is the experience that subsequently conforms his behavior to the requirement of the token milieu. The procedure provides occasions for productive social interactions and the children conform to a controlled environment which we judge to be therapeutic.

Frequently Miss Simons will deprive a child of his freedom or an article of clothing and make their return contingent on a particular performance. One day when William, a verbal autistic child, screamed, kicked and in general thrashed about, Miss Simons first took his shoes off. Then she held him by a sheet around his waist, his arms free, so that she could hold him at arm's length without being kicked or bitten. As he calmed down, she loosened her hold and as he behaved primitively she tightened it until finally the conditions for going over to the sofa where he could get his shoes were that he walk calmly, holding her hand lightly. Another time when Miss Simons had also taken off his shoes, he demanded she put them on him. She compromised by putting his shoes on (after all, *she* had taken them off) if he put his socks on (which *he* had taken off).

Initially, William's tantrum was an aversive stimulus which strongly controlled the behavior of all of those around him. Adults around William either stepped out of his way as he attacked or they tried to stop the tantrum. When they stepped out of his way, William was controlling them by presenting an aversive stimulus which was terminated by their escape. When they remained and interacted with William's tantrum he was also controlling since the tantrum provided many aversive stimuli which they would have to terminate or escape from if they remained in the vicinity. Miss Simons first reversed William's control of her by taking his shoes off and restraining him. The restraint gave her a reinforcer which she could apply to some behavior of her choice. So long as the boy behaved primitively she held him tightly. When he relaxed, she released him. This experience provided a series of contingencies in which tantrum behavior was not reinforced (the sheet remained tight). Walking toward the sofa "voluntarily" was reinforced by escape from the restraint. His shoes served as a reinforcer probably

161

because they were necessary before he could leave the room where he was under close and continuous control by Miss Simons. The procedures used in this episode reinforced productive social behaviors and extinguished tantrums and other atavisms. The environment was designed to weaken the primitive behaviors because the operants which were reinforced were incompatible with them. So long as the tantrum persisted, the restraint was maintained. The operant behavior of walking to the couch was reinforced by termination of the restraint.

A similar rearrangement of the environment was carried out with a 3½ year old autistic girl. Kathy had already developed a substantial relationship with Miss Simons and she had a considerable disposition to remain with her. The episode began with a reaction in pique when Jeanne Simons took away one of two cups from Kathy when she began banging them on the table. Kathy then took a plate with a half sandwich which she had not yet eaten and threw them on the floor. Within 15 seconds after Kathy had dropped the food and plate, Miss Simons began a set of procedures, lasting for approximately 27 minutes, during which she remained continuously with the child. She prevented any activity other than picking up the sandwich including completion of the lunch, further interpersonal reaction, or any kind of play. All of these restrictions precipitated a period of intense intermittent crying, foot stamping, and thrashing about. All this time Miss Simons kept Kathy near the sandwich or the sandwich near Kathy. There was a steady verbal interchange in which she spoke of picking up the sandwich or remarks like, "No, no, you'll have your milk after you pick up the sandwich." The episode was terminated when Kathy handed the plate approximately four inches toward Miss Simons. This was a compromise and an adjustment of the criterion toward what Miss Simons thought Kathy capable of, but next time she would require more.

These procedures had several results. First, they provided an opportunity for extinguishing or weakening primitive ways of social action, such as screaming or crying. Second, there was an aversive consequence of throwing food on the floor which may have had some effect in weakening the subsequent disposition to throw food down. Third, the final result of the episode was the reinforcement of a social operant response, picking up the sandwich, under Jeanne Simons's control.

All of these behavioral episodes described behaviors and reinforcers which were natural. The behaviors were natural because many alternative environments could also support the same behaviors. Other sweaters in other places would reinforce the same behavior as in the treatment center. If a child will not spend its life in an institution, the most useful repertoire to develop in the clinic is one that will be effective in the home. If the parental milieu is at all adequate, the success of the child's repertoire lies in performances which meet reinforcers that the parents will ultimately supply. Conversely, for a new performance from the treatment center to continue in the home, the parents' repertoire may need to be changed to maintain the child's new behavior.

162

Even behaviors under the control of natural reinforcers depend on the parental environment to be of therapeutic help for the child. Ultimately it is the parental environment which must maintain the child's behavior. Performances which are generated in a treatment center will disappear if the parents' behavior or other aspects of the home do not provide contingencies to maintain it. Conversely, primitive behaviors such as tantrums or self destruction, which may be extinguished or weakened in the treatment center, will be reinstated if the parents continue to react to these performances as they did originally. It might be possible, however, that changes in the child's behavior from the treatment center will influence a change in the parents' practices at home. Whether the child's behavior will reinforce new parental behavior depends, in turn, on the particular ways the child's behavior provides reinforcers for the parents.

## REFERENCE

BIRNBRAUER, J. S., BIJOU, S. W., WOLF, M., & KIDDER, J. D. 1965. Programmed instruction in the classroom. In L. P. Ullman and L. Krasner (Eds.) *Case studies in behavior modification.* New York: Holt, Rinehart & Winston.

GIRARDEAU, F., & SPRADLIN, J. 1964. Token rewards in a cottage program. *M. R. J.*

HARRIS, FLORENCE, JOHNSTON, K., SUSAN, C., & WOLF, M. 1964. Effects of social reinforcement on regressed crawling of a nursery school child. *J. ed. Psychol.,* 55, 35-41.

LOVAAS, I., FREITAG, G., GOLD, VIVIAN, & KASSORLA, IRENE. 1965. Experimental studies in childhood schizophrenia: Analysis of self-destructive behavior. *J. exp. Child Psychol.,* 2, 67-84.

LOVAAS, I., SCHAEFFER, B., & SIMMONS, J. In press. Experimental studies in childhood schizophrenia: Building social behaviors in autistic children using electric shock. *J. exp. Stud. Pers.*

WOLF, M., MEES, H. I., & RISLEY, T. R. 1964. Application of operant conditioning procedures to the behavior problems of an autistic child. *Behav. Res. Ther.,* 1. 305-312.

ZIMMERMAN, ELAINE & ZIMMERMAN, I. 1962. The alteration of behavior in a special classroom situation. *J. exp. Anal. Behav.,* 5, 59-60.

# MEDIATED LANGUAGE ACQUISITION FOR DYSPHASIC CHILDREN

### B. B. GRAY and L. FYGETAKIS

Monterey Institute for Speech and Hearing, Monterey, California

THE TERM "dysphasic child" is often used to designate the child with normal intellectual potential who evidences a significant lack in linguistic performance resulting from neurological impairment. This deficient linguistic performance is usually accompanied by a similar pattern of behavior in the perceptual areas as well. The behavioral corollaries to this neurologically defined deficit are hyperactivity, distractibility and perseveration.

In our school systems the educational process is based to a very large degree upon language. The main tool for information transfer is language. Therefore, the dysphasic child will, from the very beginning, experience a compounding of educational problems which will result in a failure of our educational system for him.

Especially at the pre-school level, language is very important not only for the acquisition of information but also for the development of higher order language. The latter, in turn, facilitates the intellectual assimilation of more abstract and complex ideational units.

The inability to handle the basic tools of education, i.e. language, will certainly preclude much success for the child in academics. Social defranchisement will follow closely the pattern set down as a result of poor performance in early school experiences. A major concern of any program directed at these children, then, should stress early identification and training. In this way, hopefully, early school experiences for the child will be positive and educational rather than negative and confusing.

Since the late 1950's there has been a growing interest in a behavioristic approach to many problems in human behavior and learning. The beginning of this increased attention to behavioristic application of learning theory and conditioning is most notably marked by Wolpe (1958) and Eysenck (1960, 1964, 1965). The name behavior therapy was coined by Lazarus (Wolpe and Lazarus, 1966) to refer to that group of learning theory based procedures which could be effectively applied to human behavior. This categorization, sometimes called behavior modification instead, included both instrumental and classical procedures.

Within this philosophy, behavior is viewed in terms of stimuli, response and consequence. The consequence may result in a greater likelihood that the response will reoccur in future similar situations—a reward—or conversely in a lesser likelihood that the response will occur in future similar situations—a punishment. Procedurally, then, one

BEHAVIOR RESEARCH AND THERAPY, 1968, Vol. 6, pp. 263-280.

way to modify or control the response would be to have control over either or both the stimulus and the consequence.

Numerous examples of the efficiency and effectiveness of this approach have been published. Many compendium volumes have been published, each of which offers many different authors, many different behavior therapy examples, and many different classifications of human problems (Eysenck, 1960, 1964; Eysenck and Rachman, 1965; Ullmann and Krasner, 1965; Krasner and Ullmann, 1965; Ulrich, Stachnik and Mabry, 1966). Within this and other literature there are many articles dealing with children. As an example, some of the authors have used conditioning methods to deal with emotional and behavioral problems (Patterson, 1965; Allen *et al.*, 1965). Some have concentrated upon the verbalization of mute children (Kerr *et al.*, 1965; Salzinger *et al.*, 1965). Still others have been primarily concerned with language (Risley and Wolfe, 1967; Schell, Stark and Giddan, 1967).

One noteworthy point is that in many of these and other papers, regardless of other problems in these children, concern centers upon language performance and its improvement. This observation not only points up the universality of language to human behavior but also gives us some idea of the breadth and diversity of specific learning techniques which can be effectively utilized in modifying language behavior. Much of behavior modification is concerned with delineating very carefully those overt acts to be changed. This type of preoccupation with fractionization can and does lead to a series of highly conditioned language responses which are only loosely connected to each other. The child often lacks the base language structure which is necessary for the spontaneous generation of new correct grammatical constructions. The result is an automatic type speech.

Programmed instructional techniques represent the most sophisticated method of organizing and pacing the presentation of educational materials. Programmed instruction is continuing to play an important role in the education process. Since the beginning overtures (Skinner, 1958) along this theme, the number and sophistication of programmed instruction materials has steadily increased. Hendershot (1964) lists over 100 publishers and manufacturers and more than 400 programs. Topics include nearly all of the standard educational subjects. In terms of language, they offer only vocabulary and reading skills programs.

In speech pathology there have appeared in the commercial market types of programmed booklets and tapes for various articulation disorders (Sound Production Associates, 1967; General Electronics Laboratories, Inc., 1967). The most common element to be found in this classification of material is a sequential presentation of work assignments, or problems, or auditory signals.

Almost all good programs are effective to one degree or another, but only for the adult or child *who already has a basic competence in the language*. Language serves as an interface between the information and the student. There are, to our knowledge, no programmed instruction materials for the acquisition of basic language.

For language learning purposes the typical textbook types of programs are ineffective in at least four aspects. (1) The written program booklet does not monitor the student's responses. Language is an overt transitory act and requires an immediate feedback from some external source concerning its correctness. This cannot be done initially by the child himself and a booklet provides no method of doing it. (2) The standard program has no method for confirming understanding on each frame. The building block method

165

of most programs assumes that successful completion of one frame is adequate evidence for moving to the next slightly more difficult frame. In fact, if a frame is worked incorrectly the student often proceeds ahead anyway. There is little opportunity for practice and little provision for achieving a level of competence or a strengthening of the stimulus-response bond at any one frame in a program. (3) Written programs are non-flexible. Virtually all programs are linear. Indeed, the most efficient program is a linear program. Yet the complexity and variety of options associated with language acquisition argues against a linear program. As such, the linear program would either become ineffective or it would become a branching program. Although much more difficult to design and execute, the well planned branching program is superior to an improvisation of a linear one. (4) Programs tend to minimize the critical role of meaningful reward. The basic element in learning is the response-reward contingency. Yet the program booklet relies on a subtle and highly intellectualized feeling of accomplishment on the part of the student when he moves the slider and looks at the correct answer. The effect of this bland treatment of reward can be seen in the many statements of teachers who use programmed texts. Often they remark that with some of their children the books just don't seem to be effective. The child appears to have no interest or motivation. From a learning theory point of view this situation is not unexpected. No doubt even the performance of the "good" students could be improved with some attention to the giving of meaningful and effective rewards for correct responses. Reward is such a basic element that it should not be left to chance.

Generally, then, it may be said that with behavior therapy techniques we have highly efficient procedures for modifying and/or "implanting" specific behavior. On the other hand, with programming we have a highly organized structure which can pace and grade and co-ordinate material.

If the highly efficient conditioning techniques could be "fitted" into an organizational plan (programming) which would closely co-ordinate each response to be conditioned with every other response to be conditioned, then it might be possible to create a situation wherein the child in a maximal learning situation would be able to select out those cues necessary to construct a base language as well as generate a surface language at the performance level.

The application of this proposition follows from the assumption that the dysphasic child was initially unable to extract from his normal linguistic environment those significant cues to form his base language structure. This environment in normal situations is reasonably complex, ambiguous, filled with distractions, and full of apparent contradictions. Thus, possibly in habilitation if some of these cues were re-presented to him in a highly organized, structured, and controlled environment he could, with the aid of conditioning, acquire the necessary basic and surface language structure and performance.

This paper, then, is a report of our initial efforts to construct a method of language acquisition which is based upon the best aspects of conditioning procedures and programming methods. The procedure is referred to as programmed conditioning.

## METHOD

*Ss and facilities*

The Ss for this study were students enrolled in Children's House—a facility operated by the Monterey Institute for Speech and Hearing. The training center is a day program for pre-school dysphasic children. There is a maximum enrollment of six children per class at any one time. To be placed there a child must be between the ages of three and seven with a diagnosis of aphasia or dysphasia from a neurologist, a psychologist and from a speech pathologist. In the class used for this study there were five boys and one girl. The age range was 4·0–6·1 yr with a mean age of 4·8. The range of expressive language age for the group as per standardized diagnostic testing was 2·0–5·3 yr with a mean age of 3·7 yr. Their language was characterized by fractional sentences consisting of two or three word units. Their language was further characterized by the fact that they did not use function words and inflections, such as articles, prepositions, the verb "to be". past tense, negatives, etc. In general, their syntactical and morphophonemic constructions were quite poor. Also, their language was characterized by the use of jargon. All of the Ss evidenced numerous articulation problems which further reduced intelligibility. Typical utterances would consist of formations such as "Mommy home" for Mommy is at home, or "Billy hat" for That is Billy's hat. Although these children could communicate on a very primitive and restricted level they would not be able to succeed in a normal kindergarten class or first grade—even permitting a 1- or 2-yr span for maturation. They did not have sufficient language to deal effectively with such a situation or their present environments.

The main clinical room at Children's House was used for this study. It is a room 20 × 20 ft. The perimeter of this room is bound on all sides by an area 7 ft in depth. This additional space could be left open, thus increasing the space of the central room; or it could be closed off forming six small individual work areas around the central room.

The daily routine was carried out by a trained professional speech and language teacher who was assisted by two trained volunteers. It was the task of the teacher to administer the programmed conditioning procedures and to supervise the volunteers in their administration of similar procedures. The program at the school went from 9.00 a.m.–12.00 noon five mornings a week. The basic schedule of activities for the daily session was as follows:

 9.00– 9.10   Free play (for observation of spontaneous language)
 9.10– 9.30   Calendar, show and tell (for observation of spont. language)
 9.30–10.05   Expressive language (programmed conditioning)
10.05–10.20   Juice and cookies (for observation of spont. language)
10.20–10.45   Visual motor (programmed conditioning)
10.45–11.15   Gross motor
11.15–11.40   Individual help (programmed conditioning)
11.40–11.50   Articulation (programmed conditioning)
11.50–12.00   Receptive language (Story—spontaneous language)

The procedures were administered by the teacher or by the volunteers to groups of from two to six children. Each child advanced at his own rate within the same activity. Only during occasional instances were the programs given to one child individually. The volunteers worked with groups of up to four children. The teacher worked with groups of up to the maximum, which was six. The only time that the groups were in units of less than six was during the individual help time. This period was often used to help a child "catch up" or to work on a particular problem which was unique to one or two members of the class.

167

### Behavioral control

The characteristics of hyperactivity and distractibility which were present in all of the children created particular problems. Very definite measures had to be used to gain control over the activity of the children, whether on the playground or in class. If not controlled, the situation would become a vicious circle between increased distractibility and increased hyperactivity. Not only was control desirable from a social point of view but it was very necessary in order to arrive at a preparatory set to attend for learning. It was deemed frivolous to attempt any type of language learning in an environment which did not include the attention of the children.

All activities during the morning were under behavioral control and reinforcement contingency. Discipline as well as language performance was under this reinforcement contingency. Verbal social approval was given randomly and frequently for any desired behavior and/or language performance. Also, styrofoam tokens, in the shape of thickened three pointed stars, were used as reinforcers. A child could receive a star for a correct response during programmed conditioning or for desired behavior on the playground. These were accumulated by each child in paper cups with 15 stars to a cup. When a cup was filled, it was stored and replaced with an empty cup. At the end of the week each child turned in his accumulated full cups for a toy. Various inexpensive toys were graded as to desirability and "priced" in terms of cups of stars.

Very definite and concrete rules for behavior in and outside of the classroom were established. When necessary, a star was removed from a child's cup for inappropriate behavior . . . but never for an error response during programmed conditioning. If behavior problems became so severe as to cause a disruption in the routine of the day then the child was placed in a "time out" situation. This consisted of removing the child from the group to a quiet, non-distracting place for a period of 5 min. At the end of that time the child had the option of returning to the group or remaining in the "time out" situation for an additional 5-min period. Both the teacher and the volunteers dispensed and removed stars. Only the teacher could send a child to "time out".

### Delivery system

Once the children were under operant control for their general behavior, it was then possible to activate the mechanism or the vehicle by which the desired information would be transferred to the child. The present method is called programmed conditioning.

The most obvious fact is that any program in this situation will have to be administered in some non-reading manner. One method would be for the teacher to act as an "interpreter" between the program and the child. Thus, the program could become a set of instructions for the teacher as well as a template of subject activity.

Figure 1 is an example of the programmed conditioning procedure for acquisition of the verbal-linguistic unit "is".

These programs take into account the eight variables of the learning situation which are thought to be the most influential in this situation. These are then "regulated" by the format of the program. In Fig. 1 under the column labeled *Step* can be found numerical notations for each line of the program. These Steps are similar to a frame in a regular program. Occasionally to the left of the Step column will be indications of different *Series*. Series A, B, C, etc., refer to roughly homogeneous activities which are then broken down into the smaller Steps. A Series heading is similar to a chapter heading in a book.

Goal: Use of *is* in spontaneous language    G: Star–tokens and social approval

Comments: np–vp repeated twice    Date:

|  | Step | Stimulus | Response | M | Sch | C | SM | RM | Cx |
|---|---|---|---|---|---|---|---|---|---|
| Series A | 1 | objects np–vp | is | I | C | 5 | V/V | V | 1–1 |
|  | 2 | objects np–vp | is–pred. nom | I | C | 10 | V/V | V | 2–? |
|  | 3 | objects np–vp | sub–is–pred. nom | I | C | 10 | V/V | V | 3–3 |
| Series B | 1 | pictures np–vp | sub–is-pred. nom | I | 50 | 10 | V/V | V | 3–3 |
|  | 2 | pictures np–vp | sub–is–pred. nom | IE (art.) | 50 | 10 | V/V | V | 4–3 |
|  | 3 | pictures np–vp | sub–is–pred. nom | DE (art.) | 50 | 10 | V/V | V | 4–3 |
|  | 4 | pictures np–vp | sub–is–pred. nom | IT (sub.) | 50 | 10 | V/V | V | 1–3 |
| Series C | 1 | pictures np–vp | is-prep, noun | I | C | 10 | V/V | V | 3–3 |
|  | 2 | pictures np–vp | sub–is–prep, noun | I | 50 | 10 | V/V | V | 4–4 |
|  | 3 | pictures np–vp | sub–is–prep, noun | IE (art.) | 50 | 10 | V/V | V | 1–4 |
|  | 4 | pictures np–vp | sub–is–prep, noun | DE (art.) | 50 | 10 | V/V | V | 6–4 |
|  | 5 | pictures np–vp | sub–is–prep, noun | IT (sub.) | 50 | 10 | V/V | V | 6–4 |
| Series D | 1 | pictures non–rep questions | sub–is–pred. nom– prep, noun | N | C | 10 | V/V | V | — |
|  | 2 | pictures non–rep questions | sub–is–pred. nom– prep, noun | N | 50 | 10 | V/V | V | — |
|  | 3 | objects non–rep questions | sub–is–pred. nom– prep, noun | N | I | 10 | V/V | V | — |
|  | 4 | story+pictures non–rep questions | sub–is–pred. nom– prep, noun | N | I | 15 | V/V | V | — |
|  | 5 | spontaneous language | sub–is–pred. nom– prep, noun | N | O | — | O/O | V | — |

Fig. 1. Procedural plan for programmed conditioning of the verbal-linguistic verb "is".

Immediately to the right of the Step column is a *Stimulus* column. Under this heading is listed the state or description of the stimuli being used. In Step 1 Series A the notation indicates that stimulus items will include objects which will be accompanied by an appropriate noun phrase and verb phrase (which will be repeated twice as per *Comments* at top of page). Under the heading *Response* are the descriptions of the minimally acceptable responses to the appropriate stimuli. In our example of Series A Step 1 it is the verbalization of the word *is*.

The next column *M* refers to the model being used. More specifically, during some portions of the program it is desirable for the teacher to "act out" certain aspects of the response which she is requiring the child to give. Sometimes she will act out the exact entire response, sometimes only a portion of it, sometimes none of it. The various permutations of the modeling procedure to be followed are listed in the *M* column. Various symbols are used to designate the type of modeling procedure to be used. They are: I = immediate complete model, IT = immediate truncated model (only part is given—that which appears in the parentheses), IE = immediate expanded model (more is given in the model than is required in the response), D = delayed model—same as immediate except that the model and the request for a response from the child are separated by a short time pause, DT = delayed truncated, DE = delayed expanded, N = no model.

Under *Sch* is found the reinforcement schedule to be followed on that particular step (C = continuous reinforcement, 50 = a ratio schedule of 50 per cent reinforcement, I = intermittent reinforcement, and O = only social reinforcement). Any contingency that satisfies the definition of a reward may be used as a reinforcement. In this particular case it is the star tokens. In other instances it may be candy or anything else that is appropriate. The next heading, *Criteria*, gives the number of successively correct responses required before the program is advanced to the next step. *SM* refers to stimulus mode or the method of delivery of the stimulus. A "V" preceding the slash mark indicates that the stimulus is presented visually. A "V" following the slash mark indicates that the stimulus is presented verbally. A V/V indicates that the stimulus is presented both visually and verbally. An "O" in place of a "V" means that characteristic is not present in the stimulus presentation. *RM* stands for the response mode. NV is for nonverbal responses and V is for verbal responses. The final heading *Cx* stands for stimulus complexity and refers to the numerical notation of the number of stimuli which are defined as competing with the target stimulus—the complexity of the stimulus field. The number preceding the hyphen refers to the number of defined stimuli. The number following the hyphen refers to the number of units in the response.

The ideal program will be one in which the child is always successful. Its progression is scaled to the learning ability of the child. Realization of this ideal in real life would be quite the exception rather than the rule. This means that there is a very high probability that at some point in time a given child will not continue to progress through a given program. When failure occurs and the progression is halted the obvious question becomes—what or how should the program be changed?

The answer depends in large measure upon the philosophy governing the procedures. The present philisophy is that a clinical program should move vertically through material of increasing complexity at maximum efficient speed. Horizontal movement—intense specific work—should be administered only when needed. Thus, if a vertical progression through a program is stopped by the child's errors, then the teacher should undertake a logical and sequential modification of the eight variables. He should begin with the variable which is most easily altered and which changes as little as possible in the stimulus-response structure to get the correct response.

In accordance with the philosophy and the method stated above, a logic system has been developed in conjunction with the programs. The logic system instructs the teacher how to execute the program and how and when to modify the variables of the program. Figure 2 is an illustration of the logic system.

The architecture and matriculation of the logic system has been ordered according to available information where possible. However, in many instances the suggested manipulations and relationships are theoretical extrapolations which remain to be, and must be, tested and verified or modified.

Operationally the logic system instructs the teacher to begin with the first series and move vertically along the entire program. If the child reaches a point where he can no longer move forward then the logic system tells the teacher how and in what order to change the program.

Essentially the teacher changes only one variable at a time in the order—Complexity, Model, R and S Modes, Schedule, Response, Stimulus, Reinforcement. He would continue gradually to simplify the first variable until the child begins to give correct responses. If the child still is making error responses when the first variable has been reduced to its lowest point then the teacher would begin to change the second variable and so on until correct responses obtain. A technical discussion of this activity follows in the next paragraphs.

To read the system, begin at the upper right hand corner of the diagram at SE-A. The SE refers to Series and the additional letter refers to the Series letter. In this case it is Series A of any given program. This is always the starting point. If SE-A is completed then progression would be to SE-B and so on until the goal is reached. Thus, it functions essentially as a linear program.

However, if for instance SE-B is not completed because the child is unable to continue through the program, the progression would be horizontally to SE-B'. This is the notation for the first order reduction of the program. At the left hand side of the illustration can be found a list of the various reductions. From this list it can be noted that the first item to be modified is the complexity variable. The teacher would then reduce the complexity until (a) the child begins to give correct responses or until (b) the complexity is reduced to its simplest form. If situation (a) obtains, then the teacher would increase complexity until Step 1 of Series B is approximated. The progression would then continue through SE-B and so on. If situation (b) obtains, then the teacher would go to the second order reduction. The list indicates that the second order reduction is Model. Further down the list under the heading Model Reduction Series can be found the hierarchy for the various models. These models are listed from the simplest (immediate) to the most complex (none). Again, the teacher would begin to reduce the model until (a) the child begins to respond correctly, or (b) until the simplest model had been reached. If (a) obtains, then the model would be increased until the former level is reached. The program then would move to SE-B' where complexity would be increased from its simplest form to the previous level of SE-B. At this point the child would be back at his original point in SE-B and the progression would continue. If situation (b) obtains, then the next variable—R and S Mode—would be reduced until another binary choice point is reached. This method of successive modification would then continue in a similar fashion through the remaining variables. If excessive reduction of many steps should occur then the entire program should be subject to a thorough re-examination.

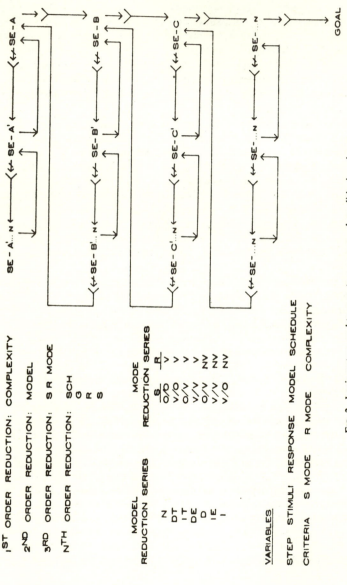

FIG. 2. Logic system used to execute programmed conditioning plans.

1ST ORDER REDUCTION: COMPLEXITY

2ND ORDER REDUCTION: MODEL

3RD ORDER REDUCTION: S R MODE

NTH ORDER REDUCTION: SCH
G
R
S

MODEL
REDUCTION SERIES

N
DT
IT
DE
D
IE
I

MODE
REDUCTION SERIES

| S | R |
|---|---|
| O/O | V |
| V/O | V |
| O/V | V |
| V/V | V |
| O/V | NV |
| V/V | NV |
| V/O | NV |

VARIABLES

STEP  STIMULI  RESPONSE  MODEL  SCHEDULE
CRITERIA  S MODE  R MODE  COMPLEXITY

172

The last type of material to be considered in this section is called the placement system. It is the purpose of this system to determine at what point in a program any given child should begin. Since not all children will need to go through the entire program, elimination of unnecessary steps will not only increase efficiency but will also decrease possible boredom on the part of the child. Figure 3 is a representation of the placement system.

Essentially it acts as a divider which successively reduces the area of uncertainty until the proper starting point is determined. Along the right hand side of the figure there is a line which has been divided into 16 equal divisions. The line from 0 to 16 represents any given program. Zero stands for the first step in the first series and 16 stands for the last step in the last series of that program. All other numbers are equidistant and represent intermediate points.

| TEST | YES | NO |
|------|-----|----|
| 1 | 2 | 5 |
| 2 | 3 | 10 |
| 3 | 4 | 12 |
| 4 | 16 | 3P |
| 5 | 6 | 8 |
| 6 | 7 | 15 |
| 7 | 7P | 6P |
| 8 | 14 | 9 |
| 9 | 9P | 0P |
| 10 | 13 | 11 |
| 11 | 11P | 1P |
| 12 | 12P | 2P |
| 13 | 13P | 10P |
| 14 | 14P | 8P |
| 15 | 15P | 5P |
| 16 | – | 4P |
| 0 | – | – |

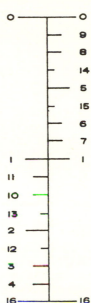

Fig. 3. Placement system used to determine starting place for programmed conditioning.

Placement testing always begins at the mid point or number 1. That is, the step which is halfway between the first and last steps is given to the child. If he can correctly perform the required response two successive times he is considered to have passed that test step. Since the program is progressive in construction it is assumed that he would have passed the preceding steps (0 to 1). By following the table on the left hand side of Fig. 3 it is possible to determine which step to test next by following the "yes" column for correct performance and the "no" column for incorrect performance. In the example, since number 1 was successfully completed the "yes" column by number 1 in the table instructs us to test number 2 next. Number 2 is mid-way between number 1 and number 16. If number 2 is failed then, following the table, we would test number 10. If number 10 is failed then we would test number 11. In the "yes" "no" column by number 11 the letter P appears by the entries. Whenever the letter P appears beside an entry in the table it

173

indicates that if the table is entered at that place the programmed conditioning should begin there. Thus, in the example, if number 11 is correctly performed by the child then the programmed conditioning should begin at the step in the program which corresponds to number 11 on the test. If the child fails number 11 then the programmed conditioning should begin at the step corresponding to number 1. A similar reduction process would occur with any combination of correct and incorrect responses.

In effect what the table does is to divide the area of uncertainty by one half each time. The programming placement is always made one level below the child's demonstrated upper limit. This is done so the child will experience success in his initial encounter with the programmed conditioning.

This entire placement test can be administered in less than 5 min. By asking only four questions it is possible to locate any child within a program within one-sixteenth of the total range of the program.

*Content material*

Once a method for delivery of information has been made available it remains to determine what material should be learned. In our particular instance we are interested in improving the base and surface language structure of these particular children. In accordance with information obtained from the initial language assessment on these children the following programs have been constructed to date: "is"; "is plus . . . ing modifier"; "regular past tense"; "articles"; "common nouns"; "what is . . . interrogative"; "auditory memory span for numbers and for letters"; and "articulation" (one program for all sounds). Basically the content material is determined by present interests or needs.

Records:

During all of the scheduled activities, various records were obtained. During the four opportunities for spontaneous language, base rates were obtained on the frequency of occurrence of a linguistic unit which was to be programmed at some time in the near future. These situations also were used to obtain frequency of occurrence measures for linguistic units which had already been conditioned and the programs terminated. During each programmed conditioning session, records were kept for the number of correct responses, the number of correct reinforced responses, the number of error responses, the type of error responses, frequency of behavior which resulted in the removal of stars, and content of spontaneous language utterances. At the end of each morning class the data were tabulated and entered on individual and group performance charts so that a running record could be maintained. This permitted analysis of day-to-day changes in performance and also permitted an exact determination of the response performance for each child on each step of each program.

## RESULTS

The behavioral control method worked extremely well. The entire class was able to sit quietly and work attentively for periods of up to 50 min. Hyperactivity and distractibility came down well into the normal range—only to reappear as the consequence of too rapidly advancing material or physical fatigue—neither of which occurred with any great frequency. The "time out" procedure was seldom needed or used. Only with one of the six children was it necessary to employ that tactic.

All children understood and responded to the token-toy method of reinforcement. After the first week all six children understood the system and were able to husband their tokens until the end of the week. There has never been any indication that the star tokens were losing their reinforcement value. This method appeared to be an acceptable means of reinforcement.

After two training sessions and 10–14 days' experience the volunteers were quite capable and able to effectively use the reinforcement contingency as well as to administer the programmed conditioning. A total of nine housewives were used as volunteers. Each one spent one or two mornings a week in the class. Since there were only two volunteers per morning this means that the children were faced with a different pair of volunteers each day. This did not appear to pose any special problem. After becoming familiar with the written form of the programmed conditioning material and symbols, the volunteers were as effective as the professional teacher in the straightforward administration of the steps in the program.

Figure 4 is a presentation of the performance of the children on the most efficient and the least efficient programmed conditioning materials. The most efficient was the "what is interrogative". An example would be "What is the boy doing?" The least efficient programmed conditioning was the "regular past tense". An example would be "He *kicked*

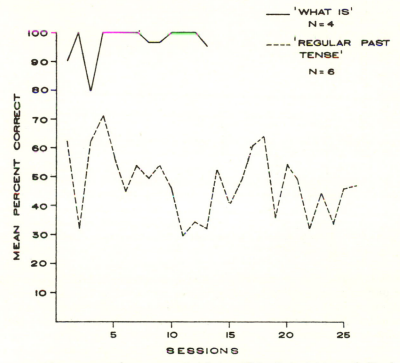

FIG. 4. Mean percentage correct responses on the most efficient ("what is interrogative") and the least efficient ("regular past tense") programmed conditioning procedures. Each session equals 25 min. Neither procedure has been completed.

the ball". At the time of this report neither program had been completed. The regular past tense procedure had been terminated and was under revision.

Figures 5 and 6 show the group performance on two highly successful programmed conditioning procedures. Both of these programs have been completed. A programmed conditioning procedure is not considered completed unless the last step has been successfully completed. The last step is always similar to the one in Fig. 1. That is, the last step is an attempt to elicit the correct response in a situation which approximates natural spontaneous speaking as closely as possible. However, it is still within the framework of the programmed conditioning and it cannot be considered to be identical with a spontaneous situation.

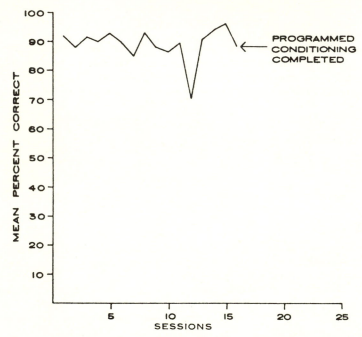

FIG. 5. Mean percentage correct responses for the "is" programmed conditioning procedure. Sessions equal 30 min each. N=6.

The periods during the morning which were designed for a freer language situation were used to determine if generalization was occurring. In all instances where a programmed conditioning procedure had been completed the target response was found to generalize to the free language periods of the morning. Also, these generalizations were found to contain spontaneous generation of grammatically correct alternate forms of the target response. Figures 7 and 8 show the performance of child M. on the programmed conditioning for the article "the" and the consequent change in target response frequency during free conversation. In no instance was there a generalization of the target response when a programmed conditioning procedure had not been successfully completed.

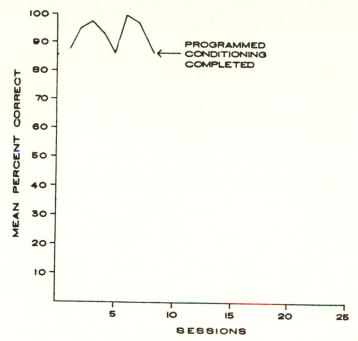

FIG. 6. Mean percentage correct responses for the "is . . . ing" programmed conditioning procedure. Sessions equal 30 min each. N=4.

Table 1 presents samples of actual language constructions of the children taken during spontaneous language opportunities. There are two examples of language samples taken before each of three programmed conditioning procedures were administered and two examples of language samples taken following the successful completion of the procedures. Language samples were taken from the same child for the before and after comparisons although different children's language samples were used for the three programmed conditioning procedures.

One item of note in Table 1 is the construction used in the "after" sample for the "the" programmed conditioning procedure. The sentence "The car is going on the floor" shows the embodiment of the two preceding programmed conditioning tasks. The spontaneous language sample from which this sentence was taken was obtained 18 weeks following the completion of "is" and 10 weeks following the completion of "is . . . ing". This example is a demonstration of the spontaneous generation of not only the article "the" but also the verb phrase "is going". This "is . . . ing" construction was dependent upon the successful acquisition of the verb "is". This demonstrates acquisition, generalization and spontaneous generation of previously programmed conditioned responses. In other words, this shows the development of a basic language structure.

At this stage, no specific procedures have been used for extending the carry-over into the home situation. As such, there is a generalization into the home situation but the

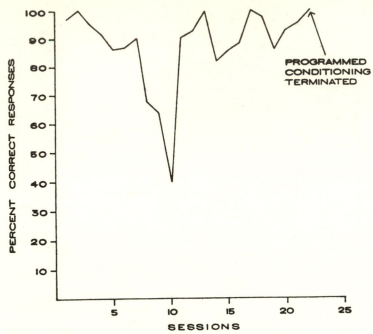

FIG. 7. Percent correct responses for child M. on the "the" programmed conditioning procedure. Each session equals 20 min.

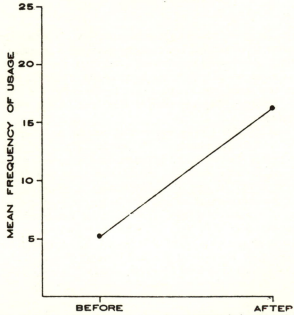

FIG. 8. Mean frequency count of correct usage of article "the" during three 10-min samples of spontaneous language before and after training on programmed conditioning procedures for child M.

178

TABLE 1. LANGUAGE SAMPLES TAKEN BEFORE AND AFTER PROGRAMMED
CONDITIONING PROCEDURES FOR THREE LINGUISTIC UNITS

| Programmed Conditioning Procedure | Before | After |
|---|---|---|
| "is" | Dad home. | He is in nest. |
| | This chip. | That is rooster. |
| "is . . . ing" | Boy sitting. | Santa Claus is going up sky. |
| | Him eating soup. | Mine jeep is rolling. |
| "the" | Sand is in jar. | The light is on the car. |
| | Choo Choo train is going. | The car is going on the floor. |

speed of the generalization and the strength of the generalization are less than for the free language situations at the school. The obvious remedy for this situation is to initiate specific procedures which will encourage a faster and stronger carry-over of the target response into the home. This is currently under development.

## DISCUSSION

Despite the newness and the unanswered questions about it, in our opinion the programmed conditioning procedure holds significant promise for effective training with language problems. This enthusiasm must be taken with a cautionary note. The procedure is new and critical portions of some of the theory behind it remain to be tested. However, if results can be used as any measure of the validity of a system then we feel that the current procedures of programmed conditioning warrant consideration.

One of the main premises of this system is that by giving these children certain function words through programmed conditioning that they would be able to generate spontaneous constructions and also be able to acquire additional basic language structure without further specific training. Without this premise the entire concept of programmed conditioning becomes nonfunctional.

One of the serious, and often valid, questions raised against a behavioral approach to language acquisition deals with the formation of a basic language structure vs. an echolalic surface language. Many linguists, such as McNeill (1966), argue that the conditioning of a number of verbal responses does not lead to the development of a base structure from which new compositions can be correctly formed. The result is that the child has a parrot-like speech. He only can elicit a variety of automatic responses to certain defined stimulus situations. It must be said that the observation of this phenomenon is not uncommon with some language conditioning procedures.

This situation led us to be particularly watchful during the free language periods. It would be in these situations where spontaneous language would first appear if the hypothesis about base structure via programmed conditioning was correct. During the free language situations, spontaneous construction of correct grammatical variations of the target response was noted. This was found in all cases of successful programmed conditioning procedures, but was not noted in situations where the programmed conditioning procedures were not completed. This observation gives support to the view that the programmed conditioning procedures do aid in the development of a basic language structure.

Another major factor in the findings was the workability of the system. If the programmed conditioning method cannot be used efficiently in the normal training setting then it has little practical value. Admittedly a first encounter with the procedures may tend to give the impression that it would be clumsy to use. Yet, teachers and clinicians who have used the procedures, found them to be very workable and suited to the actual management of the learning situation.

The best example of this is the facility with which our volunteers were able to master and to use the system. These people were housewives with no previous special training in language or psychology. They ranged from 25 yr to over 60 yr in age. After two special classes to explain the method and after 2 weeks experience assisting the teacher, the volunteers were capable of administering the programmed conditioning procedures without difficulty.

This aspect of the volunteer worker has an important implication. If non-professional people can effectively administer the programmed conditioning then this frees the time of the professional. The teacher or clinician can devote more time to construction of programs and analysis of procedures. In short, the professional has a greater opportunity to use his training and skill in a more meaningful manner.

One final observation is that these procedures appear to work effectively with a wide range of problem areas. That is, programmed conditioning appears to be a performance related activity rather than a diagnostically or disease related activity. These same procedures for programmed conditioning are being used with deaf children, autistic children, and articulation problem children. One difference is that with the deaf and autistic children we must first give content words and then function words. We have noted in these children an increment in performance level that is proportionately similar to that observed in our present population. Thus, continued support is found for the behavioral model in preference to the medical model in the achievement of goals for linguistically divergent children.

In conclusion, then, the initial results of programmed conditioning have been very promising. They have encouraged us to continue to develop and test and improve the system. The positive findings of this report must be taken in view of the fact that it is a new system. New systems need additional testing and experience; but they often hold encouragement and lead to information and understanding.

## REFERENCES

ALLEN K. E., HART B. M., BUELL J. S., HARRIS F. R. and WOLFE M. M. (1965) Effects of Positive Social Reinforcement on Isolate Behavior of a Nursery School Child. In *Case Studies in Behavior Modification* (Eds. ULLMANN L. P. and KRASNER L.). Holt, Rinehart & Winston, New York.
EYSENCK H. J. (1960) *Behavior Therapy and the Neuroses*. Pergamon Press, Oxford.
EYSENCK H. J. (1964) *Experiments in Behaviour Therapy*. Pergamon Press, Oxford.
EYSENCK H. J. and RACHMAN S. (1965) *The Causes and Cures of Neuroses*. Pergamon Press, Oxford.
GENERAL ELECTRONIC LABORATORIES, INC. (1967) *Speech Correction Series*. Boston, Massachusetts.
HENDERSHOT C. H. (1964) *A Bibliography of Programs and Presentation Devices*. Scher Printing Co., Saginaw, Michigan.
KERR N., MEYERSON L. and MICHAEL J. (1965) A Procedure for Shaping Vocalizations in a Mute Child. In *Case Studies in Behavior Modification* (Eds. ULLMANN L. P. and KRASNER L.). Holt, Rinehart & Winston, New York.

KRASNER L. and ULLMANN L. P. (1965) *Research in Behavior Modification.* Holt, Rinehart and Winston, Inc., New York.

McNEILL D. (1966) *Developmental Psycholinguistics.* The Genesis of Language. (Eds. SMITH F. and MILLER G.). The M.I.T. Press.

PATTERSON G. R. (1965) An Application of Conditioning Techniques to the Control of a Hyperactive Child. In *Case Studies in Behavior Modification* (Eds. ULLMANN L. P. and KRASNER L.). Holt, Rinehart & Winston, New York.

RISLEY T. and WOLF M. (1967) Establishing Functional Speech in Echolalic Children. *Behaviour Research & Therapy* 5, 2, 73–88.

SALZINGER K., FELDMAN R., COWAN J. and SALZINGER S. (1965) Operant Conditioning of Verbal Behavior of Two Young Speech Deficient Boys. In *Research in Behavior Modification* (Eds. KRASNER L. and ULLMANN L. P.). Holt, Rinehart & Winston, New York.

SCHELL R., STARK J., GIDDAN J. (1967) Development of Language Behavior in an Autistic Child. *JSHD* 32, 51–64.

SKINNER B. F. (1953) *Science and Human Behavior.* MacMillan, New York.

SKINNER B. F. (1958) Teaching Machines. *Science* 128, 969–977.

SOUND PRODUCTION ASSOCIATES (1967) An Automated Program in Speech Therapy. Institute of Modern Languages, Washington, D.C.

ULLMANN L. P. and KRASNER L. (1965) *Case Studies in Behavior Modification.* Holt, Rinehart & Winston, New York.

ULRICH R., STACHNIK T. and MABRY J. (1966) *Control of Human Behavior.* Scott, Foresman and Company, Glenview, Illinois.

WOLPE J. (1958) *Psychotherapy by Reciprocal Inhibition.* Stanford University Press, Palo Alto.

WOLPE J. and LAZARUS A. (1966) *Behavior Therapy Techniques.* Pergamon Press, Oxford.

# TEACHING SPEECH TO AN AUTISTIC CHILD THROUGH OPERANT CONDITIONING*

FRANK M. HEWETT, Ph.D.

The Neuropsychiatric Institute School, University of California, Los Angeles

THE AUTISTIC CHILD is a socialization failure. One of the major characteristics of autism which both illustrates and perpetuates this failure is defective speech development. The nature of speech peculiarities in autistic children has been described by Kanner,[6] and according to Rimland [12] lack of speech is found in almost one-half of all such children. The follow-up studies of Kanner and Eisenberg [7] indicate that presence or absence of speech by age five has important prognostic implications. Almost without exception the autistic child who reached his fifth birthday without developing speech failed to improve his level of socialization in later years. Even with psychotherapy, autistic, atypical children who had no speech by age three were found by Brown [1] to remain severely withdrawn and generally unimproved.

While intensification of speech training efforts with younger autistic children would seem a logical therapeutic maneuver, such children are characteristically poor pupils. Conventional teaching techniques are seldom successful because of the autistic child's profound withdrawal and preference for self rather than other-directed activities.

## BACKGROUND

The staff of the Neuropsychiatric Institute School at the University of California, Los Angeles, has been exploring operant conditioning techniques for teaching communication skills to autistic

* Presented at the 1965 annual meeting of the American Orthopsychiatric Association in New York, New York.

AMERICAN JOURNAL OF ORTHOPSYCHIATRY, 1965, Vol. 35, pp. 927-936.

children. Reading and writing have been taught to a twelve-year-old autistic boy who had never developed speech.[4] Recently a four-and-a-half-year-old, nonverbal autistic boy was the focus for a speech-training program.

In operant conditioning, the pupil learns to produce a given response (e.g., vocalization) following presentation of a cue or discriminitive stimulus (e.g., teacher's prompt) in order to obtain a desired reward or positive reinforcement (e.g., candy). In a similar manner he learns to avoid responses which lead to an undesirable consequence or negative reinforcement (e.g., isolation).

Operant conditioning techniques have been successful in increasing the frequency of vocalizations in normal infants [11] and reinstating speech in nonverbal schizophrenics.[5] An attempt to initiate speech in an autistic child is described by Weiland [13] who withheld a desired object (e.g., ball) until the child produced the word, "ball."

Speech training with animals has long involved conditioning procedures. Hayes [3] established a three-word vocabulary in his famous chimpanzee, Vicki, by making receipt of food contingent on vocalization. These vocalizations were later shaped into words by manipulating the lips of the chimp until closer and closer approximations of the desired words were obtained.

Mowrer [9] has written extensively on teaching birds to talk. According to Mowrer it is essential that the trainer's appearance become associated with positive reinforcement. He draws a parallel between this and the mother-child relationship during infancy. The mother's voice acquires secondary reinforcement value and is imitated because of its close association with food gratification and removal of pain. In a like manner presentation of food and water to birds becomes the basis for teaching speech as these positive reinforcements are paired with the trainer's presence and his verbal cues.

## THE SUBJECT

Peter is a four-and-a-half-year-old Caucasian boy diagnosed as autistic at age 2. He failed to develop speech although he said "Da-da" and "Ma-ma" during his first year. All attempts at speech ceased at one-and-one-half years and Peter was nonverbal when admitted to the Children's Service of the Neuropsychiatric Institute (NPI). Peter preferred to be left alone during infancy and became upset when picked up or cuddled. He was described as "too good," a young child who sought repetitive, mechanical activities rather than social interaction. At about age two Peter began to develop marked oppositional tendencies and became hyperactive, aggressive and uncontrollable in his behavior. His mother was constantly chasing him out of the street and away from danger. Peter's interest in mechanical gadgets increased and he developed an unusual degree of fine motor coordination. Recent neurological and laboratory tests were negative, and Peter's medical history has been uneventful. His hearing has also been judged as unimpaired. Peter has an older brother and sister who are normal.

## PROCEDURE

In planning the program of speech training, provision had to be made for gratifying and controlling Peter. Gratification and control are basic ingredients in all effective learning situations. Children learn those tasks which prove rewarding and which are taught in a systematic and structured manner. Autistic children, left to their own devices, are highly selective learners who obtain gratification by bizarre, inappropriate means; set their own limits, and consequently learn a restricted number of socialization skills. Before such children can be trained, the teacher must discover ways of providing gratification and establishing control. With respect to the latter, Phillips [10] has emphasized the importance of consistent and direct intervention of the autistic child's demands if behavioral changes are to be effected.

Food and candy are generally effective positive reinforcers, although autistic children may be quite variable in their preference. Peter was apathetic about food but displayed a consistent desire for candy as well as other positive inforcers to be described later.

Candy, however, would not control Peter's behavior. He was highly distractable, and his attention could only be engaged for brief periods with the promise of a candy reward. In an effort to reduce extraneous stimuli to a minimum and to introduce negative reinforcement as a lever for establishment of control, a special teaching booth was constructed for Peter.* The booth was divided into two sections, joined by a movable shutter (2 x 2½ feet) which could be raised and lowered by the teacher. The teacher occupied one-half of the booth and Peter the other half. Each section of the booth was four feet wide, three and one-half feet in length

and seven feet high. The only source of light came from the teacher's side and was provided by two spotlights which were directed on the teacher's face. When the shutter was down, Peter's side of the booth was dark. When it was raised, light from the teacher's side flooded through the opening and illuminated a shelf in front of Peter. To the left of the shelf was a ball-drop device with a dim light directly above it. This device consisted of a box into which a small wooden ball could be dropped. The ball rang a bell as it dropped into the box and was held inside the box until released by the teacher. When released, the ball rolled out into a cup at the bottom of the box where it could be picked up. This ball-drop device was Peter's "key" for opening the shutter. When the ball was released into the cup, he picked it up and dropped it into the box. At the sound of the bell, the teacher raised the shutter and initiated contact between the two of them.

In this setting the teacher not only provided candy and light as positive reinforcers but also used music, a ride on a revolving chair, color cartoon movies and a Bingo number-matching game which Peter liked. Isolation and darkness served as negative reinforcers and were administered when Peter failed to respond appropriately within a five-second period. Pilot trials with Peter and four other autistic children revealed the positive reinforcers to be effective in varying degrees and that all subjects would "work" to avoid isolation and darkness.

The training program with Peter can

* The author wishes to acknowledge the contribution of Mr. Frank M. Langdon, vice principal of the NPI School, in the design and construction of this booth.

be divided into four phases: introduction, social imitation, speech training and transfer.

## PHASE ONE—INTRODUCTION

When Peter was brought by his parents for admission there was a noticeable lack of separation awareness on his part. Despite the fact that he never had been away from home before, he walked away from his parents and into the ward without any visible reaction. Peter immediately was isolated in a room with an individual nurse where he remained for the first week of hospitalization. He was only taken from this room at mealtimes, when he accompanied the teacher to the teaching booth where he was fed. Peter quickly learned the mechanics of the booth. During this introductory phase he obtained each mouthful of food or drink of liquid by using the ball-drop "key." The shutter would be open when Peter was placed in the booth. The teacher fed him a portion of food and then lowered the shutter, releasing the ball into the cup. Peter picked the ball up and dropped it into the opening. At the sound of the bell, the shutter opened bringing the teacher's lighted countenance into view and providing another mouthful of food for Peter. This process was repeated mouthful by mouthful and sip by sip for one week.

By the third day of this first phase the teacher held food or liquid out for Peter but did not deliver it until eye contact was established. This first task of looking the teacher directly in the eye before getting food and drink was learned quickly, and immediate eye contact upon presentation of food was established 83 per cent of the time by the twentieth feeding.

The initial phase served not only to introduce Peter to the booth environment in which speech training would later be attempted, but also to acquaint him with the teacher. At first the teacher often would encounter resistance as he attempted to lead Peter from his ward room because of the change in activity involved. But by the fourth day of this phase Peter responded to the teacher's verbal command and walked to the door to meet him. During the course of his feeding sessions Peter remained in his chair directly in front of the teacher 57 per cent of the total time on the first day to 90 per cent on the day of the final feeding.

Throughout this paper, references are made to various positive reinforcers such as candy and food as providing necessary gratification for Peter. The teacher-child relationship which began at this early stage is not discussed. It is definitely felt, however, that the teacher acquired secondary reinforcement properties through constant association with primary reinforcers as described by Mowrer. While no attempt was made to control the teacher's facial expressions, physical contact with Peter and verbalization, these undoubtedly played an increasing role in motivating and controlling him as the training process progressed.

## PHASE TWO—SOCIAL IMITATION

Once Peter had been introduced to the booth, he was removed from isolation on the ward and allowed to participate in activities with the other children. Twenty-minute social imitation training sessions (in the booth) were held both morning and afternoon. During these sessions Peter learned to follow simple verbal directions and to imitate the teacher's hand movements. A variety of positive reinforcers was used at the beginning of this phase so that candy, the most potent reward, could be used during the speech-training phase.

Peter learned to place his hand on the teacher's face in order to obtain a segment of childrens' music. The music would continue so long as Peter kept his hand on the teacher's head. Peter appeared to enjoy testing this routine by quickly withdrawing his hand and replacing it to see if he could change the pattern.

The next task given Peter was that of clapping his hands in imitation of the teacher. Such a response would be rewarded by a single rotation of a motorized chair on which Peter sat. The hand-clap imitation proved a difficult task for him, and the shutter frequently was lowered because he was inattentive or failed to respond within the five-second limit. Once Peter learned the imitative hand-clap, another response was introduced. This required him to place both of his hands on his face in order to see a sequence of a color cartoon movie shown on a small screen to his right. This response was learned in one day. Additional social imitation training was done with the revolving chair as a reward. Peter readily learned to touch any part of his head (e.g., ear, nose) in imitation of the teacher. Each correct response within a five-second time limit earned a single rotation of the chair.

This phase was accomplished during the first month of the training program. Only those responses which Peter gave in direct imitation of the teacher were rewarded, and random responses were ignored. The main goal of this phase was to develop a reciprocal imitative relationship as a basis for speech training.

## PHASE THREE—SPEECH TRAINING

Peter had begun to vocalize spontaneously during phases one and two. He emitted 23 random spontaneous vocalizations on the first day of the booth feeding, and 79 random vocalizations during the final feeding day. In addition, music appealed to Peter, as it does to many autistic children, and he had been heard humming parts of familiar childrens' songs. He also had spontaneously hummed a few bars of the tune used as music reinforcement during phase two. The teacher selected the first three notes of this tune as the initial response in the speech-training phase, and candy was introduced as a positive reinforcer. A small lighted window was placed on Peter's side of the booth. A piece of candy could be dropped behind the glass where it remained in view until the teacher flipped it out to Peter.

The speech-training phase began with the teacher's placing a piece of candy behind the window and flipping it out. Peter was immediately drawn to this source of candy. Another piece of candy then was placed behind the window where it remained in view while the teacher hummed the first notes as an imitative cue. Peter was resistant to responding and only after several shutter drops did he imitate on cue and receive his candy reinforcement.

Once this response was established, the teacher began work on the first word. Peter had randomly made a shrill, undifferentiated vowel sound (ē-oö) during his spontaneous vocalizations in phases one and two. The teacher produced this vocalization and expected Peter to imitate it on cue for a candy reward. This was quickly established and actual speech training was under way.

Shaping this undifferentiated vowel sound into a word was the task at hand. The method of *successive approximation* described by Isaacs was used. The word "go" was selected for shaping because it denoted action and would lend itself to meaningful transfer in phase four. The teacher began by providing an imitative cue slightly in the direction of "go-o-o-o-o." Peter willingly approximated it. On successive trials, the teacher's cue moved more and more toward the word "go." The shaping of this word was accomplished dramatically in two days, and Peter consistently produced a well-articulated "go" on cue in order to obtain candy.

Overoptimism in such cases is inevitable but seldom warranted. Establishing the first conditioned word may be deceivingly simple, but retaining it is another matter. For five days, Peter readily responded with an imitative "go" to receive candy and quickly transferred this response to make the revolving chair "go." On the sixth day, however, he refused to respond appropriately. Instead of "go" he produced the vocalization, dä-dē. For the next seven days he refused to say "go."

Peter would be given five seconds to respond. If an inaccurate response was given, the shutter was dropped and a five-second penalty of isolation and darkness was administered. If the next trial produced the same response, an additional five-second increment was added and a penalty of ten seconds ensued. This increase was cumulative, and longer and longer periods were spent with Peter

and the teacher separated. At the close of the penalty period, the ball was released, Peter dropped it into the box, rang the bell, and contact with the teacher resumed.

A power struggle had begun. In an effort to resolve it, the teacher went back to providing the undifferentiated vowel sound (ē-oö) as a cue. But Peter did not respond. The major concern at this time was that the teacher would become an aversive reinforcer and that the positive relationship previously established would be negated. It was decided to wait out this resistance and to handle each inaccurate response in the prescribed manner. Finally, on the eighth day Peter began to imitate the undifferentiated vowel sound. This was quickly shaped back into the word "go," and at no time in the program did Peter display this marked resistance again.

In our previous pilot speech conditioning with autistic children, introduction of the second word often eliminated the initially learned word from the child's repertoire. It was, therefore, with some concern that the second word "my" was introduced in connection with a Bingo number-matching game which Peter liked. In order to obtain a Bingo marker, Peter was held for successive approximations of the word "my." This word was selected for its usefulness in denoting possession in the later transfer phase. During training on the new word, careful attention was given to systematically reviewing the previously learned word "go," and Peter discriminated well between the two words. The giving of an alternate reinforcer for the new word (e.g., Bingo marker) instead of candy appeared important in aiding discrimination.

The speech-training phase lasted six months during which time Peter acquired a 32-word vocabulary: go, my, see, candy, shoe, key, I, want, hi, bye-bye, mama, daddy, water, toilet, food, eye, ear, nose, mouth, hair, Peter, fine, please, juice, cracker, cookie, milk, Johnny, Marguerite, yes, no, school.

Once the first two words "go" and "my" were learned, Peter's speech became echolalic and he readily attempted to imitate all words the teacher said. However, improvement of his articulation of the 32-word vocabulary was emphasized rather than the building of a larger vocabulary.

Following the acquisition of "my," candy reinforcement was provided on a periodic basis for all new words learned.

Photographs were taken of Peter, his mother, father, brother and sister and he learned the name for each picture. In addition, pictures of Peter eating ("food"), drinking ("water") and going to the bathroom ("toilet") were used as cues. An attempt was made to break the echolalic pattern of Peter's speech, and he learned to answer the direct questions: "How are you? What's your name?" The technique used to teach Peter the appropriate responses to these questions (e.g. "Fine" and "Peter") was developed by Lovaas.[8] First, Peter was given both questions and answer for imitation (e.g., "How are you fine"). Gradually the teacher faded the question portion by saying it softly and quickly while emphasizing the answer (e.g. "How are you, FINE!"). Peter soon made a clear imitation of "fine" while paying less and less attention to the question. In a single training session, he learned to respond appropriately to these two direct questions.

The speech-training and transfer phases overlapped as Peter was required to use his conditioned words in a meaningful social context from the beginning of phase three.

## PHASE FOUR—TRANSFER

As soon as Peter had learned the word "go," transfer from the teaching booth to the hospital ward was emphasized. Each day when the teacher arrived Peter was required to say "go" as the teacher turned the key in the ward door lock to take him out for a training session.

A ward nurse later was brought into the teaching booth with the teacher. She immediately gained Peter's cooperation for social imitation tasks and the word "go." After working several sessions the nurse held Peter for the word before he was taken through the dining room door and out of the ward on walks. Peter was enrolled in the preschool program with another teacher, and she also participated in several booth-training sessions. Later Peter was required to say "go" in order to enter the schoolroom door. He also was held for "my" before he could obtain a desired object during school periods.

As Peter's vocabulary began to increase, he was required to ask for water, the toilet and food by preceding these words with the phrase, "I want." Also receipt of each periodic candy reinforcement was contingent on "I want candy." Such items as juice and crackers served in the preschool also were given to Peter only when he asked for them. These words were not introduced in the booth. Verbal imitation generalized from the teacher and the booth to other adults and even children in the ward environment.

The children in the preschool became very interested in Peter's attempts at speech and provided constant reinforcement of his words by prompting him. One older boy would hold a toy car at the top of a slanting block runway and let it "go" only when Peter directed him verbally. Peter proved a willing participant in such games.

The major effort during the transfer phase was undertaken with Peter's family. When Peter was permitted six-hour visits twice a week during the seven months of the program, he was not allowed to go home overnight. His parents knew that speech training was being attempted with Peter but not the exact nature of the program. On one occasion, however, while he was on a walk and his parents were moving more slowly than he desired, Peter spontaneously said, "go."

Once he had mastered the 32-word vocabulary Peter's parents were allowed to observe a training session through a one-way vision screen. Most of Peter's training sessions at this point were held outside the booth since he no longer needed the controlled teaching environment. Later both parents were brought into the room and directly observed the training session. Peter performed well with his parents at his side.

When the teacher pointed to Peter's mother and asked "Who's this?" Peter immediately said, "Mama," and took the photograph of his mother and placed it on her lap. He responded in a like manner for "Daddy." His parents then took the place of the teacher and evoked Peter's verbal repertoire using the photographs, Bingo game, candy and water. The transfer from teacher to parents was uneventful.

After this introduction to the speech program, Peter's parents (and occasionally his brother and sister) joined the teacher for weekly training sessions. Peter also was sent home on weekend visits, and the parents were advised regarding ways in which his newly acquired speech could be used at home. The entire family became involved in reinforcing his speech.

From this point on, Peter had great difficulty separating from his parents and often cried and clung to them as he was to report back into the hospital. Once the parents had left, Peter was given to long periods of crying on the ward. These reactions were in marked contrast to the detachment and apathy he exhibited upon separation following visits during early stages of the program.

A notable event occurred when Peter spontaneously imitated his mother's saying "money" and subsequently added, "I want money," in order to get coins to operate a vending machine. Shortly thereafter he approached the ward nurse saying, "I want toilet," or, "I want school," at the appropriate time, and his conditioned speech began to take on properties of meaningful language.

Peter remained in the speech-training program for eight months following phase three. For most of that period he participated as an outpatient, living at home, and attending the NPI School three times weekly for a two-hour preschool program and 40-minute, speech-training sessions. His speaking vocabulary grew to 150 words, and he demonstrated an insatiable desire to learn new words and phrases. Reading lessons also were introduced at this time as a means of enlarging his vocabulary.

At the time of discharge, Peter was returned to the care of the referring psychiatrist, enrolled in a private nursery-kindergarten, and placed with a speech therapist who had observed the speech-training procedures in the NPI School.

## DISCUSSION

In reviewing the significance of the conditioned speech which Peter acquired during the program it is important to consider the difference between speech and meaningful language.

Speech can be defined as articulated vocal utterances which may be the basis for communication, but meaningful language implies expression of thought and emotion in an appropriate and integrated manner. Birds may acquire speech but not true language skills.

Peter's rapid acquisition of words in association with visual and auditory cues is viewed as an important stage in the development of language. Although he did not systematically acquire the readiness for speech as does the normal child whose socialization experiences from early infancy are intimately involved with words, Peter learned to value and use word symbols. He also generalized an experimentally acquired vocabulary to the larger environment and used it to verbally express his needs (e.g., "I want toilet," or, "I want water").

How successful Peter will be in expanding his speech and converting it to truly meaningful language remains to be seen. That a sizeable communication breakthrough has occurred between an isolated, autistic boy and the social environment, however, cannot be denied.

Not only did this breakthrough make Peter more aware of his social environment, but it also altered the reaction of others toward him. This was clearly seen when nursing staff sought him out for verbal interaction, providing cues for imitation and holding him for speech before granting requests. Although many problems exist between Peter and his family, his newly acquired speech seems to hold promise for improving their relationship and facilitating limit-setting at home.

Goldfarb [2] has suggested that the response of others to the speech defects of schizophrenic children actually may reinforce such defects. Thus, the nature of the relationship between a nonverbal schizophrenic child and the environment may not be conducive to improved socialization. Meeting the needs of such a child by responding to his primitive and often bizarre attempts at communication may merely make an unsocialized existence more rewarding. In addition, the nonverbal schizophrenic child may be perceived as so atypical and difficult to reach that others develop less personal and involved means of relating with him.

The speech-training program described in this paper represents an intensive effort to establish the vital link of speech and language between a nonverbal, autistic boy and his environment during the critical period of early childhood. Peter's success in acquiring the beginnings of spoken language appears to warrant further investigation of operant techniques for establishing communication skills in autistic children.

## REFERENCES

1. BROWN, J. 1960. Prognosis from presenting symptoms of preschool children with atypical development. Amer. J. Orthopsychiat. 30: 382–390.

2. Goldfarb, W., P. Braunstein and I. Lorge. 1956. A study of speech patterns in a group of schizophrenic children. Amer. J. Orthopsychiat. **26:** 544–555.

3. Hayes, C. 1951. The Ape in Our House. Harper and Co., New York.

4. Hewett, F. 1964. Teaching reading to an autistic boy through operant conditioning. The Reading Teacher. **17:** 613–618.

5. Isaacs, W., J. Thomas and I. Goldiamond. 1960. Application of operant conditioning to reinstating verbal behavior in psychotics. J. Spch and Hring Dis. **25:** 8–12.

6. Kanner, L. 1948. Child Psychiatry (Second edition). Charles C Thomas Co., Springfield, Illinois.

7. ———— and L. Eisenberg. 1955. Notes on the Follow-up Studies of Autistic Children in Psychopathology of Childhood. Hoch and Zubrin, eds. Grune and Stratton, New York.

8. Lovaas, O. 1965. Teaching intellectual skills to schizophrenic children. (Unpublished manuscript.)

9. Mowrer, O. 1950. Learning Theory and Personality Dynamics. Ronald Press, New York.

10. Phillips, E. 1957. Contribution to a learning theory account of childhood autism. J. Psychology. **43:** 117–124.

11. Rheingold, H., J. Gewirtz and H. Ross. 1959. Social conditioning of vocalization in the infant. J. Comp. and Physio. Psych. **52:** 68–73.

12. Rimland, B. 1964. Infantile Autism. Appleton-Century-Crofts, New York.

13. Weiland, H., and R. Rudnick. 1961. Considerations of the development and treatment of autistic children. The Psychoanalytic Study of the Child, International Universities Press, New York. **16:** 549–563.

K. DANIEL O'LEARY
WESLEY C. BECKER

# Behavior Modification of an Adjustment Class:
# A Token Reinforcement Program

Praise, teacher attention, stars, and grades provide adequate incentive for most pupils to behave in a socially approved way. However, for some students—notably school dropouts, aggressive children, and some retarded children— these methods are relatively ineffective. Where the usual methods of social approval have failed, token reinforcement systems have proven effective (Birnbrauer, Bijou, Wolf, and Kidder, 1965; Birnbrauer and Lawler, 1964; Birnbrauer, Wolf, Kidder, and Tague, 1965; Quay, Werry, McQueen, and Sprague, 1966). Token reinforcers are tangible objects or symbols which attain reinforcing power by being exchanged for a variety of other objects such as candy and trinkets which are back up reinforcers. Tokens acquire generalized reinforcing properties when they are paired with many different reinforcers. The generalized reinforcer is especially useful since it is effective regardless of the momentary condition of the organism.

For the children in this study, generalized reinforcers such as verbal responses ("That's right" or "Good!") and token reinforcers such as grades had not maintained appropriate behavior. In fact, their teacher noted that prior to the introduction of the token system, being called "bad" increased the children's inappropriate behavior. "They had the attitude that it was smart to be called bad. . . . When I tried to compliment them or tell them that they had done something well, they would look around the room and make faces at each other." It is a moot question whether the poor academic performance of these children was caused by their disruptive social behavior or vice versa. It was obvious, however, that the disruptive behaviors had to be eliminated before an academic program could proceed.

Although classroom token reinforcement programs have proved effective in modifying behavior, the pupil teacher ratio has usually been small. In the study by Birnbrauer, Wolf, et al. (1965), a classroom of 17 retarded pupils had four teachers in the classroom at all times. Quay (1966) had one teacher in a behavior modification classroom of five children. One purpose of this project was to devise a token reinforcement program which could be used by one teacher in an average classroom; a second pur-

EXCEPTIONAL CHILDREN, 1967, Vol. 33, pp. 637-642.

pose was to see if a token system could be withdrawn gradually without an increase in disruptive behavior by transferring control to teacher attention, praise, and grades, with less frequent exchange of back up reinforcers.

## Subjects

The subjects for this study were 17 nine year old children described as emotionally disturbed. They had IQ scores (Kuhlmann-Anderson) ranging from 80 to 107. They had been placed in the adjustment class primarily because they exhibited undesirable classroom behaviors such as temper tantrums, crying, uncontrolled laughter, and fighting. The children were in the classroom throughout the day with the exception of some remedial speech and reading work. Although the token reinforcement system was in effect for the whole class, the study focused on the eight most disruptive children.

## Method

The children's deviant behaviors were observed by two students in the classroom from 12:30 to 2:10 three days a week. A third student made reliability checks two days a week. Among the behaviors recorded as deviant were the following: pushing, answering without raising one's hand, chewing gum, eating, name calling, making disruptive noise, and talking. Each student observed four children in random order for 22 minutes each session. Observations were made on a 20 second observe/10 second record basis. Deviant behaviors were recorded on observation sheets. During the observations, the children had three structured activities: listening to records or stories, arithmetic, and group reading. During these activities, instruction was directed to the whole class, and the children were expected to be quiet and in their seats.

*Base Period.* The teacher was asked to handle the children as she normally did. To obtain data which reflected the frequency of deviant pupil behavior under usual classroom procedures, a base period was used. The observers were in the classroom for three weeks before any baseline data were recorded. At first the children walked up to the observers and tried to initiate conversation with them. As the observers consistently ignored the children, the children's approach behaviors diminished. Thus, it is likely that initial show-off behavior was reduced before baseline measures were obtained.

The average interobserver reliability for individual children during the four week base period, calculated on the basis of exact agreement for time interval and category of behavior, ranged from 75 to 100 percent agreement (Table 1). A perfect agreement was scored if both observers recorded the same behavior within a 20 second interval. The reliabilities were calculated by dividing the number of perfect agreements by the number of different responses observed. The percentage of each child's deviant behavior for any one day was calculated by dividing the number of intervals in which one or more deviant behaviors occurred by the number of observed intervals for that day. As can be seen from Figure 1, there was a fairly stable base rate of deviant behavior with a slight increasing trend.

*Token Reinforcement Period.* On the first day of the token period the experimenter placed the following instructions on the blackboard: In Seat, Face Front, Raise Hand, Working, Pay Attention, and Desk Clear. The experimenter then explained the token procedure to the children. The tokens were ratings placed in small booklets on each child's desk. The children were told that they would receive ratings from 1 to 10 and that the ratings would reflect the extent to which they followed the instructions. The points or ratings could be exchanged for a variety of back up reinforcers. The reinforcers consisted of small prizes ranging in value from 1 to 29 cents, such as candy, pennants, comics, perfume, and kites. The total cost of the reinforcers used during the two months was $80.76. All the pupils received reinforcers in the same manner during class, but individual preferences were considered by providing a variety of items, thus maximizing the probability that at least one of the items would be a reinforcer for a given child at a given time.

The experimenter repeated the instructions at the beginning of the token period each day for one week and rated the children to provide a norm for the teacher. It was the teacher, however, who placed the ratings in the children's booklets during the short pause at the end of a lesson period. The ratings reflected the extent to which the child exhibited the appropriate behaviors listed on the blackboard. Where possible, these ratings also reflected the accuracy of the child's arithmetic work.

The number of ratings made each day was gradually decreased from five to three, and the number of points required to obtain a prize gradually increased. For the first three days, the tokens were exchanged for reinforcers at the end of the token period. For the next four days, points were accumulated for two days and exchanged at the end of the token period on the second day. Then, for the next 15 days, a three day delay between token and reinforcers was used. Four day delays were employed for the remaining 24 school days. During the three and four day delay periods, tokens were exchanged for reinforcers at the end of the school day. By requiring more appropriate behavior to receive a prize and increasing the delay of reinforcement it was hoped that transfer of control from the token reinforcers to the more traditional methods of teacher praise and attention would occur.

After the first week, the teacher made the ratings and executed the token system without aid. Procedures were never discussed when the children were present.

The children also received group points based on total class behavior, and these points could be exchanged for popsicles at the end of each week. The group points ranged from 1 to 10 and reflected the extent to which the children were quiet during the time the ratings were placed in the booklets. The number of group ratings made each day were gradually decreased from five to three as were the individual ratings. However, since the children were usually very quiet, the number of points required to obtain a popsicle was not increased. The points were accumulated on a thermometer chart on the blackboard, and the children received popsicles on seven of the eight possible occasions.

At first the teacher was reluctant to accept the token procedure because of the time the ratings might take. However, the ratings took at most three minutes. As the teacher noted, "The class is very quiet and usually I give them a story to read from the board while I give the ratings. One model student acts as the teacher and he calls on the students who are well-behaved to read. . . . This is one of the better

parts of the day. It gave me a chance to go around and say something to each child as I gave him his rating. . . ."

The rating procedure was especially effective because the teacher reinforced each child for approximations to the desired final response. Instead of demanding perfection from the start, the teacher reinforced evidence of progress.

In addition to the token procedure, the teacher was instructed to make comments, when appropriate, such as: "Pat, I like the way you are working. That will help your rating." "I am glad to see everyone turned around in their seats. That will help all of you get the prize you want." "Good, Gerald. I like the way you raised your hand to ask a question."

A technique used by the teacher to extinguish the deviant behavior of one child was to ignore him, while at the same time reinforcing the appropriate behavior of another child. This enabled the teacher to refrain from using social censure and to rely almost solely on positive reinforcement techniques, as she had been instructed.

The investigators also were prepared to use time out from positive reinforcement (Wolf, Risley, and Mees, 1964) to deal with those behaviors which were especially disruptive. The time out procedure involves isolating the child for deviant behavior for a specified period of time. This procedure was not used, however, since the frequency of disruptive behavior was very low at the end of the year.

The average interobserver reliability for individual children during the token period ranged from 80 to 96 percent. As indicated in Table 1, the reliabilities were recorded separately for the base and token periods because reliabilities were higher during the token period when the frequency of deviant behavior was low.

**Results**

As can be seen from Figure 1, the average percentage of deviant behavior at the end of the year was very low. The daily mean of deviant behavior during the token procedure ranged from 3 to 32 percent, while the daily mean of deviant behavior during the base period ranged from 66 to 91 percent. The average of deviant

## FIGURE 1

**Average Percentages of Deviant Behavior during the Base and Token Periods**

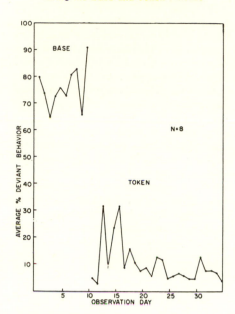

## FIGURE 2

**Percentages of Deviant Behavior for Individual Children during Base and Token Periods**

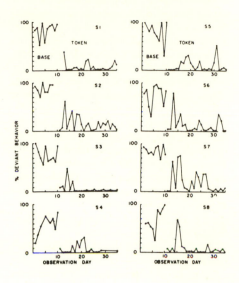

## TABLE 1

### Average Interobserver Reliabilities during Base and Token Reinforcement Periods

| | Base Period | | Token Reinforcement Period | |
|---|---|---|---|---|
| Subject | Percentage of Perfect Agreement | Number of Reliability Checks | Percentage of Perfect Agreement | Number of Reliability Checks |
| 1 | 85 | 3 | 88 | 9 |
| 2 | 82 | 2 | 94 | 9 |
| 3 | 92 | 3 | 96 | 9 |
| 4 | 100 | 1 | 93 | 5 |
| 5 | 77 | 3 | 87 | 9 |
| 6 | 75 | 4 | 87 | 9 |
| 7 | 80 | 4 | 80 | 8 |
| 8 | 75 | 3 | 88 | 8 |

## TABLE 2

### Analysis of Variance on Deviant Behavior Scores (N = 8)

| Source | df | MS | F |
|---|---|---|---|
| Between Subjects | 7 | 72.86 | |
| Within Subjects | 8 | 2203.00 | |
| Treatment | 1 | 17424.00 | 609.87* |
| Residual | 7 | 28.57 | |

\* $p < .001$

195

behavior for all children during the base period was 76 percent as contrasted with 10 percent during the token procedure. As can be seen from the $F$ ratio (Table 2), the change from the base period to the token period was highly significant ($p < .001$). Using an omega squared, it was estimated that the treatment accounted for 96 percent of the variance of the observed deviant behavior.

An examination of the individual records (Figure 2) shows the small degree of individual variation and differences in deviant behavior from the base to the token period. Although subjects 2 and 7 exhibited more deviant behavior than others during the token period, the percentage of deviant behavior was obviously less than during the base period. The percentage of deviant behavior declined for all pupils from the base to the token period.

## Discussion

At least two variables in addition to the token procedure and social reinforcement possibly contributed to the change in the children's behavior. First, during the baseline and token phases of this demonstration, the teacher was enrolled in a psychology class which emphasized operant and social learning principles. The influence of this class cannot be assessed, although the dramatic and abrupt change from the base to the token phase of the demonstration makes it seem highly implausible that the psychology class was the major variable accounting for the change. However, in a replication of this study now being planned, the teacher will receive only a short introduction to the basic principles and subsequent instruction by the experimenter throughout the procedure.

Secondly, the reduction in deviant behavior enabled the teacher to spend more time giving children individual attention during the token phase of the experiment. She had time to correct and return the children's work promptly, thus giving them immediate feedback. She was also able to use teaching materials not previously used. Some children who had not completed a paper for two years repeatedly received perfect scores. The immediate feedback and new materials probably contributed to the maintenance of appropriate behavior.

An experiment within the Skinnerian paradigm involves the establishment of a stable base rate of behavior; next, environmental contingencies are applied and the maladaptive behavior is reduced. The contingencies are then withdrawn and there is a return to base conditions. Finally, the environmental contingencies are again instituted and the maladaptive behavior decreased. This procedure of operant decrease, increase, and finally decrease of maladaptive behavior in association with specific environmental conditions demonstrates the degree of stimulus control obtained by the technique.

A return to base conditions early in the treatment period of this study was not carried out because of a concern that the enthusiasm and cooperation generated by the program throughout the school system might be severely reduced. There is little doubt that a return to base conditions following three or four weeks of the token procedure would have resulted in an increase in disruptive behavior. When a reversal was used by Birnbrauer, Wolf, et al. (1965), a number of children showed a decline in the amount of studying and an increase in disruptive behavior. As an alternative, it was planned to return gradually to baseline conditions during the following fall, but radical changes in pupil population prevented this reversal.

Without a reversal or a return to baseline conditions it cannot be stated that the token system and not other factors, such as the changes that ordinarily occur during the school year, accounted for the observed reduction of deviant behavior. To demonstrate clearly the crucial significance of the token procedure itself, a systematic replication with different children and a different teacher is planned. As Sidman (1960) noted, "An investigator may, on the basis of experience, have great confidence in the adequacy of his methodology, but other experimenters cannot be expected to share his confidence without convincing evidence (p. 75)."

Two interesting implications of this study are the effects of delay of reinforcement and generalization. The use of tokens provides a procedure which is intermediate between immediate and delayed tangible reinforcement. In Birnbrauer, Wolf, et al.'s (1965) class of severely retarded children this delay was extended from a few seconds to over an hour. Some educable children studied for many days for check marks only and, presumably, the knowledge that they were approaching a goal. All the children in the present study worked for four days without receiving a back up reinforcer. In addition, more than one child made the comment toward the end of school that next year they would be old enough to behave and work well without the prizes.

Anecdotal records indicate that after the token procedure was put into effect, the children behaved better during the morning session, music, and library periods. These reports suggest that a transfer to normal classroom control using social reinforcement and grades would not be very difficult. Also, the gang behavior of frowning upon "doing well" disappeared. Some children even helped enforce the token system by going to the blackboard just before class began and reading the instructions to the class.

## References

Birnbrauer, J. S., Bijou, S. W., Wolf, M. M., and Kidder, J. D. Programmed instruction in the classroom. In L. P. Ullman and L. Krasner (Eds.), *Case studies in behavior modification*. New York: Holt, Rinehart and Winston, 1965. Pp. 358-363.

Birnbrauer, J. S., and Lawler, Julia. Token reinforcement for learning. *Mental Retardation*, 1964, 2, 275-279.

Birnbrauer, J. S., Wolf, M. M., Kidder, J. D., and Tague, Cecilia E. Classroom behavior of retarded pupils with token reinforcement. *Journal of Experimental Child Psychology*, 1965, 2, 219-235.

Quay, H. C., Werry, J. S., McQueen, Marjorie, and Sprague, R. L. Remediation of the conduct problem child in the special class setting. *Exceptional Children*, 1966, 32, 509-515.

Sidman, M. *Tactics of scientific research*. New York: Basic Books, 1960.

Wolf, M. M., Risley, T. R., and Mees, H. L. Application of operant conditioning procedures to the behavioral problems of an autistic child. *Behavior Research and Therapy*, 1964, 1, 305-312.

K. DANIEL O'LEARY *is Instructor, and* WESLEY C. BECKER *is Professor, Psychology Department, University of Illinois, Urbana. This study was supported in part by Research Grant HD 00881-04 from the National Institutes of Health.*

# DEVELOPING APPROPRIATE CLASSROOM BEHAVIORS IN A SEVERELY DISTURBED GROUP OF INSTITUTIONALIZED KINDERGARTEN-PRIMARY CHILDREN UTILIZING A BEHAVIOR MODIFICATION MODEL

*Ethel Rabb, Frank M. Hewett*
*Neuropsychiatric Institute, University of California, Los Angeles, California*

A program was established at the Neuropsychiatric Institute School in the Center for Health Sciences, University of California Los Angeles, to engage hospitalized children diagnosed as autistic, atypical, schizophrenic, minimally neurologically impaired and severe primary behavior disorders, in a group learning situation.

The program was developed as an alternative to the traditional nursery school model, which was used previously for these children, whose social and communication skills fell in the two- to five-year age range although their chronological ages were from five to nine. Major criteria that the program was expected to meet were as follows:

1. Program was to focus on increasing the task oriented attention of the child.
2. Activities were to permit learning to take place at individual rates and to provide rewards for the individual learner.
3. Group and individual tasks were to be chosen for their usefulness in building greater competency in group learning situations.
4. Program was to operate with one teacher and four to six children.
5. Successful program management was to be possible for a variety of kindergarten and primary teachers.

The experimental kindergarten-primary program took place five days a week for a 45-minute session. Individual and group activities chosen to foster behaviors and skills the children would be expected to have in a normal kindergarten or primary grade class were presented on a specific schedule. Three phases were included in the experimental program. The first phase lasted for three months, during which baseline data on the child's task oriented attention were collected. Phase two lasted for five months, during which tokens in the form of poker chips were dispensed on a specific schedule to reinforce attention and attempts to perform activities assigned. Within a four-week period immediate exchange of chips for small candy units was replaced by delayed exchange for small trinkets and toys. During phase three, which is still in progress, token reinforcement was withdrawn.

An Esterline-Angus events pen recorder, operated by a trained research assistant was used to record the occurrence and duration of task oriented attention engaged in by the child, and teacher attention to the child, during each phase of the program. Rater reliability between two trained observers recording simultaneously at four different sample sessions ranged between 86 and 96 per cent.

Changes in the behavior of two subjects who have continued in the program for the eight-month period that it has been in progress, indicate that the presence of token reinforcers maintains higher and less variable rates of task oriented attention. The data indicate that token reinforcement was more significant than teacher attention in maintaining the child's task oriented attention. Changes in the data on three occasions when substitute teachers were engaged were minimal.

Conclusions of the study must await completion of phase three of the study. A major finding of this study that can be made at this date, however, is that a severely disturbed group of four to six children functioning at the two- to five-year level in social and communication skills, can be profitably involved in a learning situation with one teacher.

# BEHAVIOR CHANGE IN A THERAPEUTIC SUMMER CAMP: A FOLLOW-UP STUDY

*University of Alabama*

HENRY C. RICKARD AND MICHAEL DINOFF

In recent years a number of summer camping programs have been developed specifically for the troubled child. For example, the Michigan Fresh Air Camp which began as a camp for underprivileged children in 1921 has more recently evolved (1961) as an effective program for the diagnosis and treatment of emotionally disturbed boys (2). Myers (3) has prepared a report of the proceedings of two camping workshops which brought together directors of camps for emotionally disturbed children from several states. Summary statements are presented on numerous topics, including staff training, selection of campers, program planning, and the value of the camp setting itself as being intrinsically therapeutic. The workshop report emphasized the therapeutic advantages of summer camping. An entire issue of the *Journal of Social Issues* has been devoted to a discussion of therapeutic camping (1). Authorities in the field attest to the effectiveness of therapeutic camping, but stress the need for continued research and exploration.

Located in northeastern Alabama is a specialized summer camping program for emotionally troubled boys. During the 1963 camping season, the initial year of operation, 11 boys were accepted for the two-month session. The boys ranged in age from 8 to 14 and were average to superior in intelligence. Most of the campers exhibited difficulties in their interpersonal relationships and in their school work. The camp was directed by two clinical psychologists aided by consultants in psychiatry, social work, speech therapy, and psychology. A favorable camper to counselor ratio of three to one was maintained.

Each boy received considerable individual and group psychotherapy, but, more importantly, he was treated as an individual toward whom the entire staff directed common attitudes and behavior. For example, staff decisions were made as to what classes of behaviors would be rewarded and what limits would be imposed for each child. A full schedule of activities was maintained, and each boy was expected to take part in work assignments as well as play activities. Attempts to control and shape behavior took three major forms: (*a*) stage setting for the emergence of adaptive behavior, within the advantages

JOURNAL OF GENETIC PSYCHOLOGY, 1967, Vol. 110, No. 2, pp. 181-183.

of the camp environment; (*b*) social reinforcement of adaptive patterns; and (*c*) various forms of psychotherapy. Counseling sessions were held with the parents, and follow-up reports were sent to referring agencies in an effort to promote the transfer of adaptive camp behavior to the home environment.

During the 1963 season the impression was gained that the majority of the campers had shown improvement in their social relations and had emerged from the camping experience better able to accept limits and to function in a group. A follow-up questionnaire was sent to the parents three months after the camp closed to obtain their appraisal of the camping program. The following instructions were typed on the questionnaire: "Please circle the rating in each category which best describes your son's behavior now compared to his precamp behavior. Please make your choices as objectively and sincerely as possible. Please make comments where you feel they would be helpful."

Table 1 presents the parents' responses to the questionnaires. In terms of overall behavior with family members, 10 campers were reported improved or much improved and one was reported as unchanged. In overall behavior with peers, nine campers were reported improved or much improved and two were reported unchanged. Eight campers were reported to have improved in the quality of their work, while three remained unchanged. Question 4 indicated that all of the parents believed their child gained to some extent from his experiences at camp. If they had it to do over again, nine of the parents would have sent their child to the camp: two other parents might have sent their child. Eight couples believed that they profited from counseling with the directors, while three couples felt they gained very little or not at all. Parent responses to an additional question, "What did you like best about Camp Ponderosa?" were quite consistent. Seventeen comments centered around what the parents considered to be favorable attitudes and activities on the part of the staff. On the other hand, the parents were very inconsistent in replying to the question, "What did you like least about Camp Ponderosa?" Comments to this question appeared to reflect personal tastes, and no common thread was discernible.

The entire population of the questionnaires was returned. The results of the follow-up study, while encouraging, are obviously difficult to evaluate. A good measure of rapport had been established between the parents and the directors, and the parents may have been reluctant to express negative results. The categories to be rated were gross and in some cases presented problems in rating. In addition, a control group was not available. On the other hand, the questionnaires have served as a sort of standardized subjective parental report. It is concluded, with caution, that the majority of the parents were

## TABLE 1
### PARENTS' RESPONSES TO FOLLOW-UP QUESTIONNAIRE
### (N = 11)

| Question | Category | Response |
|---|---|---|
| 1. Overall behavior with family members | Much improved | 3 |
| | Improved | 7 |
| | Unchanged | 1 |
| | Worse | |
| | Much worse | |
| 2. Overall behavior with peers | Much improved | 2 |
| | Improved | 7 |
| | Unchanged | 2 |
| | Worse | |
| | Much worse | |
| 3. Quality of school work | Much improved | 1 |
| | Improved | 7 |
| | Unchanged | 3 |
| | Worse | |
| | Much worse | |
| 4. Did your child profit from his experience at Camp Ponderosa? | Very much | 4 |
| | Much | 5 |
| | Some [a] | 2 |
| | Little | |
| | Very little | |
| | None | |
| 5. Knowing what I know now about Camp Ponderosa I _____ sent my child | Would have | 9 |
| | Probably would have | |
| | Might have | 2 |
| | Probably would not have | |
| | Would not have | |
| 6. Did you as parents profit from counseling with the directors? | Very much | 1 |
| | Much | 6 |
| | Little | |
| | Very little | 2 |
| | None | 1 |

[a] Two respondents added the category "Some" when rating Question 4.

pleased with the program and that they perceived their sons as having made progress associated with the summer camping experience.

## REFERENCES

1. McNeil, E. B. (Ed.). Therapeutic camping for disturbed youth. *J. Soc. Issues*, 1957, **13**, 1-62.
2. ————. Forty years of childhood. *Mich. Quart. Rev.*, 1962, **1**, 112-118.
3. Myers, T. Camping for Emotionally Disturbed Boys. Bloomington, Ind.: Indiana Univ. Press, 1961.

SAUL AXELROD

# Token Reinforcement Programs in Special Classes

A RECENT extension of the principles of operant conditioning includes the use of token reinforcement as a means of modifying behavior in the special education classroom. Token reinforcers are objects or symbols which in and of themselves probably have little or no reinforcing value (Birnbrauer, Wolf, Kidder, & Tague, 1965). However, they may be exchanged for a variety of objects or privileges which are reinforcing. For example, an individual might use his tokens to purchase several different kinds of candies, toys, or a trip to the zoo. As a result of this association with different types of reinforcement, the tokens should become generalized reinforcers which are independent of any particular state of deprivation or satiation which an individual is experiencing. The superiority of the token reinforcement system over other systems employing a particular primary reinforcer is considerable. For example, if food is used to reinforce a certain behavior, the effectiveness of the reinforcement procedure is greatly dependent upon the state of deprivation of the individual. Tokens, on the other hand, are not so limited, since they can be used to purchase several different types of reinforcers or can be saved until a later time when a particular state of deprivation does exist. In addition, several tokens can be accumulated and exchanged for some item that has more reinforcing value for an individual than a single piece of candy.

A significant advantage of token reinforcers over the use of grades in maintaining appropriate behavior in the classroom was reported by McKenzie, Clark, Wolf, Kothera, and Benson (1968). These investigators pointed out that grades have traditionally been the token reinforcement system of schools. However, the effectiveness of grades is often minimal since the amount of time between behavior and reinforcement is frequently between 6 and 9 weeks. As a result, an association between responding and reinforcement is unlikely. In accordance with this notion, Clark, Lachowitz, and Wolf (1968) pointed out that a major benefit of a token program is that the token can be used as an immediate reinforcer of a response and thus can close the time lapse between the appropriate response and the backup reinforcer. For example, it would be difficult to provide a trip to the circus as an immediate reinforcer for completing a difficult reading assignment. However, it would be quite easy to administer a sufficient number of tokens for this trip immediately following the appropriate behavior.

Token reinforcement programs have generally been employed in classroom situations in which teacher attention has been

SAUL AXELROD is Assistant Professor, Department of Educational Psychology, University of Connecticut, Storrs.

EXCEPTIONAL CHILDREN, 1971, Vol. 37, No. 5, pp. 371-379.

ineffective in controlling the students' behavior (Kuypers, Becker, & O'Leary, 1968). The administration of a token is usually preceded by some type of approval (e.g., "good boy") so that teacher praise will eventually become a conditioned reinforcer. It is often intended (Kuypers et al., 1968) that control over student behavior will be transferred from the tokens to the teacher through this conditioned reinforcement procedure.

## Increasing Academic Performance

### Mentally Retarded Populations

*Severely retarded class.* A study by Birnbrauer and Lawler (1964) appears to be the first published investigation of the use of a token reinforcement system in a special education classroom. Subjects for this experiment were 37 severely retarded children who were divided into classes of 6 to 13 pupils. Each teacher conducted his class without the help of teaching assistants. Of the 36 subjects, 14 had never attended school before, three had been dropped from school due to "incorrigibility," and four were "severe behavior problems." All had IQ's of 40 or less. The children were gradually introduced to a token reinforcement program using poker chips which could be exchanged for a variety of backup reinforcers. Chips were awarded for clearly defined behaviors. At the end of the school year, 33 of the 37 pupils hung up their coats upon entering the classroom, sat down quietly, and waited for their assignments. In addition, 11 worked without assistance on programed reading material which required 10 to 30 minutes to complete. It was found, however, that many of the children did not change their behavior outside the classroom.

*Programed material.* Birnbrauer, Bijou, Wolf, and Kidder (1965) discussed a special education classroom in which a token reinforcement system was combined with programed instructional material (PI) to teach various school subjects (reading, writing, and arithmetic) and related practical skills (e.g., telling time). Subjects for the study were eight boys ranging in chronological age (CA) from 9 to 13 and in mental age (MA) from 5-5 to 7-3 (Peabody Picture Vocabulary Test: PPVT). Their clinical diagnoses included brain damage and familial retardation. A token reinforcement system was instituted after the discovery that the pupils would not work effectively for approval and knowledge of results. The student to teacher ratio was frequently one to one. The authors reported that within 5 months, seven of the eight pupils were "good students." It was claimed that the subjects studied longer, accomplished more work, and exhibited a minimal number of disruptive behaviors.

*Tokens vs teacher attention.* The question of whether the reinforcement program or the greater attention paid to students' problems is responsible for producing increased student output is frequently raised. A study by Birnbrauer, Wolf, Kidder, and Tague (1965) shed some light on this matter. The purpose of this investigation was to determine the effectiveness of the reinforcers in maintaining appropriate behavior on the Sight Vocabulary Program by systematically withdrawing and reapplying the reinforcers. Of the 17 mentally retarded children who took part in this study, two were mongoloid, three were familial, nine were brain damaged, and three had no available diagnosis. IQ's ranged from 50 to 72 (PPVT). The study consisted of three conditions: The first (B) paired social approval with tokens; the second (NT) used teacher approval but no tokens; the third condition ($B_2$) was the same as the first. The study used one male certified teacher and three female assistants. The results indicated that five children showed no decrement in performance during NT. Six children made more errors during NT, but completed the same or a greater number of items and presented no greater number of behavior problems. Four children made more errors, did less work, and presented serious disciplinary problems during NT. After tokens were reinstated all subjects returned to the original level or better. It appeared, therefore, that the token reinforcement procedures rather than teacher attention accounted for the behavioral changes.

Bijou, Birnbrauer, Kidder, and Tague (1966) reported on 3 years of research in which a token reinforcement system was applied to teaching reading, writing, and arithmetic to retarded children. Subjects consisted of 27 boys and girls ranging in CA from 8-7 to 14-9. The average IQ (PPVT) for the group was 63. Eleven of the subjects were diagnosed as brain damaged, three as mongoloid, four as cultural-familial, and nine as uncertain or unknown. Although no mention was made of the number of teachers who were involved, the classroom situation was structured so that a newly admitted student would receive almost constant attention from a teacher. The authors implied that the results of this study were quite favorable, but failed to include objective data.

*Other Populations*

*Multiply handicapped teenagers.* Nolen, Kunzelman, and Haring (1967) performed a study which was directed toward improving the academic and social behavior of junior high age children with a variety of disorders. Subjects ranged in age from 12 to 16 years and in achievement levels from preschool to sixth grade. Etiologies included a variety of emotional and learning disorders, as well as mental retardation. The authors stressed, however, that their program centered on the diagnosis of skill problems rather than on physical or psychological deficits. Following the development of skill sequences and the determination of the students' functioning levels within these sequences, individual programs were devised. The teacher allotted points, which were exchangeable for reinforcers appropriate to teenagers, for each of a number of academic tasks. After 100 days, a median of 2.7 years gain in arithmetic and 2.05 years gain in reading was found. To test the effectiveness of the reinforcement, the experimenters administered rewards on a noncontingent basis for a period of time. This technique produced a significant decrease in appropriate academic behavior which was quickly resumed once reinforcement was reinstituted on a contingent basis. Followup studies of three students who were transferred from this classroom indicated that their performances were lower in the traditional classroom than in the experimental classroom. However, their productivity was still superior to other students' in their new class.

*Urban underachievers.* In accordance with current national problems, Wolf, Giles, and Hall (1968) conducted a program which was intended to improve the academic performance of low achieving children from an urban poverty area. Fifteen of the subjects for this study were from the sixth grade while the sixteenth was from the fifth grade. All subjects scored at least 2 years below their grade level on the reading portion of the *Stanford Achievement Test* (SAT). According to school records, IQ's ranged from 73 to 104. Classes, which were conducted by one teacher with two teaching assistants, were held after school hours and during summer months. In addition, students attended regular classes during school hours. A token reinforcement program which included a wide range of backup reinforcers was instituted. The first of two experiments concerned two subjects and attempted to determine whether the rate of reading certain material was a function of the distribution of points. It was found that manipulation of the number of points earned by reading significantly affected the reading rate of both children. In one case, doubling the number of points the child could receive produced a significant level of response even though he had not responded at all under the original conditions. In the second experiment, subjects were given their choice of types of academic materials with which to work. However, the number of points which could be earned for completing various units was changed periodically. For example, at one time reading units were worth 5 points, while arithmetic and English units were worth 2 points. At another time, reading was worth 8 points, arithmetic was worth 2 points, and English was worth one-half a point. The material a child chose varied according to the number of points that could be earned. At the end of the year the data indicated that the control group, which only attended regular classes, gained a median of .8 year on the SAT, while the experimental group showed a median gain of 1.5 years. These results were significant at the .01 level of confidence. In addition, subjective teacher remarks indicated that the children from the experimental group performed better while in the regular school classroom than they had previously.

*Dropouts.* A study by Clark and his colleagues (1968) also employed a population representative of contemporary problems. This investigation was directed toward improving the academic skills of school dropouts by means of a token reinforcement program. Subjects for the study were two groups of five girls matched according to differences between their number of years of formal education and their scores on the *California Achievement Test* (CAT). All the girls were between 16 and 21 years old. One group was termed the classroom group and received the token reinforcement program. The second group was designated the job group and received job placement. The classroom group subjects were given their choice of a variety of instructional materials. Points, which were exchangeable for money, were awarded on the basis of performance on these materials.

As the study progressed, the distribution of points was shifted to increase the probability of a student's working in an area in which she was deficient. For example, if a girl were deficient in arithmetic, more points would be awarded for appropriate arithmetic performance. One, and often two teachers were in the classroom. Four girls in the classroom group attended class for 8 weeks and 4 days while the fifth attended 24 days. According to the CAT pretest and posttest scores, the classroom subjects gained a median of 1.3 years while the job group gained only .2 year.

*Learning disabled.* In order to improve the level of academic achievement in a learning disabilities class, McKenzie and his coworkers (1968) introduced a token reinforcement system. Subjects for this study were ten students ranging in age from 10 to 13 years. Although their ability levels did not indicate mental retardation, their achievement levels were retarded by at least 2 years in one or more academic areas. All were diagnosed as having minimal brain damage and emotional disturbance. Based on their academic performance, the children were reinforced with recess, special privileges, weekly grades, et cetera. Achievement under these conditions was judged to be less than optimal. A program conducted by a teacher and teacher aides was then instituted in which the amount of allowance a child would receive from his parents was determined by his weekly grades. Since the parents were already accustomed to giving their children allowances, a burden was not added to the parents' budgets. A significant increase in arithmetic and reading achievement was observed while using weekly allowances as backup reinforcers. Due to the risk involved, no reversal of reinforcement conditions was attempted.

*Reading disabled.* Haring and Hauck (1969) did a study concerned with improving the reading achievement level of four elementary school boys through a combination of PI material and token reinforcement. Subjects for this investigation were disabled in reading, but average or above in intelligence. According to the *Gates-McKillop Diagnostic Reading Tests,* reading development showed a lag of from one to 5 years. Several experimental conditions were employed. During condition A the material was presented without the answers. During the second condition (B), correct answers were provided following a response by the subject. Condition C included a counter which tallied the number of correct responses. This count was available both to the boys and the experimenters. Condition D provided continuous token reinforcement for correct responding, whereas condition E programed reinforcement on a variable ratio schedule (e.g., an average of every five correct responses was reinforced). A transfer from PI material to work lists, basal readers, and library books was involved in condition F. The teacher's role in this program was minimal since much of the material was automated. The study consisted of 91 sessions of 65 minutes each. The data showed that the later conditions produced higher rates of correct responding than conditions A and B. In addition, it was found that the boys gained from 1.5 to 4.0 years in reading achievement during the 5 months of the study, according to the *Sullivan Placement Test.* Transition to the more traditional situation in condition F was reported as successful, but definitive data were lacking.

*Emotionally disturbed.* Hewett, Taylor, and Artuso (1969) used an engineered classroom design with "emotionally disturbed" students. A total of 54 children were assigned to six classrooms with nine students in each. Each class had a teacher and a teacher aide. Children ranged in CA from 8-0 to 11-11 years with Full Scale WISC IQ scores between 85 and 113.

Nearly all showed academic retardation. The experimental condition involved the use of checkmarks and backup reinforcers for appropriate behavior. Any instructional approach which the teacher chose to follow except the use of tangible or token rewards was used in the control condition. Class 1 (E) stayed in the experimental condition for 32 weeks. Class 2 (C) stayed in the control condition for 32 weeks. Classes 3 and 4 (CE) and classes 5 and 6 (EC) were in the control condition for 16 weeks and the experimental condition for 16 weeks. The dependent variables were reading and arithmetic achievement measured by the CAT and task attention. A comparison of classes E and C indicated that the experimental condition produced superior task attention and arithmetic achievement but not reading achievement. The data of class C and classes CE verified these findings. The data of classes EC indicated that removal of the experimental condition resulted in improved task attention and did not affect reading or arithmetic achievement- levels. To account for these surprising observations, Hewett and his associates (1969) hypothesized that (a) the teachers became more effective secondary social reinforcers, and (b) the competence of group EC increased as a result of the experimental condition.

### Reducing Disruptive Behaviors
*Mentally Retarded Populations*

*Hyperactivity.* The purpose of a study by Patterson, Jones, Whittier, and Wright (1965) was to condition the attending behavior of a hyperactive child in a classroom situation. In addition, it was intended that the effect generalize to situations in which the conditioning apparatus was not being used. An experimental subject (ES) and a control subject (CS) were employed. ES was a brain injured, mentally retarded boy with a WISC IQ of 65. CS was a brain injured boy with a range in IQ scores from the eighties to the low nineties according to the PPVT and *Raven Matrices Test.* During conditioning trials ES wore an earphone into which a signal was passed for each 10 seconds during which ES attended properly. Later a variable interval schedule was used. Each buzz indicated that a piece of candy or a penny

was accumulated toward a total which was to be shared by the entire class. Following conditioning, the apparatus was removed and a 4 week extinction period was begun. Differences between ES and CS were insignificant during baseline. However, after conditioning sessions were started, it was found that ES performed significantly more attending behaviors than did CS. These measurements were taken during the period prior to which ES would wear the conditioning apparatus for that day. During extinction, ES maintained a significantly higher rate of attending than did CS. Patterson therefore obtained generalization of the conditioning effect.

*Obscene conduct.* Sulzbacher and Houser (1968) used a group contingency procedure to eliminate a disruptive behavior in a classroom. This design was constructed so that the rewards of each depended upon the behavior of the group as a whole. Subjects for this study were 14 educable mentally retarded children, seven of whom were boys. Ages ranged from 6-7 to 10-5. The problem behavior was the frequent occurrence of an obscene gesture. The children were informed that there would be a 10 minute recess at the end of the day. However, each display or reference to the obscene gesture by any member of the class decreased recess time by one minute for the entire class. The program was designed so that one teacher could carry out the entire procedure without assistance. The frequency of undesirable behaviors decreased from a mean of 16 per day to 2.11 per day. After removal of the contingency, the behavior increased, but to a lower level than the baseline level.

*Maladaptive behaviors.* Perline and Levinsky (1968) attempted to determine the effect of token reinforcement on the maladaptive behaviors of severely retarded children in a residential preschool setting. Subjects ranged in age from 8 to 10 years and in social quotient from 22 to 38. Five maladaptive behaviors were defined including aggression toward peers and throwing objects. Two experimental conditions were applied concurrently for 10 days. All children were given tokens for lack of maladaptive behaviors and lost a token if they misbehaved. However, for half the children, each deviant behavior led to a time-out period consisting of 5 to 15 minutes during which the child was not allowed to move from a certain area. For the other half of the children, no additional contingencies were used. The data indicated that a decrease in maladaptive behaviors for each of the five categories occurred. However, there were no appreciable differences between using token reinforcement and token reinforcement with time-out.

## Other Populations

*Hyperactivity.* Patterson (1965) devised a token reinforcement program to control the disruptive behaviors of a child in a classroom setting. The subject was a 9 year old boy in the second grade, who demonstrated hyperactive behavior and academic retardation. Neurological signs indicated minimal brain damage while IQ scores were in the borderline range. After observing the boy for several hours, it was decided that the greater part of his hyperactivity could be broken down into talking, pushing, and hitting. A small box with a flashlight bulb and an electric counter was then placed on the boy's desk. If he did not perform any disruptive behaviors for a period of time (which increased as trials progressed) the light flashed and the counter clicked. At the end of each session, all members of the class divided up the amount of candy or pennies corresponding to the number of points on the electric counter. This program required the presence of the teacher and an experimenter. The data indicated that 8.4 fewer disruptive responses per minute occurred during conditioning. This result was at the .01 level of significance. After the experiment was completed, the teacher reported that the boy was less disruptive and played more with other children.

*Emotionally disturbed.* An extension of the Patterson (1965) study was performed by Quay, Werry, McQueen, and Sprague (1966). Although an explicit description of the children was not given, it appears that the children were emotionally disturbed. Each student was given a box containing a light which could be flashed following attending behaviors of a fixed duration. The children were later given a piece of candy for each light flash. The program, which was conducted by one teacher and an experimenter, increased attending from 41 percent during baseline to

71 percent during the last 20 days of reinforcement. A return to baseline conditions was not attempted.

O'Leary and Becker (1967) attempted to devise a token reinforcement system which could be used by one teacher in an average size classroom. In addition, the authors were interested in the possibility of gradually withdrawing the tokens without an increase in deviant behavior by transferring control to teacher attention and grades. Subjects for this study were 17 nine year old children described as "emotionally disturbed." Kuhlmann-Anderson IQ scores ranged from 80 to 107. After the baseline period, the experimenter placed the following instructions on the blackboard: "In Seat, Face Front, Raise Hand. . . ." The children were told that they would receive points (which were determined by the experimenter) depending on how well they followed instructions. These points could be exchanged for a variety of backup reinforcers. The number of ratings made each day gradually decreased and the number of points required to obtain a prize gradually increased. By requiring more appropriate behavior to receive a reward and increasing the delay of reinforcement, it was hoped that transfer of control from tokens to teacher praise and attention would occur. During baseline, the daily mean of deviant behaviors varied between 66 and 91 percent. This decreased to a range of 3 to 32 percent during the token procedure. This result was significant at the .001 level. A return to baseline conditions during school sessions during the following fall was planned. However, extensive changes in the pupil population prevented this possibility. Anecdotal evidence, however, indicated that after the procedure was put into effect, the students behaved better during class sessions in which tokens were not used than they had previously.

*Out-of-seat behavior.* A group contingency procedure was utilized by Gallagher, Sulzbacher, and Shores (1967) to reduce disruptive behaviors in a classroom. The subjects were five boys who were enrolled in an intermediate class for emotionally disturbed children. The boys ranged in age from 7-11 to 11-8. It was hypothesized that more deviant behaviors occurred when at least one member of the class was out of his seat. Hence, an attempt was made to eliminate out-of-seat behavior. The children were informed that they could have a 24 minute coke break at the end of the day if they did not leave their seats without permission. A chart was posted which displayed 2 minute segments from 24 to 0. Each child's name was assigned a different color chalk. When a child left his seat without permission, the teacher marked off 2 minutes with the designated color from the entire class's coke time. The frequency of the boys' being out of their seats decreased from an average of 69.5 to 1.0 times per day. In addition, an overall decline in disruptive classroom behaviors was reported. Although the program used one master and three student teachers, it would appear that it could have been conducted by one teacher without assistance.

*Socially maladjusted.* Kuypers, Becker, and O'Leary (1968) performed an experiment to reduce the number of disruptive behaviors in an adjustment class through the use of a token reinforcement program. Subjects for this study were six third grade and six fourth grade children who were described as socially maladjusted. Data were collected on only the six most disruptive children. They were given tokens (which could be used to purchase various items) for staying in their seats, facing front, and other attending behaviors. During baseline, deviant behavior occurred 54 percent of the time. This decreased to 27.8 percent during the token period and then increased to 41.5 percent when the tokens were removed. Generalization to other situations was minimal. The authors admitted that these results were less impressive than those obtained by O'Leary and Becker (1967). Kuypers attributed the limited success to the following: (a) the tokens were awarded on an absolute basis rather than for individual improvement, (b) the teacher was not trained in the use of operant conditioning techniques, and (c) the observers tended to be a disturbance to the class.

### Criticisms

Although the studies reviewed above are almost unanimous in revealing the ability of token reinforcement to produce favorable changes in the special education classroom, the area has not been free of methodological and engineering difficulties. A frequent problem with many of the studies has been the failure of the experimenters to clearly demonstrate that contingent token reinforcement was responsible for the academic changes which occurred.

In an operant conditioning experiment, the researcher typically notes the frequency of the behavior of interest under normal or baseline conditions. He then applies some consequence to the behavior in an attempt to alter its rate of occurrence. If the rate changes in the predicted direction, the experimenter still cannot be certain that this change was due to the consequence which was applied to the behavior. It is possible that the alteration of the rate was due to the passage of time, maturation of the subjects, increased teacher effectiveness, or many other ongoing factors. To circumvent this difficulty, the experimenter will frequently return the subjects to the conditions which existed before the reinforcement techniques were applied. A return of the behavior to the original baserate lends credence to the idea that it was the contingent reinforcement or punishment which accounted for the behavioral change.

Nevertheless, many of the token studies have failed to include a reversal to baseline conditions (e.g., Birnbrauer & Lawler, 1964; Perline & Levinsky, 1968). It might be argued that the ability of operant principles to alter behavior has been demonstrated in a sufficient number of cases that a reversal phase is unnecessary, especially in a purely therapeutic situation. As Sidman (1960) noted however, "An investigator may, on the basis of experience, have great confidence in the adequacy of his methodology, but other experimenters cannot be expected to share his confidence without convincing evidence [p. 75]" (cited by O'Leary & Becker, 1967).

The manner in which many of the studies were conducted raises questions as to their usefulness in the special education classroom. One problem has been the use of a large number of personnel in order to execute the programs. Birnbrauer's (1965) study used three teachers in a classroom of eight boys, whereas the Patterson (1965) study required the presence of a teacher and an experimenter. Although it is desirable that such a personnel-teacher ratio exist ordinarily, it is unrealistic to expect this situation in many special education classrooms. A somewhat promising solution to this problem is given in the group contingency design used by Gallagher's group (1967) and by Sulzbacher and Houser (1968). These studies treated the entire class as a unit and thus simplified the administration of reinforcement and the bookkeeping procedures.

Another limitation of some of the above studies is that electronic equipment was required for their execution (e.g., Patterson, 1965; Patterson et al., 1965). Although it could be argued that this equipment is not complex, it is doubtful that the necessary apparatus would be installed by many special education teachers without the assistance and encouragement of a researcher. The availability of the appropriate researcher is often limited.

## Future Research

The Kuypers (1968) study stated that "a general goal of token systems is to transfer control of responding from token systems to other conditioned reinforcers such as teacher praise and grades [p. 101]." If this is an accepted aim of token reinforcement programs, future research must be conducted in this direction. The most frequently stated suggestion (e.g., Kuypers et al., 1968) for achieving transfer from the token system to the more traditional classroom situation is to precede the delivery of tokens with praise. This arrangement is intended to eventually establish social events as conditioned reinforcers and to allow a teacher to maintain student behavior with social reinforcement alone.

Another proposal concerning the removal of tokens was given by O'Leary and Becker (1967). By requiring progressively more behavior to receive a prize and by increasingly delaying reinforcement, the authors claimed that a transfer from tokens to teacher praise could be achieved eventually.

Which, if either, of these proposals will be fruitful will be determined by future investigation. The question seems an important one, since it is unlikely that a token system would be applied indefinitely in any school setting.

In the present author's opinion, future token experiments should employ reinforcers already available in the classroom. Studies which are dependent on the introduction of candies and toys into the classroom can only be applied for a limited period of time because of the strain eventually placed on the school's or teacher's budget. Most special education teachers permit their students to have free play time, field trips, and games. Rather than permitting the students to engage in such activities independent of classroom performance, the privileges could be used as reinforcers in the token program. This approach has been successfully employed by Sulzbacher and Houser (1968) and offers the most economical and easily transferred system of behavior modification.

## References

Bijou, S. W., Birnbrauer, J. S., Kidder, J. D., & Tague, C.E. Programmed instruction as an approach to the teaching of reading, writing, and arithmetic to retarded children. *Psychological Record*, 1966, 16, 505-522.

Birnbrauer, J. S., Bijou, S. W., Wolf, M. M., & Kidder, J. D. Programmed instruction in the classroom. In L. P. Ullmann and L. Krasner (Eds.), *Case studies in behavior modification*. New York: Holt, Rinehart & Winston, 1965. Pp. 358-363.

Birnbrauer, J. S., & Lawler, J. Token reinforcement for learning. *Mental Retardation*, 1964, 2, 275-279.

Birnbrauer, J. S., Wolf, M. M., Kidder, J. D., & Tague, C. Classroom behavior of retarded pupils with token reinforcement. *Journal of Experimental Child Psychology*, 1965, 2, 219-235.

Clark, M., Lachowitz, J., & Wolf, M. A pilot basic education program for school dropouts incorporating a token reinforcement system. *Behavior Research and Therapy*, 1968, 6, 183-188.

Gallagher, P., Sulzbacher, S. I., & Shores, R. E. A group contingency for classroom management of emotionally disturbed children. Paper read to Kansas Chapter, The Council for Exceptional Children, Wichita, March, 1967.

Haring, N. G., & Hauck, M. Improved learning conditions in the establishment of reading skills with disabled readers. *Exceptional Children*, 1969, 35, 341-352.

Hewett, F., Taylor, F., & Artuso, A. The Santa Monica project: Evaluation of an engineered classroom design with emotionally disturbed children. *Exceptional Children*, 1969, 35, 523-529.

Kuypers, D. S., Becker, W. C., & O'Leary, K. D. How to make a token system fail. *Exceptional Children*, 1968, 35, 101-109.

McKenzie, H. S., Clark M., Wolf, M. M., Kothera, R., & Benson, C. Behavior modification of children with learning disabilities using grades as tokens and allowances as back up reinforcers. *Exceptional Children*, 1968, 34, 745-752.

Nolen, P., Kunzelmann, H. P., & Haring, N. G. Behavioral modification in a junior high learning disabilities classroom. *Exceptional Children,* 1967, 34, 163-168.

O'Leary, K. D., & Becker, W. C. Behavioral modification of an adjustment class. A token reinforcement program. *Exceptional Children,* 1967, 33, 637-642.

Patterson, G. R. An application of conditioning techniques to the control of a hyperactive child. In L.P. Ullmann and L. Krasner (Eds.), *Case studies in behavior modification.* New York: Holt, Rinehart & Winston, 1965. Pp. 370-375.

Patterson, G. R., Jones, R., Whittier, J., & Wright, M. A. A behavior modification technique for the hyperactive child. *Behavior Research and Therapy,* 1965, 2, 217-226.

Perline, I. H., & Levinsky, D. Controlling behavior in the severely retarded. *American Journal of Mental Deficiency,* 1968, 73, 74-78.

Quay, H. C., Werry, J. S., McQueen, M., & Sprague, R. L. Remediation of the conduct problem child in the special class setting. *Exceptional Children,* 1966, 32, 509-515.

Sidman, M. *Tactics of scientific research.* New York: Basic Books, 1960.

Sulzbacher, S. I., & Houser, J. E. A tactic to eliminate disruptive behaviors in the classroom: Group contingent consequences. *American Journal of Mental Deficiency,* 1968, 73, 88-90.

Wolf, M. M., Giles, D. K., & Hall, R. V. Experiments with token reinforcement in a remedial classroom. *Behavior Research and Therapy,* 1968, 6, 51-64.

211

DAVID S. KUYPERS
WESLEY C. BECKER
K. DANIEL O'LEARY

# How to Make a Token System Fail

TOKEN systems of reinforcement have usually been implemented in classrooms when the available social reinforcers such as teacher praise and approval have been ineffective in controlling the behavior of the children. Token systems involve the presentation of a "token" (e.g., a checkmark) following the emission of specified responses. When the child has accumulated a sufficient number of tokens, he is then able to exchange them for "back up" reinforcers (e.g., candy, toys). The tokens initially function as neutral stimuli, and they acquire reinforcing properties by being exchangeable for the back up reinforcers. Teacher praise and approval are often paired with the tokens, in order to increase the effectiveness of praise and approval as conditioned reinforcers. A general goal of token systems is to transfer control of responding from the token systems to other conditioned reinforcers such as teacher praise and grades.

Different investigators have reported upon the success of token systems in controlling the behavior of children in classrooms where the usual social reinforcers were ineffective (Birnbrauer, Bijou, Wolf, & Kidder, 1965; Birnbrauer & Lawler, 1964; Birnbrauer, Wolf, Kidder, & Tague, 1965; O'Leary & Becker, 1967).

Teachers operating successful token programs in these studies have usually been explicitly trained in the systematic use of principles of operant behavior, and much of the success of the programs is most likely due to the general application of principles other than those governing the use of tokens per se. The central aspect of a token system is the pairing of teacher praise with tokens which are backed up by an effective reinforcer. In most effective studies, however, many other procedures have also been used. For example, praise for appropriate behavior and ignoring of disruptive behavior are used at times when tokens are not being dispensed. Time out (or isolation) is often used when intensely disruptive behaviors occur. Systematic contingencies in the form of privileges are often applied throughout the day. The children following the rules are the ones who get to help teacher, to be first in line, to choose an activity, etc. The principle of shaping is also systematically applied. Praise, privileges, and tokens are not administered for achieving an absolute standard of performance, but for improving behavior or for maintaining a high level of acceptable behavior.

The present study is one of several aimed

EXCEPTIONAL CHILDREN, 1968, Vol. 35, pp. 101-109.

at clarifying the important components of effective token systems. The authors' objective is primarily to make clear to those who might adopt such systems where things can go wrong if a token system is attempted without full consideration of the many variables important to success. The study uses a general procedure which was shown to be very effective when coupled with training in behavior theory, a time out procedure, shaping, and differential social reinforcement throughout the day (O'Leary & Becker, 1967). The present study, however, examines the effectiveness of the token system by itself in a classroom in which no other modifications were made in the teacher's handling of the class. The study approximates what might happen if a teacher read about a token system and tried to use it mechanically without a fuller understanding of those basic principles and supplementary procedures which are often used in successful studies but which are not emphasized or made explicit.

The study was planned to include additional phases to train the teacher in behavior principles; following this, a more effective program would have been established. However, at the request of the teacher, it was necessary to terminate the study prior to its completion. We will come back to this point in the discussion.

## Method

The subjects who participated in this study were six third grade and six fourth grade children who were described as socially maladjusted. The children were typically assigned to an adjustment class when they showed such behaviors as temper tantrums, fighting, failure to pay attention in class, inability to work on their own, and academic retardation. While the token system of reinforcement was in effect for the entire class, observations were conducted on only three of the children at each grade level—six children in all. Four of the children were selected because they engaged in a high rate of inappropriate and disruptive behavior, and two were selected because the teacher reported a low incidence of highly disruptive behavior in relation to the other class members. Two of the children

had previously attended a classroom at another school in which a token system of reinforcement had been used (O'Leary & Becker, 1967).

### Observations

The incidence of inappropriate classroom behaviors of the four highly disruptive children was recorded by two undergraduate students during the morning between 9:30 and 11:30. Between 1:00 and 2:00 in the afternoon, three undergraduate observers recorded the behavior of six children who included the four observed in the morning plus two children who were reported by teacher not to show much disruptive behavior. Deviant behaviors were defined as behaviors likely to be incompatible with group learning conditions. Definitions used for six classes of deviant behaviors, and one class of relevant behavior, are as follows:

Coding Categories for Children
Deviant Behavior
*Gross motor behaviors.* Getting out of seat, standing up, walking around, running, hopping, skipping, jumping, rocking chair, moving chair, knees on chair. Include such gross physical movements as arm flailing, feet swinging, and rocking.
*Disruptive noise.* Tapping feet, clapping, rattling papers, tearing papers, throwing book on desk, slamming desk top, tapping pencil or other objects on desk. Be conservative, rate what you hear, not what you see, and do not include accidental dropping of objects or noise made while performing gross motor behaviors.
*Disturbing others.* Grabbing objects or work, knocking neighbor's books off desk, destroying another's property, throwing objects at another without hitting, pushing with desk. Only rate if someone is there.
*Contact.* Hitting, pushing, shoving, pinching, slapping, striking with objects, throwing object which hits another person, poking with object. Do not attempt to make judgments of intent. Rate any physical contact.
*Orienting responses.* Turning head or head and body to look at another person, showing objects to another child, attending to another child. Must be of 4 seconds duration to be rated and is not rated unless seated. Any turn of 90 degrees or more from desk while seated is rated.
*Verbalizations.* Carrying on conversations with other children when it is not permitted, calling out answers to questions or comments without being called on, calling teacher's name

213

to get her attention, crying, screaming, singing, whistling, laughing, coughing, or blowing nose. Do not rate lip movements. Rate what you hear, not what you see.

Relevant Behavior

Time on task, e.g., answering questions, listening, raising hand for teacher attention, working at assigned task, reading. Must include whole 10 second interval except for orienting responses of less than four seconds duration.

The children were observed in a fixed order for 22 minutes each session, three times a week. Observations were made on a 20 second observe, 10 second record basis. Each observer had a clipboard with a stop watch and a recording sheet. Simple symbols were used to indicate the occurrence of a particular class of behavior. A given class of behavior could be rated only once in an observation interval.

Percentage of deviant behavior was defined as the percentage of intervals in which one or more deviant behaviors occurred. Reliability was checked on the average of once a week, and was calculated by dividing the number of agreements on behavior code and time interval by the number of agreements plus disagreements.

## Class Activities

For most of the day the children were in a single classroom with one teacher. During the morning the children's activities consisted of group reading lessons and individual seat work. During the afternoon the first 40 minute period consisted of a group arithmetic lesson and the second 40 minute period consisted of either art or music in another room for the fourth graders and art or spelling for the third graders.

## Experimental Phases

*Baseline.* During the baseline phase, the teacher was asked to handle the children according to her usual techniques and procedures. Observers had recorded the children's behavior for approximately three weeks before the collection of baseline observations was begun. This initial period was instituted in order to allow the children to adapt to the observers' presence in the classroom.

*Token reinforcement phase.* The following written instructions were given to the teach-

er and discussed with her. These instructions were used as the basis for the token reinforcement stage.

A. *Instructions for initial introduction of token program.*

1. Prior to the explanation of the token economy to the children, a list of rules should be written on the blackboard and left there while the program is in effect. (The rules worked out with the teacher were: *stay in seats, raise hand, quiet, desk clear, face front,* and *work hard.* For the art period for the third graders the rules were: *quiet, work hard,* and *be polite.*)

2. Explain to the children that they will be rated on how well they follow the rules from 1:00 to 2:30. Spiral notebooks will be attached to their desks, and every rating period the teacher will put a number from 1 to 10 in their notebooks. The better a child follows the rules the higher the number he will receive.

3. By earning points in this way, the children will be able to win prizes. They must have a certain number of points in order to win a prize. Show the children the prizes and explain that 10 points earns a prize from this box (show an example) and 25 points earns a prize from this box. Do not let the children handle the prizes.

4. Emphasize that at all other times when the children are not being rated their behavior will not affect their rating during the afternoon period.

5. Explain to the fourth graders that their other teachers will rate them when they leave the classroom, and that they will have to bring back a slip with their number on it signed by their teacher. If they do not bring back this slip, they will not receive any points that day. Also explain that the other children in the art and music class will not be told about their point system.

6. Emphasize that they will not receive prizes every day, and that sometimes they will have to collect points over two or more days in order to obtain prizes. However, they will be told how long they have to work to earn a prize.

B. *General instructions for operation of token program.*

1. Each day before the rating period, go over the rules with the children. Point out that they can earn prizes, tell them how many points they must have to win different types of prizes, and then show them some of the prizes they can win.

2. When rating a child, point out the rules he followed in order to receive the points he

did. "I'm giving you 8 points because. . . ," "I'm not giving you 10 points because. . . ." Also indicate what behaviors could be improved on to earn full points.

3. At all times, except when prizes are being shown to the class or when the children are picking out the prizes they have earned, the prizes should be stored in a location where the children cannot reach them.

4. If the children mention certain types of prizes they would like to be able to earn or if they do not appear interested in any of the prizes available, please notify the investigator as soon as possible.

5. Record points on two pages. One will be picked up each day. Enter ratings from art and music teachers into the book also.

6. Except for the first day of the token program, prizes should be given out at the end of the school day. On the first day give out prizes after the third rating period.

7. The children will be rated from 1 to 10 on how well they follow the classroom rules and behave in class. Rules can be modified or changed, but if this is done, notify the class and put the change on the blackboard.

8. The value of the prize will be changed as the children are required to earn more points to win prizes. The number of points required will be indicated on the appropriate boxes.

9. A child should be very well behaved to earn the highest value prizes. Do not allow the children to try to talk you into giving them more points. Make a judgment and then explain that he earned only so many points, but he can earn more by behaving better.

Two values of prizes were used—one group in the 5¢ to 10¢ range, and one group in the 15¢ to 19¢ range. They included such things as candy, gliders, balls, pencils, and clay.

For third graders ratings were given after each 30 minute period. Since the fourth graders left for art or music during the second '30 minute period, the problem was initially handled by doubling the points earned in the first period and by having the art or music teacher give a rating for that period. After four days the system was changed so that both third and fourth graders were rated after two 40 minute periods. During the first four days prizes were distributed each day. After that they were distributed every other day. The number of points required to earn prizes was gradually increased from 10 to 30 for lower value prizes and 25 to 35 for higher value prizes.

The teacher used her own judgment in making ratings within the guidelines given above. She was informed of how the observers rated the children the first few days of the program, but no attempt was made to determine her ratings. In all other aspects of her behavior, the teacher was expected to continue as she had before.

*Baseline two.* The token system was withdrawn for two weeks and baseline conditions reestablished. It was during this period that the teacher decided not to continue with the study.

## Results

### Reliability

During the afternoon observations, interobserver reliability for individual children for the 13 day baseline period ranged from 64 to 98 percent agreement with an average of 80 percent. During the token period the interobserver reliability ranged from 69 to 100 percent with an average of 87 percent. For the second baseline, the range was 68 to 100 percent with an average of 82 percent. The reliabilities for morning observations ranged from 52 to 100 percent with an average of 85 percent.

### Group Data

For all six children in the afternoon, the average percentage of deviant behavior during the baseline period was 54. During the token period the average decreased to 27.8 percent and then increased to 41.5 percent when the tokens were removed. The daily averages for the different periods have been plotted graphically in Figure 1. If fewer than four children were observed on any day, then that day was eliminated from the analysis. The single day that a substitute teacher was in the classroom was also eliminated. An analysis of variance, using the average percentage of deviant behavior for each child during each period, indicated that the effects of periods were significant beyond the .01 level ($F = 11.27$, $df = 2$).

The average daily percentage of deviant behavior for the four children observed both in the morning and afternoon is plotted graphically by days for the different periods for

215

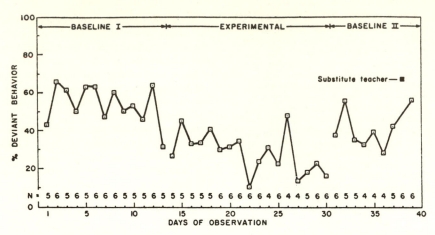

Fig. 1. Percentage of deviant behavior as a function of experimental conditions for children observed during the afternoon.

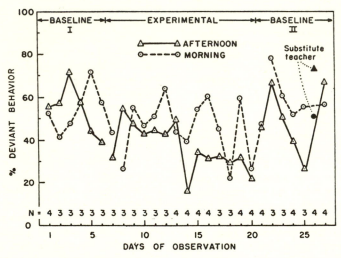

Fig. 2. Percentage of deviant behavior as a function of experimental conditions for children observed during morning and afternoon.

both the morning and afternoon observations (see Figure 2). A child had to be observed in both the morning and afternoon for his percentage of deviant behavior to be included in the analyses, and if fewer than three children were observed on any day, then that day was eliminated from the analysis. The average percentage of deviant behavior for the first baseline period was 53.2 for morning and 54.3 for afternoon observations. For the token pe-

riods the percentages were 45.0 (AM) and 35.5 (PM); and for the second baseline they were 58.5 (AM) and 50.4 (PM). These data show little, if any, generalization of improved behavior from the afternoon period when the token system was in effect to the morning period when the token system was not in effect. No statistical tests were carried out on the generalization data because of wide individual variations in effect. The important results of the

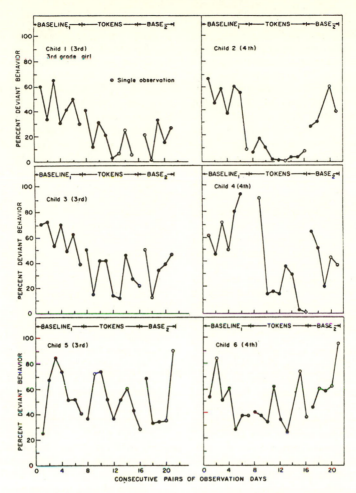

Fig. 3. Percentage of deviant behavior for individual children based on afternoon observations.

study are made clear by examination of the individual graphs.

### Individual Data

The individual graphs show that four children (1 through 4, Figure 3) improved considerably under the token system, and two showed at best occasional good days. No consistent individual gains occurred during the morning period when individual data were examined (these graphs are not presented). Of interest is the fact that children 4 and 6 had partici-

pated in the earlier program by O'Leary and Becker (1967). Child 6 rarely responded to the new program, and often would not even keep his point book on his desk.

### Discussion

Although an average significant effect of the token program was demonstrated, it is quite clear from the individual graphs and the generalization measures that the program was only marginally effective. Many interpretations are always possible when there is a failure to establish experimental control over behavior; however, a number of the findings when compared with those from the earlier study by O'Leary and Becker (1967) suggest some reasonable conclusions. The reader should first keep in mind that the formal token system was very similar to that used by O'Leary and Becker, including the shift to a two day delay in back up reinforcers after the first four days. The programs were carried out at similar times during the day, on similar children in adjustment classes. In the first study (O'Leary & Becker, 1967) there were more Negro children and the general level of deviant behavior was higher during baseline. The token system in the first study produced a dramatic shift from approximately 80 percent deviant behavior to under 10 percent, and it was effective for all children. Furthermore, although generalization measures were not taken, repeated reports by diverse observers indicated a dramatic change in the behavior of the children throughout the day. Some of the keys to the differences in findings include the following:

1. Tokens or points were given for meeting an absolute standard in the present study, rather than for improvement. A shaping procedure was not used by the teacher. Under these conditions, the two children who were considered by the teacher to be less troublesome to begin with (children 1 and 2) responded very well to the program. While these two children had an average percentage of deviant behavior during baseline approximating that of the other children, it was qualitatively different behavior. Their behaviors involved talking and turning around in their seats rather than fighting, making loud noises, and wandering around the room. It was easy for the teacher to give them high ratings and for them to respond to the reinforcement system. The children who could not as easily meet the standards set by the teacher could have been punished for improved behavior by receiving low point scores. The high degree of variability over days and between children is precisely what would be expected when an absolute standard is applied.

2. No attempt was made to have the teacher systematically apply differential social reinforcement in between the times when points were awarded or at other times during the day. This aspect of the earlier program was probably responsible for much of its effectiveness. Points which are awarded 30 or 40 minutes later are not enough to help a child learn more appropriate behaviors. With effective and continuous use of praise for good behaviors and ignoring of deviant behaviors, immediate consequences can be brought to bear on such behavior, especially when praise has been made important to the children through its pairing with tokens. The lack of generalization effects are most likely due to this difference in procedures. (We had hoped to clearly show this by introducing systematic social reinforcement in the next stage of the experiment.) Observations of the teacher throughout the day indicated that she would intermittently pay attention to deviant behaviors and would often ignore the children when they were behaving well. If paying attention is reinforcing and if ignoring amounts to an extinction condition, these teacher behaviors would be affecting the children in a way opposite to that desired.

3. The teacher in this study was not trained through a workshop in the systematic application of behavioral principles. Such training may be important in knowing how to shape behavior and how to effectively use differential social reinforcement.

4. Some initial difficulties were encountered in getting the fourth graders to respond to the program (children 2, 4, and 6, Figure 3). They typically received high ratings (appropriately given) by their art and music teachers which made it less necessary for them to behave in the classroom to earn points. The point system was eventually changed so that good behavior in both periods was essential (in the move to 30 points for a lower prize and 35 for a higher one).

5. Another potential problem was that during baseline the teacher considered the level of deviant behavior to be close to an acceptable level. She had a great capacity

for tolerating disruptions in the class as long as they did not interfere with her work with an individual child. Also, in making judgments about following the rules, she was much more lenient than our judgment would deem appropriate. Her frame of reference would likely foster the reinforcement of deviant behaviors, as defined in the present study, and leave the level of improvement at a low level.

The authors titled this paper, "How to make a token system fail." In actuality, the system functioned as expected—as far as it went. The minimal token system employed was statistically effective and could not have been much more effective, if differential social reinforcement and shaping must be a central part of a workable system. The real failure in this experiment was the failure to give the teacher sufficient support and information to keep her working with the researchers so that subsequent phases of the study could demonstrate more definitively the importance of additional procedures. The behavior of the morning observers was a particular source of irritation for the teacher. Although instructed to fade into the background, two of them did not. Chewing and cracking gum, talking, and obviously watching the children were among their behaviors found irritating by the teacher. Her warnings were not responded to soon enough, although eventually one of the observers was fired. By then it was too late to save the study. There were other failures in the administration of the study which produced unnecessary irritations for the teacher, such as intruding on her evening and weekend time to discuss problems.

We explicitly point out these problems so that others may profit from our mistakes. Great care should be exercised in selecting and training observers, in providing guidelines for the supervisory staff, and in preparing the teacher for what is coming. While the teacher emphasized the role of the observer's behavior in her decision to stop the study, the study was not stopped until we had withdrawn the token system for about four days. Problem behavior as well as the concerns of the teacher had increased. Although the teacher agreed to let us finish the second baseline period, better

preparation of the teacher on our part could have saved the study.

## Implications

A token system is usually designed to make more usual social reinforcers effective for children and lead to an elimination of the token system. These objectives involve the use of a complex set of procedures. The findings of this study when contrasted with those from O'Leary and Becker (1967) should suggest to the reader who is interested in applying a token system some of the important procedures which may be missed or not thought important in looking at the literature on token systems. If the token system involves delays in giving tokens or points (to simplify the procedure for the teacher), it is probably very important to use differential social reinforcement at all times. Explicitly, this involves giving praise and privileges for improvement in behavior, and ignoring (rather than criticizing or distracting) children showing deviant behaviors—unless someone is being hurt. In the latter case, withdrawal of all social attention and loss of the opportunity to earn tokens by isolating the child (time out) is the procedure of choice. It is also important to use tokens and praise to shape improved behavior, so that all children can be affected by positive reinforcement. Catch the child being good. Focus on that aspect of behavior which is an improvement (e.g., in seat rather than out, even if not yet working) and reinforce it. Look for sequential steps toward improvement which can be successively reinforced (in seat, not turning and talking to neighbors, desk cleared of excess materials, paying attention, working, working diligently).

A token system is not a magical procedure to be applied in a mechanical way. It is simply one tool within a larger set of tools available to the teacher concerned with improving the behavior of children. The full set of equipment is needed to do the job right.

## References

Birnbrauer, J. S., Bijou, S. W., Wolf, M. M., & Kidder, J. D. Programmed instruction in the classroom. In P. L. Ullman and L. Krasner (Eds.), *Case studies in behavior modification.*

New York: Holt, Rinehart and Winston, 1965. Pp. 358-363.

Birnbrauer, J. S., & Lawler, J. Token reinforcement for learning. *Mental Retardation*, 1964, **2**, 275-279.

Birnbrauer, J. S., Wolf, M. M., Kidder, J. D., & Tague, C. E. Classroom behavior of retarded pupils with token reinforcement. *Journal of Experimental Child Psychology*, 1965, **2**, 219-235.

O'Leary, K. D., & Becker, W. C. Behavior modification of an adjustment class: A token reinforcement program. *Exceptional Children*, 1967, **33**, 637-642.

---

DAVID S. KUYPERS *is Graduate Student, Department of Psychology, and* WESLEY C. BECKER *is Professor of Educational Psychology, Bureau of Educational Research, University of Illinois, Urbana;* K. DANIEL O'LEARY *is Assistant Professor of Psychology, State University of New York at Stony Brook, Long Island, New York.*
*This study was supported by the National Institutes of Health, Grant No. HD 00881-05.*

H. G. WADSWORTH

# A Motivational Approach Toward the Remediation of Learning Disabled Boys

*Abstract: A group of unmotivated third grade boys was diagnosed as having learning disabilities and was taught under three conditions. The boys served as their own controls. The dependent variables were reading level and school behavior. The independent variables were, in order of presentation, reading tutoring at a private clinic, reinforcement techniques in a self contained classroom, and intermittent reinforcement (via a resource room) during reintegration into a regular classroom. Clinic tutoring resulted in no significant gains in reading; reinforcement approaches, however, produced significant gains. Appropriate school behavior was significantly related to reading level.*

THERE is little debate that schools across the nation are generally unsuccessful with significant proportions of the children they serve. On the whole, school personnel are dissatisfied with the inability to change seemingly intractable characteristics of children whose performance is academically and socially inadequate. There are various areas of exceptionality under which many school children with problems have been subsumed.

An apparent new malady has emerged and is known by such names as perceptual handicap, minimal brain dysfunction, learning disability, etc. (Reger, Schroeder, & Uschold, 1968). The most popular label seems to be "learning disability" and has been adopted by the Department of Health, Education, and Welfare. The National Advisory Committee on Handicapped Children (1968) says, "A learning disability refers to one or more significant deficits in essential learning processes requiring special educational techniques for its remedia-

tion [p. 34]." Programs for children with learning disabilities are springing up in many communities to reach those children who are not best served by other special education programs. There is probably also a significant number of parents who prefer their children to be called "learning disabled" rather the more stigmatized "emotionally disturbed" or "mentally retarded"; thus they are pushing for this new classification. Actually this "new malady" is not new but represents an attempt to encompass and cover all the previously existing problems.

This study examined a remediation approach which has received scant attention in the learning disability field (McCarthy & McCarthy, 1969). The central feature of the approach was to utilize knowledge from learning theory (behavior modification) for the benefit of 15 elementary school boys who had learning disabilities. These boys were diagnosed by a certified school psychologist as having visual-motor integration difficulties, auditory discrimination problems, reading disabilities, and other related disorders.

### Overview of Learning Disabilities

Teachers and parents have long been concerned about the considerable percent-

H. G. WADSWORTH *is Assistant to the Director, Pupil Personnel Department, District 59, Elk Grove Village, Illinois, and Doctoral Student, Department of Studies in Behavioral Disabilities, University of Wisconsin–Madison.*

EXCEPTIONAL CHILDREN, 1971, Vol. 38, No. 1, pp. 33-42.

age of children who have difficulty learning for one reason or another. A diagnosis of "learning disabilities" provides a vindication for many school failures. Some pediatricians (de la Cruz & La Veck, 1965) explain that learning disorders are symptoms of a great variety of functional and organic conditions. They say that various disciplines have approached the problem, each with their special viewpoints, "and findings have not been integrated into a rational and workable form [p. 31]." The pediatrician remains the key to any successful effort since the causes are primarily motor and sensory deficit, malnutrition, organicity, diseases, and metabolic disturbances. Michal-Smith and Morgenstern (1965) give more credit to the ego and therefore emotional factors in the discussion of causes.

Clements (1964) is well noted for his work with learning disorders and considers this problem within the area of minimal brain dysfunction. Children with this impairment are of at least average intelligence and have mild to severe genetically and neurologically based school problems. Clements reports that in the past these children have shown up in psychiatric clinics or classes for the retarded, or were retained as children who were simply lazy. Graduate schools of psychology, social work, education, and medicine are faulted for not having provided information in this area. The diagnosis of the learning disordered child, which Clements considers crucial, is made on the basis of clinical behavior, history, psychological evaluation, and neurological signs. Treatment depends on proper medication and educational planning along with psychotherapy where indicated. However, Haring and Hauck (1969) are not concerned about causes. They feel that by the time reading behavior, for example, becomes important for children, it is too late to be concerned about etiology. Johnson (1968) shows some disfavor with the diagnostic process because he feels such terms as "perceptually handicapped" are frequently and unfortunately used as "global explanations of complex behavior [p. 62]."

Kephart (1960) says about this type of child that he needs to have experiences which train his perceptual-motor skills and that he needs to practice these experiences

often. It can also be said, and this was our implicit supposition, that the child needs to first have an orderly educational plan and then to have *motivation to practice,* because he may regard as monotonous the experiences which are necessary in order to improve. This statement is at issue with Edgington (1968) when she comments on the child with reading disabilties. "He is not lazy; he is not retarded; he is not able to do better if he just would; he is not likely to outgrow his disability without special help [p. 7]. . . ." The author contends that he *is,* in a sense, lazy and is able to do better if he wants to. His "wanting to" depends on motivating factors, and motivation does not come from within the child; it comes from experiences and environmental manipulation.

### Setting of the Study

The learning disabilities (LD) program in the district chosen for this study is large and serves a school system of 12,000 children in 20 buildings (grades K-8). Each building has its own LD teacher who is permitted a maximum enrollment of 10 children. These children go to a resource room for periods varying from 20 to 45 minutes per day for remedial work pertaining to their disability as diagnosed by a student-services team (nurse, psychologist, social worker). The primary treatment mode is the use of special materials including such things as pegboards, lacing cards, blocks, tracing items, shape patterns, walking boards, and Language Masters.

The program assumed that lack of experience in certain areas causes the child to do poorly in reading, arithmetic, and writing, and auditory difficulties hamper oral understanding. Likewise, it is assumed that emotional factors enter into a child's school performance and his parents' reaction to it. Unfortunately, the success of this approach has not been validated because of a lack of research on it in the district. It is known, however, that some LD teachers are unsure of their effectiveness, that some do not feel the child benefits significantly, and that some regular classroom teachers are dubious about the program and its carryover for the child in the regular classrooms.

Because of an interest in the above mentioned concerns, one of the LD teachers

222

agreed to participate in a small project. One of the central premises of the project was that it is not necessary to be concerned with extensive diagnostic findings regarding the causes of the disability, but to view the problem as an educational one and to seek better programing and motivating factors for the children.

### A Motivational Approach

Behavior modification had been used in the school district in classes for the emotionally disturbed and the socially maladjusted, with individual children in regular classrooms, and with individual children through their parents at home. (For a fuller understanding of behavior modification, see Thomas, 1967; Ullmann & Krasner, 1965; Ulrich, Stachnik, & Mabry, 1966). In using these methods for children with learning disabilities, it is necessary to consider two broad types of maladaptive behavior—social and academic. Social maladaptive behavior includes such things as hitting or talking without permission. Academic maladaptive behavior covers such responses as pronouncing words incorrectly or misspelling words.

The LD teacher wanted to try a motivational approach on half of her children with whom she worked individually. (The terms behavior modification and operant conditioning were avoided because of their negative connotations to some.) A point exchange system was set up with the children earning points for such behaviors as reading, sounding out words, and working with flash cards. In an attempt to transfer the children's gains to the regular classroom, they were also reinforced for correct answers on spelling and math tests and for turning in assignments. The points, which were accompanied by praise, were exchangeable for primary reinforcers such as toys and candy. Criticism or calling attention to poor work was avoided. The LD teacher worked with these five children on this basis for the last 3 months of the school year. She and the regular classroom teachers felt the results were good. These subjective feelings were substantiated by the objective data of better grades, more assignments turned in, and a higher achievement level. The extra cost for this experiment was very small—less than $25.

Other researchers (McKenzie, Clark, Wolf, Kothera, & Benson, 1968) comment on token systems straining school budgets. This project demonstrates however, that it is not so much the retail value of the items that motivates children, but the aspect of a consistent, positive approach including verbal and tactile praise with the relative immediacy of reinforcement for their accomplishments.

It was unusual to see five children who had been classified as perceptually handicapped significantly improve upon or even overcome their "learning disability" so rapidly. Therefore, a more sophisticated project was instituted involving better controls. The director of special education authorized a self contained LD class, with eligibility for the class being determined by the severity of the child's disability and concomitant behavioral problems.

### Evolution of the LD Class

*Subjects and their history.* The subjects were 10 boys of middle class, suburban background who were in the third grade and were 8 and 9 years old. When these boys entered the third grade in the fall of 1968, they were quickly identified by the teacher as children who had severe reading problems.

Midway in the third grade their teacher requested special help since she was not being successful within the regular classroom. She felt the children's academic problems far exceeded any she had ever experienced. A number of behavior problems were also surfacing. However, the academic difficulties—especially reading—were such that the teacher believed the 10 boys would not be able to pass the third grade academic requirements and should therefore be retained at the end of the year.

Reading disability is probably the most difficult problem facing schools. The consequences of being unable to read can be everlasting to the individuals involved—not to mention to society. School systems are concerned for at least three reasons. One is that poor reading reflects on the effectiveness and efficiency of the educators. Second, difficulties in reading frequently lead to behavioral problems which upset teachers and parents. Third, educators are dedicated to help children have happy and successful school experiences. During the last months of the school year, special education services were approved. The school staff obtained agreement from the district administration that the district would assume responsibility to help these boys despite budget limitations.

### Procedure

Efforts with the subjects were divided into four stages. The boys were used as their own controls, and reading performance was a dependent variable throughout the entire project. School behavior was not a dependent variable for Stage II as will be explained later. The stages are outlined as follows:

Stage I  : LD consultation, April, 1969–June, 1969.

Stage II : reading clinic, June, 1969–September, 1969.

Stage III: self contained LD class, September, 1969–December, 1969.

Stage IV: resource room, December, 1969–May, 1970.

*Stage I.* This stage did not involve a major effort by the specialists and covered a 2 month period from April to June, 1969. Baseline measurements were taken in April. After extensive observation the LD teacher rated the 10 boys with the *School Behavior Test* (see chart 1) and the social worker administered the *Slosson Oral Reading Test* (SORT). During the 2 month period, the only intervention was the LD teacher's consultation with the regular classroom teacher.

*Stage II.* Before Stage II began, the SORT and *School Behavior Test* (SBT) were administered again. Stage II extended from June to September during which time the boys received tutoring—three 45 min-

CHART 1

**School Behavior Chart**

| Student_____ | Teacher_____ | | Date_____ | |
|---|---|---|---|---|

| Behavior | Almost Always (0) | Frequent (1) | Occasional (2) | Seldom (3) | Almost Never (4) |
|---|---|---|---|---|---|
| 1. Stays in seat, moves around with permission. | | | | | |
| 2. Does not hit, push, disturb others. | | | | | |
| 3. Talks with permission. | | | | | |
| 4. Quiet, does not cry, scream, whistle, or make other oral noise (excluding talking). | | | | | |
| 5. Does not make noise deliberately with objects. | | | | | |
| 6. Pays attention. | | | | | |
| 7. Turns in homework and assignments. | | | | | |
| 8. Prepared for classwork (paper, pencils, etc.). | | | | | |
| 9. Answers teacher's questions and follows directions. | | | | | |
| 10. Participates in class. | | | | | |

ute sessions per week—from a reading clinic (paid for by the district). Just prior to the tutoring, the boys were tested by the reading clinic, using various psychological and reading tests including the *Wechsler Intelligence Scale for Children* (WISC). the *Bender-Gestalt Test for Young Children,* and the *Wide Range Achievement Test* (WRAT). (The SORT significantly correlated with the reading section of the WRAT: rho = .65, $p < .05$, means identical.)

*Stage III.* The SORT was administered again during early September before Stage III began. However, the children were not rated with the SBT because they had not been in school during the summer months and the LD teacher had no information on which to rate them. Stage III involved the self contained LD class beginning in early September and ending in early December, 1969. The purpose of this 3 month period was to determine if significant change could result over a short period of time.

Before the class began at the start of the school year, the social worker met casually with the boys' parents both individually and in groups to inform them of the nature of the class and to determine if there were any significant home problems. No important problems were uncovered through this approach, i.e., there were no discoveries of severe medical problems or family disorganization. After these initial meetings, no further counseling or psychotherapeutic sessions were scheduled with parents or children.

The class was organized to focus on the amelioration of reading and school behavior problems. Other necessary school subjects were also taught. Traditional LD materials (e.g., pegboards) were not used. The teacher drew on the existing school environment to provide perceptual training and experiences. A point exchange system provided the motivation. The procedure included:

1. Outline for the children (on a blackboard or poster) the rules or social and academic behavioral expectations.
2. Reinforce with points (and praise) behavior according to the rules. Points are later exchangeable for tangible items.
3. Give little or no attention to the break-

## CHART 2

**Point Exchange System for LD Class**

| Behaviors to be Reinforced | Points |
|---|---|
| Social: | |
| Being on time | 5, morning and following breaks |
| Talking with permission | Maximum of 3 per hour (use timer) |
| Moving around with permission | Maximum of 2 per hour (use timer) |
| Academic: | |
| Spelling worksheets (10 per week) | 4 per page |
| Handwriting worksheets (5 per week) | 4 per page |
| Reading worksheets (15 per week) | 4 per page |
| Spelling test (20 words per week) | 3 per correct word |
| Reading out loud | 3 per page |
| Phonic questions | 1 per correct answer |

ing of rules unless the child becomes exceedingly disruptive whereupon he could be given a "time-out" and sent into the hall for 2 to 5 minutes. The breaking of rules is, in a sense, self punishing in that the child loses the opportunity to be positively reinforced.

4. Reintegration into the regular classroom, when ready, is the ultimate goal for this class. This is accomplished through gradual exposure to regular classrooms and through the gradual termination of tangible reinforcers.

Behaviors to be reinforced and the corresponding points given are shown in Chart 2.

Points were recorded on 200 point cards which were placed on each child's desk. The value of tangible items was determined by their retail value, for example 100 points equaled a 5 cent value; 1,000 points equaled a 50 cent value. Free time privileges were also earned. For example, if an assignment was to be finished within a 15 minute time period and the child finished within 10 minutes (the assignments could always be finished much faster than the allowed time period), the balance of time could be used to draw, read a book of his choice, or play quiet games.

Initially, the social worker observed frequently in the classroom to work out problems that might arise. For example, one boy approached the teacher's desk several times an hour and bothered her with meaningless questions. The technique used to extinguish this behavior was to compliment the child whenever he was appropriately sitting at his desk working, and to totally ignore him when he tried to get the teacher's attention at her desk. Since the attention he got was achieved while he was at his desk and none was achieved when he went without permission to the teacher's desk, this behavior was almost totally eliminated within 2 days.

*Stage IV.* In December Stage IV began and SBT and SORT scores were again obtained. Following these measurements, a reintegration process (into the regular fourth grade) was begun. When the boys spent time in the regular class, they were not reinforced with points. However, reinforcers were continued in the resource room. The resource room was actually the same as the LD self contained room (same teacher, etc.), but the boys only visited this room for a short time each day. By January the group was spending only 80 minutes per day in the resource room, and by the end of March, they had all been completely reintegrated. In a sense, then, they were being intermittently reinforced from December through March. Further-

more, the points became increasingly more difficult to earn as determined by the LD teacher's judgment of each child's need for tangible reinforcers for motivation. In early May the final SORT and SBT posttests were administered.

What was primarily investigated in this study was the influence of behavior modification techniques to overcome the effects of "learning disabilities" on behavior and reading. Therefore, this aspect (Stages III and IV) was emphasized rather than the tutoring program.

## Results

*Reading.* Table 1 shows the changes in reading level. The rate of learning (Libaw, Berres, & Coleman, 1966), based on past learning speed, was used to measure the boys against themselves. The nonparametric $t$ test and Wilcoxon were utilized for statistical verification. Improvement in reading level was not statistically significant ($p < .05$) during Stages I and II. Significant differences were found for Stages III and IV. In the 3 month span of Stage III, the group gained 8 months in reading performance. During the 5 month period of Stage IV, a gain of 9 months in reading level was made.

The last phase of intermittent rein-

**TABLE 1**

**Expected and Actual Reading Levels of the 10 Boys**

| Boys | Reading level base | Rate of learning[a] | Stage I Expected | Actual | Stage II Expected | Actual | Stage III Expected | Actual | Stage IV Expected | Actual |
|---|---|---|---|---|---|---|---|---|---|---|
| 1 | 2.6 | .70 | 2.7 | 2.7 | 2.8 | 3.1 | 3.0 | 3.7 | 3.4 | 4.3 |
| 2 | 1.3 | .35 | 1.4 | 2.2 | 1.4 | 2.1 | 1.5 | 2.9 | 1.7 | 3.8 |
| 3 | 2.2 | .60 | 2.3 | 2.3 | 2.4 | 2.7 | 2.6 | 3.2 | 2.9 | 4.5 |
| 4 | 3.1 | .84 | 3.3 | 2.6 | 3.4 | 2.4 | 3.6 | 2.8 | 4.0 | 3.7 |
| 5 | 3.0 | .80 | 3.2 | 3.1 | 3.2 | 3.6 | 3.4 | 4.9 | 3.8 | 5.2 |
| 6 | 2.6 | .70 | 2.7 | 3.4 | 2.8 | 3.6 | 3.0 | 4.4 | 3.4 | 5.9 |
| 7 | 2.0 | .54 | 2.1 | 1.9 | 2.2 | 2.1 | 2.4 | 2.1 | 2.6 | 3.0 |
| 8 | 1.5 | .41 | 1.6 | 2.1 | 1.6 | 2.4 | 1.8 | 3.2 | 2.0 | 3.9 |
| 9 | 2.2 | .60 | 2.3 | 2.4 | 2.4 | 2.4 | 2.6 | 3.5 | 2.9 | 4.3 |
| 10 | 2.1 | .57 | 2.2 | 3.9 | 2.3 | 3.8 | 2.5 | 5.3 | 2.7 | 6.4 |
| Mean | 2.3 | .62 | 2.4 | 2.7 | 2.5 | 2.8 | 2.6 | 3.6 | 2.9 | 4.5 |
| SD | .56 | | .58 | .60 | .61 | .62 | .62 | .94 | .70 | .97 |
| Wilcoxon | | | NS | | NS | | $p = .01$ | | $p < .005$ | |
| $t$ | | | $1.07\ p > .10$ | | $1.03\ p > .10$ | | $2.25\ p < .025$ | | $4.05\ p < .005$ | |

[a] Base level divided by population norm level (3.7); expected levels determined by this rate.
Note: One-tailed tests used, nonparametric.

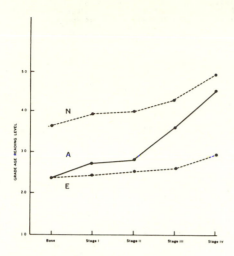

**FIGURE 1.** Comparison of the boys' expected (E) and actual (A) reading levels with population grade norms (N) for children their age.

forcement generated significant results. Even if a new expectation baseline had been calculated as of December, 1969 (increasing the group's rate of learning from .62 in April, 1969 to a new rate of .84), the Wilcoxon would indicate significant changes between December and May ($p < .005$). However, there were not significant differences between December and May scores according to the $t$ test (1.06, $p > .10$).

Figure 1 reflects the gains and the narrowing of disparity between the actual and norm reading levels. Although all boys were fully reintegrated in May, 1970, the individual results of two boys (numbers 4 and 7) warranted some reading assistance when they entered the fifth grade.

*School behavior.* All of the boys were not behavior problems as can be noted in Figure 2. The Wilcoxon, nevertheless, was used to determine if there were significant positive directional changes in behavior as measured by the SBT. This was administered by the LD teacher based solely on her observations of the boys in regular and special classes. It was expected that with no intervention, behavior would do no better than remain the same (and probably worsen). There were statistically significant differences in the direction of improvement during Stages I and III (see

Table 2). Behavior was not considered a problem at the end of Stage III. Thus, no further improvement was expected or achieved in Stage IV. Incidentally, although only three social behaviors were specifically reinforced (see Chart 2), there appeared to be effective generalization to other behaviors.

**TABLE 2**

**School Behavior Test Scores of the 10 Boys**

| Boys | Base | Stage I | Stage III | Stage IV |
|---|---|---|---|---|
| | | *SBT Scores* | | |
| 1 | 0 | 0 | 0 | 0 |
| 2 | 33 | 26 | 2 | 4 |
| 3 | 35 | 22 | 6 | 9 |
| 4 | 23 | 20 | 1 | 4 |
| 5 | 25 | 18 | 3 | 3 |
| 6 | 5 | 4 | 1 | 0 |
| 7 | 26 | 23 | 5 | 4 |
| 8 | 27 | 27 | 0 | 1 |
| 9 | 0 | 1 | 0 | 0 |
| 10 | 26 | 21 | 2 | 1 |
| Mean | 20.0 | 16.2 | 2.0 | 2.6 |
| Wilcoxon[a] | | $p < .01$ | $p < .005$ | NS |
| rho[b] | $-.60, p < .05$ | $-.65, p < .05$ | $-.17$, NS | $-.21$, NS |

[a] Wilcoxon tested the two adjacent scores i.e., Base with Stage I, Stage I with Stage III, etc.
[b] Spearman rank correlation coefficient of subjects' SBT scores with SORT scores.
Note: One-tailed tests used, nonparametric.

*Association between behavior and reading.* The SBT and SORT correlated significantly initially (April, 1969) and before Stage II began (June, 1969).* (See Table 2.) Subjects with lower reading levels tended to have more behavior problems. It may be concluded, at least for this study, that poor behavior is associated with poor reading level. Bateman (1966) states that since boys outnumber girls 10 to 1 in primary reading retardation, a sex-linked factor is strongly indicated. On the other hand, it could be hypothesized that boys, who generally have more behavior problems than girls, are retarded in reading because of behavioral interferences rather than from hereditary disadvantages attrib-

---

* Note that the correlations between the SBT and SORT as of December, 1969 and May, 1970 were not significant. It is assumed the lack of association is due to the factor that behavior was no longer a problem.

227

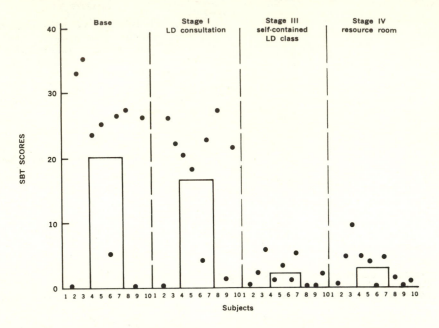

**FIGURE 2.** Illustration of group average (bars) and individual scores (dots) on the *School Behavior Test.*

uted to their sex (e.g. slower matura-tion). McCarthy and McCarthy (1969) in their review point out that disturbed be-havior is not the direct consequence of brain damage but is the result of patterns developed in the course of a typical rela-tions with the developmental environment. Likewise it is presumed, but not known for certain, that the behavioral problems were not a direct result of the learning dis-ability but did develop because of frustra-tions associated with learning and emanat-ing from the disability.

*Diagnostic appraisal.* The results of this study appear to be important in light of the lack of understanding about what ap-proaches are best for the "learning disabil-ity" child. Consequently, it would not be unreasonable to question the original di-agnoses. Were these children representative of the learning disordered? During Stage I the boys were given a battery of psychologi-cal tests by a certified school psychologist to help assess the nature of their problems. WISC scores ranged from 89 to 110 with a mean of 100. There were no significant correlations between the Verbal Scale, Per-formance Scale, and Full Scale of the WISC and reading level. There were also no sig-nificant differences between Performance Scale (mean = 102) and Verbal Scale (mean = 95). The three following sum-maries by the psychologist further substan-tiate the learning disability diagnoses:

Billy exhibits reading performance a full three grade levels below his potential abil-ity as demonstrated by listening compre-hension. Basic word attack skills appear to be missing. Performance on the *Wepman Auditory Discrimination Test* was poor. Analyzing parts auditorily and visually seemed to be a problem area. Billy's left to right working direction is inconsistent. Reversal patterns occurred several times. He performed better in most sections of the *Gates Test* but exhibited difficulty in recognizing and blending common word parts.

Mark is a boy of average intelligence with a reading disability. Oral reading is at least one grade level below school placement and two levels below his potential level as demonstrated by listening comprehension.

Mark's distractibility and short attention span further complicate his reading efforts. Testing reveals weakness in auditory discrimination skills and possible difficulties in eye-motor coordination. Mark has a medical history of allergies and asthma and has been treated with hormones for a thyroid problem. He is easily discouraged and lacks confidence with new learning tasks.

Joe's testing indicates problems in visual and auditory perception. Reversal rotation problems, incorrect working directional sense, with very slow progress in formal reading activities further suggest that there may be deep seated, neurologically based problems. Indicative of good potential are his superior performance in some areas of the WISC and good listening comprehension. He has a wandering right eye which, according to an oculist, needs fusion training.

### Discussion

This project attempted to investigate the application of reinforcement techniques to learning disabilities. Although the design of this project was not ideal, it is a beginning in an area which is in the incipient stages.* It can be argued that variables other than the primary one discussed (reinforcement techniques) accounted for the significant improvements in the boys' reading level and social behavior. The improvements could have been attributed to the small classroom setting, the teacher's personality, the newly found enjoyment of school, or parental support via the home. Improvement could also have occurred because of high experimenter expectations: "When programs of change or treatment are instituted, expectations for their effectiveness are very likely to be involved . . . [Rosenthal & Jacobson, 1968, p. 166]." The success with the original five boys increased the confidence toward the program with the 10. It is likely that the positive changes were due to several variables; however, most of the credit is given to the motivational approach.

There is no effort to interpret the data as giving support to the "special education"

classroom. The author's bias is that children's problems can be solved as well or better in the regular classroom or on a resource room basis (Wadsworth, 1970), but perhaps a short period of intensive work in a self contained atmosphere provides a strong counteractive foundation. The results after a year's duration appear significant, but the stability of the subjects' progress continues to be checked.

The educational programing of disabled learners is crucial. The tutoring given these children from an outside clinic was presumed to have been unsuccessful because of unsatisfactory motivating techniques. Once children become interested in learning—have a reason that is valid to them, e.g., pleasant things happen when they work—then they can learn at an accelerated pace. As they spend more time on their tasks, less time is available for maladaptive behavior. There is, of course, wide disagreement on how to solve reading difficulties. Nevertheless, Haring and Hauck (1969) are speaking for a growing number of specialists when they say the etiology of the problem should be ignored and emphasis should be given to the improvement of instructional conditions.

### References

Bateman, B. Learning disorders. *Review of Educational Research*, 1966, **36**, 93–119.
Clements, S. The child with minimal brain dysfunction—A profile. In S. Clements, L. Lehtin, and J. Lukens (Eds.), *Children with minimal brain injury*. Chicago: National Society for Crippled Children and Adults, 1964. Pp. 1–15.
de la Cruz, F., & La Veck, G. The pediatricians' view of learning disorders. In J. Hellmuth (Ed.) *Learning disorders*. Seattle: Straub and Hellmuth, 1965. Pp. 31–47.
Edgington, R. *Helping children with reading disability*. Chicago: Developmental Learning Materials, 1968.
Haring, N., & Hauck, M. Improved learning conditions in the establishment of reading skills with disabled readers. *Exceptional Children*, 1969, **35**, 341–352.
Johnson, O. Testing the educational and psychological development of exceptional children. *Review of Educational Research*, 1968, **38**, 61–70.
Kephart, N. *The slow learner in the classroom*. Columbus: Charles E. Merrill, 1960.
Libaw, F., Berres, F., & Coleman, J. Evaluating the treatment of learning difficulties. In N. J. Long, W. C. Morse, and R. G. Newman (Eds.), *Conflict in the classroom: The education of emotionally disturbed children*. Belmont, Cal.: Wadsworth Publishing, 1966. Pp. 505–508.

---

* Behavior modification researchers will need to give, where possible, greater emphasis to designs which are more methodologically tight than the one used here. Essentially this involves randomization of subjects to treatment and control groups.

McCarthy, J. J., & McCarthy, J. F. *Learning disabilities*. Boston: Allyn & Bacon, 1969.

McKenzie, H., Clark, M., Wolf, M., Kothera, R., & Benson, C. Behavior modification of children with learning disabilities using grades as tokens and allowances as back up reinforcers. *Exceptional Children*, 1968, **34,** 745–752.

Michal-Smith, H., & Morgenstern, M. Learning disorders—An overview. In Jerome Hellmuth (Ed.), *Learning disorders*. Seattle: Straub and Hellmuth, 1965. Pp. 171–196.

National Advisory Committee on Handicapped Children. *Special education for handicapped children*. First annual report. Washington, D. C.: Department of Health, Education, and Welfare, Office of Education, 1968.

Reger, R., Schroeder, W., & Uschold, K. *Special education: Children with learning problems*. New York: Oxford University Press, 1968.

Rosenthal, R., & Jacobson, L. *Pygmalion in the classroom*. New York: Holt, Rinehart & Winston, 1968.

Thomas, E. (Ed.) *The socio-behavioral approach and applications to social work*. New York: Council on Social Work Education, 1967.

Ullmann, L., & Krasner, L. (Eds.) *Case studies in behavior modification*. New York: Holt, Rinehart & Winston, 1965.

Ulrich, R., Stachnik, T., & Mabry, J. *Control of human behavior*. Glenview, Ill.: Scott Foresman, 1966.

Wadsworth, H. Initiating a preventive-corrective approach in an elementary school system. *Social Work*, 1970, **15** (3), 60–66.

HUGH S. McKENZIE
MARILYN CLARK
MONTROSE M. WOLF
RICHARD KOTHERA
CEDRIC BENSON

# Behavior Modification of Children with Learning Disabilities Using Grades as Tokens and Allowances as Back up Reinforcers

A NUMBER of investigations have indicated that behavior modification techniques can be highly effective in the beneficial change of social and academic behaviors of both normal and exceptional children. Recent research has applied these techniques to bright, preschool children (Bushell, Wrobel, and McCloskey, 1967); to school dropouts (Clark, Lackowicz, and Wolf, in press); to emotionally disturbed children (O'Leary and Becker, 1967); and to low achieving culturally deprived children (Wolf, Giles, and Hall, in press). More extensive reviews of this growing body of experimental literature may be found in Anderson (1967) and Whelan (1966). The approach that these investigations have taken has been to employ token reinforcers such as colored chips or point cards to improve and maintain improvement of social and/or academic behaviors.

Items such as candy, gum, toys, and money have served as back up reinforcers to these tokens, since tokens are exchanged for them.

The problems which can be created, even by an effective token reinforcement system, may be numerous. Not only can token systems be costly in terms of teacher time, but they also may involve an additional burden to already strained school budgets. The administration of tokens such as colored chips and the overseeing of the exchange of tokens for back up reinforcers such as toys may be an unfamiliar role for teachers. Also, parents may be given no function in a token system, although it is recognized that parents can play an integral part in an effective program for children with special needs (Cruickshank, 1967).

These considerations mean that a token system must make a contribution to the ameliora-

EXCEPTIONAL CHILDREN, 1968, Vol. 34, pp. 745-752.

tion of the children's learning difficulties which is significantly greater than that possible with less costly procedures. As O'Leary and Becker (1967) have indicated, the rationale usually offered for employing token systems is that other incentives available to the school, such as teacher attention and grades, have not been effective, since the children involved still exhibit a high frequency of asocial and nonacademic behaviors.

The primary goal of the present research was to assess whether a pay for grades token reinforcement system could increase academic behavior to levels higher than those achieveable with the usually available school incentives. Another aim was to reduce the problems often associated with token systems. By employing grades as tokens, the teacher was not subjected to an unfamiliar role. With weekly allowances as back up reinforcers for grades, parents were able to administer the exchange aspect of the system and were consequently involved in the program. Because parents managed the exchange of tokens for back up reinforcers, and because corrections and some form of grades are an integral part of almost any instructional program, the teacher spent little extra time in the execution of this system. Since the parents of the children of the present study were accustomed to giving their children allowances, neither parents nor school assumed added costs.

**Method**

*Subjects.* The subjects were ten students in a learning disabilities class which was held in Skyline Elementary School, Roesland School District #92, Shawnee Mission, Kansas, during the 1966-1967 school year. This class was one of several special classes operated by the Northeast Johnson County Cooperative Program in Special Education, Johnson County, Kansas.

These ten students, eight boys and two girls, ranged in age from ten to 13 years and were selected for a learning disabilities class on the basis that although their ability levels were above the educable mentally retarded range, their achievement levels were retarded by at least two years in one or more academic areas. All students had received medical and/or psy-chological evaluations which had suggested minimal brain damage with accompanying emotional disturbance. Case histories reported all students to be highly distractible and prone to engage in disruptive behaviors.

Data are reported on eight of the ten students, as data were incomplete on two students who returned to regular classes after the first week of the pay for weekly grades period.

*Teacher.* Prior to teaching the Skyline special class, the teacher had had five years of full time teaching and five years of teacher substitute work in grades K-8. She had obtained her M. Ed. in Special Education from the University of Kansas, with the major part of the academic work for this degree involving courses in behavior modification and operant psychology. Her master's thesis dealt with a basic education program for school dropouts employing a token reinforcement•system (Clark, Lackowicz, and Wolf, in press).

Volunteers from a women's service organization also participated in the program as teacher aides. These aides served mainly to correct and grade the children's academic work.

*Classroom.* The skyline special classroom is similar to self contained classrooms found in many elementary schools. With the exception of desk shields extending about 20 inches above and on three sides of a desk's writing surface, no effort was made to reduce stimuli in the room to a bare minimum, as is sometimes recommended (Cruickshank, 1967). Decorative curtains served as window drapes; different colors surfaced walls, floor, and ceiling; books, teaching materials, and art supplies were always in full view. Walls served as display areas for the children's art work and construction projects. The room often had a festive air as the children decorated it for the various seasons.

*Instructional Materials and Programing.* The commercially available academic materials used were those which might be found in any elementary classroom. Where possible, the children worked on programed instructional materials (e.g., the SRA reading series). Otherwise children did workbook assignments (e.g., Ginn's arithmetic workbooks). Such materials were used because they require overt responses.

232

Prior to the beginning of school and during the first two days of school, the teacher tested the children with the Durrell Analysis of Reading Difficulty and the SRA Achievement Tests. On the basis of these measures, children were placed at academic levels in each of the five instructional areas of the class: reading, arithmetic, spelling, penmanship, and English composition and grammar.

Children were given weekly assignments in each of these five instructional areas, with one assignment sheet for each area. Assignment sheets listed the materials to be worked on each day and the total number of responses assigned, and provided space for the child to record his starting and finishing time and for the teacher (or aide) to record daily the number of responses completed, the number correct, and the child's grade. In each academic area, children were required to complete all previous assignments before going on to new work. If any work was not completed by the week's end, it was assigned for the following week as a new assignment.

*Observations and Recording Procedures.* Children were observed by a research assistant through the one way mirror of a room adjacent to the classroom. A sound system was arranged so that the assistant could hear what occurred.

Observation time covered the first three hours of every morning: the reading and arithmetic periods, together with a short break between these periods in which the children had physical education or recess. Attending was defined as direct orientation toward work materials, i.e., a child was scored as attending if he was sitting at his desk with materials open and before him, and eyes directed toward these materials. Any contact with teacher or aide (raising hand for teacher help or discussion of assignment) was likewise scored as attending. In group work, a child was scored as attending if he was oriented toward work materials, to a reciting fellow student, or to the teacher, or if he himself was responding orally to a lesson. All behaviors other than those specified above were scored as nonattending.

An attending score was obtained for each child once every three minutes. From 90 to 120 seconds were required to observe and score the entire class. The remaining 60 to 90 seconds of the three minute period were used to note teacher and aide behaviors and prepare for the next group of observations.

The reading period lasted about 80 minutes and the arithmetic 60, so that approximately 26 and 20 measures of attending to reading and arithmetic, respectively, could be made on each child on each school day. A child would at times finish an assignment early, resulting in fewer observations of that child for that assignment period. The observer stopped recording the behavior of a child when he had turned his materials in to the teacher or aide and these materials had been certified as complete.

Although the observer was aware of the general orientation of the investigation, he was informed neither of the details of the pay for grades procedure, nor of when it was put into effect.

*Baseline Period.* Incentives available in the school were employed as described below.

1. *Recess.* The children earned recess by the successful completion of all of their assignments for the given assignment week up to the point of a given recess period. Children were required to work through recess if their work was not complete.

2. *Free Time Activities.* When a child had completed all of his assigned work before a given academic period had ended, he was free to go to a free time table to draw, paint, or construct, or he could read a book of his choice at his seat. Free time activities were not available to children until all work was complete.

3. *Special Privileges.* School errands were run by those children who were working hard and well, or who had shown recent improvement in the quality of their work. Line leaders and monitors were chosen on the same basis.

4. *Group versus Individual Lunch.* Children who had all of their work complete by lunchtime earned the privilege of eating in the school cafeteria with the rest of the school. Those whose work was incomplete ate at their desks, in silence.

5. *Teacher Attention.* The attention of the teacher was contingent upon appropriate working behaviors of the children. For ex-

ample, the teacher would say to a hard working child, "Good for you, you're working well, and that's the way you'll become smart in arithmetic and return to regular class sooner." Inappropriate behavior was either ignored or, if disruptive, was punished.

6. *Weekly Grades.* Every week children were given grades to take home to their parents. The parents signed the grade sheets, which the children then returned to the teacher. Both daily and weekly grades were included on these grade sheets. *A* grades indicated that a child had finished his work with 90 percent correct, *B* indicated 80 to 90 percent, *C* indicated 79 percent and below, and *Incomplete* indicated that a child had failed to finish his assigned work.

The teacher conducted group parent conferences once a month at the school, during which time the parents were instructed to praise grades of *A* and *B* and to compliment children for their hard work. Grades of *C* were acceptable, while brief expressions of sorrow were to be paired with grades of *Incomplete* (e.g., "That's too bad you didn't finish all your work in reading this week"), and children were to be encouraged to finish all work for the next week.

Discussions about academic behaviors and their reinforcers were undertaken by the teacher with individual children as well as with the entire group. These discussions were kept brief and never were held when a child was emotionally upset. Through these discussions it was hoped that the children would gain a further awareness of how they could succeed academically and what rewards would accompany such achievement.

To be maximally effective, reinforcers must be consistently applied. In this case, academic behaviors were consistently reinforced, while nonacademic behaviors were extinguished (not reinforced) or punished (resulting in the removal of some reinforcer). To ensure consistency, both the observer and the first author observed the teacher (and aides, where appropriate) and made at least one report a day to the teacher concerning her application of behavior modification techniques. For example, a tally sheet was kept of the number of times the teacher attended to academic behaviors during the school day and of the number of times she incorrectly attended to inappropriate, nonacademic behaviors. By daily discussion of this tally sheet, the teacher was able to increase her frequency of attending to good behaviors and could virtually ignore the unacceptable ones.

The teacher was likewise informed if a child had earned but not been awarded the opportunity to run a school errand, and if a child should not have been allowed recess because of incomplete work. With this information feedback, the teacher appeared to increase her behavior modification skills.

*Pay for Weekly Grades Period.* All procedures employed during the baseline period were continued in identical fashion during the pay period. However, the weekly grades of the baseline period now acquired an additional back up reinforcer: the payment of a weekly allowance to children by their parents on the basis of the children's grades for all subject areas. All the children had received some allowance previous to this period, but the amount received had not depended on their weekly grades. Children were paid for the average weekly grade of each subject area.

At a parent teacher conference toward the end of the baseline period, parents were instructed in the pay for grades procedures. As an example, parents were told that a child might be paid ten cents for *A's*, five cents for *B's*, and one cent for *C's*, while *Incompletes* would lead to a subtraction of the *A* amount, or minus ten cents. The parents determined the precise amounts on the basis of how much money their child was accustomed to having and the cost of the items he would be expected to purchase from his earnings. Amounts actually paid by parents for the weekly grades ranged from the values in the above example up to five times each grade amount in the example. Thus, with the five areas of the special class, plus physical education and music which the children took with the other children in the school, children's maximum earnings varied from $.70 to $3.50. With *Incompletes* being subtracted from earned allowance, it was possible for a child to owe his parents money. Toward this eventuality, parents were told to allow such an indebted child

234

to perform some household chores over the weekend to square his debt. No money beyond the debt was to be earned, however. One indebted child, during the early part of the pay period, settled the debt by cleaning the garage.

Parents were asked to sit down with their child each Friday afternoon when the child brought home his weekly grades, calculate with the child the amount earned, and then pay him this amount. This was to be made an important weekly event. Parents were also asked to see that a large portion of the allowance be immediately consumed, and that the child be expected to pay with his earnings for all items he valued highly. Such things as movies, sweets, models, dolls, horseback riding, the purchase and care of pets, makeup, and inexpensive clothes were to be the children's financial responsibility. The children were not allowed to earn other money about the home, and any added money which came as presents or which was earned outside the home was to be banked. Such procedures helped to maintain the child's need and desire for money at high levels so that money would continue to serve as an effective reinforcer for academic behavior.

Parents informed their children of the pay procedure on the day before the start of the week which would lead to the first payment for weekly grades. Parents also told their children what items the child would be expected to purchase with his earned allowance.

The pay procedure was continued for the remainder of the year for all children, including children who returned to regular classes. Regular classroom teachers were instructed to give these children grades of D and F, as well as higher grades, when their work was at these levels. A grade of D substracted the B amount from a child's allowance, while a grade of F subtracted the A amount. When a child had successfully made the transition to regular class and had performed well for an extended period of time, the length of grade periods was increased, e.g., from once a week to once every two weeks, with appropriate increases in amounts paid for grades. In this way it was hoped to strengthen the child's academic behavior further and to prepare him for the longer grading periods he would encounter in his future schooling.

## Results

A marked increase in attending to reading occurred in the pay period compared with the baseline period (see Figure 1). Overall medians increased from 68 percent in the baseline period to 86 percent in the pay period.

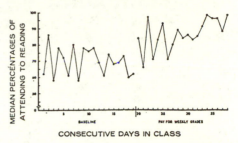

**Figure 1. Patterns of Medians in Attending to Reading**

It is necessary to be certain that the increases in the pay period cannot be attributed to progressive, though perhaps gradual, increases during the baseline period, since the consequences employed during the baseline period may have been increasing attending. Since the most powerful test for such trends was desired, an analysis of variance, rather than a nonparametric test, was performed on the baseline data, yielding an F ratio of less than one (see Table 1) which allows the retention of the hypothesis that the baseline procedures had no tendency to increase attending to reading. By computing eta square, it was estimated that trends accounted for only 6 percent of the variance of the baseline period.

### TABLE 1
### Analysis of Variance for Baseline Trends of Percentages of Attending to Reading

| Source | SS | df | MS | F |
|--------|-----|-----|-----|-----|
| Between Subjects | 32345.368 | 7 | | |
| Within Subjects | 36351.684 | 144 | | |
| Trends | 4337.302 | 18 | 240.96 | $<1$ |
| Residual | 32014.382 | 126 | 254.08 | |

The increase in attending to reading from the baseline period to the pay period was significant (see Table 2); $p < .005$, one tailed Wilcoxon Matched Pairs Signed Ranks Test (Siegel, 1956). The data for each student conformed very closely to the pattern of medians shown in Figure 1. Thus, it can be inferred that the token reinforcement system led to substantial gains in attending to reading for all students.

### TABLE 2
### Subjects' Median Percentages
### of Attending to Reading

| Subjects | Baseline | Pay | Increase |
|---|---|---|---|
| S1 | 71 | 89 | 18 |
| S2 | 82 | 95 | 13 |
| S3 | 23 | 77 | 54 |
| S4 | 83 | 93 | 10 |
| S5 | 72 | 83 | 11 |
| S6 | 72 | 79 | 7 |
| S7 | 75 | 83 | 8 |
| S8 | 62 | 75 | 13 |

*Note:*—Wilcoxon $T = 0$; $p < .005$ (one tailed test)

### TABLE 3
### Analysis of Variance for Baseline Trends
### of Percentages of Attending to Arithmetic

| Source | SS | df | MS | F |
|---|---|---|---|---|
| Between Subjects | 36957.158 | 7 | | |
| Within Subjects | 51337.684 | 144 | | |
| Trends | 7265.842 | 18 | 403.678 | 1.154* |
| Residual | 44071.842 | 126 | 349.776 | |

*$p > .25$

Similar results were obtained in arithmetic (see Figure 2). Overall medians increased from 70 percent in the baseline period to 86 percent in the pay period. The analysis of variance for trends during the arithmetic baseline period also yielded an insignificant $F$ ratio (see Table 3; $F = 1.154$, $p > .25$). Through eta square, it was estimated that only 8 percent of the baseline arithmetic variance could be accounted for by trends.

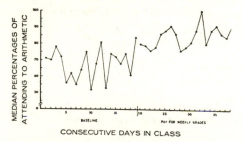

CONSECUTIVE DAYS IN CLASS

**Figure 2. Patterns of Medians in Attending to Arithmetic**

Attending to arithmetic also showed significant increases for the pay period over the baseline period (see Table 4; $p < .005$, one tailed Wilcoxon Test). Six subjects' graphs showed the same general form as the median graph in Figure 2. Thus, it can be inferred that the token system led to substantial gains in attending to arithmetic for these six subjects. The remaining two subjects (Subjects 2 and 7) showed gradual but steady increases in attending to arithmetic for the last ten days of the baseline period. Consequently, it cannot be concluded that the increases in attending to arithmetic shown by these two subjects for the pay period over the baseline period can be attributed solely to the pay for weekly grades procedure.

### TABLE 4
### Subjects' Median Percentages
### of Attending to Arithmetic

| Subjects | Baseline | Pay | Increase |
|---|---|---|---|
| S1 | 67 | 88 | 21 |
| S2 | 89 | 94 | 5 |
| S3 | 36 | 79 | 43 |
| S4 | 80 | 91 | 11 |
| S5 | 83 | 88 | 5 |
| S6 | 63 | 76 | 13 |
| S7 | 64 | 81 | 17 |
| S8 | 53 | 68 | 15 |

*Note:*—Wilcoxon $T = 0$; $p < .005$ (one tailed test)

Percentages of attending were determined in the following way: if a total of 20 observations were made on a child in arithmetic, and if, of these, ten were scored as attending, the child's percentage of attending to arithmetic on that day was $10/20 \times 100$ or 50 percent. Reliability checks were made between the first author and the observer on four occasions, two for reading and two for arithmetic. Reliability coefficients, estimated by the Pearson product moment formula and calculated across subjects with day and academic area held constant, were .91 and .95 for reading and .88 and .90 for arithmetic.

The attending data were obtained during October, November, and part of December, 1966. The month of September was used to refine the observational techniques and to ensure that instructional procedures and materials were adequate to meet each child's needs.

Although the observations were stopped after Christmas vacation, the number of *Incompletes* (with the exception of Subject 8) and the percentages of correct responses indicated that subjects maintained for the remainder of the school year the level of academic behavior attained during the pay period. Students' earnings varied from week to week and ranged from 30 to 85 percent of maximum possible earnings.

As the working efficiency of the students increased, larger assignments were given. At the end of the school year, all ten students were working successfully one to four levels above their starting levels in all academic areas. Six of the ten students were returned full time to regular classes to one grade higher than the ones they had been in during the previous school year. For two of these six, grading periods were extended to four weeks and for one, to two weeks, while the other three remained on the one week period since they were returned to regular classes with only two months of the school year left. In spite of the fact that regular classroom teachers were instructed to give grades of *D* and *F* when appropriate, half of the returned students consistently earned *B* averages and half earned *C* averages. At the close of the school year, all six of the returned students were again promoted, this time by their regular classroom teachers.

## Discussion

The present study demonstrated that a token reinforcement system with grades as tokens and allowances as back up reinforcers can significantly increase levels of academic behavior beyond those maintained by the systematic application of other reinforcers available to a school.

All students, with the exception of Subject 8, maintained these increased levels of academic behavior. This subject, with the pay still in effect, would alternate several weeks of complete work and high grades with several weeks of incomplete work. His parents reported that they had never reached agreement on the proper administration of the pay procedures and were, consequently, very inconsistent in its application. The subject was originally required to purchase his weekly movie and a construction model, yet his parents said that they gave him these rewards even when his earnings were insufficient to purchase them. One parent, on several occasions, had claimed all of his earnings as payment for misdemeanors committed at home. In the spring of the year he acquired a high level of social and academic behavior which was maintained for the remainder of the school year. This change in his behavior was coincidental with the death of one of his parents.

Grades have long been the token reinforcement system of schools. But as a reinforcer's effectiveness is directly proportional to its immediacy of presentation (Bijou and Baer, 1961), an apparent weakness of this grade system has been that grade reports are presented to children every six to nine weeks, a long delay of reinforcement for a child of elementary school age.

Teachers must correct children's work to ensure learning, and it is but a small step from corrections to grades. Although the teacher of the present study had volunteer aides to assist in the grading, the teacher felt that she could carry out the daily grading and weekly reports, and actually did for the many days that aides were absent.

No test was made to test the effect of the allowance back up reinforcer in the maintenance of high levels of academic behavior for the remainder of the school year. This effect could have been tested by paying the children their allowances independently of their weekly grades. If attending to academic materials had decreased significantly with this change, evidence would have been provided for a maintaining effect for this back up reinforcer. The risk of returning students to their less efficient levels of the baseline period overruled the possible gains in scientific information, and this analysis was not made.

## Conclusion

The token reinforcement system used in the present study increased levels of academic behavior with highly distractible and disruptive children. Several additional advantages are inherent in this token system. First, teachers need not spend valuable time in overseeing the exchange of tokens for back up reinforcers. Parents can manage this task at home. Secondly, parents are frequently able to bear the cost of the allowance back up reinforcer, as many parents provide allowances for their children anyway. For parents unable to bear this cost, it seems likely that a service organization could be found which would contribute funds which parents could then pay to their children on the basis of weekly grades. Finally, the present system can open, as it did in this case, an effective channel of communication and cooperation between parents and teachers of children with special educational needs.

## References

Anderson, R. C. Educational psychology. In P. R. Farnsworth (Editor), *Annual Review of Psychology*. Volume 18. Palo Alto, California: Annual Reviews, 1967. Pp. 129-164.

Bijou, S. W., and Baer, D. M. *Child development*. Volume 1. New York: Appleton-Century-Crofts, 1961.

Bushell, D., Wrobel, P. A., and McCloskey, M. L. Some effects of normative reinforcement on classroom study behavior. Unpublished manuscript, Webster College, 1967.

Clark, M., Lackowicz, J., and Wolf, M. A pilot basic education program for school dropouts incorporating a token reinforcement system. *Behavior Research and Therapy*, 1968, 6 (2), in press.

Cruickshank, W. M. *The brain-injured child in home, school, and community*. Syracuse, New York: Syracuse University Press, 1967.

O'Leary, K. D., and Becker, W. C. Behavior modification of an adjustment class: a token reinforcement system. *Exceptional Children*, 1967, **33**, 637-642.

Siegel, S. *Nonparametric statistics*. New York: McGraw-Hill, 1956.

Whelan, R. J. The relevance of behavior modification procedures for teachers of emotionally disturbed children. In P. Knoblock (Editor), *Intervention approaches in educating emotionally disturbed children*. Syracuse, New York: Syracuse University Press, 1966. Pp. 35-78.

Wolf, M. M., Giles, D. K., and Hall, V. R. Experiments with token reinforcement in a remedial classroom. *Behavior Research and Therapy*, 1968, **6**, 51-64.

HUGH McKENZIE *is Assistant Professor of Education, University of Vermont, Burlington; this research was conducted when he was Research Fellow, Bureau of Child Research, University of Kansas.* MARILYN CLARK *is Special Education Teacher, Skyline School, Shawnee Mission, Kansas.* MONTROSE M. WOLF *is Associate Professor of Human Development and Research Associate in the Bureau of Child Research, University of Kansas, Lawrence.* RICHARD KOTHERA *is Superintendent of Schools, Roesland District #92, Shawnee Mission, Kansas.* CEDRIC BENSON *is Director of Special Education, West Suburban Association for Special Education, Oak Park, Illinois; this research was conducted when he was Director of Special Education, NEJC Cooperative Program in Special Education, Johnson County, Kansas.*
*This study was supported in part by grants 5 T01 NB05362-05 and 3 P01 HD00870-04SI from the National Institutes of Health.*

FRANK M. HEWETT
FRANK D. TAYLOR
ALFRED A. ARTUSO

# The Santa Monica Project:
# Evaluation of an Engineered Classroom Design
# with Emotionally Disturbed Children

APPLICATION of behavior modification methodology in educational programs for children with emotional disturbance has provided evidence that systematic manipulation of stimuli and consequences in the classroom often result in significant behavioral and academic improvement (Patterson & Ebner, 1965; Quay, Werry, McQueen, & Sprague, 1966; Whelan, 1966; Nolen, Kunzelmann & Haring, 1967). The teacher approaches the disturbed child as a behavior and learning problem rather than an "ill" or "impaired," and while demands which the child cannot handle emotionally or which call for competencies he lacks are not arbitrarily made, appropriate and reasonable behavioral and academic goals are established. In general, selection of these goals is based on a desire to aid the child in changing maladaptive behavior to adaptive behavior. At best, these concepts of "maladaptive" and "adaptive" provide only the broadest of guidelines for selection of specific behavioral goals. In this sense the powerful methodology of the behavior modification approach is not matched by concern with goals in learning. Teachers are

provided with an efficient means of taking emotionally disturbed children someplace but are not substantially aided in the selection of where to go.

It is this lack of balanced emphasis on goals and methods that may preclude the acceptance of behavior modification in the field of education, particularly in the public school, and thereby may greatly limit its usefulness. An interesting parallel to this state of affairs can be drawn with reference to psychoanalytic theory and psychodynamic psychology. These approaches have had an important influence on special education for the emotionally disturbed over the past several decades, but their preoccupation with therapeutic goals to the almost complete exclusion of concern with educational methodology has restricted their acceptance and effectiveness in public school programs for these children.

### Engineered Classroom Design

The engineered classroom design attempts to approach education of the emotionally disturbed with a balanced emphasis on goals and

EXCEPTIONAL CHILDREN, 1969, Vol. 35, pp. 523-529.

methods. The disturbed child is viewed as a socialization failure and assessed in terms of his developmental learning deficiencies. These deficiencies are determined with reference to a developmental sequence of educational goals (Hewett, 1968) which postulates that in order for the child to learn successfully he must pay *attention*, make a *response*, *order* his behavior, accurately and thoroughly engage in multi-sensory *exploratory* behavior, gain *social* approval, and require *mastery* of self care and cognitive skills. Finally he must function on a self motivated basis with *achievement* in learning providing its own reward.

The room arrangement, teacher pupil ratio, schedule, and operations of the engineered classroom support attainment of these goals, and manipulation of stimuli and consequences in the program is done in accord with the behavior modification methodology. The room is divided into three major centers: (a) the mastery and achievement center including the students' desks and two study booths where academic assignments are given; (b) the exploratory-social center where science, art, and communication activities take place; and (c) the attention-response-order center which provides simple direction following tasks. There are nine students, a teacher, and an aide in each classroom. The 4 hour class day is divided into 2 hours of reading, written language, and arithmetic; one hour of exploratory activities; and a total of one hour of physical education and recesses. Each child carries a Work Record Card with him throughout the day, and earns a possible 10 checkmarks every 15 minutes. Checkmarks are given for starting and working on tasks and for behavior related to the levels on the developmental sequence which are most critical for each individual child. Completed Work Record Cards may be exchanged weekly for tangible rewards in Phase I of the program, for time to pursue self selected activities in Phase II, and for daily graphing of total checkmarks earned in Phase III. The Santa Monica Project as reported here utilized only the Phase I approach. Throughout the day, a given child may be assigned tasks relating to any level on the developmental sequence in an effort to keep him learning and earning checkmarks as a successful

student. A complete description of the program and the planned interventions directed toward assuring students success has been reported elsewhere (Hewett, 1966, 1967, 1968a, 1968b).

The Santa Monica Project was undertaken by the authors to assess the effectiveness of the engineered classroom design in maintaining student attention to tasks and in improving academic achievement level. It was done in the Santa Monica Unified School District, Santa Monica, California, during 1966-1967. Santa Monica is a coastal community near the city of Los Angeles with a broad range of socio-economic levels similar in proportion to the greater Los Angeles county area.

### Subjects

Fifty-four children with learning and behavior problems, the majority of which were considered "emotionally disturbed," were assigned to six project classrooms with nine students in each. These children ranged in age from 8-0 to 11-11 years and ranged in Full Scale IQ score from 85 to 113 as determined by the Wechsler Intelligence Scale for Children. Academically the children were functioning in reading from 0 to 6.2 grade levels and in arithmetic fundamentals from 0 to 5.2 grade levels, as measured by the California Achievement Test (elementary level). With the exception of five children, all students were 2 or more years below their expected grade level in reading and all but seven were 2 or more years below in arithmetic fundamentals.

In the assignment of individual children to project classrooms, an attempt was made to arrive at comparable class groupings with respect to IQ, age, and reading and arithmetic achievement. Since so few girls were located, control could not be exerted over the variable of sex. Table 1 reports the mean values for IQ, age, and achievement level in each of the six project classrooms.

### Teachers

Six female elementary school teachers were selected from teaching applicants to the Santa Monica District prior to the 1966-1967 school year. None had taught previously in the dis-

# TABLE 1

## Mean Values for IQ, Age, and
## Achievement Level for the Six
## Project Classrooms

| Class | Mean IQ | Mean Age | Mean Total Reading Grade Equivalent | Mean Total Arithmetic Grade Equivalent |
|---|---|---|---|---|
| 1 | 93 | 10-4 | 3.0 | 3.9 |
| 2 | 95 | 10-6 | 2.9 | 3.4 |
| 3 | 92 | 10-8 | 2.5 | 3.0 |
| 4 | 96 | 10-1 | 3.2 | 3.3 |
| 5 | 98 | 9-9 | 3.0 | 3.4 |
| 6 | 93 | 10-4 | 2.3 | 3.0 |

# TABLE 2

## Assignment of Project Classes to Experimental and Control Conditions

| Class | Fall Semester | Spring Semester |
|---|---|---|
| 1 (E) | Experimental | Experimental |
| 2 (C) | Control | Control |
| 3 and 4 (CE) | Control | Experimental |
| 5 and 6 (EC) | Experimental | Control |

trict, one had never taught before, and the teaching experience of the others ranged from 3 to 8 years. Only one teacher had worked before with emotionally disturbed children. Their final selection was made by the Santa Monica School District personnel office on the basis of strong qualifications and an expression of willingness to participate in the project. Six female teacher aides (without prior teaching experience) were also selected from a group of housewives and graduate students who applied.

A 2 week training program was conducted prior to the beginning of the school year to acquaint all of the teachers and aides with the goals and methods of the engineered classroom design. This training program included lectures, group discussions, and demonstrations conducted by the authors. Following this training program each teacher and aide was randomly assigned to a project classroom which had previously been designated as either experimental or control.

## Procedure

The experimental condition of the project involved rigid adherence to the engineered classroom design and systematic reliance on the giving of checkmarks. The control condition of the project consisted of any approach the teacher chose to follow, including aspects of the engineered design except use of tangible or token rewards. Conventional grading, verbal praise, complimentary written comments on completed assignments, and awarding privileges for good work were all acceptable. To facili-

tate assessment of the effect of introducing and withdrawing the experimental and control condition, the project classes were assigned as shown in Table 2.

Class E maintained the experimental condition for the entire project year while Class C maintained the control condition during that time. Classes CE began as control, but abruptly introduced the experimental condition at midyear. The reverse was true for Classes EC which started as experimental and then abruptly shifted to control at the project's midpoint.

As has been stated, the independent variable in the project was rigid adherence to the engineered design and use of the checkmark system. The dependent variables also were briefly mentioned—student task attention and academic functioning level in reading and arithmetic.

Two observers sat in front of each project classroom for 2½ hours daily during the 34 week project period. These observers were undergraduate college students recruited and trained for this assignment. Each observer held a stopwatch and was assigned four or five children to observe regularly. The children were observed for 5 minute segments throughout the observation period in random order so that at least five separate samples of task attention were obtained on each student each day. Observers recorded the number of seconds the student's eyes (or in some cases his head and body) were appropriately oriented toward an assigned task. Specific criteria for crediting a student for "task attention" were established. The project observers were trained by two graduate students who had reached a 90 percent or better agreement between themselves for task attention measurement. Each observer was then paired with one of the graduate students until reliability was established at a level of 90 percent or better. Every 2 weeks the graduate students rotated through the classrooms rechecking reliability and at no point in the project was agreement found to be below the 85 percent level. Daily individual task attention percentages were obtained on each child, these percentages were totalled for all the children in a class, and a weekly task attention percentage mean was obtained for each project class.

All students were retested twice with parallel forms of the California Achievement Test used in the initial screening—once at midyear and once at the close of the project.

The six project classrooms were visited each week by the authors and the project coordinator. Weekly meetings were held with the teachers, at which time problems with individual students were taken up with the project coordinator. In general he continually referred to the engineered design and its resources for handling problems presented by experimental teachers. With the control teachers he made similar suggestions (without reference to the giving of tangible or token rewards) but usually offered several alternatives. Separate meetings of the project staff and the parents of children enrolled in each class were held near the start of the project. The class program was presented and questions brought up by the parents were discussed at this time. There was no other systematic attempt to meet or work with the parents during the project.

On the first Monday morning of the spring semester the teachers in Classes CE introduced the engineered design to their students. At the same time, the teachers in Classes EC an-nounced that checkmarks would not be used any more. These teachers had altered the room arrangement and were free to conduct the program from that point on any way they wished but without the previous reward system. Class E continued as a year long experimental class and Class C continued using the control condition for the remainder of the year.

## Results

The results of the Santa Monica Project evaluation will be discussed in reference to three main questions:

1. What was the effect on task attention and achievement level of introducing the experimental condition to emotionally disturbed children who had previously been in a regular class?
2. What was the effect on task attention and achievement level of introducing the experimental condition to emotionally disturbed children who had previously been in a small, individualized class under the control condition?
3. What was the effect on task attention and achievement level of abruptly withdrawing the experimental condition from a class of emotionally disturbed children who had become accustomed to it over a semester?

Table 3 presents the mean task attention percentages for all project classrooms, averaged for 4 week intervals during the fall and spring semesters. The mean task attention percentages are based on five daily 5 minute observations made on each child in a given class; in most cases at least 100 such observations were made on every child during each 4 week

### TABLE 3

**Mean Task Attention Percentages for All Classes, Averaged for 4 Week Intervals During Fall and Spring Semesters**

| Class | Fall Semester | | | | Spring Semester | | | |
|---|---|---|---|---|---|---|---|---|
| | *1*<br>*weeks*<br>*2-5* | *2*<br>*weeks*<br>*6-9* | *3*<br>*weeks*<br>*10-13* | *4*<br>*weeks*<br>*14-17* | *5*<br>*weeks*<br>*2-5* | *6*<br>*weeks*<br>*6-9* | *7*<br>*weeks*<br>*10-13* | *8*<br>*weeks*<br>*14-17* |
| E | 82.3 | 87.6 | 94.2 | 93.8 | 92.0 | 93.9 | 94.8 | 94.0 |
| C | 90.7 | 84.5 | 81.1 | 89.0 | 86.7 | 86.3 | 86.7 | 84.4 |
| EC | 85.5 | 85.8 | 87.7 | 86.6 | 85.6 | 90.0 | 91.8 | 91.3 |
| CE | 76.2 | 78.0 | 84.3 | 81.6 | 84.5 | 91.0 | 92.0 | 90.5 |

242

TABLE 4

## Mean Raw Scores and Grade Equivalents in Reading and Arithmetic
### for All Project Classes

| Test | Initial Screening | | | | Midyear | | | | End of Year | | | |
|---|---|---|---|---|---|---|---|---|---|---|---|---|
| | E | C | EC | CE | E | C | EC | CE | E | C | EC | CE |
| CAT Total Reading | 31.4 (3.2)ᵃ | 23.1 (2.8) | 28.1 (3.1) | 24.8 (2.9) | 33.1 (3.3) | 34.4 (3.4) | 32.9 (3.3) | 33.4 (3.3) | 38.0 (3.6) | 30.6 (3.2) | 35.9 (3.5) | 37.8 (3.6) |
| CAT Arithmetic Fundamentals | 15.1 (3.9) | 10.5 (3.4) | 10.7 (3.4) | 11.1 (3.5) | 20.7 (4.6) | 13.9 (3.8) | 15.2 (3.9) | 13.5 (3.8) | 24.9 (5.0) | 11.7 (3.6) | 19.8 (4.5) | 19.7 (4.5) |

ᵃ Figures in parentheses represent grade equivalents.

interval. Figure 1 shows these 4 week interval mean task attention percentages.

**FIGURE 1. Mean task attention of Class E, Class C, Classes EC, and Classes CE averaged for 4 week intervals during the fall and spring semesters.**

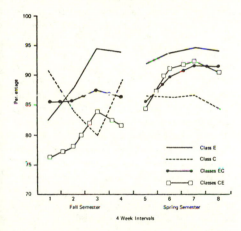

Table 4 reports the achievement data obtained during initial screening, at the midyear point, and at the end of the project year.

In the discussion which follows a difference reported as "significant" represents the .05 level of confidence or better. Specific reference to the statistical method used to evaluate project data (analysis of variance, covariance, and *t* test) will not be made nor will the complete data from the evaluation be presented. How-

ever, this has been reported elsewhere (Hewett, Taylor, & Artuso, 1967).

Classes E and C provide information with reference to question one cited earlier. While Class C enjoyed a significant task attention advantage over Class E during interval 1 in Figure 1, this disappeared in interval 2. Beginning with interval 3 Class E maintained superiority in task attention for the remainder of the project year.

Achievement data in Table 4 reveal no significant difference in reading between the classes, but a significant difference in arithmetic fundamentals in favor of Class E is seen. Class E showed a 1.2 year gain while Class C gained only 0.4 year during the project. The experimental condition, then, was related to significantly higher task attention among students coming from regular classes from interval 3 on, and was also related to a significant gain in arithmetic over the year.

Question 2 may be considered by comparing Class C and Classes CE. During the fall semester, all three classes utilized the control condition. At midyear Classes CE shifted to the experimental condition, thus providing evidence regarding the effect of this condition on children already enrolled in a small class group. Class C maintained a significantly higher task attention percentage during intervals 1, 3, and 4 during the control phase over Classes CE. But by interval 5 when Classes CE introduced the experimental condition there was no such difference, and during intervals 6, 7, and 8 these classes attained a significantly higher task attention level than Class C. While no significant differences emerged in reading, Classes CE made a significant gain over Class C in arithmetic fundamentals during the spring semester when they utilized the experimental condition. Therefore both task attention and arithmetic gains were related to the introduction of the experimental condition.

In relation to question 3, Class E and Classes EC provided information. All three classes utilized the experimental condition during the fall semester but at midyear Classes EC eliminated rigid adherence to the experimental condition and use of checkmarks and tangible rewards. Evidence was then obtained regarding the effect of abrupt withdrawal of the experimental condition on a small class that had become accustomed to it. Except for intervals 1 and 2, Class E achieved a significantly higher task attention level during the fall semester than Classes EC when all were using the experimental condition. This continued during intervals 5 and 6 but ceased to exist during the last half of the spring semester. During these intervals Classes EC attained their highest task attention level, indicating with respect to task attention that removal of the experimental condition had a facilitating effect. There were no significant differences in reading or arithmetic between Class E and Classes EC either semester. Class E and Classes EC made their gain in arithmetic consistently over the entire year. In summary, removal of the experimental condition resulted in improved task attention in Classes EC but did not affect achievement levels in reading or arithmetic.

## Discussion and Conclusions

The major findings of the Santa Monica project can be summarized as follows: task attention of students was significantly facilitated by the experimental condition when that condition was introduced to emotionally disturbed children following placement in either a regular or control condition class. Task attention was also facilitated by removal of the experimental condition from classes which had become accustomed to it over a one semester period. Reading achievement was not significantly affected by either the experimental or control condition but gains in arithmetic fundamentals were significantly correlated with the presence of the experimental condition.

The facilitating effect of the experimental condition on student task attention is seen as related to the emphasis in the engineered design on building *attention*, *response*, and *order* behaviors. The planned routine of the classroom, the provision for systematic acknowledgment of functioning level by means of the checkmark system, and continual reassignment to tasks promoting success undoubtedly contributed to students becoming more willing, efficient, and consistent in paying attention. The teacher in Class C, which enjoyed a significant task attention advantage over Class E during interval 1, was concerned with maintaining her students at a high task attention level since she, as did all the other teachers, knew this was being measured by the observers. Without the checkmark system she had to use considerable verbalization and social reinforcement in controlling student behavior. While this technique made her initially more effective in orienting them toward assigned tasks, its effectiveness quickly diminished following the first 4 weeks. This may be related to the questionable responsiveness of emotionally disturbed children to social reinforcement, which has been reported by Levin and Simmons (1962) and Quay and Hunt (1965). The more objective and neutral checkmark system, while admittedly providing reinforcement on a more primitive level, may be better suited for initiating contact with disturbed students and starting them toward success in school.

The correlation between arithmetic improvement and presence of the experimental condition is also probably a reflection of the emphasis on attention, response, and order behavior present in classes utilizing this condition. The building of these basic learning competencies may more directly and immediately apply to arithmetic than to language arts subjects such as reading.

Perhaps the most interesting and somewhat surprising finding was that Classes EC actually improved in task attention following removal of the experimental condition. This change was apparently not just due to time in a special class alone since Class E and Class C showed no such improvement during the second half of the year. Another hypothesis to explain Classes EC improvement under the control condition might center on a novelty effect; any major innovation, even the taking away of something supposedly desirable such as tangible rewards, might be expected to bring about an initial change in student behavior. This hypothesis is rejected because of the long period of time covered in the evaluation. A novelty effect might exert influence over the first several weeks but it is doubtful it would be maintained over a 17 week period. A more logical explanation is to view the improvement of Classes EC in task attention under the control condition as resulting from (a) the increased effectiveness of the teachers in these classes to function as secondary social reinforcers due to their semester long association with a success oriented approach using a primary reward system, and (b) the investment made in building competencies at the attention, response, and order levels during the experimental condition which readied the students for participation in a teacher centered, more traditional educational program utilizing exploratory, social, and mastery tasks and rewards.

Certainly evidence was provided that the use of tangible rewards on a temporary basis does not doom children to dependence on them. On the contrary, it appears such rewards may be extremely useful in launching children with behavior and learning problems into successful learning in school.

The engineered classroom design as evaluated in the Santa Monica Project appears basically a launching approach. Its provision for increasing the teacher's effectiveness as a social reinforcer through systematic association with student success and primary rewards and for building fundamental learning competencies often forgotten about in education past the primary grades may greatly aid the disturbed child in taking the first step toward achieving success in school.

### References

Hewett, F. The Tulare experimental class for educationally handicapped children. *California Education*, 1966, 3, 6-8.

Hewett, F. Educational engineering with emotionally disturbed children. *Exceptional Children*, 1967, 33, 459-467.

Hewett, F. An engineered classroom design for emotionally disturbed children. In J. Hellmuth (Ed.), *Educational therapy.* Vol. 2. Seattle: Special Child Publications, 1968. (a)

Hewett, F. *The emotionally disturbed child in the classroom: A developmental strategy for educating children with maladaptive behavior.* Boston: Allyn and Bacon, 1968. (b)

Hewett, F., Taylor, F., & Artuso, A. *The Santa Monica Project: Demonstration and evaluation of an engineered classroom design for emotionally disturbed children in the public school, phase 1: Elementary level.* Final Report. Project No. 62893, Demonstration Grant No. OEG-4-7-062893-0377, Office of Education, Bureau of Research, US Department of Health, Education and Welfare, 1967.

Levin, G., & Simmons, J. Response to praise by emotionally disturbed boys. *Psychological Reports*, 1962, 11, 10.

Nolen, P., Kunzelmann, H., & Haring, N. Behavioral modification in a junior high learning disabilities classroom. *Exceptional Children*, 1967, 34, 163-169.

Patterson, G., & Ebner, M. Application of learning principles to the treatment of deviant children. Paper presented at the meeting of the American Psychological Association, Chicago, September 1965.

Quay, H., & Hunt, W. Psychopathy, neuroticism and verbal conditioning: A replication and extension. *Journal of Consulting Psychology*, 1965, 29, 283.

Quay, H., Werry, J. S., McQueen, M., & Sprague, R. L. Remediation of the conduct problem child in the special class setting. *Exceptional Children*, 1966, 32, 509-515.

Whelan, R. J. The relevance of behavior modification procedures for teachers of emotionally disturbed children. In P. Knoblock (Ed.), *Intervention approaches in educating emotionally disturbed children.* Syracuse: Syracuse University Press, 1966.

FRANK M. HEWETT *is Associate Professor of Education and Psychiatry and Chairman, Area of Special Education, University of California, Los Angeles;* FRANK D. TAYLOR *is Director of Special Services, and* ALFRED A. ARTUSO *is Superintendent, Santa Monica Unified Schools, California. The work reported herein was performed pursuant to a grant from the US Office of Education, Department of Health, Education, and Welfare.*

PATRICIA A. NOLEN
HAROLD P. KUNZELMANN
NORRIS G. HARING

# Behavioral Modification in a Junior High Learning Disabilities Classroom

New evidence supporting behavioral modification techniques in special education classrooms is reported almost monthly. Those who have extended operant behavioral principles to classroom learning have suggested that complex academic response repertoires may be amenable to a methodology based on a functional analysis of behavior (Bijou and Sturges, 1958; Birnbrauer, Bijou, Wolf, and Kidder, 1966; Staats, Finley, Minke, and Wolf, 1964; Lindsley, 1964; Whitlock, 1966). Whether or not this approach can be applied to situations beyond the short-term clinical or tutorial periods, however, has been the basis for continuing doubt. The heterogeneous enrollments and complex curriculum requirements in most regularly scheduled classrooms have seemed to limit the functionality of operant behavioral analysis to appropriate social behaviors or to short sequences of the program. Preliminary findings from the classrooms of the University of Washington Experimental Education Unit, however, have suggested otherwise. Here ongoing investigations seem to indicate that any limitations imposed upon behavioral analysis at the outset may be premature (Haring and Kunzelmann, 1966; Haring and Lovitt, 1967).

The Experimental Education Unit was organized to provide for the study, assessment, and remediation of educational retardation. Because its research responsibilities are diverse, and because it provides services for teacher training as well as services for exceptional children, the behavioral deviancies of its children span a wider range than is found within the usual special education classrooms. Diagnostic categories represented within any one class are further differentiated as a result of the school unit's involvement in the multidisciplinary Mental Retardation and Child Development Center. Despite the multiplicity and heterogeneity of learning problems, however, each of the unit's five classrooms has provided sufficient evidence in one school term to warrant further investigation of functional behavioral analysis as a classroom teaching and management technique.

The data reported here were taken from the junior high classroom during its first year of operation. Students enrolled in this class were 12 to 16 years in age, with individual achievement levels ranging from preschool to sixth grade. Diagnostic categories and recorded behavioral deviancies covered as wide a span for the one grouping as did the achievement levels. On the referrals, students were listed as "passive-aggressive," "psychotic," "dyslexic," "aphasic," having "generalized mental retardation," being

EXCEPTIONAL CHILDREN, 1967, Vol. 34, pp. 163–168.

"emotionally disturbed," or "neurologically impaired," together with a generally pessimistic prognosis for any long term effect of remedial teaching. Such classifications are not used as criteria for the school unit's enrollment; demonstrated learning deficits are the preferred criteria. With these deficits as primary concerns, the educational diagnostician seeks to identify deficiencies the child may have in content or extent and/or rate of learning within any one or a number of specific academic or social behavioral skill areas. This diagnosis by skill specifics, rather than by physical or psychological deficit, is considered fundamental to the application of behavioral management techniques in the unit's classrooms. It has allowed a much broader view of remedial teaching, which, contrary to the popular notion, has not seemed to neglect the web of dynamic interrelationships posed by such factors as "motivation" or "inadequate self concept." Although these factors have been included within the teaching context, they have been considered as "the ability to respond successfully and effectively." By standards of skill specifics, then, the frequency of accurate academic responses is of primary consideration here.

Initial organization of the classroom entailed an extensive tabulation and compilation of all skills that could be identified within any one academic area. Standard test achievement levels such as "third grade reading comprehension" or "first grade computational ability" simply did not supply the teacher with the precise information on which remediation as behavioral modification could be based. In place of the broad summarization of standardized tests, behavioral definitions of skill sequences were abstracted largely from programed academic curricula for which adequate developmental and field testing data were available. Eventually this detailed outline was expanded to include both teacher designed steps and an increased number of contingencies advocated for optimal learning (Homme, Debaca, Devine, Steinhorst, and Rickert, 1963). An interesting outcome of the analysis was the finding that, for most learners, an optimal program requires less of the former and more of the latter.

It is not new to note that present knowledge allows only an approximation of the structure of any one content area. Within these limitations, an attempt was made to define as many steps in a particular learning sequence as could be identified. It is believed that this may be necessary before attempting to order classroom learning situations for the employment of behavioral modification techniques.

Observers invariably made remarks about the lengthy and detailed skill sequence sheets (University of Washington College of Education, 1966), saying that although the idea was praiseworthy, a teacher could not possibly know every child's attainment or exact direction of skills at any one time. Those who had the opportunity to test this assumption, however, found that the unit's teachers did in fact know a child's skills and would use and often revise these skill outlines. In the junior high class, for example, a student was not merely "working on multiplication," he was working with multiplication of whole numbers defined in terms of repeated addition or reconstructing multiplication equations with a missing product or missing factor in combinations through 5 x 9 or studying in another area which had been analyzed with similar detail. Answers also referred to comparative rates of performance, computed not between students but between any two performances of the same student.

## Program Stimuli

Once both skill sequences and the student's functioning at some point in the sequence were identified, the designation of the program was no simple task of matching student and workbook at some certain grade level. On the contrary, completely individual programs were organized. These were built largely from commercially programed materials together with selections from traditional texts and workbooks. Often the linear progression was achieved only with the design of supplements programed to overcome deficits in the sequence. During the second year of operation, while refinements in programing continued, individualization of instruction for a student became less of a problem than individualization of a particular content area. From these initial programs, preliminary task analyses of specific and generic teaching points were outlined in terms of their distribution and interrelation.

## Reinforcement Contingencies

Although the stimulus program (an attempt to define and arrange academic responses) played an important role in the organization of an operant classroom, reinforcement contingencies were the major concern. Two principles guided the exploration of reinforcement contingencies in the unit's classrooms: the first, what is known as "high probability behavior," is a concept well substantiated by the work of Premack (1965) and Homme et al. (1963). This behavior occurs at a high rate prior to educational or clinical intervention; it consists of those things the student most often chooses to do, providing a source for "natural" consequences for the manipulation and acceleration of low probability behavior; the second requirement was that both high probability behavior and any other consequences assumed to be "secondary reinforcers" were ultimately acceptable in a traditionally organized classroom. This second principle precluded at the outset the use of money, candy, or trinkets, the "consumable/manipulatable" classifications of the laboratories (Bijou and Sturges, 1958). Further, the singular use of social approval as a durable reinforcing consequence did not seem to offer the initial control needed for programing the multiple contingencies of a group situation. Moreover, it did not seem that classroom management could be optimally based on the assumption that social approval was a reinforcer for those adolescents with a history of school and interpersonal failure (Bijou and Baer, 1966).

In an attempt to standardize the number of stimuli presupposed to be "natural" consequences of high strength behavior, the teacher allotted points for the child's successful completion of each of a number of gradually lengthening academic tasks. A running record of these points was kept at each child's desk, and these points were negotiable at any time for play periods analogous to school recesses or for a variety of enrichment or practical studies in the public schools (Haring and Kunzelmann, 1966). The junior high students' most preferred choices for contingent high strength behavior centered on handicrafts, typing, woodworking, organized games, or science units. These choices were somewhat surprising to the teaching staff, who had made an effort to supply what are considered culturally determined "reinforcers" for adolescents by extending the available consequences to include slot cars, models, popular recordings, and teen magazines, on the assumption that such choices would be replaced only by gradually shaping preferences for the more traditional school activities.

## Data Collection

Unlike procedures used in the majority of operant studies, the experimenter-teacher did not have the exclusive function of establishing individual behavioral baselines. Using service as one of the operational criteria, baseline or "operant level" was determined by (a) anecdotal records and achievement test scores from the student's school records prior to enrollment in the unit, and (b) rate of daily academic responses recorded on the first day of enrollment. It seemed advisable to begin the teaching method on the first day, with concomitant manipulation of high and low strength behaviors not only from a first day service viewpoint but also due to the ease of its application to a group admitting new members during the school year. The data were recorded in terms of both subject matters and total academic responses for each student over a period of 100 days.

## Indications

The resulting data from the first year's efforts at organizing a special education classroom on a behavioral basis are shown in Figure 1. These records include only reading and arithmetic responses, excepting the modification of social behaviors which accompanied remedial skill instruction. Throughout the 24 week instructional period, an effort was made to define "academic response" individually for each student and for each particular subject area. In the initial stages of reading, for example, the correct association of a letter shape with a sound was an adequate response for the application of negotiable consequences. Later, however, once the association had been cued, prompted, and practiced without prompts, the single element became part of a chain included in the definition of a succeeding response. In other words, sound-symbol relationships, phonic blending and sight words, and eventually oral reading of a complete sentence were all progressively defined as a single response for recording purposes and for consequence application.

In like manner, arithmetical functioning was ordered in successive stages which began with the manipulation of actual concrete physical quantities, followed by the manipulation of physical representations, then abstract repre-

## FIGURE 1. Cumulative Academic Record

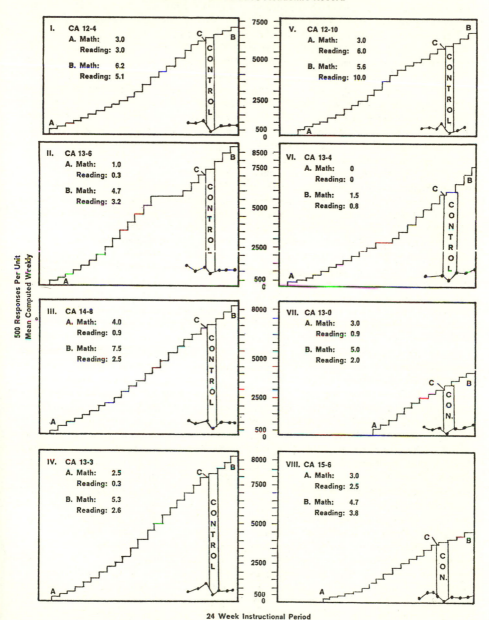

24 Week Instructional Period

249

sentations prior to any association of numerals with numbers or symbols with operations. As in reading, antecedent steps in any arithmetical sequence were considered chained in subsequent, more complex responses.

Each graph in Figure 1 represents one student's weekly cumulative record of frequency of correct academic responses in reading and mathematics during that part of the instructional period in which he was enrolled. After a high rate of responding had been established, the procedure was altered in an attempt to isolate the function of contingent delivery of the points negotiable for high strength activities. During this control period, four time allotments for high strength activities were scheduled daily for each student. Unlike the organization of the school day prior and subsequent to the control period, the high strength activities at this time were contingent neither upon accuracy nor on rate of responding. In this way, the free time followed not as a consequence upon completion of work but upon mere passage of time. Point C on each record identifies the cumulative responses during this interval of reversal. A graph of the drop in the mean number of responses during the five day control period and the subsequent rise during reinstatement of contingencies is displayed at the base of each record.

Notations accompanying response records of eight of the junior high students show beginning achievement levels on the basis of referral reports (A), and achievement levels at the close of the first instructional period of approximately 100 days (B). Even though the programs were based largely on a structural linguistic approach in reading and the "new" mathematics process in arithmetic, terminal levels have been determined on the basis of scores on the Metropolitan Achievement Tests, an instrument which does not always reflect the newer instructional emphasis on process as well as product.

While the original records note any absences from the classroom during the school day as a result of illness, clinic visits, or scheduled appointments with any of the unit's supporting services, no compensations for resulting discrepancies in response frequencies have been included. Nor do these records show one of the most welcome by-products of the use of high strength activities to reinforce a low entering level of responding. Seldom if ever did observers to the classroom fail to note the personal pride in achievement evidenced verbally by students. Surprisingly, this came not only as a result of a more generous allotment for minimal functioning in a new skill sequence, but also for the gradual reduction in allotment of points for review work of an increasingly complex and time consuming nature.

Not included in this report is a study of the modification of inappropriate classroom social behavior as the primary goal for a 13 year old male prior to an analysis of subject matter functioning. Whereas this particular student was withdrawn by parental request, it must also be noted that his reinstatement was requested by the parent within a short time.

## Conclusion

The acceleration of academic response rates of adolescent students with learning disorders participating in this limited application of functional behavioral analysis to academic performance has stimulated wide interest among personnel in surrounding school districts. Reports indicate that similar behavioral management techniques are either under consideration or in practice at this time. Followup studies of three of the students who have been transferred from this classroom show that, although the acceleration of their rates to peaks of 500 or more responses per day have not been maintained under traditional classroom contingency arrangements, in each case levels of achievement have been maintained and response rates have exceeded those of other members of the transfer classrooms. For those students who were maintained for a second teaching session at the unit, a nine week summer vacation did not interrupt the individual response patterns or rates of acceleration.

In addition, the records from the junior high teacher's parental conferences show that there have been changes in the verbal content of the conferences which have accompanied the increases in individual response rates. The most consistent change recorded is a decrease in parental requests for such conferences on the basis of a student's functioning and an increase in parental requests for detailed explanations of the techniques of classroom management.

As a result of such parental demands, study groups for parental education have been planned for those parents asking to participate. A decrease in parental requests for conferences concerning academic progress, and an increase in their requests for management information, seem to indicate that the behavioral changes of the students are, in fact, generalizing to situations other than the controlled environment of the classroom.

## References

Bijou, S. W., and Baer, D. M. Operant methods in child behavior and development. In W. K. Honig (Editor), *Operant behavior*. New York: Appleton-Century-Crofts, 1966. Pp. 778-782.

Bijou, S. W., and Sturges, P. T. Positive reinforcers for experimental studies with children—consumables and manipulables. *Child Development*, 1958, **30**, 151-170.

Birnbrauer, J. S., Bijou, S. W., Wolf, M. M., and Kidder, J. D. Programmed instruction in the classroom. In L. P. Ullman and L. Krasner (Editors), *Case studies in behavior modification*. New York: Holt, Rinehart and Winston, 1966. Pp. 358-366.

University of Washington College of Education. *Experimental Education Unit mathematics skill sequence sheet*. Seattle, Washington: Author, 1966.

Haring, N. G., and Kunzelmann, H. P. Finer focus of therapeutic behavior management. In J. Hellmuth (Editor), *Educational therapy*. Seattle, Washington: Special Child Publications, 1966. Pp. 225-251.

Haring, N. G., and Lovitt, T. C. Operant methodology and educational technology in special education. In N. G. Haring and R. L. Schiefulbusch (Editors), *Methods in special education*. New York: McGraw-Hill, 1967. Pp. 12-48.

Homme, L., Debaca, P., Devine, J., Steinhorst, R., and Rickert, E. Use of the Premack principle in controlling the behavior of nursery school children. *Journal of Experimental Analysis of Behavior*, 1963, **6**, 544.

Lindsley, O. R. Direct measurement and prosthesis of retarded behavior. *Journal of Education*, 1964, **147**, 62-81.

Premack, D. Reinforcement theory. In D. Levine (Editor), *Nebraska symposium on motivation*. Lincoln, Nebraska: University of Nebraska Press, 1965. Pp. 123-189.

Staats, A. W., Finley, J. R., Minke, K. A., and Wolf, M. Reinforcement variables in the control of unit reading response. *Journal of the Experimental Analysis of Behavior*, 1964, **7**, 139-149.

Whitlock, Sister Carolyn. Note on reading acquisition: an extension of laboratory principles. *Journal of Experimental Child Psychology*, 1966, **3**, 83-85.

Patricia A. Nolen *is Teacher*, Harold P. Kunzelmann *is Principal*, Norris G. Haring *is Director of the University of Washington Experimental Education Unit, Seattle, Washington.*

# Treatment of Nonreading in a Culturally Deprived Juvenile Delinquent: An Application of Reinforcement Principles

Arthur W. Staats, *University of Hawaii*
William H. Butterfield, *University of Michigan*

Staats has previously discussed behavior problems and their treatment in terms of learning principles (1964c, 1963). In doing so it was indicated that problem behaviors can arise in part (1) because behavior that is necessary for adjustment in our society is absent from the individual's repertoire, (2) because behaviors considered undesirable by the society are present in the individual's repertoire, or (3) because the individual's motivational (reinforcement) system was inappropriate in some respects.

Although a complete account is not relevant here, several points pertinent to the above conceptions will be made in introducing the present study. The notion that many behavior problems consist of deficits in behavior is important in the study of child development.

---

The present methods of reading training were formulated, and the present paper written, by the first author as part of a long-term project applying learning principles and procedures to the experimental study of language-learning and reading. The methods were applied by the second author in his position as an officer of the Maricopa County Juvenile Probation Department. The second author also collected and tabulated the data and aided in its graphic presentation. Appreciation is expressed to Chief Probation Officer John H. Walker for lending cooperation in the conduct of the study. In addition, Mary J. Butterfield made important contributions in the preparation of the reading materials used in the study, Brenda Shields typed the materials, and Janet Munir typed the present manuscript.

CHILD DEVELOPMENT, 1965, Vol. 36, pp. 926–942.

Behaviorally speaking, a child is considered to be a problem when he does not acquire behaviors as other children do. It is conceivable that a deficit in behavior could arise because the child simply cannot acquire the behavior involved, even though the conditions of learning have been entirely adequate.

It would be expected, however, that behavioral deficits would also arise in cases where the conditions of learning have been defective. Learning conditions can be defective in different ways. For example, the child may never have received training in the behavior he must later exhibit. Or the training may be poor, even though the "trainers," parents or teachers, and so on, have the best intentions.

In addition, however, a child may be exposed to learning conditions that are appropriate for most children but, due to the particular child's past history of learning, are not appropriate for him. It is especially in these cases that people are most likely to conclude erroneously that since other children learn in the same circumstances, the child's deficit must be because of some personal defect. For example, in cases where the training is long term, adequate reinforcement must be available to maintain the attentional and work behaviors necessary for learning. As Staats has indicated (1964c, 1963, 1962), the reinforcers present in the traditional schoolroom are inadequate for many children. Their attentional behaviors are not maintained, and they do not learn. Thus, a deficit in an individual's behavioral repertoire may arise although he has been presented with the "same" training circumstances from which other children profit. Learning does not take place because the child's previous experience has not provided, in this example, the necessary reinforcer (motivational) system to maintain good learning behaviors. It would seem that in such a circumstance the assumption that the child has a personal defect would be unwarranted and ineffective.

However, after a few years of school attendance where the conditions of learning are not appropriate for the child, he will not have acquired the behavioral repertoires acquired by more fortunate members of the class—whose previous experiences have established an adequate motivational system. Then, lack of skilled behavior is likely to be treated aversively. That is, in the present case, the child with a reading deficit (or other evidence of underachievement) is likely to be gibed at and teased when he is still young, and ignored, avoided, and looked down upon when he is older. Although the individuals doing this may not intend to be aversive, such actions constitute the presentation of aversive stimuli. Furthermore, this presentation of aversive stimuli by other "successful" children, and perhaps by a teacher, would be expected to result in further learning, but learning of an undesirable nature. These successful children, teachers, academic materials, and the total school situation can in this way become learned negative reinforcers, which may be translated to say the child acquires negative attitudes toward school (see Staats, 1964b).

At this point, the child is likely to begin to escape the school situation in various ways (daydreaming, poor attendance, and so on) and to behave aversively in turn to the school and its inhabitants (vandalism, fighting, baiting teachers and students, and the like). Thus, a deficit in behavior, resulting from an inappropriate motivational system, can lead to the further development of inappropriate reinforcers and inappropriate behaviors.

The foregoing is by no means intended as a complete analysis of delinquency, dropouts, and the like. However, it does indicate some of the problems of learning that may occur in school. In addition, it does suggest that an analysis in terms of laboratory-established learning principles, when applied to problems such as in classroom learning of the above type, can yield new research and applied hypotheses. It was with this general strategy that the study of reading acquisition employing learning principles and reinforcement procedures were commenced (Staats, 1964a, 1964d, 1964c, 1962). The present study is a replication and an extension of these various findings to the development of a program for training nonreaders to read. The program, which adapts standard reading materials, is based upon the principle of the reinforcer system employed in the previous studies with the younger children, thus testing the principles of reinforcement in the context of remedial reading training, as well as the feasibility of using the type of reinforcement system with a new type of subject. As such, the study has implications for the study of nonreading children of pre-adolescent, adolescent, and young adult ages. In the present case, the subject was also a culturally deprived delinquent child — and the study thus involves additional information and implications for the special problems associated with education in this population of children.

## Methods

### Subject

The subject was fourteen years and three months old. He was the fifth child in a Mexican-American family of eleven children and the mother and father. The parental techniques for controlling their children's behavior consisted of physical and verbal abuse. Both parents described their own childhood conditions as primitive. The father was taken out of school after completing the fifth grade to help with his father's work. Each of the subject's four older brothers had been referred to the juvenile court for misbehavior. The parents appeared to be at loss as to how to provide effective control for family members.

The subject had a history of various miscreant behaviors, having been referred to the juvenile department nine times for such things as running away, burglary, incorrigibility, and truancy. During the

254

course of the study the subject was again referred (with three other boys) on a complaint of malicious mischief for shooting light bulbs and windows in a school building with a BB gun. He associated with a group of boys who had been in marked difficulty with the law. The subject smoked and on occasion he drank excessively.

The study commenced when the subject was residing with his family. However, after the complaint on malicious mischief he was sent to a juvenile detention home. During his stay there he was allowed to attend school in the daytime. The study was finally concluded when he was committed to an industrial school for juvenile delinquent boys. This occurred because he baited the attendants at the detention home and caused disturbances which, although not serious, were very unpleasant and disruptive.

On the Wechsler Bellevue Form I, given when the subject was 13-10, he received Verbal and Performance IQ's of 77 and 106, respectively, for a Full Scale IQ of 90. The examiner concluded that the subject was probably within the normal range for this test. On the basis of this test and HTP Projective Drawings, the subject was characterized as having a poor attention span and poorly integrated thought processes and as lacking intellectual ambitiousness. He was also described as seeking satisfaction in fantasy and as having good conventional judgment.

The subject had continually received failing grades in all subjects in school. He was described as having "been incorrigible since he came here in the second grade. He has no respect for teachers, steals and lies habitually and uses extremely foul language." The subject had been promoted throughout his school career simply to move him on or to "get rid of him." He was disliked by the teachers and administrators in grade school because of his troublesome behavior and was described by the principal as mentally retarded even though one of the tests taken there indicated a score within the normal range. Another test taken there gave him an IQ of 75. During the study the subject was attending a local high school and taking classes for low-level students.

### Reinforcer System

In previous studies (Staats, 1966, 1964d, 1964e), a reinforcer system was demonstrated that was capable of maintaining attention and work behaviors for long term experimental studies. This system worked well with preschool children of ages 2 to 6 and with educable and trainable retardates of ages 8 to 11. The principle of the system was based upon token reinforcers. The tokens were presented contingent upon correct responses and could be exchanged for items the child could keep. In the previous studies toys of various values could be obtained when a sufficient number of tokens had been accrued in visible containers.

This system was adapted for use with the adolescent of the present study. In the adaptation there were three types of token, distinquished by color. The tokens were of different value in terms of the items for which the tokens could be exchanged. A blue token was valued at $1/10$ of one cent. A white token was valued at $1/5$ of a cent. A red token was worth $1/2$ of a cent.

The child's acquisition of tokens was plotted so that visual evidence of the reinforcers was available. The tokens could be used to purchase a variety of items. These items, chosen by the subject, could range in value from pennies to whatever the subject wished to work for. Records were kept of the tokens earned by the subject and of the manner in which the tokens were used.

## Reading Materials

The reading material used was taken from the Science Research Associates reading-kit materials. The SRA kits consist of stories developed for and grouped into grade levels. Each story includes a series of questions which can be used to assess the reader's comprehension of the story. The reading training program was adapted from the materials as follows:

*Vocabulary words.* A running list was made of the new words that appeared in the series of stories. The list finally included each different word that appeared in the stories that were presented. From this list, the new vocabulary for each story was selected, and each word was typed on a separate $3 \times 5$ card.

*Oral reading materials.* Each paragraph in the stories was typed on a $5 \times 8$ card. Each story could thus be presented to the subject paragraph by paragraph.

*Silent reading and comprehensive-question materials.* Each story, with its comprehensive questions, was typed on an $8^{1}/2 \times 13$ sheet of white paper.

## Procedure

*Vocabulary presentation.* The procedure for each story in the series commenced with the presentation of the new words introduced in that story. The words were presented individually on the cards, and the subject was asked to pronounce them. A correct response to a word-stimulus card was reinforced with a mid-value token. After a correct response to a word, the card was dropped from the group of cards yet to be presented. The subject was instructed to indicate words that he did not know the meaning of, and this information was provided in such cases.

When an incorrect response to a word stimulus occurred, or when the subject gave no response, the instructional technician gave the correct response. The subject then repeated the word while looking at the stimulus word. However, the word card involved was returned to the group of cards still to be presented. A card was not dropped from the group until it was read correctly without prompting. After an error on a word stimulus, only a low-value token was given on the next trial when the word was read correctly without prompting. The vocabulary-presentation phase of the training was continued until each word was read correctly without prompting.

*Oral reading.* Upon completion of the vocabulary materials, each paragraph was individually presented to the subject in the order in which the paragraph occurred in the story. When correct reading responses were made to each word in the paragraph, a high-value token was given upon completion of the paragraph. When a paragraph contained errors, the subject was corrected, and he repeated the word correctly while looking at the word. The paragraph was put aside, and when the other paragraphs had been completed, the paragraph containing errors was again presented. The paragraph was repeated until it was done correctly in its entirety—at which time a mid-value token was presented. When all paragraphs in a story had been completed correctly, the next phase of the training was begun.

*Silent reading and comprehensive questions.* Following the oral reading the subject was given the sheet containing the story and questions. He was instructed to read the story silently and to answer the questions beneath the story. He was also instructed that it was important to read to understand the story so that he could answer the questions.

Reinforcement was given on a variable interval schedule for attentive behavior during the silent-reading phase. That is, as long as he appropriately scanned the material he was given a low-value reinforcer an average of every fifteen seconds. The exact time for reinforcement was determined by a table of random numbers varying from one to thirty seconds. Whenever he did anything else than peruse the material, no reinforcement was given. The next interval was then timed from the moment he returned to the silent reading, with the stipulation that no reinforcement be given sooner than five seconds after he returned to the reading. If the interval was less than five seconds, a token was not given until the next interval had also occurred. Timing was done by a continuously running stop-watch. The subject was also given an extra mid-value token at the end of the silently read story on those occasions where he read without moving his lips.

Upon completion of the story, the subject wrote his answers to the questions typed below the story and gave his answers to the technician. For each correct answer, the subject received a high-value token. For an answer with a spelling error, he was reinforced with a mid-value token when he had corrected the answer. For incorrect answers the subject had to reread the appropriate paragraph, correct his answer, and he then received a mid-value token.

*Vocabulary review.* Some of the vocabulary words presented to the subject in the first phase of training were words he already could read. Many others, however, were words that the procedure was set up to teach. The oral reading phase performance indicated the level of the subject's retention of the words he had learned—and also provided further training trials on the words not already learned. A further assessment of the subject's retention of the words that he did not know in the vocabulary training was made after each twenty stories of the SRA materials had been read. This test of individually presented words for each story was started about three days after completion of the twenty stories and constituted fairly long-term retention.

This test was also used as a review for the subject, and further training on the words was given. This was first done by reinforcing with a low-value token for every word he read correctly. However, the subject's attention was not well maintained by this reinforcement, and the procedure was changed to provide a mid-value token for correctly read words. When he could not read a word, or missed one, he was prompted and had to correctly repeat the name of the word while looking at the word. This word card was then put aside and presented later, at which time the subject was reinforced with a low-value token if he read it correctly. If not, the procedure was repeated until a correct unprompted trial occurred.

*Achievement tests.* Prior to the commencement of the training, the subject was tested to assess his reading performance, and during the period of experimental training he was given two additional reading-achievement tests. The first one given was the Developmental Reading Test. (At this time his vision and hearing were also tested and found to be normal.) After forty-five training sessions another reading test was given, this time the California Reading Test, Form BB, for grades 1, 2, 3 and L-4. Twenty-five sessions later, just before the termination of the study, the subject was given the California Reading Test, Form BB, for grades 4, 5, and 6. His performance on the three reading tests constituted one of the measures of his progress. The tests were given at the Arizona State University Reading Center.

*Training sessions.* The training sessions would ordinarily last for one hour or less, although a few sessions were as short as thirty minutes or as long as two hours. Not all of this time was spent in reading, however. A good deal of time was spent in arranging the materials, recording performance, keeping count of the reinforcers, plotting the reinforcers accrued, and so on. The time spent actually reading was tabulated. During the 4½-month experimental period seventy training sessions were conducted, with an average of about thirty-five minutes spent per session, or a total of forty hours of reading training.

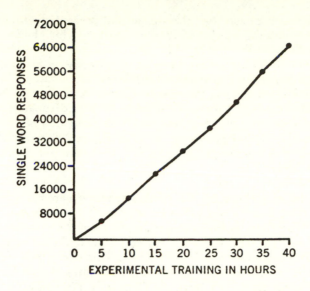

**Fig. 1.** Number of single-word reading responses as a function of the time in experimental reading training

During the period of training the subject made many reading responses. Figure 1 shows the number of single-word reading responses the subject made as a function of the hours of time spent in training. An estimate of the number of single-word reading responses was obtained from tabulating each presentation of a word card, the number of words in the stories, and the reading comprehension questions at the end of each story, as well as the words presented in the later single-word retention test. Actually, the number of words in the stories is an estimate obtained from the mean number of words in two out of each five stories. Thus, rather than giving the true absolute number of reading responses made, the figure gives an estimate. However, the most important aspect of the figure is to indicate the rate of this single-word reading-response measure as a function of time in experimental training. As can be seen, as the training progressed the subject covered the reading material at a slightly more rapid rate, as is shown by the slight positive acceleration in the curve. The importance of this result is to indicate that the child's behavior of attending to the task and making the appropriate reading responses did not diminish throughout the period of training. Thus, the reinforcement system employed was capable of maintaining the behavior for a long period of time. During this time the attentional and cooperative behaviors instigated resulted in many, many learning trials—*sine qua non* for the acquisition of achievement in any skill.

Before reading each story the subject was presented with individual cards for all the words included in that story which had not been presented in a previous story. When these words were presented, the subject would read a certain proportion correctly on first presentation, the other words being missed on the first presentation. The ones missed were considered to be new words, words that he had not previously learned. These words were tabulated separately. The cumulative number of these new words as a function of every five stories read is shown by the top curve of Figure 2. (The data for the first ten stories are not presented since they were not available for all three curves.) As this curve indicates, 761 new words were presented during the training.

Thus, the subject missed 761 words when they were first presented to him. However, he was given training trials on these words, and then he read them again in the oral reading of the paragraph. The number of these words that he missed in this oral reading phase is plotted in the bottom curve of Figure 2. This curve then indicates the number of errors made on the second reading test of the words that had been previously learned. Thus, only 176 words out of 761 (about 23 percent) were missed in the oral reading phase—showing retention for 585 words. The results indicate that the criterion of one correct unprompted reading trial in the original vocabulary-learning phase produced considerable learning when the words were read in context.

The middle curve in Figure 2 involves a measure of long-term retention of the words that had been learned. This measure was obtained by testing the subject on the words, presented singly, that had been learned in the preceding twenty stories. This test was given 10 to 15 days after the training occurred. The training thus included the previous single-word presentations of the words, as well as those same words read orally and silently. In addition, however, the subject had also learned a considerable number of other words by the time of this test. As the middle curve shows, when tested 10 to 15 days later, he read 430 of the 761 words correctly, or, conversely, 331 words (about 43 percent) were missed. Thus, the procedures produced retention when the words were later presented out of context after a considerable intervening period.

The results appearing in Figure 2 indicate that the child covered a considerable amount of reading material, that he learned to read a number of new words when presented individually or in context, and that he retained a good proportion of what he had learned. The results also indicate that the child improved during the training in his retention. That is, his rate of getting new words in the first-presentation phase continued at a high rate throughout the study. (This supports the results shown in Figure 1 indicating that the child's behavior did not weaken during the training.) However, his "rate" of missing the new words on the second and third presentations decreased; that is,

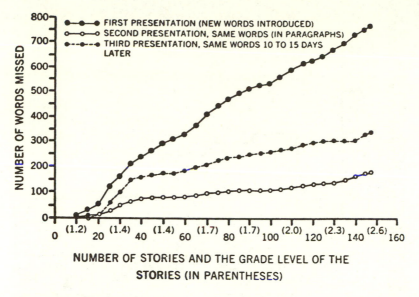

**Fig. 2.** Number of words missed on first, second, and third presentations for the 150 stories

he retained more of the words he had learned. Thus, tabulation indicated that for the first thirty-five stories only about 33 percent of the words learned were retained 10 to 15 days later, whereas the subject's subsequent retention increased to about 55 percent. It should be noted that this improvement occurred even though the difficulty of the words (as shown in Figure 2 by the numbers in parentheses) became progressively greater during the training, moving from the 1.2 grade level of difficulty to the 2.6 grade level.

These results receive support from the data presented in Figure 3. As already indicated, on the first presentation of the vocabulary of a story, some words were missed out of the total presented—and the subject was then presented with training on these words. Figure 3 shows the number of the words presented and missed in ratio to the total number presented as this ratio is related to the number and difficulty of the stories presented. A smaller ratio indicates that the subject missed fewer of the total vocabulary words when they were presented for the first time. As can be seen in Figure 3, as the child read more stories in his training (even though they became more difficult), he missed fewer and fewer words that were presented to him. It should be stressed that he was thus improving in the extent to which he correctly responded to new words on *first* presentation. This improvement appeared to be correlated with other observations that indicated the subject was also beginning to learn to sound out words as a function of the training. For example, he remarked

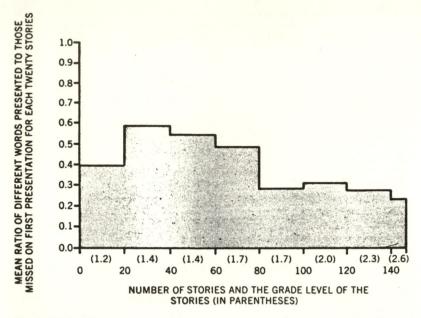

**Fig. 3.** Ratio of words presented to those missed on first presentation for the 150 stories

that when in the judge's office he thought a sign said "information" because he could read the "in" and the "for" and the "mation." In addition, he reported a number of times that the training was helping him in school, that reading was getting easier for him in school, that he liked the reading training better as he went along, and so on. It would be expected (as will be supported by other data) that as the reading training improved his reading in school, the things he learned in school would also improve his performance in the reading training. It is this effect that may also be reflected in his increasing ability to read the new words presented to him.

In addition to this direct evidence of the child's progress in reading training, and the foregoing indirect evidence that the reading training was having general effects upon the child's behavior, the study was formulated to obtain other sources of information concerning the child's progress. One means of doing this was to give the child reading achievement tests before beginning the reading training as well as during the training. The results of these tests are shown in Figure 4. The first point on the curve is a measurement obtained by use of the Developmental Reading Test giving a total score of reading achievement showing that the subject was performing at the grade 2 level. After forty-five reading-training sessions, the subject's performance on the California Reading Test shows a gain to the 3.8 grade level. By the end of the training, after twenty-

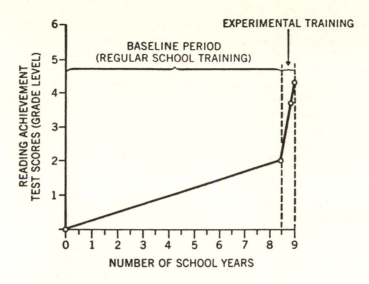

**Fig. 4.** Reading-achievement test scores as a function of 8½ years of school training and 4½ months of experimental training

five more training sessions, he had advanced to the 4.3 grade level on the California Reading Test.

Another indication of the general effect of the reading training came from the child's performance in school, both in school achievement and deportment. The period of reading training coincided with a school term. The boy received passing grades in all subjects: C in Physical Education, D in General Shop, D in English, and D in Mathematics. It should be emphasized that these grades represent the first courses that this child had ever passed, and thus his finest academic performance.

Furthermore, the subject began to behave better while in school. The boy had always been a behavior problem in school, and this continued into the period during which he received reading training. As Figure 5 shows, during the first month of the training he committed ten misbehaviors that resulted in the receipt of demerits. The behaviors were as follows: disturbance in class (two times), disobedience in class (five times), loitering (two times), and tardiness. In the second month he was given demerits for scuffling on the school grounds and also for creating a disturbance. In the third month he was given demerits for cutting a math class and for profanity in class. As the figure shows, however, no misbehaviors occurred in the fourth month or in the half month before the conclusion of the school term.

The subject requested that the tokens be exchanged for items that he wanted in sessions 12, 17, 25, 31, 35, 43, 49, 55, and in the last session he was given the value of the remaining tokens in cash. Items included were a pair of "Beatle" shoes, hair pomade, a phonograph record, an ice cream sundae, a ticket to a school function, money for his brother who was going to reform school, and so on. Further information regarding the reinforcement system is given in Figure 6. The vertical axis of the graph represents the ratio of the number of tokens obtained by the subject relative to the number of single-word reading responses which he emitted. Lesser ratios thus indicate more reading responses per reinforcer. This ratio was plotted as a function of the progress made in the training program, as given by the number of SRA stories he had completed. As the training progressed the subject gradually made an increasingly greater number of reading responses per reinforcer. This effect was not accomplished by changing the rules by which the reinforcers were administered. The effect, which was planned in the training program, resulted from the fact that the stories became longer as the grade level was raised. Since, for example, paragraph reading was reinforced by the paragraph, the longer the paragraph, the greater the number of reading responses that had to be emitted before reinforcement was obtained. Thus, at the end of training the subject was getting about half as much reinforcement per response as at the beginning of training. It should also be indicated that the stories were more difficult as the training progressed, so the effort involved in reading was increasing —although reinforcement for the reading was decreasing.

During the 4½ months of training, which involved forty hours of reading training and the emission of an estimated 64,307 single-word reading responses, the subject received $20.31.

### Discussion

In this section the various aspects of the reading training procedures will first be discussed. Then the implications of the results and analysis will be outlined both for further studies of remedial reading training as well as for a learning conception of certain aspects of cultural deprivation and delinquency.

The method of reading training used in the present study was derived from previous studies (Staats, 1964a; 1962) with preschool children in which words were first presented singly, then in sentences, and finally in short stories. The present study indicated that SRA materials can be adapted for a similar type of presentation in conjunction with the type of reinforcer system previously developed. From the SRA materials it was possible to present single-word training trials and oral-reading training and to develop a silent reading training procedure, all involving reinforcement.

When the training of reading, at least in part, is considered as

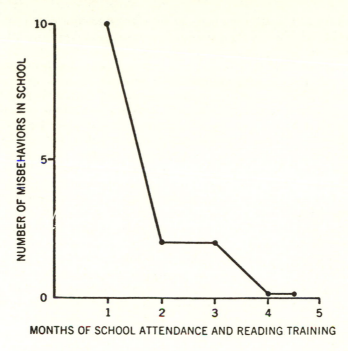

**Fig. 5.** Number of official misbehaviors in school as a function of time in the experimental training

instrumental (operant) discrimination learning, the learning task consists of having the subject emit the correct speech response while looking at the verbal stimulus — this process being followed by reinforcement. This basic procedure was elaborated in the present study to include two levels of reinforcement. An unprompted reading response on the first trial was reinforced more heavily than one that had been previously missed. This procedure appeared to produce learning that was retained very well when the child later read the words orally in a paragraph, with considerable retention also occurring when the child was tested on the individual words 10 to 15 days later.

It may seem incongruous at first to attempt to reinforce silent reading since this behavior is not observable. However, it should be remembered that the subject actually has two types of behavior in the silent reading act. He looks at the verbal stimuli — that is, attends — and he makes "reading" verbal responses to the verbal stimuli. While the reading responses cannot be monitored when they are covert, the attending behavior can be. Of course, there is a danger involved in reinforcing the behavior of just looking at something. Perhaps the child will do nothing else. If he is heavily reinforced for sitting and looking at a page, and the actual reading responses are effortful, he may not emit the reading responses. The present procedure was set up to eliminate this possibility by using a double contingency. The child was reinforced for simple attention, but the reinforcement was low in value. The opportunity for a greater amount of reinforcement came during the answering of the questions. Thus, although simple attention was reinforced lightly, attention and reading responses were reinforced much more heavily. In this way it was possible to use reinforcement in a procedure designed to maintain reading for understanding, in addition to simple "word-naming." (These results could be generalized to other types of learning.) Furthermore, this procedure provided an opportunity to train the subject to read silently. Although he had a tendency to make vocal or lip responses while reading, it was possible to strengthen reading without these other responses through differentially reinforcing the correct silent reading.

Thus, it may be concluded that the reading program increased the child's reading vocabulary as shown by the various measures of retention used in the study, the tests of reading achievement, as well as the child's improved school performance and his verbal description of improved attitude toward and performance in reading in school. There were also suggestions that the child was acquiring a "unit reading repertoire," that is, the general ability to sound out words through making the correct response to single letters and syllables. Thus, for example, the child made errors on fewer and fewer of the new words presented as the training progressed, even though the words were of greater difficulty. In addition, he retained a greater proportion of the words he learned as he went on. Further research of the present type must be conducted to test the possibilities for using a more phonic system of remedial reading training with the present type of subject.

A final point should be made concerning the training procedures used in the present study. The procedures are very specific and relatively simple. Thus it was not necessary to have a person highly trained in education to administer the training. In the present case the instructional technician was a probation officer. It might also be suggested that anyone with a high school education and the ability to read could have administered the training. This has implications for the practical application of the present methods, since one of the questions that arises in this context concerns the economy of the procedures. The procedures as described involved a ratio of one trainer to one student as many remedial teaching procedures do. But the simplicity of the procedures used in this case suggests the possibility that savings may be effected because the instructional technician need not be so highly trained. Thus, the procedures could be widely applied or adapted by various professionals; for example, social workers, prison officials, remedial teachers, tutors, and so on.

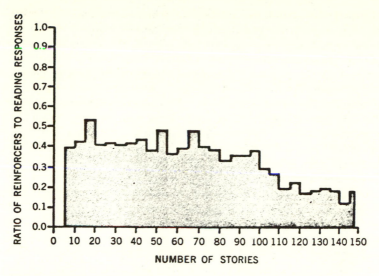

**Fig. 6.** Ratio of the number of tokens received divided by the number of reading responses made as a function of the number of stories read

In an even more economical application, helpers of professionals could be used to actually administer the procedures; for example, selected delinquents (or prisoners) could administer the procedures to other delinquents. Thus, the procedures could be utilized in various situations, such as settlement houses, homes for juvenile delinquents, prison training programs, parts of adult education, and so on. All that is needed is a suitable system of reinforcers to back up the tokens.

It is relevant to add here that the type of token-reinforcer system employed in the present study was first developed by Staats in 1959 in the context of an exploratory study of remedial reading. Communication of the efficacy of the token-reinforcer system to Jack Michael at the University of Houston began its use there in work with retarded. Further communication with Ayllon led to adoption of the token-reinforcer system in the psychiatric ward (Ayllon and Azrin, 1968). The token-reinforcer system has since been widely employed in various forms in educational and clinical behavior modification studies (for example, see Wolf, Giles, and Hall, 1968; and Ullmann and Krasner, 1969). After the initial development of the token-reinforcement system, Staats also adapted it for work with preschool children in a series of basic and behavior modification studies of various types of complex learning (see Staats, 1968; Staats, Finley, Minke, Wolf, and Brooks, 1964; Staats, Minke, Finley, and Wolf, 1964; Staats, Staats, Schutz, and Wolf, 1962).

Furthermore, additional studies have been conducted in the present project to further substantiate the general efficacy of the reinforcer system and the reading procedures, with various types of subjects. Thus, the present training procedures have been employed successfully in a study involving eighteen additional children (including seven educable retardates as well as several emotionally disturbed children) of junior high school age in Madison, Wisconsin. The instructional technicians were nine average high school students and nine adult volunteers (Staats, et al., 1967).

In a later study (Staats, Minke, and Butts, 1970) thirty-two Negro ghetto children with behavior problems were given the treatment in Milwaukee. The instructional technicians were literate Negro high school children from ghetto schools and two formerly unemployed Negro adults employed on the project in full-time positions. The treatment was conducted for a semester, and the results were again successful. Increases were shown in achievement tests, grades, attendance, and deportment, in comparison to a control group of thirty-two children. In addition, Staats (1968) has conducted a long term project with young children in the study and treatment of cognitive deficits in such areas as first reading acquisition, number skill learning, and writing acquisition. The present methods and principles receive strong support as being generally applicable from these various studies.

In the present study, it may be worth pointing out that the results indicated that the child advanced as many years in reading achievement, as measured by the tests, during the experimental training as he had in his previous school history. A comparison of the relative costs — in the present case about forty hours of time of a person not necessarily trained in teaching and $20.31 for the reinforcers versus 8½ years of trained teachers' time, albeit in a group situation — suggests that the procedure introduced in the present study may not be uneconomical, even without improvements in the method. And, as will be further described, the child's failure in school may in many cases be considered as a contributor to the child's delinquency — which also carries a high cost to society. The present results, in suggesting that the training procedures may also effect general improvements in behavior, including misbehaviors in school, thus have further implications concerning the economy of the procedures.

The present study, among other things, tests the feasibility of using the type of reinforcing system previously applied successfully to younger children to the study of learning in older children — in this case a fourteen-year-old juvenile delinquent. The reinforcer system worked very well with the present subject, maintaining his attention and working behaviors in good strength for a long period of time. And there was every reason to expect that the study could have been continued for a much longer period, probably as long as it would have taken to train the child to read normally.

It should be noted that although the amount of reinforcement given decreases during the training, as shown in Figure 6, the reading behavior is maintained in good strength throughout the study, as shown in Figures 1 and 2; thus, less and less reinforcement is needed to maintain the behavior even though the material increases in difficulty. As already described, this occurred because a progressively greater number of reading responses was necessary per reinforcer. This is analogous to gradually raising the ratio of responses to the reinforcers as considered in terms of ratio schedules of reinforcement. Staats has suggested that this type of gradual increase must occur to produce good work behaviors in humans (Staats, 1963).

This result in the present study is in part an answer to the question of whether the use of extrinsic reinforcers in training will produce a child who is dependent upon these reinforcers. It is not possible to discuss this topic fully now. However, it may be said that the extrinsic reinforcement can be gradually decreased until, as was happening with the present child, reading becomes reinforcing itself, or other sources of reinforcement maintain the behavior.

A word should be said concerning the relevance of reinforcement variables in the treatment of non-learning in culturally deprived children. Typically, as in the present case, such children do not, as a result of their home experiences, acquire "reinforcer systems" appropriate for maintaining learning in the traditional classroom. Rosen (1956) has shown that, in the present terminology, lower class children do not have experiences that make school involvement and learning itself positively reinforcing. This deficit, among others that affect the reinforcer system, can be expected to lead to poor school learning and other behavioral deficits. In such cases, there are increased opportunities for other poor social attitudes and undesirable behaviors to develop, as suggested in the introduction and exemplified in the present case.

The present study suggests that these conditions can be reversed through the application of learning principles and reinforcement variables to the task of repairing the child's behavioral-achievement deficit. There were indications that this treatment resulted in improvement in the reinforcement value of (attitudes toward) school for this child and consequently in the decrease in incidence of misbehaviors in school. The results thus suggest that under appropriate conditions the deficit in behavior stemming from the child's inadequate reinforcing system may be, at least in part, repaired by a properly administered, effective reinforcement system, resulting in a decrease in undesirable behaviors.

A comment should be made about the possibility of a Hawthorne effect; that is, that the social reinforcement provided by the instructional technician and possible extraexperimental reinforcement contributed to the results in the present study. It would be expected that such reinforcers could contribute to the overall effect — and in the present case the expenditure for the material reinforcers was small. In general, it can be expected that individuals will vary in the extent to which social reinforcers will be effective. For example, in preschool children social reinforcement is ineffective for long term training (Staats, 1964c, 1962), and the same would be expected for many individuals with behavior problems. Ordinarily, it might be expected that the weaker other sources of reinforcement are for the individual, the stronger must be the reinforcer system of the treatment procedure.

In conclusion, the present study helps support and replicate the previous findings and extends the general procedures and principles to the study of an adolescent child who is culturally deprived and is also a juvenile delinquent. The various sources of data used suggest that the present procedures and principles are applicable to this population also. Based upon these suggestions, further studies will be conducted on culturally deprived children, delinquent and non-delinquent, as well as studies of other types of nonachieving or underachieving readers.

It should also be indicated that the present study indicates the possibility for developing procedures for the objective application and testing of laboratory-derived learning principles within the context of an actual problem of behavior. As previously indicated (Staats, 1968, 1964a), verification of learning principles in the context of a problem of human behavior constitutes one way to further the generality of the principles themselves. It may thus be suggested that such studies have two types of implication: they have implications for people interested in dealing with the problems of human behavior, as well as for those interested in the extension and verification of the basic science.

# REFERENCES

Ayllon, T., and Azrin, N. H. *The Token Economy*. New York: Appleton-Century-Crofts, 1968.

Ellson, D. G., Barber, L., Engle, T. L., and Kampaerth, L. "Programmed Tutoring: A Teaching Aid and a Research Tool," *Reading Research Quarterly*, 1965, 1.

Rosen, B. C. "The Achievement Syndrome: A Psychocultural Dimension of Social Stratification," *American Sociological Review*, 1956, 21, 203–211.

Staats, A. W. "A Case in and a Strategy for the Extension of Learning Principles to Problems of Human Behavior," in A. W. Staats (ed.), *Human Learning*. New York: Holt, Rinehart and Winston, 1964. (a)

Staats, A. W. "Conditioned Stimuli, Conditioned Reinforcers, and Word Meaning," in A. W. Staats (ed.), *Human Learning*. New York: Holt, Rinehart and Winston, 1964. (b)

Staats, A. W. (ed.) *Human Learning*. New York: Holt, Rinehart and Winston, 1964. (c)

Staats, A. W. "An Integrated-functional Learning Approach to Complex Human Behavior," in B. Kleinmuntz (ed.), *Problem Solving: Research, Method and Theory*. New York: Wiley, 1966.

Staats, A. W. *Learning, Language, and Cognition*. New York: Holt, Rinehart and Winston, 1968.

Staats, A. W., Finley, J. R., Minke, K. A., and Wolf, M. "Reinforcement Variables in the Control of Unit Reading Responses," *Journal of the Experimental Analysis of Behavior*, 1964, 7, 139–149. (d)

Staats, A. W., Minke, K. A., and Butts, P. "A Token-Reinforcement Remedial Reading Program Administered by Black Therapy-Technicians to Problem Black Children," *Behavior Therapy*, 1970, 1, 331–353.

Staats, A. W., Minke, K. A., Finley, J. R., Wolf, M., and Brooks, L. O. "A Reinforcer System and Experimental Procedure for the Laboratory Study of Reading Acquisition," *Child Development*, 1964, 35, 209–231. (e)

Staats, A. W., Minke, K. A., Goodwin, W., and Landeen, J. "Cognitive Behavior Modification: 'Motivated Learning' Reading Treatment with Subprofessional Therapy-Technicians," *Behavior Research and Therapy*, 1967, 5, 283–299.

Staats, A. W. with contributions by Staats, C. K. *Complex Human Behavior*. New York: Holt, Rinehart and Winston, 1963.

Staats, A. W., Staats, C. K., Schutz, R. E., and Wolf, M. "The Conditioning of Textual Responses Utilizing 'Extrinsic' Reinforcers," *Journal of the Experimental Analysis of Behavior*, 1962, 5, 33–40.

Ullmann, L. P., and Krasner, L. *A Psychological Approach to Abnormal Behavior*. New York: Prentice-Hall, 1969.

Wolf, M. M., Giles, E. K., and Hall, R. V. "Experiment with Token-Reinforcement in a Remedial Classroom," *Behavior Research and Therapy*, 1968, 6, 51–64.

NORRIS G. HARING
MARY ANN HAUCK

# Improved Learning Conditions in the Establishment of Reading Skills with Disabled Readers

CHILDREN with severe reading disabilities are currently receiving national attention and concern. These are children who apparently have failed to acquire the necessary responses to be successful in reading. Their reading performances typically exhibit low rates of total performance, high rates of error, and marked deficiency in visual to auditory and auditory to visual association, as well as other related deficiencies in discrimination. Research providing reliable information about this serious behavior problem is extremely urgent. Neither medicine nor education has conducted research, which can be replicated and utilized in the natural school setting, that provides answers to the identification, treatment, and prevention of the problems presented by these children.

Medically oriented professionals (Critchley, 1966; Hermann, 1959; Money, 1962) have referred to these children as dyslexic, a term often meant to suggest that the child has a reading disability associated with minimal neurological dysfunctioning. This label attached to children who read poorly may or may not be appropriate, and the present investigators in no way acknowledge the existence of such a medical entity. These children, nevertheless, remain a serious problem to educators.

There are widely varying reading deficits among children which might result from either biological or experiential factors. By the time reading behavior becomes important to children, however, it is far too late to be concerned about etiology. The concern to the educator is with procedures which will predictably establish reading responses with children having severe reading disabilities. The concern of the present investigation was the establishment of reading skills in four boys with severe reading disability using systematic instructional procedures.

*Analysis of Reading Behavior*

The process of using systematic procedures began with an analysis of reading behavior. This analysis included (a) an assessment of the entering skills each student had acquired; (b) specification of terminal reading skills

EXCEPTIONAL CHILDREN, 1969, Vol. 35, pp. 341-352.

TABLE 1

Entering and Terminal Levels of Reading Skills of Subjects

| Student | | Entering Levels | | | Terminal Levels | |
|---|---|---|---|---|---|---|
| | Grade | Programed Material | Basal Reader | Word rec- ognition | Basal Reader | Programed Material |
| RD | 5 | Primer | Primer | 2.8 | 4-1 | 4.2 |
| M | 4 | Primer | Primer | 2.5 | 3-1 | 3.9 |
| R | 4 | Primer | 3.1 | 3.1 | 4-2 | 4.5 |
| P | 3 | Primer | Primer | 2.5 | 2-2 | 3.5 |

each student should acquire; (c) specification of successive approximations to these terminal reading skills that would be viewed as progress in skill development; and (d) an assessment of the kinds of stimuli which could function as reinforcing events to the individual child.

As social reinforcers had well demonstrated their weakness in shaping skill development in these boys, other stimuli which were already strong reinforcers to these four students had to be used. An extensive repertoire of skills cannot be built without the use of variables that are motivating to the child (Ferster, 1961). Although candy (Hewett, 1964), trinkets (Staats, Staats, Schutz, & Wolf, 1962), a combination of both (Bijou & Sturges, 1959), and opportunity to engage in a desired activity (Homme, deBaca, Devine, Steinhorst, & Rickert, 1963) have all been demonstrated as strong reinforcers, the most powerful extrinsic reinforcer for accelerating responses has proved to be token reinforcement (Bijou & Baer, 1966; Ferster & Skinner, 1957; Ferster & DeMyer, 1961) because it is appropriate to changing conditions of deprivation. Token reinforcement procedures use reinforcing events which have become motivating by their temporal occurrence (pairing) with other more basic reinforcers. Points (Haring & Kunzelmann, 1966), chips (Bijou, 1958), stars and checkmarks (Birnbrauer, Wolf, Kidder, & Tague, 1965), exchangeable for time to engage in an activity of one's choice (Haring & Kunzelmann, 1966) or for a wide variety of store items (Staats et al., 1962; Staats & Butterfield, 1965), have func-

tioned as powerful motivators in skill development (Zimmerman & Zimmerman, 1962).

The present investigation used token reinforcement in the form of points as counter numbers and later as marbles exchangeable for edibles, trinkets, and more expensive store items that were known to be highly reinforcing. Space and equipment were unavailable for investigating effects from tokens exchangeable for activity time. Information useful for establishing a store of reinforcers was obtained from the students and their parents during informal conversations that initiated the entering assessments.

Terminal reading goals were established as reading at grade level, as in basal readers and Sullivan Programmed Books. Successive approximations of the terminal goals were built into the commercially programed reading materials in minute and successive response requirements.

## Method

### Subjects

Four elementary school boys (grades 5, 4, 4, and 3) severely disabled in reading but average or above average in intelligence, were diagnostically evaluated by the experimenters as one to 5 years retarded in reading skills. Entering reading behaviors are categorized in Table 1 under entering grade level, word recognition level from the Gates-McKillop Diagnostic Reading Tests, instructional reading level determined by informal basal reading tests, and placement in Sullivan Programmed Reading Books determined by the Sullivan Placement Test. All four boys presented read-

**TABLE 2**

**Baseline and Modification Periods of Experiment**

| Independent Reinforcement Variables | | | Periods | | | |
|---|---|---|---|---|---|---|
| | *A* | *B* | *C* | *D* | *E* | *F* |
| | Without answers | With answers | Counters | Continuous reinforcement token reinforcement | Variable ratio token reinforcement | Variable ratio token reinforcement |
| Material | Programed Material | | | Programed Material | | Basal reader |
| Period type | Baseline periods | | | Modification periods | | |

ing skills at the primer level in Sullivan Programmed materials. Only one boy, R, read above the primer level in a basal reader.

## Materials and Apparatus

Reading materials were sequentially ordered in frames with answers adjacent to each presentation to allow for individual progress and effective sequencing of skills. A slider covered the answer until a written response was completed.

The highly structured reading environment contained a teacher station, four student stations, and a reinforcement area. A podium behind the four students served as the teacher station at which the teacher performed her observations and made verbal contact with each boy through a microphone to the headsets worn by each boy. She whispered instructions, provided directional prompting cues during oral reading, and manipulated switches to reinforce oral responses throughout the experiment. At the student stations, students completed all written and oral reading work, and manipulated a switch at the outside edge of their carrels to record correct and incorrect written responses.

The reinforcement area contained edibles, trinkets, and toys priced at various point values based on actual retail value. Items with retail value of 15 cents or more had point val-

ues based on 400 points per 15 cents. Five cent items were valued at 200 points, 10 cent items at 350 points, and one cent items at 50 points. Pellets of candy, gum, and peanuts were valued at 25 points. Reinforcers were packaged separately except for pellets of candy and gum which were bottled for dispensing one at a time.

## Design and Procedures

Obtaining continuous evaluation and making ongoing decisions for the development of terminal behaviors required that the effects of reinforcement variables on written and oral reading responses be continuously measured through each change in variables. The five periods of the design included two baseline periods and three modification periods (See Table 2). The study continued for 91 days with a 65 minute session each day—the students' only formal reading period. Reading material remained constant throughout the five periods except that content became progressively more complex.

*Response specification.* Two types of responses from each student were measured: written responses and oral responses. A written response was defined by the response requirement of each programed frame: (a) circling the correct word or picture, (b) drawing a line to the correct word or picture,

(c) writing one letter or several letters, or (d) writing a whole word. Each constituted one written response. One oral response was defined as each word read orally from (a) lists of new words, (b) word discrimination groupings, and (c) sentences appropriate to each unit in the programed books.

*Baseline periods.* The four boys served as their own controls in two ways. First, each brought with him an academic history exhibiting from one to four years of low rates of performance in reading. Secondly, during the first 2 weeks of the experiment, the students made reading responses to the programed material without receiving any reinforcement beyond what the programed format offered, i.e., immediate confirmation of answers and/or appropriate sequencing of textual material. These measures, especially the latter, were considered as representing the number of correct reading responses each student made under conditions prior to the experimental conditions—response data which served as a baseline from which to compare behavior change.

*Adaptation.* Prior to the first baseline period, 4 days of adaptation introduced procedures for: (a) written responding to programed reading, (b) oral responding to appropriate stimuli from cards and teacher directions through earphones; and (c) switch use.

*Period A.* During the 4 days of Period A, answer columns were stapled together, visible answers were blacked out, and verbal correction of oral responses was not given. Under these conditions, which approximated classroom assignments for which answer feedback is often delayed, each response was followed by the next frame and movement of a switch by the student to record his response.

$$S^D \relbar\joinrel\longrightarrow R \relbar\joinrel\longrightarrow S^r$$

| programed frame | writing answer | next frame, switch movement |

*Period B.* The 7 days of this period provided a typical programed format. After making each written response, the student obtained answer confirmation from the adjacent answer column. Verbal correction of oral responses was given by the teacher. The student recorded

the accuracy of his answer by moving a switch at his carrel to the right if he was correct and to the left if incorrect.

$$S^D \relbar\joinrel\longrightarrow R \relbar\joinrel\longrightarrow S^r$$

| programed frame | writing answer | answer feedback, switch movement, next frame |

During this period the programed format was modified permanently to avoid misuse of the answers. This enabled measurement of responses emitted before answers were known. Answers were cut from the books, perforated at the top, and hung backwards on hooks in front of the student. The cut pages were stapled into books. The modified format required the student to write responses to a complete page of frames, remove the answer column from the hook, place it next to the corresponding frames, and correct his written responses.

*Period C.* Following the baseline period, a counter, which tallied the number of correct responses being made, was installed at each carrel and functioned as the only change in variables for the next 12 days.

$$S^D \relbar\joinrel\longrightarrow R \relbar\joinrel\longrightarrow S^r$$

| programed page | writing a page of answers | answers, switch movement, counter numbers, next page |

This running account of the number of correct responses emitted proved to be important information for both the student and his neighbor.

Although the counter directly influenced behavior, the more important process for modification of the student's skills was the systematic application of reinforcement following two basic procedures: acquisition and maintenance reinforcement. During the initial modification procedures (Period D), when each student's correct reading responses occurred at a very low rate, it was necessary to reinforce each correct reading response. When each student had exhibited a high, stable rate of correct reading responses over a number of sessions, reinforcement was presented only intermittently (Period E), but no less systematically, to maintain the high output of correct responses each boy was exhibiting.

*Period D: Acquisition reinforcement.* Throughout the 21 days of Period D, counter numbers functioned as points (token reinforcement) with exchange value for edibles, trinkets, and more expensive items. Correct responses were reinforced continuously. Each correct written or oral response immediately earned one point, and each student set up his own chained reinforcement schedule of continuous reinforcement (CRF) components by his choice of the reinforcers for which he would work. During the first week, points had exchange value for store items varying from 25 points to 1,000 points. During the second week expensive items were introduced for purchase requiring point saving over many days or several weeks.

*Period E: Maintenance reinforcement.* Correct responses during the 47 days of Period E were reinforced intermittently. Arrangements for reinforcement changed progressively from presentation following a variable ratio (VR) of every two responses (VR 2) to VR 4, VR 5, VR 7, VR 10, VR 15, and VR 25, without instruction to the student. For example, arrangements for presenting points on a variable ratio of 2 correct responses entailed presenting points variably, sometimes after one correct response and sometimes after 2 correct responses. Arrangements for presenting points on a variable ratio of 10 correct responses meant that on the average each tenth correct response received a point, although in fact sometimes a marble would be earned after one response, or after 3 responses, or sometimes only after 20 correct responses.

The objective of intermittent reinforcement was to maintain, as the number of reinforcements per responses progressively decreased, the high stable rate of performance which developed during continuous reinforcement. Intermittent reinforcement of correct responses initially was very frequent, but progressively became less frequent as responding appeared to stabilize with each change in schedule. Except for the initial instructions indicating that sometimes, following a number of correct responses, the student would earn a marble worth 10 points, no instructions were given

when reinforcement arrangements changed.

Marbles worth 10 points each took the place of counter points as token reinforcement to give the experimenters the flexibility necessary for intermittent reinforcement with crude, nonautomatic equipment. The series of numbers within a ratio schedule were determined randomly to enable randomly varied reinforcer presentation controlled from the teacher's podium. Following a predetermined number of correct responses registered on a student's counter at the teacher's podium, the teacher flipped a microswitch which activated a stimulus light at a student carrel indicating to the student he had made enough correct responses to have earned a marble. The boy responded to the stimulus light by manipulating an apparatus attached to his carrel which dispensed a marble.

*Period F.* This month of transition was designed as another step in the reinforcement of successive approximations to the terminal behavior—"normal reader functioning under natural contingencies." The independent variables which changed were the instructional materials. As Figure 1 indicates, a three component chained sequence of responding required (a) reading a word list, (b) reading a story from the basal reader, and (c) making a choice between reading in a basal book or a library book. Silent reading preparation preceding the opportunity to read orally for points constituted the basic procedure in each component. The points earned and the reinforcement given for correct oral reading were credited to the student contingent on daily completion of all three components. Word lists containing words not known during silent preparation or oral responding were grouped to emphasize common word parts, derivations, and/or syllable division. Comprehension was measured by responses to oral questions from the teacher after oral reading and by answers to written multiple choice questions following story completion.

Initially, the students were assigned to read only one basal reader page silently before having the opportunity to read orally for points. But within one week, this requirement had changed to silently reading 3 pages before oral reading and, finally, they were re-

FIGURE 1. Chained sequence of responding required in Period F.

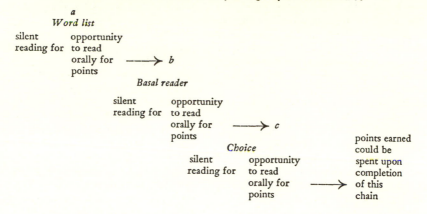

quired to read a complete story. Initially, when a student orally read a randomly selected paragraph for points, he earned one point per word in each line of print read correctly. But within a week, reading the total paragraph correctly was required before any points were earned. This incorporated an essential feature of skill development: progressive increase in task difficulty as performance data exhibit readiness.

Reinforcement was provided only for correct oral responding, as follows: (a) from the word list, 5 points per word within each group of similar words read correctly, but no points for words in a group if errors occurred within it; (b) from the basal reader, initially one point per word from a line of print read without error and later from a paragraph read without error, but no points if any errors were made in either instance; (c) during the "choice" component, 2 points per word from a paragraph read without error if the basal reader was chosen, and one point per word from a paragraph or page if a library book was chosen. All material to be read orally was randomly selected from pages already read silently, except the words on the word list. Correct oral answers to oral comprehension questions received 5 points. Correct written answers to written comprehension questions received 10 points. Follow-

ing Period F, the same reading procedures were continued but under the direction of the teacher in the student's public school classroom.

*Teacher Instruction*

The teacher paced the students together through side one of the Sullivan Primer the first 2 days of the adaptation period to establish the procedural chain for functioning in the experimental environment. From that time on each student progressed individually.

All other reading instruction from the teacher was given given during oral reading in the Sullivan material for Periods A through E and in the basal readers and word lists during Period F. When a student mispronounced a word while reading orally, the teacher directed him to the word for another try by repeating the word immediately preceding the word mispronounced. With this cue, the student returned to the mispronounced word for a second try. If he failed on this try, the teacher provided directional cues highlighting the beginning, middle, or ending of the word. For example, the teacher would say, "Look at the beginning of the word again." If the student failed with this cue, he was told the sound of the part missed, and finally told the word, if necessary. The first cue was often sufficient; the latter two were rarely needed. Mispronounced words were programed for a word list the next day.

The teacher diagnostically recorded mispronunciations during oral reading. With microswitches she recorded the interval and content of her verbal interaction with a student as well as the number of correct oral responses a student was making. The latter data also registered on the student's counter.

## Teacher Communications

Teacher communication was almost totally preplanned and prepared in script form. Scripts controlled teacher communication for: (a) giving initial procedural directions, (b) repeating directions upon request or upon teacher observation of improper responding to directions, (c) requesting oral reading, (d) stopping behavior harmful to others or to equipment, (e) dispensing final reinforcers, and (f) commencing or dismissing class.

## Student Procedures

The two basic procedures for the students entailed writing answers in their programed books and orally reading from word cards at the teacher's requests. Oral reading was programed to correspond with progress in the books.

During reinforcement periods, points earned, spent, and saved were recorded in common bank savings books. At any time a student had earned enough points or marbles to make a purchase he had the option to make a purchase, although students usually waited until the session ended.

## Response Recording

A 20 pen event recorder automatically recorded the occurrence of correct oral responses, and the occurrence and content of teacher communication as well as correct and incorrect written responses. A daily check of the student's switch use was obtained from a book count of the actual number of correct and incorrect written responses.

## Results

Results will be discussed under three categories: (a) comparison of response data between baseline and modification periods, (b) reading skill progress and (c) reinforcer preference.

## Average Response Data

*Baseline performance.* Response data for both baseline periods (Period A, with no answer confirmation given, and Period B, with immediate answer confirmation given) were similar for all four students. Whether or not the student was provided immediate confirmation of answers, the total number of correct responses made daily was low. Correct responding, which occurred at the rate of about four per minute when the child was reading, was irregularly interspersed with responding to stimuli other than reading materials. Almost half of each session was spent in behavior incompatible with making reading responses, resulting in an overall average of 2.8 correct responses per session. Over the last few days of the baseline period, a rapid decrease in the number of reading responses and a rapid increase in the amount of time spent not reading were evident. Figure 2 exhibits for each student the average number of correct responses made each sesssion and the average number of 5 minute intervals spent not making reading responses.

*Counters (Period C).* After counters were installed, dramatic changes occurred in reading performance. Students made correct responses at the baseline rate of 4 per minute but typically made over 300 each session, resulting in an overall rate of 4.5 responses per session. Responding became stable throughout the session with very few five minute intervals when the student was not making reading responses. Although response rate varied extremely over sessions for each student, compared to rate during continuous reinforcement (Period D), counters did function as conditioned reinforcers. Average response rates were significantly higher for three of the four boys compared to baseline rates. Misuse of the programed format by the fourth boy, M, before answers were clipped from the frames prevented accurate comparison of his overall baseline rate with rates between other periods. Comparison between his rate during Period A when he could not misuse the answers and his rate during any modification

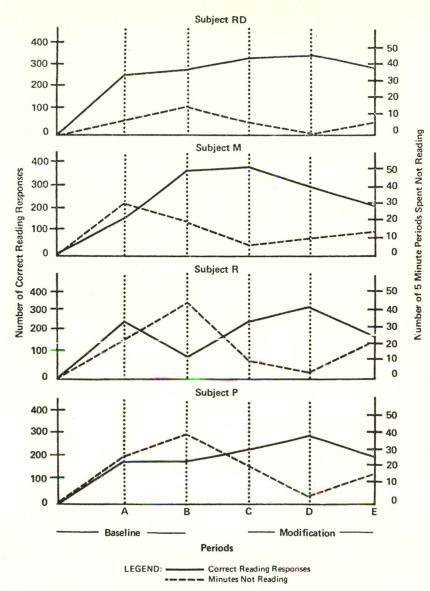

FIGURE 2. Average number of correct responses and average number of minutes spent not reading per period.

period, however, indicates a very significant difference.

*Acquisition reinforcement (Period D).* Systematic application of reinforcers following each correct response during the first week of this modification period resulted in: (a) establishing stable reading rates throughout each session; (b) accelerating response rates to 6.2

TABLE 3

## Comparison of Average Total
### Responses per Period

| Subjects | Average Total Responses | | | | |
| | Baseline Periods | | Modification Periods | | |
| | A | B | C | D | E |
|---|---|---|---|---|---|
| RD | 115 | 228 | 335* | 334* | 316* |
| M | 121 | 335a | 337* | 267 | 240 |
| R | 219 | 94 | 295* | 319* | 209* |
| P | 180 | 174 | 221* | 297* | 213* |

*Chi square test revealed significantly higher ($p < .001$) average total responses

aMisuse of answers

and 8.5 correct responses per minute; and (c) producing daily rates as high as 400 to 550 correct responses. Table 3 exhibits the significantly higher average response rates which occurred for three of the four students under continuous reinforcement compared to baseline conditions.

Two boys, P and RD, averaged about 100 more correct responses every session, while R averaged almost 200 more correct responses. It may be of importance to note that M responded during Period D almost as fast as he misused the answers during the baseline conditions of Period B.

Expensive reinforcers introduced the second week, requiring long term saving, were not effective in maintaining high response rates. Rates either rapidly decelerated or stabilized at a lower rate until the middle of the third week of Period D when three of the four students, short of the points necessary for very expensive items for which they had been saving, spent all points they had. At that time, responding again accelerated to near the high level observed the first weeks of Period D. A reinforcer too far removed from the response—too far in time from the final reinforcer—does not maintain the desired response (Kelleher & Gollub, 1962).

*Maintenance reinforcement (Period E).* As the number of reinforcements decreased gradually from one on the average of every 2 correct responses to one on the average of every 25 responses, without instruction to the student over 47 days, the significant difference between baseline response rates and changes in response rates during Period D modifica-

tion procedures was maintained. A chi square test revealed that total responses under variable ratio schedules were significantly higher (.001 level) than baseline rate for three of the four boys, although significantly lower than rate under continuous reinforcement for two of the four boys.

Although research has demonstrated that response rates are characteristically higher under intermittent reinforcement than under continuous reinforcement (Ferster & Skinner, 1957; Kelleher & Gollub, 1962; Staats, Finley, Minke, & Wolf, 1964), there are several reasons why this failed to occur in the present study. During continuous reinforcement, the student probably responded near his physiological limit as he moved through the chain of requirements for writing, correcting, and recording the answer. Secondly, response requirements had become more complex, requiring much more silent reading per written response. RD and M, for whom response requirements changed greatly during Period C but not during Periods D and E, exhibited average daily responses not significantly different between these two periods. R and P, for whom response requirements changed greatly, exhibited significantly lower rates in Period E.

Observation of the number of minutes spent reading when learning conditions were motivating reveals a marked decrease in the number of intervals spent avoiding reading. When reading was reinforcing, the reading performance of the four students exhibited both higher rates and more intervals of reading during each session. The increase in minutes spent not reading during Period E for R and P is evidence of weakening reinforcers. Certainly for R the data exhibit the effect of a visit by his mother 2 weeks before the end of the period; she told him he must not buy any more candy or other edibles. For R, edibles had been the strongest reinforcers; consequently, his rate rapidly decelerated, but all points he did earn were spent on candy.

*Maintenance reinforcement during transition (Period F.)* The chain of three silent and oral reading components, through which the child had to respond each session, using reading materials typical of the classroom, proved very effective in maintaining stable rates during the final 19 days in the experimental setting and the final 3 weeks of responding in the regular classroom. Only once out of the 19 days of the period did each boy fail to silently prepare his reading lesson carefully before having the opportunity to read orally for points. A lesson poorly prepared silently meant few points earned during oral reading.

This same three component chained assignment was used during the final 3 weeks of school within the regular classroom with equal effectiveness. At the time the students returned to the classroom, R moved out of the state. A followup letter from his mother stated he was reading above grade level in his classroom, and at home was reading "everything he could get his hands on." Reading performance back in the regular classroom actually occurred at a higher average rate than observed during the last week in the experimental setting. In the classroom, a student helper or the classroom teacher listened to the oral reading, tallied the number of words read correctly, and recorded the information in a common bankbook. The total number of correct responses was converted into "points to spend," using the same intermittent schedules from the experimental procedures. Twice a week each student was brought a supply of store items from which to make purchases. Plans for the final phase of the project require maintenance of these efficient, accurate reading performances, using systematic programing of learning conditions natural to the classroom.

## Reading Progress

Change in reading performance was not only remarkable because of the amount of change in rate of making correct responses every day and the number of 5 minute intervals spent reading, but also because of the amount of measurable skill development. Overall changes in the instructional reading levels of the four boys ranged from one and one-half years to 4 years, following 5 months of instruction (Table 1). Comparison of pre- and postmeasures of instructional basal reading levels indicated: (a) RD progressed from primer to book 4-1; (b) M progressed from

primer to book 3-1; (c) R progressed from book 3-1 to book 4-2; and (d) P progressed from primer to book 2-2 by the time the transition period began. Each student read his final programed book with less than 5 percent error rate during both oral and silent reading.

*Reinforcer preference.* Of the three types of reinforcers available for purchase, the preferred reinforcers were generally edibles and expensive items, although individual preference patterns differed. The typical daily pattern for point spending included purchase of 50 to 200 points worth of edibles and saving of the remainder toward purchase of an expensive item valued between 500 and 1,500 points.

## Summary and Conclusion

Learning conditions were individually programed in a group setting to provide sequential arrangement of reading material and systematic presentation of reinforcing events to optimize each child's performance. Arrangements of reinforcing events were designed first to accelerate performance rate, then to maintain the high rate. Learning conditions were considered optimal when the child's performance rate accelerated and stabilized at a higher rate and/or when the number of minutes spent avoiding reading greatly decreased.

When learning conditions were individually appropriate, each child averaged between 100 and 200 more correct responses every day and spent very few minutes avoiding reading. The students not only made more correct responses daily and worked longer, but also progressed in instructional reading levels from one and one-half to 4 years over 5 months of instruction. Behavior and performance in other academic areas within the regular classroom also improved markedly, according to *unsolicited* comments from the classroom teachers.

Conditions for learning were evaluated, through direct and continuous measurement of the student's performance under specified conditions, (a) in terms of effectiveness of the conditions for reading, and (b) for functional, ongoing decisions about future arrangements of these conditions.

The steps in modifying a behavior are components of a process of refining the independent variables of performance, i.e., refining reading materials for sequential skill development and refining motivational variables within the classroom for efficient performance. Both are critical to performance, as experimental results of this and other research well demonstrate. Response data from each boy indicated that attention to sequencing instructional materials without appropriate programing of motivational variables proved ineffective for establishing efficient performance.

When performance data from the child do not meet preset criteria, then learning conditions are not effective and must be changed. If the learning environment is programed appropriately, there is a high probability that the child will make more reading responses and at an accelerated rate because he is rapidly acquiring a history of reinforcement which motivates him to read. Positive reinforcement not only accelerates responding but also has the additional effect of establishing stimuli, present during reinforcement, as conditioned reinforcers, which come to maintain responding (Ferster, 1961). Specifically, the more initial pairings of the reading stimuli with events which are reinforcing to the individual child, the more motivating the reading stimuli themselves become (Staats et al., 1964; Goldiamond & Dyrud, 1966). Concomitantly, as the high rate of responding to successively more difficult material actualizes the establishment of a large repertoire of skills, "being correct" comes to gain strength as a reinforcer (Ferster, 1961).

When children encounter severe reading disabilities the teacher frequently looks to the cause of the problem as being biological or constitutional. The present investigation, however, demonstrates that rather than look to the etiology of the problem look to the systematic refinements in procedures of instruction that improve instructional conditions to the point where children who have severe reading disabilities can come to read normally in a rather short period of time. Whether or not we, as educators, recognize and systematically investigate the effects of classroom variables on performance, these variables are functionally influencing performance.

## References

Bijou, S. W. Operant extinction after fixed-interval schedules with young children. *Journal of Experimental Analysis of Behavior*, 1958, 1, 25-29.

Bijou, S. W., & Baer, D. M. Operant methods in child behavior development. In W. Honig (Ed.), *Operant behavior: areas of research and application*. New York: Appleton-Century-Crofts, 1966.

Bijou, S. W. & Sturges, P. T. Positive reinforcers for experimental studies with children—consumables and manipulables. *Child Development*, 1959, 3, 151-170.

Birnbrauer, J. S., Wolf, M. M., Kidder, J. D., & Tague, Cecilia. Classroom behavior of retarded pupils with token reinforcement. *Journal of Experimental Child Psychology*, 1965, 2, 219-235.

Critchley, M. *Developmental dyslexia*. London, England: Whitefriars Press, 1966.

Ferster, C. B. Positive reinforcement and behavioral deficits of autistic children. *Child Development*, 1961, 32, 437-456.

Ferster, C. B., & Skinner, B. F. *Schedules of reinforcement*. New York: Appleton-Century Crofts, 1957.

Ferster, C. B., & DeMyer, M. K. The development of performance in autistic children in an automatically controlled environment. *Journal of Chronic Disorders*, 1961, 13, 312-345.

Goldiamond, I., & Dyrud, J. E. Reading as operant behavior. In J. Money (Ed.), *The disabled reader*. Baltimore: Johns Hopkins Press, 1966.

Haring, N. G., & Kunzelmann, H. P. The finer focus of therapeutic behavioral management. In J. Hellmuth (Ed.), *Educational therapy*. *Vol. I.* Seattle: Special Child Publications, 1966.

Hermann, Knud. *Reading disability: A medical study of word-blindness and related handicaps*. Springfield, Illinois: Charles C Thomas, 1959.

Hewett, F. Teaching reading to an autistic boy through operant conditioning. *Reading Teacher*, 1964, 17, 613-618.

Homme, L. E., deBaca, P., Devine, J. V., Steinhorst, R., & Rickert, E. J. Use of the Premack principle in controlling the behavior of nursery school children. *Journal of Experimental Analysis of Behavior*, 1963, 6, 544.

Kelleher, R. T., & Gollub, L. R. A review of positive conditioned reinforcement. *Journal of Experimental Analysis of Behavior*, 1962, 5, 543-597.

Money, J. (Ed.) *Reading disability. Progress and research needs in dyslexia*. Baltimore: Johns Hopkins Press, 1962.

Staats, A. W., & Butterfield, W. A. Treatment of nonreading in a culturally deprived juvenile delinquent: an application of reinforcement principles. *Child Development*, 1965, 36, 925-942.

Staats, A. W., Finley, J. R., Minke, K. A., & Wolf, M. M. Reinforcement variables in the control of unit reading responses. *Journal of Experimental Analysis of Behavior*, 1964, 7, 139-149.

Staats, A. W., Staats, C. K., Schutz, R. E., & Wolf, M. The conditioning of textual responses using "extrinsic reinforcers." *Journal of Experimental Analysis of Behavior*, 1962, 5, 33-40.

Zimmerman, E. H., & Zimmerman, J. The alternation of behavior in a special classroom situation. *Journal of Experimental Analysis of Behavior*, 1962, 5, 59-60.

NORRIS G. HARING *is Professor of Education, Lecturer in Pediatrics, and Director of Experimental Education Unit; and* MARY ANN HAUCK *is Special Projects Research Teacher, Experimental Education Unit, University of Washington, Seattle.*

283

# CHILD BEHAVIOR THERAPY:
## A COMMUNITY PROGRAM IN APPALACHIA*

ROBERT G. WAHLER
The University of Tenenessee
and
MARIE ERICKSON
Bell County Health Center

COMMUNITY psychology is a currently popular concept in the "mental health" field (e.g. Sarason, *et al.*, 1966). It implies the notion that the clinician should concentrate his therapeutic and prophylactic efforts on the patient's immediate and not-so-immediate environment rather than on the patient *per se*. That is, instead of following the traditional dyadic treatment model, the clinician's role should be that of an agent for change in his client's community—community, meaning the client's relatives, friends, and working associates as well as the more impersonal aspects of his social and physical surroundings. It is clear that the clinician is seen from this point of view as an expert in human ecology; a practitioner who assumes that man's behavior is an important function of his current environment.

While a number of theoretical models could be employed to implement the community psychology concept, one is of particular relevance in view of its emphasis upon human ecology. Reinforcement theory has as one of its basic tenets the assumption that the development and maintenance of behavior is a function of stimulus contingencies set by one's environment. It is argued that man behaves as he does because of differential reinforcement, provided primarily by the social attention of other people. In the case of the child, people such as his parents, his peers, his siblings, his teachers, etc. are seen as selective dispensers of social attention; in a very real sense these social agents "teach" him which aspects of his behavior will be most instrumental in obtaining approval, reassurance, affection, nearness, and other forms of their attention. From this view, then, the question of whether the child develops normal or deviant behavior can be answered only through an assessment of his social community and how it interacts with him.

The above contention is an intriguing one and readily lends itself to research evaluation. Thus far, attempts to isolate naturalistic events which may support or maintain deviant child behavior have proved promising. For example, evidence is now available to show that parents may inadvertently support their child's deviant behavior through their social

*The authors are grateful to Ira Weinstein for his helpful suggestions in the preparation of this manuscript. Thanks are also due to Norman Teeter for his statistical analysis of the data.

BEHAVIOR RESEARCH AND THERAPY, 1969, Vol. 7, pp. 71-78.

attention to it, (Wahler *et al.*, 1965). Similar studies of teacher–child interactions in pre-school settings.have demonstrated that teachers may also function in this capacity. That is, teachers have been found to function as powerful sources of rienforcement for child behavior such as excessive crying (Hart *et al.*, 1964), isolate play (Allen *et al.*, 1964), excessive passivity (Johnson *et al.*, 1966), regressive crawling (Harris *et al.*, 1964), and aggressive behavior, (Scott *et al.*, 1967; Brown and Elliot, 1965). Finally, more recent studies have indicated that the preschool child's peer group adds a further component to these sources of control (Patterson *et al.*, 1967; Wahler, 1967).

In addition to demonstrating the roles which parents, teachers and peers may play in the maintenance of deviant child behavior, the above studies also brought to light a highly practical finding: In many cases the parents, teachers, and peers could be trained in the use of behavior modification techniques, enabling them to produce dramatic changes in the children's deviant behavior. The techniques, of course, were based on reinforce-ment theory and the previously discussed analyses of the adult–child interactions.

A community psychology program based on reinforcement theory has several features to recommend it as far as child therapy is concerned: (1) the previously discussed research findings support the assumption that social agents in the child's immediate community may be responsible for the maintenance of his deviant behavior; (2) reinforcement con-tingencies set by these social agents may often be modified, and these modifications may produce therapeutic changes in the deviant child behavior; (3) the operations involved in modifying the social reinforcement contingencies are simple, and the T requires relatively little formal training to implement them. This latter point raises the possibility of training clinically unsophisticated community members as Ts. The present program was initiated with these three points in mind.

### Community and clinic settings

Pineville, Kentucky (population, 3000) is the county-seat of Bell County, and the location of the Bell County Health Center. This clinic is state supported and serves the medical and psychological needs of residents in Bell County (population 35,000) and in Harlan County (population 65,000). As far as psychological services are concerned, the Clinic represents the only source of this type in the two counties. The staff of the psychology unit is made up of one permanent member, (a social worker) and one consulting member (a clinical psychologist) who visits the Clinic twice a month.

A picture of the two counties describes a rather typical cross-section of Appalachia. Poverty, unemployment, and low educational attainment are widespread among the residents, and many are dependent on social welfare for financial security. As might be expected, birth control is a serious problem among the poorer families.

Ninety-five percent of the referrals to the psychological clinic are children. The majority of these are from the poorer families who generally bring their children in at the urging of public health nurses or public assistance workers. Presenting complaints range from retardation and autism to less serious problems such as low achievement motivation in school settings. At the present time the Clinic charges no fees for services rendered.

### Program development and current functioning

The senior author's very limited contact with the Clinic was instrumental in the decision to develop a community program. Not only were the senior author's consulting visits restricted to two a month, but because of travel time to and from Pineville, each visit was restricted to a period of about 5 hr. It seemed obvious that a clinician would find it difficult to work therapeutically with a patient, much less handle a large waiting-list of prospective patients, on such a contact basis. Therefore, it seemed advisable to consider a program which emphasized the use of non-professionals as T's—in this case, community members who could be trained in the use of child behavior therapy techniques.

Recruitment procedures were complicated by a lack of funds to hire new clinic staff members. Since it was then apparent that staffing the program would require volunteer workers, efforts were made to obtain the cooperation of Pineville churches, the city school board, and the local mental health committee. The senior author provided these groups with mimeographed manuscripts which described the plight of the Clinic and the proposed behavior therapy program. In addition, the manuscript stated that the educational background of the volunteers was immaterial and that they would be expected to serve no more than 2 hr/week.

Within a period of 2 months following the community group effort to recruit workers, a total of thirteen volunteers were available to the Clinic. Of this number, six were public health nurses from Bell and Harlan Counties, three were public assistance workers in Bell County and four were citizens in Pineville engaged in other occupations. In addition to these regular workers, several teachers and school counselors requested to assist the Clinic on specific cases.

Training of the workers was primarily of an in-service type. Although the authors did provide interested workers with reprints of several studies cited earlier in this paper, most of the workers did not find the material to be helpful. The following steps characterized the training and the regular functioning of the workers and the Clinic staff:

(1) When a prospective child therapy case was seen at the Clinic, the child, his immediate family, and any other people who were closely involved with the child (e.g. teachers) were interviewed by the professional Clinic staff. These interviews were aimed at obtaining descriptions of the behavior which created problems at home, at school, or elsewhere. In addition, efforts were made to determine the usual consequences of such behavior–consequences provided by the child's parents, his teachers, his peers, etc. The interviews were diagnostic in the sense that their function was to provide a list of the child's deviant behavior and a list of probable reinforcers for the behavior.

(2) A volunteer worker was then introduced to the interview data by the Clinic psychologist. Discussion of the case emphasized descriptions of those physical and verbal responses of the child which were considered deviant in his regular environment. Following this description, the clinician emphasized the notion that the behavior was probably being maintained by people in the child's environment. Then followed a brief essay on reinforcement theory, with emphasis on the concepts of reinforcement, extinction, and punishment. Finally, the clinician pointed to those social agents whom he suspected to be responsible for the maintenance of the deviant behavior; therapy for the child was described as a process of modifying the probable reinforcement contingencies currently provided by these social agents.

(3) Prior to step 3, the volunteer worker obtained at least two 1-hr observations of the child's behavior within the problem setting (e.g. home or classroom). These observational procedures will be described later. Second interviews were then scheduled for those social agents who seemed to provide clear and potentially modifiable contingencies for

the child's deviant behavior. The volunteer worker and the clinician conducted these interviews together. Essentially, these social agents were given descriptions of the child's deviant behavior and they were then advised that their social attention to such behavior was a likely cause of their maintenance. The social agents were then told to ignore the child's deviant behavior but to respond as usual to his other behavior patterns, especially those which seemed incompatible with the deviant behavior. In cases where the deviant behavior involved highly aggressive or oppositional actions, a punishment procedure was suggested as well. In all instances this suggested procedure involved social isolation of the child for short periods of time following his deviant behavior. It was then made clear to the social agents that the volunteer worker would make weekly visits to observe interactions between them and the child and to point out needed corrections in social contingencies.

(4) For an inexperienced volunteer worker, these interviews were continued on a twice a month basis until the clinician felt confident in the volunteer worker's understanding of the therapeutic process as it applied to the child. When this occurred, the clinician met only with the volunteer worker on the same time basis. Discussion centered around the child's progress and the progress of the social agents in maintaining their "therapeutic" contingencies for the child.

The following case study is cited to illustrate these procedures: Ricky (age 8) was referred to the Clinic by his school principal because of his disruptive behavior in the classroom. According to his teacher, Ricky would frequently tease the other children in a variety of ways. Following an interview with the teacher, numerous examples of Ricky's disruptive behavior were recorded; in addition, the interview revealed that the teacher's usual response to this behavior was to shout at Ricky, argue with him and at times to spank him. The teacher also admitted that her usual response to Ricky's infrequently cooperative behavior was to ignore him; she pointed out that Ricky irritated her so much of the time that she found it exceedingly difficult "to be nice to him" even when his behavior was appropriate. Since Ricky's parents were unwilling to come to the Clinic, the therapy program focused on the school setting.

The volunteer behavior T was a young public health nurse who normally visited the school on a weekly basis. This was her first behavior therapy case. She and the psychologist discussed the interview data for about 30 min prior to the second meeting with Ricky's teacher. During the discussion, Ricky's disruptive classroom behavior was described in detail and the psychologist emphasized the possibility that the teachers' attention (admittedly negative) could be maintaining this behavior. The psychologist pointed out that if the teacher could ignore it. However, it was evident that this procedure would be impractical in terms of maintaining any semblance of classroom routine. Therefore, a punishment technique was outlined by the psychologist. Essentially, the proposed procedure involved isolating Ricky from his peers and his teacher for short time periods following the occurrence of his disruptive behavior. The psychologist speculated that if the punishment procedure could suppress Ricky's disruptive behavior, the teacher might find it much easier to provide positive social attention following his appropriate behavior.

The second interview with Ricky's teacher included the volunteer behavior T. Prior to the interview, the psychologist urged the T to comment whenever possible on the therapeutic procedure. In beginning the interview, the psychologist reviewed Ricky's problem behavior and then briefly outlined the proposed behavior therapy program for Ricky.

During the ensuing discussion of the program, Ricky's teacher offered suggestions for implementing the procedures—particularly the punishment portions. It was decided to use the teacher's lounge (a former cloakroom adjacent to the classroom) as the isolation area in the punishment program. The teacher agreed to attempt the program and to work closely with the volunteer T, who would visit the classroom twice weekly.

After the program had been in effect for two weeks, a third Clinic meeting was scheduled for the teacher and the therapist. However, since the teacher was unable to attend, only the psychologist and the T were present. According to the T's report, little change had occurred in Ricky's disruptive behavior; both she and the teacher were quite discouraged. The T's reports revealed that the teacher had used the punishment procedure for 5 days with little success. At the end of that time she decided, "it wouldn't work" and discontinued its use.

A careful analysis of the T's classroom observations provided a possible explanation for the program's failure. Two features of her report were of interest: (1) the teacher's use of the punishment procedure was inconsistent. That is, only about 60 per cent of Ricky's disruptive episodes were followed by social isolation; (2) when she did use the procedure, it was not used promptly upon the occurrence of the disruptive behavior. Often the teacher would first warn Ricky or argue with him before ordering him to the isolation room. The T agreed to discuss these problems with the teacher and to monitor the teacher's behavior more carefully in the next 2 weeks.

At the next interview, both the teacher and the T were present. Both were enthusiastic about the marked improvement in Ricky. According to the report, Ricky's disruptive behavior had dropped from about twenty episodes a day to only one or two. The teacher also reported that her attitude toward Ricky had changed to the point that she could now offer genuine approval for his appropriate behavior.

The T agreed to continue her observations on a weekly basis and to meet twice a month with the psychologist to describe her experiences. Two months later, therapeutic changes in Ricky were still in evidence and his case was closed.

*Program effectiveness*

The program has now been in effect for over 2 yr and fourteen volunteer workers are now actively involved in it. In all cases treated, the deviant behavior was in evidence either in the child's home or in his school. Therefore, most of the social agents were either the child's parents or his teachers, or both.

The major claims of the program's effectiveness rest on observational reports of improvement by the volunteer workers, the number of cases seen by the Clinic, and the time spent treating these cases.

Observational data were collected in the following manner: after a volunteer worker became familiar with the behavioral problems presented by her case, she was introduced to a check-list method of recording the behavior. This method, similar to one described by Zeilberger *et al.*, (1968), required the observer to make coded checks for the occurrence or non-occurrence of the problem behavior and the stimulus contingencies, within successive 20-sec intervals. For each case, the worker obtained two 1 hr observations prior to treatment and two 1-hr observations just after termination of treatment. These observations were made in the child's home or classroom or both, depending on the stimulus location of the presenting problem.

Because of time and scheduling problems, it proved possible to assess the scoring reliability of approximately half of the volunteer workers. In assessing observer reliability, observers worked in pairs; an agreement or disagreement was tallied for each 20-sec interval and the percentage of agreements for the two observers was computed for each response and stimulus class. All reliability tests showed agreement levels of 85 per cent or better; since all behavior categories were based on quite distinct physical and verbal behaviors, this kind of reliability is not particularly surprising.

It proved possible to classify the presenting problems for all cases in five general categories: (1) classroom disruptive behavior; this category included fighting with other children, shouting, and not obeying teacher instructions. (2) classroom study behavior; this category included attending (i.e. looking) to either the teacher or to the learning materials. (3) school absences; this record was obtained from teacher attendance records. (4) home disruptive behavior; this category included fighting with siblings, parents, or other people in the home, destruction of property, and not obeying parent instructions. (5) home study behavior; this category included attending to school homework materials.

Table 1 describes pre- and post-treatment measures of the above behavior problems over 2 yr of the community program. As this table indicates, many of the 66 cases handled during this time were deviant in terms of more than one of the problem categories. An examination of mean differences in the problem behavior categories before and after

TABLE 1. MEAN NUMBER OF PROBLEM BEHAVIOR EPISODES BEFORE AND AFTER TREATMENT

| | Mean variance | | | | $F$ test | $t$ Test | Corrected $t$ test | Number of cases |
| | Pre-treatment | | Post-treatment | | | | | |
|---|---|---|---|---|---|---|---|---|
| Classroom disruptive behavior | 25.77 | 128.70 | 7.77 | 27.83 | 4.62* | | 4.03* | 35 |
| Classroom study behavior | 51.68 | 660.22 | 95.12 | 1366.68 | 2.28* | | 10.70* | 50 |
| School absences (Days absent) | 7.60 | 5.69 | 1.66 | 4.67 | 1.22 | 2.68* | | 15 |
| Home study behavior | 13.49 | 120.35 | 59.67 | 1075.00 | 8.93* | | 8.37* | 45 |
| Home disruptive behavior | 29.87 | 259.10 | 9.88 | 76.40 | 3.39* | | 7.87* | 52 |

*$P < 0.05$

treatment revealed significant changes in the frequencies of these behaviors; all categories displayed marked changes in the therapeutic direction. Unfortunately, because of a lack of personnel, an appropriate control group was not included to evaluate the causal influence of the treatment procedures. Thus, although the children *did* show improvement, the role of the volunteer workers in producing the improvement is not clear.

During the senior author's first year at the Clinic, he and the junior author engaged in fairly traditional techniques of diagnosis and therapy; no attempts were made to assess the effectiveness of these procedures. Table 2 presents a description of the number of cases seen during this initial year compared to the community program years; in addition, the same comparison is made for time between the screening of a case and its termination. As Table 2 indicates, the mean treatment time for the community program years was significantly shorter than that for the initial year—and a larger number of cases were seen during each program year.

TABLE 2.  MEAN NUMBER OF TREATMENT WEEKS PER PATIENT OVER 3 yr

| | Number of cases | Weeks between screening and termination | | F test | Corrected t test |
|---|---|---|---|---|---|
| | | Mean | Variance | | |
| Traditional treatment year (T) | 17 | 19.00 | 20.88 | | |
| First community program year (C1) | 31 | 8.63 | 5.08 | | |
| Second community program year (C2) | 35 | 9.17 | 5.00 | | |
| T vs. C1 | | | | 4.11* | 8.50* |
| T vs. C2 | | | | 4.17* | 8.40* |
| C1 vs. C2 | | | | 1.02 | .01 |

*$P < 0.05$

Although no great emphasis can be placed on the correlational improvement data, results based on the number of cases treated and on the time between screening and termination of cases must be considered compelling.  There are certainly many treatment facilities in the United States which are similar to this Appalachian unit in terms of the undesirable ratio between patients and professional workers.  Since it is unlikely that many of those units will obtain an adequate number of professional workers in the near future, programs emphasizing the use of indigenous non-professional workers must be considered; as the present results show, a reinforcement theory based training program can lead to highly desirable outcomes.  Thus, in terms of efficient use of the professional clinician's time, such a community program has much to recommend it.

## REFERENCES

ALLEN K. E., HART B. M., BUELL J. S., HARRIS F. R. and WOLF M. M. (1965) Effects of social reinforcement on isolate behavior of a nursery school child. *Child Dev.* 35, 511–518.
BROWN P. and ELLIOT R. (1965) Control of aggression in a nursery school class. *J. Exp. Child Psychol.* 2, 103–107.
HARRIS F. R., JOHNSON M. K., KELLEY C. S. and WOLF M. M. (1964) Effects of positive social reinforcement on regressed crawling of a nursery school child. *J. Educ. Psychol.* 55, 35–41.
HARRIS F. R., WOLF M. M. and BAER D. M. (1964) Effects of adult social reinforcement on child behavior. *Young Child.* 20, 8–17.
HART B. M., ALLEN K. E., BUELL J. S., HARRIS F. R. and WOLF M. M. (1964) Effects of social reinforcement on operant crying. *J. Exp. Child Psychol.* 1, 145–153.

HAWKINS R. P., PETERSON R. F., SCHWEID E. and BIJOU S. W. (1966) Behavior therapy in the home: amelioration of problem parent-child relations with the parent in a therapeutic role. *J. exp. Child Psychol.*
**4**, 99–107.

JOHNSON M. K., KELLEY S. C., HARRIS F. R. and WOLF M. M. (1966) An application of reinforcement
principles to development of motor skills of a young child. In *Control of Human Behavior*, pp. 135–136.
(Eds. ULRICH R., STACHNIK T. and MABRY J.). Scott, Foremsan and Company.

PATTERSON G. R., LITTMAN R. A. and BRICKER W. (1967) Assertive behavior in children: A step toward
a theory of aggression. *Soc. Res. Chiid Dev. Monogr.* **32**, No. 5.

SARASON S. B., LEVINE M., GOLDENBERG I. CHERLIN D. L. and BENNETT E. M. (1966) *Psychology in Community Settings: Clinical, Educational, Vocational, Social ffspects.* John Wiley, New York.

SCOTT P. M., BURTON R. V. and YARROW M. R. (1967) Social reinforcement under natural conditions.
*Child Dev.* **38**, 53–63.

WAHLER R. G. (1967) Child-child interactions in free field settings: some experimental analyses. *J. exp.
Child Psychol.* **5**, 278–293.

WAHLER R. G., WINKEL G. H., PETERSON R. F. and MORRISON D. C. (1965) Mothers as behavior therapists for their own children. *Behav. Res. & Therapy* **3**, 113–124.

ZEILBERGER J., SAMPEN S. and SLOANE H. (1968) Modification of a child's problem behaviours in the home
with the mother as therapist. *J. app. Behav. Anal.* **1**, 47–53.

# USE OF BEHAVIORAL TECHNIQUES IN A CASE OF COMPULSIVE STEALING[1]

RALPH WETZEL

*University of Arizona*

Several investigators have demonstrated the effectiveness of behavioral techniques in the modification of so called deviant behaviors. These demonstrations have involved settings varying from the hospital (Ayllon & Michael, 1959; Wolf, Risley, & Mees, 1964) and the nursery school (Harris, Wolf, & Baer, 1964) to the clinician's office (Wolpe, 1958) and the home (Boardman, 1962). Likewise, the modifications have varied from the establishment of new behavioral repertoires to the elimination of whole classes of behavior.

An important feature of many demonstrations is that the change in behavior is often accomplished by relatively untrained, non-professional individuals. Hospital attendants, nursery school teachers, parents, and others have all been effective in the modification of deviant behaviors heretofore considered the domain of highly skilled and usually highly paid professional individuals. Usually these nonprofessionals have received very little special training. The implications for the efficient use of consultant time, the reduction of treatment costs, and the dispersion of therapeutic effectiveness are obvious. Bandura (1962) has pointed out that the professional individual can best spend his time instructing others in the application of behavioral principles and the work of several authors has suggested some very practical and ingenious

consulting procedures (Phillips, 1960; Williams, 1959; Wolf, 1965).

The efficiency of behavioral techniques usually depends upon the control of specific response contingencies and has been most successfully applied in controlled environments. Outside of the laboratory, hospitals appear to provide the best control although the nursery school studies of Harris, Wolf, and Baer (1964) demonstrate the achievement of control in a relatively free environment. Boardman (1962), in spite of the relative lack of control in the "natural" environment of a young boy, was able to significantly modify aggressive acting-out behavior using behavioral techniques, and Wolf (1965) has shown that parental cooperation can provide excellent control of specific behavior in the home.

In his discussion of Boardman's demonstration, Bandura (1962) is critical of the use of punishment for several very valid reasons and suggests that it is more desirable to remove reinforcers maintaining the target behavior and reinforce alternative behaviors. His suggestion, however, becomes more difficult to implement as the environment becomes more natural. In these situations there are probably multiple reinforcers controlling a behavior, many of which cannot be identified, much less controlled. On the school ground, for example, behavior which is under the control of other children is often difficult to handle because the situation requires modifying the behavior of several other individuals. Further, the natural environment

[1] The author is grateful to the director and staff of the Arizona Children's Home for their cooperation. Special thanks to Catherine Randall and the Child Care Workers for their splendid effort and, in particular, to Maria who really made the study possible.

JOURNAL OF CONSULTING PSYCHOLOGY, 1966, Vol. 30, pp. 367-374.

frequently prohibits the use of potentially effective reinforcement contingencies. Although there are certain behaviors upon which parents and teachers may make meals contingent (such as handwashing), the use of food as a reinforcer is generally restricted. Thus, the general use of behavior principles in the more open, natural situation is often hampered by the existence of these multiple reinforcers and by a restriction in the range of reinforcers available for modifying the target behavior.

The present study further demonstrates the use of behavior principles in the modification of a deviant behavior. The "compulsive" stealing of a 10-year-old resident of a home for mildly disturbed children was successfully eliminated over a $3\frac{1}{2}$-month period. Records indicate that the behavior had been a source of difficulty for at least 5 years. The behavior "therapy" was carried out in a field situation and made minimal use of professional time. The study demonstrates the use of nonprofessional individuals in the modification, observations, and recording of behavior and indicates some of the hazards involved in so doing. Hopefully it also suggests some solutions to the problems involved.

## SUBJECT AND HISTORY

The subject, who will be called Mike, was a Mexican-American boy, age 10 at the beginning of this study. He first came to the attention of professional individuals when school authorities expelled him from the first grade and referred his mother to a child guidance clinic. He had already long been a disciplinary problem to his mother who found him "impossible." She had had many complaints of stealing and destructive behavior from neighbors but was unable to exert any control over Mike. She most frequently resorted to locking Mike in his bedroom, but he usually tore open the screen and escaped through the window. On one occasion he left after setting fire to his bed. The father was hospitalized for a chronic condition resulting from a war injury and the family was considered by caseworkers as "marginal." The mother had four children, little money, and was described by the psychiatrist at the guidance clinic as "inadequate."

In the first grade Mike continued to steal,

was destructive of school property, disturbed other children, and made no academic progress. At the child guidance clinic, at age 7, he was given a psychiatric and psychological examination. He was described as a nonpsychotic, anxious, "slow learner" with "poor impulse control." His Stanford-Binet IQ was 78. He was diagnosed "passive-aggressive personality, aggressive type, severe." A special education class was recommended from which Mike was expelled 1 month later because the teacher was unable to handle him. He was placed in a foster home by the public welfare agency.

In the first half of his eighth year, Mike alternately lived in foster homes or under juvenile detention. The complaints from the foster homes were consistently about his stealing and destruction (in one home he chopped up a dining room chair with an ax). Due to his inability to adjust to foster homes and the undesirable effects of his long-term detention residence, Mike was made a ward of the court at age $8\frac{1}{2}$ and was placed in the Children's Home, a residential treatment center for mildly disturbed children. The records of Mike's first few weeks at the Children's Home indicate the absence of destructive behavior but a high rate of tantrum behavior, bedwetting, and stealing. In his first interview with the consulting psychiatrist he complained of being picked on by the other children and accused of stealing. He admitted that he just could not stay out of their lockers. The psychiatrist felt that he had "many qualities of a full-blown psychopath" but that he was essentially workable and looking for controls. He was described by the staff as "charming," with little conscience and a tendency to "project his faults to others."

During the ensuing 9 months Mike was described as making some adjustment to the home. He saw a caseworker once or twice a week, entered special classes of a nearby public school, and gradually established some relationships with the staff. The latter were almost exclusively with the women child care workers with whom he made himself ingratiating and useful. He was variously described by them as "a charmer," "adorable," and "a manipulator." At the same time there was a noticeable reduction in the staff reports of tantrums and daywetting.

His relationships with the other children at the home remained poor, apparently because he continued to steal. More and more the discussions with his caseworker took up the topic of stealing. The casework notes record Mike saying such things as, "I know I shouldn't steal people's things. I know it's wrong, so I am not going to do it." He complained about his inability to get along with "Englisher kids" because they picked on him for stealing. In spite of his complaints and promises, however, the incidence of stealing increased and spread to the school. He frequently brought home from the school toys, books, and assorted objects from the teacher's desk and the school bulletin board.

Various attempts were made to curb the stealing. It was noted, for example, that he frequently gave the objects he stole to another person. Suspecting that he was buying affections, his caseworker spent several sessions discussing Mike's need for affection with him and suggesting to Mike that his stealing enabled him to win affection from others. Mike usually replied by saying he was sorry and that he would not do it again. Another time a child care worker suggested that Mike might derive some satisfaction from the attention his stealing brought and thought they should "simply see that he returns what he takes." This plan was never put into effect although it had merit.

At the end of his first 9 months in the home, Mike showed definite improvement in all behaviors except stealing and bedwetting. His stealing was by far the most serious since it had prohibited his establishing rewarding relationships with his peers and had alienated most of the staff. At this time, his behavior was described as "kleptomania" in his records. The case work notes of this period reflect the general pessimism over his stealing:

Mike has come to me almost every day saying, "I didn't steal at school," sometimes he has and sometimes he hasn't. I feel our sessions are a "front." He simply wants me to feel he is trying even though he isn't.

The optimism expressed in the last summary in regard to Mike's "sticky fingers" was apparently premature since soon after the end of October he started stealing both from school and again from the home (whenever a closet was left open) and from the other children.

After 9 months in the Children's Home, Mike was recommended for foster home placement. It was the general consensus that his behavior had improved considerably and that his stealing represented a bid for affection. It was hoped that the latter would improve in a home atmosphere with a "loving maternal figure." He was described as "a chronic bedwetter with occasional wet pants . . . seeking out women and relating to them in an immature way . . . . Lovable but often like a little pack rat." He was placed with a Mexican-American family described as "exceptionally warm," living on the Arizona desert with three boys and horses.

One can only speculate what happened in the foster home. Five months later the Children's Home received a letter from welfare stating that "Mike's behavior in his foster home suggests further deterioration in his capacity to adjust" and requesting that he be readmitted. He entered for the second time at the age of 9 years, 10 months.

After readmission, the frequency of stealing appeared to be greater than ever before. It was reported at staff conferences that he was stealing nearly every day and on each shopping trip. The other children had begun to blame him for every missing article and, according to staff notes, "the articles are invariably found in his locker, on his person, or located with another individual who states that they are gifts from Mike."

At one staff conference the rationale for the present study was suggested by the author. Though there was not complete agreement about the method, the nearly 5-year history of previous failure and the shortage of staff for casework and interview therapy contributed, perhaps, to its acceptance.

## METHOD

*Training the staff.* Since the individuals in constant contact with Mike, the child care workers, were relatively untrained and unsophisticated in psychological theory and technique, it was first necessary to acquaint them with a few behavior principles. This was done in a series of four 1½-hour conferences. These covered the nature of reinforcement, the effects of behavior consequences, and the recording of behavior. In addition, the film "Reinforcement in Learning and Extinction" (McGraw-Hill, 1956) was shown. Discussion was focused on the possible application of these principles to Mike's stealing behavior. The reactions of the staff were varied. Some were enthusiastic, others stated that behavior principles are just "common sense," while others stated that the approach was "too scientific," meaning apparently, that it was too remote and "disregarded feelings." The intention was to convey in these sessions three essential points: (a) the consequences of behavior can control the behavior; (b) recording of the behavior is essential to the success of the study; (c) the study is experimental and there may be a period of trial and error. It will be seen that these points were not completely conveyed.

*Selecting the reinforcer.* The staff argued that punishment of the stealing was not desirable. Mike had shown himself resistant to the usual consequences of stealing. Scoldings and disapproval by the child care workers, the anger of peers, the return of the objects all had no effect on the stealing rate. The history indicates that assorted punishments (including spanking and isolation) prior to his admission to the home had been ineffective. The general policies of the home, moreover, encouraged only the most minimal and judicious use of punishment. Extinction by removal of the consequences thought to maintain the stealing was also ruled out. There was no question but that a great deal of attention was paid to Mike's stealing. He had developed an extensive repertoire of excuses and explanations which could hold the attention of a child care worker often for an hour. However, the removal of these consequences was difficult. Much of the attention came from peers, school children, and teachers and was difficult to control. An attempt by the supervisor of the child care workers to reduce the attention paid to the stealing had no effect. It was thus decided to withdraw positive reinforcement contingent on stealing.

The initial task was to find a positive reinforcer that could be conveniently and effectively removed. The child care workers agreed that there was nothing Mike cared enough about that he would stop stealing to maintain. An examination of his personal relations indicated that he had no particular rapport with the child care workers but that he did occasionally talk to one of the cooks, a Spanish-speaking Mexican-American woman who seemed fond of Mike. The decision was made to make the relationship with the cook the positive reinforcer.

*Establishing the reinforcer.* Since Mike's relationship with the cook, Maria, was casual and tenuous at best, it was necessary to intensify it to give it effective reinforcing value. It was explained to Maria, through a translator, that she seemed to play an important role in Mike's life at the Children's Home and that it would be helpful if she could become even more important to him. It was also explained that she would eventually be asked to help Mike with his principal difficulty, stealing. Maria was very willing and a plan was devised whereby she saw Mike daily. He was invited into the kitchen, prepared Mexican foods, and taken to Maria's home for visits. Maria mended his clothes, took him shopping and to church. In a few days, Mike apparently was looking forward to his visits and Maria, in turn, became especially fond of him.

*The contingency.* Maria was told that it was possible she could help Mike with his stealing. It was explained that whenever Mike stole she would be informed and that as soon as possible she was to say to him in Spanish: "I'm sorry that you took *so-and-so's blank* because now I can't let you come home with me tonight." It was emphasized that she should say nothing else, should listen to no explanations or excuses but should turn and walk away. The following day she was to resume her usual warm relationship with Mike and maintain it until the next stealing incident.

*Recording behavior.* The child care workers were told that whenever the property of another person, the school, or the home was found on Mike's person, in his locker, or in his room, and it was determined that the property had not been legitimately given to him, they were to (a) record a stealing incident on a daily chart and (b) when the time came, report the incident to Maria. Maria was instructed to keep a record of sessions she missed with Mike because of his stealing.

## RESULTS

Once a week the charts were collected and transferred to the cumulative record shown in Figure 1. Each step up represents *one or more* stealing incidents for a given day. The period of observation covers approximately 5 months and 1 week. The 4 days around Christmas which Mike spent out of the home are not recorded since observation was impossible.

It was planned to allow 4 weeks for the relationship with Maria to develop. The child care workers were instructed to continue the recording they had begun in the training sessions during this time. They were told, also, to handle the stealing in whatever way they were accustomed.

*The baseline.* The beginning of the record to *b* constitutes the baseline recording. At *a* Mike began his visits with Maria and the

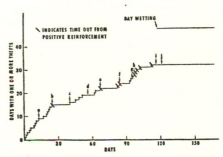

FIG. 1. A cumulative record showing the effects of withdrawal of a positive reinforcer on the stealing behavior of a 10-year-old boy. The upper right line indicates the absence of day wetting as a substitute "acting-out" behavior.

supervisor of the child care staff began to keep daily records of the interactions between Mike and Maria as well as others. Some quotations from these records will clarify the nature of the relationship between Mike and Maria.

11/10 Began daily hour with Maria—very pleased. 11/11 Went for five hours (in the) afternoon— brought me some homemade tortilla from Maria's. 11/12 Clothes shopping with Maria. Pleased and made certain I marked (them) properly in big letters, happy Maria bought him shirts and took home and shortened sleeves before return—impressed on me what a good mother Maria is. I agreed. 11/13 Related he is teaching Maria English—he really likes to go with her because she has tortillas every day. Liked warm jacket Maria gave him. It was her boy's that he outgrew.

Although there was a reduction in stealing behavior immediately following the beginning of the visits with Maria, the rate soon returned to its original level. Since the record only indicates *one or more* stealing incidents per day, it does not accurately reflect the amount of stealing within days. The following lists the objects stolen in the five incidents tween $a$ and $b$: ($a$) a ten cent store ring, a ball, a pin, five pencils, all belonging to other children; ($b$) three rolls of toilet paper, three sweaters, and 12 pairs of socks belonging to other children; (c) some underwear, three bars of soap, and a model airplane; ($d$) a quarter; ($e$) a child care worker's keys.

*The first contingency.* At $b$, 12 days after the beginning of his sessions with Maria, Mike gave the supervisor such a difficult time that she decided to deny him his visit with Maria even though it was premature according to the general program. Her notes are explanatory:

I left linen closet door open in process of getting towels to boys who went to shower without. Next thing I knew, Mike was having a tooth paste-squirting game all over the room. (He said) he took from closet—I had him clean up. After shower, rash of bandaids appeared all over. Mike admitted taking at same time as tooth paste. Said didn't have p.j.'s. At this point, I went to drawer and pulled (them) out wherein I found a pearl-handled pocket knife which belonged to George, and Playboy magazine. Said he took these from (child care worker's) room when I went into relief room to answer telephone. I recognized with him I was very tired and really should know better than to ever leave a door open. . . . told him I considered this deliberate stealing four times within a half hour

and I would tell Maria and he would not go with her Monday."

Since this occurred late one evening, Maria was not informed until the next day nearly 20 hours after the behavior. Hence, the first contingency was hardly contingent, though the supervisor's threat certainly was.

The next day at dinner time Mike went into the kitchen as usual. He was followed by several child care workers who were anxious to see what would happen. They reported that Maria looked "stern" as she spoke to Mike in Spanish. Mike, however, remained in the kitchen and seemed so unaffected that one of the child care workers urged Maria to tell Mike again. Accordingly, Maria repeated the routine, turned and went about her work in the kitchen. Mike wandered into a nearby sitting room where he had been allowed to wait. About 5 minutes later, a child care worker told him he would have to return to his cottage. He was described as "pouty" the rest of the evening and throughout the next day. In the evening, he met Maria in the kitchen as usual. For the next 13 days, no stealing was reported. It was apparently the longest he had gone without stealing at the home.

*Removal of the contingency.* A new problem arose in the period represented by the interval $c$ to $e$ in Figure 1. Mike began to appear with assorted articles which seemed so minor to the child care staff that they were not reported to Maria. Some matches which he said he found, some cookies which "a nice lady had given him," a little Christmas tree from the infirmary all seemed too innocent to report. The child care staff offered two reasons for feeling lenient: ($a$) Mike already seemed better; ($b$) It was so close to Christmas that they hated to deny him his visit. $d$ marks Christmas, and it can be seen that, like most children, Mike was especially good the few days on either side of this date.

*The second contingency.* At $e$ several articles belonging to other children were found in Mike's locker and he was denied his visit. This was followed by 10 days of nonstealing. At $f$, the supervisor, disturbed at the increasing rate in the previous days in spite of the contingency urged the child care staff to continue reporting and showed Mike the charts they were keeping, explaining how stealing eliminated his visit for that day.

At *g* the author was called in to consult. Mike had taken his roommate's jacket on one day and his hair brush, the next. The child care workers were concerned about reporting these incidents since it was not uncommon behavior in the home and they did not wish to penalize Mike unfairly. The author discovered at this time that the staff had recently changed, and there were some child care workers who knew little about the program. The next day, Mike stole a pass key, a serious offense, but was not reported. At *h* the final meeting with the child care staff was held at which it was stressed that the contingency must be used consistently and that the recent alternation might make Maria less effective. It was agreed to report the possession of anything not belonging to him. Although this seemed unfair in view of the borrowing behavior of the other children, it was felt that Mike had more to gain by nonborrowing. Beginning at *h* he was denied Maria for possessing someone's clothing and for the two subsequent incidents involving his roommate's hairbrush and some pictures from the school bulletin board. The last incident involved some toys belonging to another child at the home. Although he promised to return them and not "steal again," Maria was denied.

*Nonstealing behavior.* In the consulting sessions, stress had been laid on the positive reinforcement of appropriate alternative behaviors. The staff was urged to praise and otherwise reinforce all of Mike's socially appropriate behavior. This proved difficult for nonstealing, however, and the only solution seemed to be to reinforce at certain intervals as long as he did not steal. The problem was resolved on "bank day" when the children bank part of the money they have earned for chores or otherwise accumulated. At *i* instead of banking, Mike divided his money between two boys, stating that it was to replace some articles he had previously taken and lost and announced that he was "not stealing anymore." It was the first instance of denotable "nonstealing" behavior and was heavily reinforced by the supervisor and child care staff with praise throughout the day.

At *j* a similar incident occurred. Mike took a text book he owned to the public school where the teacher questioned him about it. Mike stated that he had not stolen it but bought it. The teacher, aware of the efforts to help him, verified the story, took Mike to the principal and explained the incident. The principal praised Mike for not stealing and being honest and gave him a set of bird pictures for being a "good boy." The display of these brought praise from the child care staff.

Periodically over the last recorded month, Mike reminded the staff that he had not stolen or lied. Toward the middle of the last recorded month, he asked the child care supervisor to tell Maria he was going to the carnival with the other boys and would not be able to visit with her. His times with Maria have since dropped to two to three times a week. Anecdotal evidence indicates that his relationships with peers have been improving.

*Pants wetting.* At a staffing shortly after it became apparent that Mike had improved, it was suggested that he might have begun to wet his pants. A child care worker thought he detected dampness. Many staff members agreed that pants wetting might be a substitute acting-out behavior to replace the stealing. Recording was begun to determine the increase. As Figure 1 shows, there have been no wet pants since the date of the first record.

## DISCUSSION

If, as suggested, the professional individual is to spend increasing amounts of time instructing others in the application of behavior principles, effective methods of consultation must first be developed. Most often, the individual who is to mediate the change in behavior is unsophisticated in behavioral techniques. In some cases (Boardman, 1962; Wolf, 1965), the "mediator" is simply given a set of specific instructions by the consultant who maintains frequent contact, often by phone, to insure that the instructions are carried out. This can be effective when the number of mediators involved is small (e.g., parents), but is inefficient if the number of individuals involved is large as in the study above, which involved 16 people. It seemed desirable in this case to give the group enough of a foundation in behavior techniques to allow it to function at least semi-

297

autonomously. For this reason, the brief training session was instituted.

The training presented several difficulties. The time available and the educational backgrounds of most of the individuals prohibited anything but a rather superficial review of behavior principles. As such, the principles sounded deceptively simple and common-sensical and the systematic characteristic of the techniques tended to be missed. It was difficult, for example, for the child care workers to understand the necessity of reinforcing immediately and consistently. Reinforcement was anything but systematic at the beginning of the program. The study points up the need for long-range staff-improvement programs in behavior principles and techniques if these are to be applied at the institutional level. The development of these can be an important part of the consultant's role.

The training of mediators in the observation and recording of behavior is essential. Accurate records can detect changes in behavior which otherwise might be missed and provide daily feedback on program effectiveness. The use of behavior records presented difficulties for the staff in this study, initially. First of all, record keeping disrupted ongoing routines and was viewed as bothersome. Further, some tended to regard them as a "criminal record" and were hesitant to report stealing incidents for fear of getting Mike into trouble. Eventually, however, the record came to be the principal source of reinforcement to the child care workers since it provided feedback on their effectiveness. Thus, training mediators in record keeping not only provides the consultant necessary information but also provides a source of reinforcement for the mediator himself. The consultant can make his praise contingent on a good record or approximations to it.

Maintaining a systematic program involving several people is made considerably easier if the consultant can find an individual to act as coordinator. For example, in this case the supervisor of the child care workers was invaluable. It is particularly important to be advised of important changes in the environment, illnesses, changes in personnel, and the like. Also, a coordinator can do much toward insuring that records are kept and the contingencies applied. This relieves the consultant from a great deal of "legwork."

If the behavior is to be modified by reinforcement contingencies, the choice of the reinforcer is crucial. The consultant must evaluate the availability of effective reinforcers in the environment and his ability to make them contingent on specific behavior. In situations where the target behavior is maintained by recognizable and controllable reinforcers, extinction coupled with reinforcement of alternate behavior is probably most desirable, as Bandura (1962) suggests. Punishment of the behavior tends to be used more when the consequences maintaining the behaviors are unknown or uncontrollable. Punishment, however, is not only not permissible in many settings but also has several undesirable side effects (Bandura, 1962). Removal of a positive reinforcer, as in this study, is usually not so aversive, often more natural, and within the permissible range. It can also be used when the maintaining consequences are unknown. In all cases special care should be taken to encourage mediators to reinforce desirable alternate behaviors.

The use of relationships as a source of reinforcement has long been a part of behavior modification. "Building rapport" is one way of establishing a reinforcer, as in this study. The consultant should be on the lookout for naturally existing reinforcers in the environment of the target individual. Maria, the reinforcer used in this example, was a "natural." She required no training in how to become reinforcing to Mike. Her usual warmth and interest were entirely sufficient and the training of Maria, upon whom the success of the program rested, took no more than 20 minutes. The important factor was to make the relationship contingent on Mike's nonstealing. Just providing Mike with a warm mother figure, as suggested in his earlier therapy, was not sufficient. Even though his stealing rate dropped immediately after he began his visits with Maria, it quickly rose again. As a mother of a hospitalized patient known to the author recently remarked, "It's not just loving; it's what you love them for."

It is probably desirable to keep generalizability in mind when selecting reinforcers. Mike's nonstealing behavior appears to be coming under the control of the child care worker and peer relationships which may be effective enough to maintain it. Whether or not his nonstealing can be maintained outside of the Children's Home is questionable. However, it can be now stated with some degree of assurance that Mike's stealing is sensitive to its consequences and at least one effective consequence can be specified. Such information should prove useful when future placement is considered for Mike, so that, whatever environment is eventually selected, socially appropriate behaviors leading toward a more rewarding life for Mike can be developed and maintained.

Finally, it should be pointed out that the successful application of behavioral techniques to the modification of deviant behavior probably depends on several conditions not specified by principles of reinforcement. For example, in the middle of this study Mike was shown the charts and informed of how his stealing eliminated a visit with Maria for the day. Although this event was not dictated by reinforcement principles, it very well might have influenced the effectiveness of the contingency. James and Rotter (1958), in fact, have demonstrated that the reinforcing value of a stimulus may be a function of whether or not the subject perceives the reinforcement to depend on his own behavior (skill) or the whims of the environment (chance). Likewise, contingencies imposed in a natural setting tend to generate several changes in the articulation of an individual and his environment well beyond the scope defined by the target behavior. The nature of these changes and their contribution to the outcome are seldom described or evaluated in most studies of environmental manipulation. Thus, though the technique of intervention may be the establishment of a particular reinforcement contingency, several other factors must be considered if the success of the technique is to be evaluated. So far, these additional conditions have been "played by ear" or handled through "clinical intuition."

The James and Rotter study and others (Phares, 1957, 1962; Rotter, Liverant, & Crowne, 1961) indicate that conditions which augment or limit the effectiveness of environmental manipulation can be specified and suggest that behavioral principles can be extended eventually into a technology of intervention.

## REFERENCES

AYLLON, I., & MICHAEL, J. The psychiatric nurse as a behavioral engineer. *Journal of Experimental Analysis of Behavior*, 1959, 2, 323–334.

BANDURA, A. Punishment revisited. *Journal of Consulting Psychology*, 1962, 26, 298–301.

BOARDMAN, W. K. Rusty: A brief behavior disorder. *Journal of Consulting Psychology*, 1962, 26, 293–297.

HARRIS, F. R., WOLF, M. M., & BAER, D. M. Effects of adult social reinforcement on child behavior. *Young Children*, 1964, 20, 8–17.

JAMES, W. H., & ROTTER, J. B. Partial and 100% reinforcement under chance and skill conditions. *Journal of Experimental Psychology*, 1958, 55, 397–403.

PHARES, E. J. Expectancy changes in skill and chance situations. *Journal of Abnormal and Social Psychology*, 1957, 54, 339–342.

PHARES, E. J. Perceptual threshold decrements as a function of skill and chance expectancies. *Journal of Psychology*, 1962, 53, 339–407.

PHILLIPS, E. L. Parent-child psychotherapy: A follow-up study comparing two techniques. *Journal of Psychology*, 1960, 49, 195–202.

ROTTER, J. B., LIVERANT, S., & CROWNE, D. P. The growth and extinction of expectancies in chance controlled and skilled tasks. *Journal of Psychology*, 1961, 52, 161–177.

WILLIAMS, C. D. The elimination of tantrum behaviors by extinction procedures. *Journal of Abnormal and Social Psychology*, 1959, 59, 269.

WOLF, M., RISLEY, T., & MEES, H. Application of operant conditioning procedures to the behavior problems of an autistic child. *Behaviour Research and Therapy*, 1964, 1, 305–312.

WOLF, M. Reinforcement procedures and the modification of deviant child behavior. Paper read at Council on Exceptional Children, Portland, Oregon, 1965.

WOLPE, J. *Psychotherapy by reciprocal inhibition.* Stanford: Stanford University Press, 1958.

# The Effects of Reward
# and Level of Aspiration
# on Students with Deviant Behavior

*Abstract: The purpose of this study was to test the efficacy of rewards and level of aspiration with children classified by a behavior problem checklist. Forty-five junior high age, potential dropout students were classified according to deviant classroom behaviors. They were then tested in several different levels of aspiration and reward treatment combinations. Results showed no differences between classifications of students and no hypothesized differences in the differential effectiveness of level of aspiration and reward for the types of students. The results also showed that setting a high level of aspiration had a significant positive effect.*

FOR years the fields of special education, psychiatry, and psychology have been concerned with the task of developing diagnostic and treatment procedures for emotionally disturbed children. The field has gained expertise in the area of diagnosis of children with disturbing behaviors but apparently has not been able to develop treatment procedures which have demonstrated greater effectiveness than control group situations (Levitt, 1957; Lewis, 1965; Rubin, Simpson, & Betwee, 1966).

One effort to make teaching the disturbing child more effective has been the development of functional classification systems of disturbing behaviors which have a demonstrated relationship to learning in the classroom (Quay, 1968; Spivak & Swift. 1967). While the evidence for the success of this strategy of intervention is meager at this point, it provides hope that more than

administrative shuffling of children can be accomplished in special education.

The problem is twofold, involving first the establishment of functional classification procedures and, second, the provision of educational methods, which are differentially effective within the classifications. There is a need for relevant categories of disturbing behavior in children which can serve as the basis for planning differential educational procedures.

### Purpose

The purpose of this study was to investigate the efficacy of rewards and level of aspiration as relevant educational procedures with children classified by a behavior problem checklist. This was done by the study of three independent dimensions: (a) classification by type of predominant deviant classroom behavior—hyperactive-aggressive, anxious-withdrawn, and no deviant behaviors (control), (b) a motivation dimension involving types of reward—monetary, verbal, and no apparent reward, and (c) a motivation dimension involving different levels of aspiration—free level of aspira-

THOMAS NOFFSINGER *is Director, Lake County Regional Program for Handicapped Children, Garfield Elementary School, Mentor, Ohio.*

EXCEPTIONAL CHILDREN, 1971, Vol. 37, No. 5, pp. 371 371-379.

tion, controlled positive, and no stated level of aspiration. The types of predominant classroom behaviors are not an attempt to group invariant personality traits, they are merely classifications based on teacher observed behaviors.

A visual tracking task (Geake & Smith, 1966) was selected as the dependent variable since it could be easily quantified and simulated in an educational setting. It is a task involving performance and speed.

## Related Research

The classification scheme in this investigation (Quay, 1966) is based on statistical analysis using factor analytic techniques. With the use of these techniques, Quay and others have been able to investigate behavioral and psychological traits in a wide variety of sample populations.

In an attempt to provide theoretical basis for expecting different educational performance, Quay (1965) suggests that people displaying the first major cluster of behaviors, hereafter called hyperactive-aggressive, are similar to those who traditionally have been called psychopathic personalities. He theorizes that the psychopathic person is reacting to either a lowered arousal level or excessive stimulation seeking and thus exhibits behaviors observed as aggressive and hyperactive. The interaction of this lowered arousal or stimulation seeking tendency and the particular environmental contingencies of a person could form relatively stable patterns of behavior. Hyperactive-aggressive behavior as a result of stimulation seeking is also suggested by Cromwell (1963), Skrzypek (1967), and Eysenck (1957).

The second major cluster of behaviors consistently found in behavior ratings is called anxious-withdrawn (Quay, 1968). This classification includes behaviors such as hypersensitivity, social withdrawal, self consciousness, fear, and anxiousness. Quay suggest that children with these behaviors respond to verbal praise more often than do children with hyperactive-aggressive behaviors.

In summary, the hyperactive-aggressive pathological stimulation seeker should prefer the complex over the simple, the novel over the expected, and physical reward over verbal reward. The anxious-withdrawn subject should respond to the less stimulating situations of maximum verbal reinforcement.

### Level of Aspiration (LOA)

Using level of aspiration or goal setting as a motivation variable has been suggested by Fryer (1964) and Locke (1966a). Locke and Bryan in a series of investigations dealing with setting goals and its effect on performance found that specific, quantitative goals led to higher performance levels than goals which were stated in terms of "do your best" (Bryan & Locke, 1967a, 1967b; Locke, 1966a, 1966b; Locke & Bryan, 1966a, 1966b).

Locke, Bryan, and Kendall (1968) report the results of five experiments dealing with level of aspiration (goal setting) incentives and monetary incentives on performance of college undergraduates. Consistent findings showed that goal setting incentives are the mechanism by which monetary rewards influence behavior. All five studies showed significant relationships between goals or intentions and behavior within and/or between different monetary incentive conditions. It was demonstrated that if goal setting was controlled there was no effect of amount of monetary incentive on behavior. Locke, Bryan, and Kendall would predict that high goal setting would produce equally high performance regardless of the reward situation.

The previous level of aspiration research has not investigated differential effects of setting goals on hyperactive-aggressive or anxious-withdrawn subjects. However, the possibility of level of aspiration as a motivational variable for educational procedures warrants its inclusion in this research.

## Method

*Subjects.* The subjects for this experiment were 45 boys of average intelligence enrolled in six junior high schools in the Nashville Metropolitan School System. All of the subjects took part in a special Work Education Employment Program (WEEP) which was connected with an Elementary and Secondary Education Act Title I project. The WEEP program was designed to maintain the school related interests of potential dropout students by combining academic and occupational educational goals. All of the WEEP classes were in metropolitan area poverty sections.

301

The 45 experimental subjects were classified on the basis of their homeroom teacher's assessment of their predominant disturbing behaviors using Quay's Behavior Problem Checklist. The subjects were divided into three groups selected on the basis of their observed excess and lack of certain behaviors. That is, those subjects who displayed a preponderance of hyperactive-aggressive behaviors (above the 60 percentile in their class) and a lack of anxious-withdrawn behaviors (below the 40 percentile in their class) were grouped together (N = 15) in the hyperactive-aggressive classification. Those subjects who displayed a preponderance of anxious-withdrawn behaviors (above 60 percentile in their class) and a lack of hyperactive-aggressive behaviors (below the 40 percentile in their class) were grouped together (N = 15) in the anxious-withdrawn classification. Those subjects who showed a lack of any disturbing behaviors (below the 10 percentile in their class) were grouped into a third group (N = 15) and classified as no deviant behaviors. Table 1 presents a description of each of the three groups.

The average reading level of each group using the *Wide Range Achievement Test* was, as expected, below the grade level of junior high students. The differences between groups was significant with an $F$ value equal to 4.52 exceeding the 3.23 required at the .05 level of significance. Further breakdown of this relationship showed the hyperactive-aggressive and anxious-withdrawn groups not significantly different from each other but the no deviant behavior group significantly higher than the deviant behavior groups. Although there was a significant difference in reading level at the time of the study, the relationship

of reading to total score on the dependent variable was negligible (Pearson $r$, .097). Analysis of covariance techniques was not useful since little variance is accounted for with such a low correlation (Feldt, 1958).

Although race was not an experimental variable, the random assignment of subjects to groups provided approximately equal Negro and Caucasian subjects. A chi square analysis revealed a value of 1.61 which did not exceed the 3.8 value needed for significance at the .05 level.

The range in ages was from 12 years 10 months to 16 years 10 months. The average ages of the groups were not significantly different ($F$ value of 1.06).

**Procedure**

Each subject was tested individually on three successive school days. The testing session, held in a quiet comfortable schoolroom, lasted approximately 12 to 15 minutes each. Care was taken to insure that each subject was tested at approximately the same time each day and under as similar conditions as were possible in the public school setting.

All of the testing was done by one experimenter (the author) to insure as similar experimental conditions as possible between subjects. The author is aware of the possibility of experimenter effects (Rosenthal, 1967) and thus took care to minimize this variable. Included in these precautions was a "blind" experimenter variable. The experimenter did not know which subjects belonged to which behavioral classification. Performance expectations on the basis of knowledge of the stated hypotheses were thus minimized.

The 15 subjects who displayed a preponderance of hyperactive-aggressive behaviors were randomly assigned to three groups,

**TABLE 1**

**Descriptive Data of Subjects**

| Group | Total N | Race W | Race N | Age Mo. $\overline{X}$ | Age SD | Reading Level $\overline{X}$ | Reading Level SD |
|---|---|---|---|---|---|---|---|
| Hyperactive-aggressive | 15 | 7 | 8 | 170.1 | 12.0 | 5.2 | 5.1 |
| Anxious-withdrawn | 15 | 10 | 5 | 176.3 | 12.8 | 4.3 | 3.8 |
| No deviant behaviors | 15 | 7 | 8 | 176.2 | 14.9 | 6.4* | 5.2 |
| Total | 45 | 24 | 21 | | | | |

* $p$ <.05 level

302

each of which received three particular combinations of the reward in a particular sequence. This method of presentations was replicated across the other two classifications of subjects.

## Reward Variable

*Monetary reward.* It was assumed that money would be reinforcing to these students from low socioeconomic conditions. In addition to the money, the examiner's presence and verbal comments may have been a reinforcing (positively or negatively) factor. The examiner attempted to keep verbal comments to a minimum to isolate the effects of the monetary reward as much as possible.

*Verbal reward.* The examiner encouraged each subject to perform as well as he could. Verbal rewards such as "good," "very good," and "nice try" were offered when appropriate, that is, when the subject reached, exceeded, or came close to his aspiration. Between trials the examiner made comments such as "You sure are doing a nice job," "It makes me feel good to see you doing so well," or a similar positive verbal comment. In general, the examiner tried to be very supportive verbally.

*No apparent reward.* In any social situation, all of the reinforcing contingencies are impossible to predict. The effort in this situation was to eliminate as many as possible. Verbal and social contact was held to a minimum. The examiner was cordial and business-like proceeding from trial to trial with the comment "Now, let's go on to the next."

## Level of Aspiration Variable

*Controlled positive LOA.* A scale was reproduced at the top of each visual tracking exercise with which the subject estimated his expected performance each time he began each excercise. The controlled positive LOA scale allowed the subject to predict that he would do the "same" as the last performance, a "little better" than the last time, or "much better" than the last time. The subject marked on the scale the number of letters he expected to find in the next performance in terms of a numerical figure.

*Free level of aspiration.* The free LOA allowed the subject to state his expectations on a continuum from "much worse" to "much better" in terms of the exact number of letters he expected to find. A scale was included prior to each exercise.

*No stated level of aspiration.* The no stated LOA situation consisted of a series of similar visual tracking tasks with no expectancy scale or opportunity for the subject to state his expected performance. This variable provided a control situation to test the relative effectiveness of a LOA motivation procedure.

## The Experimental Task

The experimental task was a series of visual tracking exercises (Geake & Smith, 1966) in which the subject had to find and mark letters in alphabetic sequence in a series of make believe words. Each treatment combination included eight visual tracking exercises. Each exercise had a time limit of 45 seconds. There was a possible range of scores for each subject on each exercise of 0-26 and on each treatment combination 0-208. Total scores on each treatment combination were used in analysis of the data.

## Results

*Experimental design.* The experimental design for this study was one in which the 15 subjects from each of the three types of predominant behavior classifications were randomly assigned to three groups. The three groups of five subjects each were then placed in a 3 x 3 Greco-Latin square arrangement so that no group received more than one treatment in each of the LOA (A1, A2, A3) and reward (B1, B2, B3) categories (see Figure 1). This Greco-Latin square arrangement counterbalanced the order effects of LOA and reward. An order variable which represents particular LOA and reward treatment combinations is shown as D1, D2, and D3 in Figure 1.

This basic three factor counterbalanced design was replicated across different classifications of children (represented in Figure 1 by C1, C2, and C3). The design is a Plan 13 analysis (Winter, 1962) with reward, LOA, and order as within subject effects, and types of classroom behaviors as between subject effects. Analysis of variance was used for the overall total analysis (Table 2). Orthogonal comparisons were used to analyze the simple effects (Table 3).

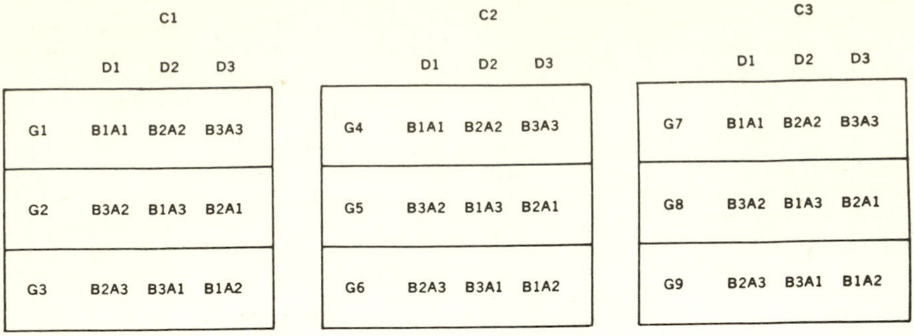

FIGURE 1. Graphic representation of the experimental design.

An *F-Max* test of homogeneity of variance for each treatment combination resulted in a ratio of 2.10. The hypothesis of unequal variance was rejected and homogeneity of variance was concluded.

Table 2 shows the breakdown of the variance found in this study. Three significant results were found: (a) an order of treatment combinations effect ($F = 87.59$), (b) a classification by reward effect ($F = 5.98$), and (c) a classification by order effect ($F = 4.27$).

*Hypothesis.* It was hypothesized that there would be no difference in performance between classifications of predominant types of classroom behaviors. This hypothesis was accepted since an $F$ score of .25 was not significant.

The significant classification X reward interaction ($F = 5.98$) was a predicted finding. That is, on the basis of the Quay research, it was hypothesized that aggressive-hyperactive subjects would respond differently to different rewards than anxious-withdrawn or no deviant behavior subjects (see Figure 2).

The direction of the difference between hyperactive-aggressive and anxious-withdrawn subjects is, however, opposite to the predicted results for money (B1) and verbal (B2) rewards. That is, hyperactive-aggressive subjects performed most poorly under money reward and best under verbal reward, anxious-withdrawn performed best under money reward and most poorly under verbal reward. None of the simple effects at any B level reaches the .05 level

TABLE 2
Total Analysis of Variance

| Source of Variation | df | $x^2$ | $s^2$ | F |
|---|---|---|---|---|
| Between subjects | 44 | 40376.26 | | |
| Classifications (C) | 2 | 493.73 | 246.86 | .25 |
| Sequence effects | 2 | 1178.80 | 589.40 | .59 |
| Classification X sequence | 4 | 2826.53 | 706.63 | .71 |
| Error between | 36 | 35877.20 | 996.59 | |
| Within subjects | 90 | 26178.67 | | |
| Order effects (D) | 2 | 15453.90 | 7726.95 | 87.59** |
| LOA (A) | 2 | 480.04 | 240.02 | 2.72 |
| Reward (B) | 2 | 33.91 | 16.95 | .19 |
| Classification X LOA (CXA) | 4 | 243.56 | 60.89 | .69 |
| Classification X reward (CXB) | 4 | 2109.42 | 527.35 | 5.98* |
| Classification X order (CXD) | 4 | 1506.23 | 376.56 | 4.27* |
| Error within | 72 | 6351.61 | 88.22 | |
| Total | 134 | 66554.93 | | |

* $p < .005$
** $p < .001$

of significance. This indicates that children with different behavior patterns did not respond significantly differently to different rewards. But since the performance is exactly opposite to the predicted direction, it is an interesting finding. The significant difference in this interaction lies in the difference between withdrawn and no deviant behavior subjects. As Figure 2 indicates, the differences between these groups are similar for money (B1) and verbal (B2) reward but different at the no reward situation. This indicates that the difference between the responses of subjects identified by the checklist were different for the various reward situations.

The overall effects of LOA as shown in Table 2 were nonsignificant ($F = 2.72$). However, it was hypothesized that the effect of positively controlled LOA on the visual tracking scores would be significantly greater than the effect of free LOA. Table 3 shows that an $F$ value of 4.04 was significant and the hypothesis was accepted. As Figure 3 indicates the motivation situation of "no stated LOA" was also higher than "free LOA."

### Post Hoc Results

The remainder of the results presented represent post hoc findings. Although there

### TABLE 3
#### Orthogonal Comparisons of LOA

| Hypothesis | df | $s^2$ | F |
|---|---|---|---|
| Positive LOA <> free LOA | 1 | 356.01 | 4.04* |
| No LOA < LOA | 1 | 124.03 | 1.41 |
| Error—total within | 72 | 88.22 | |

* $p < .05$

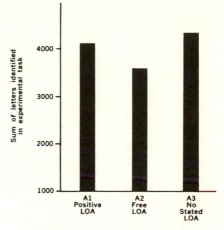

FIGURE 3. Level of aspiration dimension.

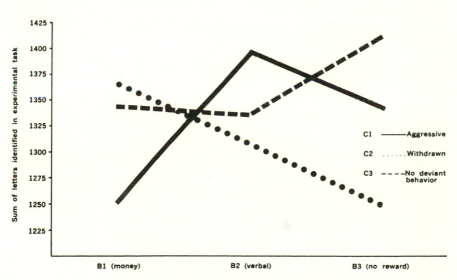

FIGURE 2. Classification X reward interaction.

was no hypothesis testing the order effect of treatment combinations, Table 2 shows that there was a significant effect ($F = 87.59$). This means that the overall effect of order of presentation of treatment combinations (level of aspiration X reward) contained a significant difference. To find the location of the differences, orthogonal comparisons were used to test treatment combinations in D1 against D2 and D3 against the average of D1 and D2. Significant differences on both of the tests would indicate a linear effect of order of presentation. Table 4 indicates that both comparisons were significant and, since D3 > D2 > D1, it was concluded that there is a progressively increasing effect probably due to practice or learning.

The total analysis of variance (Table 2) also revealed a significant classification X order (CXD) effect. This indicates that subjects classified on the basis of predominant classroom behaviors responded differently to the effects of order of presentation of treatment combinations. Figure 4 shows this effect.

The difference between C3 and the average of C1 and C2 at D1 is significant with an $F$ value of 5.18 (see Table 5). That is, at the first trial, the deviant behavior subjects performed more poorly than the no deviant behavior subjects. On trial two (D2) it is apparent that there were no significant differences between classifications. On trial three (D3) the hyperactive-aggressive group exceeded the other two groups. The anxious-withdrawn subjects increased performance to equal that of the no deviant subjects. These differences in D3 did not reach the .05 level of significance (Table 5).

## Discussion

It is apparent from the results of this study that the Problem Behavior Checklist was not effective in differentiating subjects *in support* of the Quay theory. That is, the hyperactive-aggressive subjects did not respond better to the monetary reward situation and poorer to the verbal reward situation and anxious-withdrawn subjects did not respond better to verbal reward than to monetary reward.

The author feels that these results

### TABLE 4
**Orthogonal Comparisons of Order of Presentation**

| Hypotheses | df | $s^2$ | F |
|---|---|---|---|
| H: D1 = D2 | 1 | 8027.8 | 90.9** |
| H: $\dfrac{D1 + D2}{2}$ = D3 | 1 | 7426.1 | 84.2** |
| Error—total within | 72 | 88.22 | |

** $p$ <.001

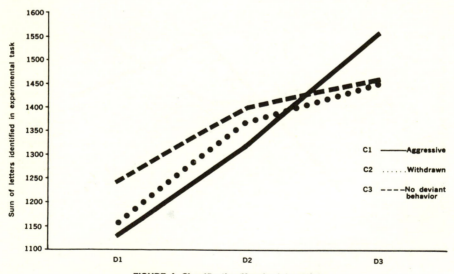

FIGURE 4. Classification X order interaction.

306

TABLE 5
**Orthogonal Comparisons of the Effects of Deviant
and Nondeviant Behaviors at the First and
Third Orders of Presentation**

| Hypotheses | df | $s^2$ | F |
|---|---|---|---|
| H: $\left(\dfrac{C1 + C2}{2}\right)D_1 = (C3)D_1$ | 1 | 1488.4 | 5.18* |
| Error—within for D1 only | 42 | 287.5 | |
| H: $\left(\dfrac{C1 + C2}{2}\right)D_3 = (C3)D_3$ | 1 | 106.7 | .26 |
| Error—within for D3 only | 42 | 413.7 | |

* $p < .05$

should not be interpreted to be a disconfir-
mation of the validity for classification for
differential response of the Problem Behavior Checklist since the significant reward X
classification interaction means that, in
fact, the groups of subjects did respond
differently to the rewards. The fact that
the classification system did not predict behavior in the hypothesized direction does
not mean that it did not differentiate subjects. The difference between anxious-withdrawn and no deviant behavior groups was
different across the reward dimension. The
greatest difference between these groups
was found in the no apparent reward situation (see Figure 2).

These results are logical if the no apparent reward situation can be seen as producing a relatively high amount of anxiety
as a result of minimal feedback to the
subjects about their performance. In such
a situation, subjects who have few anxious
behaviors (no deviant behaviors) could be
expected to perform better than subjects
who exhibit a great deal of anxious behavior. There are three major implications
here. First, it may be beneficial for future
research in this area to look at the anxiety
level of the subjects, measured by the
amount of feedback they receive. It might
be expected that where there is an excess
of feedback about a subject's own performance, those subjects who are relatively secure (no deviant behavior) are not motivated to perform at a higher level since
they are receiving rewards for their present
level. These subjects, when placed in a situation of relatively little feedback, will
presumably be motivated to higher performance (Figure 2 indicates such a relationship).

Subjects, on the other hand, who are relatively insecure (anxious-withdrawn),
perform best when feedback is the strongest (monetary reward). This may lower
their anxiety since feedback lets them
know exactly how they are doing. With increasingly less feedback (no apparent reward) anxiety increases and inhibits performance. What seems to be demonstrated
in this interaction is that the subjects with
anxious behaviors perform more poorly
when there is less feedback about their
performance. Subjects with no deviant behaviors perform better with less feedback.

What may be occurring here is a curvilinear relationship of anxiety to performance. If the amount of anxiety in the
condition of no reward with anxious subjects can be seen as extremely high, poor
performance would be expected. As feedback increases (no reward to verbal reward to physical reward) anxiety of these
subjects decreases and performance increases. The lesser amount of anxiety at
the monetary reward situation helps the
anxious-withdrawn subject at this point
but the subject who has little initial anxiety (no deviant behavior) experiences
minimal motivation here. It is only when
the situation invokes anxiety for him (increasingly less feedback) that he is motivated to better performance. The total
amount of anxiety is experienced differently for anxious-withdrawn and no deviant behavior groups.

The second implication of this interaction is that the Problem Behavior
Checklist did identify these subjects. It,
therefore, may be a useful instrument for
differentiating subjects if these findings are
found to be reliable in future research. It
must be remembered that the subjects in
this study represent a special subgroup of
the population. Sociocultural background
may have been a factor in the results. To
investigate this factor, replication of the
reward by classification dimension is suggested with similar populations and with
populations of different sociocultural backgrounds.

The third implication from the reward
X classification interaction has relevance
for the classroom teacher. If these results
are reliable, a teacher should not dispense
rewards (in the form of feedback) indiscriminately. A child who displays few anxious behaviors may be more highly moti-

vated if he receives little feedback about his performance. This child may possess other motivation and reward systems which cause him to perform maximally when there is little outside influence. It may prove harmful to praise him continuously or reinforce him with monetary rewards. On the other hand, the highly anxious child should receive external feedback to support and increase his performance.

The performance of the hyperactive-aggressive subjects in this reward X classification interaction is difficult to explain. Poor performance in the monetary reward situation may be due to the fact that being paid for school related performance caused students to be suspicious or created so much feedback that their performance was decreased. The finding that their response was opposite to the hypothesized direction and different from the other two types of students is reason to suspect that these subjects are somehow a different type of student and thus provide relevant inquiry for future investigation.

The fact that setting only positive LOA produces significantly higher performance than free LOA (being able to aspire to poorer or better performance) is of considerable importance to the educator. It is in support of Locke's research concerning the value of stating high specific goals prior to the task. If this is a reliable finding, it would indicate that the explicit, positive goals which were set influenced the actual performance in a positive direction. One implication of this is that a very important part of teaching is helping the student expect better performance from himself. Care must be used by the teacher because if the possibility of negative expectation is introduced performance level may decline.

The fact that the no LOA situation (see Figure 3) was also significantly better than the free LOA situation can be in harmony with this effect of positive and negative expectation if one assumes that there were implicit internal positive goals set by the subjects in the no LOA situation. In this series of exercises the subject does not take time with estimating future performance on an expectancy scale. However, his previous performance is recorded before him and, because of the 45 second time factor, he is placed in a rapid perform, score, record, perform cycle. In this situation he

quite logically remembers past performance and could set implicit or explicit positive goals for his immediate performance. Of course, he could also set negative goals but in the rapid game-like procedure where external reward effectiveness would be minimized he probably would be trying to increase his performance. This positive expectancy for better performance could very well produce it.

In summary, the implications of this research are:

1. The Problem Behavior Checklist did not predict performance based on the Quay theory.
2. The Problem Behavior Checklist may be a useful experimental tool since it did differentiate subjects in combination with rewards.
3. Future research should look at the feedback which different reward contingencies provide for different subjects. A hierarchy of reward effectiveness for different subjects in different situations should be established.
4. The curvilinear relationship of anxiety to performance should be kept in mind when teachers reinforce students for certain behaviors. This may best be thought of as the amount of feedback needed to balance anxiety for maximal performance.
5. Future research in the LOA dimension should attempt to delineate more clearly the effects of positive and negative expectations and also attempt to manipulate implicit and explicit goal setting.
6. Teachers should become proficient in helping the student expect better performance from himself.

### References

Bryan, J. F., & Locke, E. A. Goal setting as a means of increasing motivation. *Journal of Applied Psychology*, 1967, **51**, 274-277. (a)

Bryan, J. F., & Locke, E. A. Parkinson's law as a goal setting phenomenon. *Organizational Behavior and Human Performance*, 1967, **2**, 258-275. (b)

Cromwell, R. L. A social learning approach to mental retardation. In N. Ellis (Ed.), *Handbook of mental deficiency*. New York: McGraw-Hill, 1963. Pp. 41-91.

Eysenck, H. J. *The dynamics of anxiety and hysteria*. New York: Praeger, 1957.

Feldt, L. S. A comparison of the precision of three experimental designs employing a concomitant variable. *Psychometrika*, 1958, **23** (4) , 335-353.

Fryer, F. *An evaluation of aspiration as a training procedure.* Englewood Cliffs, N. J.: Prentice-Hall, 1964.

Geake, R., & Smith, D. *Visual tracking: A self-instruction workbook for perceptual skills in reading.* Ann Arbor, Mich.: Ann Arbor Publishers, 1966.

Levitt, E. E. The results of psychotherapy with children. An evaluation. *Journal of Consulting Psychology*, 1957, **21**, 189-196.

Lewis, W. W. Continuity and intervention in emotional disturbance: A review. *Exceptional Children*, 1965, **31**, 465-475.

Locke, E. A. A closer look at level of aspiration as a training procedure: A reanalysis of Fryer's data. *Journal of Applied Psychology*, 1966, **50**, 417-420. (a)

Locke, E. A. The relationship of intentions to level of performance. *Journal of Applied Psychology*, 1966, **50**, 60-66. (b)

Locke, E. A., & Bryan, J. F. The effects of goal-setting, rule-learning and knowledge of score on performance. *American Journal of Psychology*, 1966, **79**, 451-457. (a)

Locke, E. A., & Bryan, J. F. Cognitive aspects of psychomotor performance: The effects of performance goals on level of performance. *Journal of Applied Psychology*, 1966, **50**, 286-291. (b)

Locke, E. A., Bryan, J. F., & Kendall, L. M. Goals and intentions as mediators of the effects of monetary incentives on behavior. *Journal of Applied Psychology*, 1968, **52**, 104-121.

Quay, H. C. Psychopathic personality as pathological stimulation seeking. *American Journal of Psychiatry*, 1965, **122**, 180-183.

Quay, H. C. Dimensions of problem behavior in children and their interaction in the approaches in behavior modification. *Kansas Studies*, 1966, **16**, 6-13.

Quay, H. C. Dimensions of problem behavior and educational programming. In P. S. Graubard (Ed.) , *Education of the disturbed and delinquent child.* New York: Follett, 1968.

Rosenthal, R. The effect of the experimenter on the results of psychological research. In B. A. Maher (Ed.) , *Progress in experimental personality research.* Vol. 1. New York: Academic Press, 1967.

Rubin, E. Z., Simpson, C. B., & Betwee, M. C. *Emotionally handicapped children in the elementary school.* Detroit: Wayne State University Press, 1966.

Skrzypek, G. J. The effect of perceptual isolation and arousal on anxiety, complexity preference, and novelty preference in psychopathic and neurotic delinquents. Unpublished doctoral dissertation, University of Illinois, 1967.

Spivak, G., & Swift, M. The Devereaux Elementary School behavior rating scales: A study of the nature and organization of achievement related disturbed classroom behavior. *Journal of Special Education*, 1967, **1**, 71-90.

Winer, B. J. *Statistical principles in experimental design.* New York: McGraw-Hill, 1962.